In the Beginning

Herman Bavinck (1854–1921)
Graphite sketch by Erik G. Lubbers

In the Beginning

Foundations of Creation Theology

Herman Bavinck
Edited by John Bolt
Translated by John Vriend

 Baker Books

A Division of Baker Book House Co
Grand Rapids, Michigan 49516

© 1999 by the Dutch Reformed Translation Society, P.O. Box 7083, Grand Rapids, MI 49510

Published by Baker Books
a division of Baker Book House Company
P.O. Box 6287, Grand Rapids, MI 49516-6287

Printed in the United States of America

Library of Congress Cataloging-in-Publication Data is on file at the Library of Congress, Washington, D.C.

Sketch of Herman Bavinck © 1996 by Erik G. Lubbers.

For information about academic books, resources for Christian leaders, and all new releases available from Baker Book House, visit our web site:
http://www.bakerbooks.com

Contents

Dutch Reformed Translation Society
Board of Directors

Preface

The financing for the translation and editing of *In the Beginning* was provided by the Dutch Reformed Translation Society. The DRTS was formed in 1994 by a group of businesspeople and professionals, pastors, and seminary professors, representing five different Reformed denominations, to sponsor the translation and facilitate the publication in English of classic Reformed theological and religious literature published in the Dutch language. It is incorporated as a nonprofit corporation in the State of Michigan and governed by a board of directors.

Believing that the Dutch Reformed tradition has many valuable works that deserve wider distribution than the limited accessibility of the Dutch language allows, Society members seek to spread and strengthen the Reformed faith. The DRTS's first project is the definitive translation of Herman Bavinck's complete four-volume *Gereformeerde Dogmatiek (Reformed Dogmatics)*. This volume on creation is the second installment of that project. The Society invites those who share its commitment to and vision for spreading the Reformed faith to write for additional information.

Editor's Introduction

In July 1925, Dayton, Tennessee, high school biology teacher John T. Scopes was brought to trial for teaching the theory of evolution to his students in violation of state law. The resulting famous Scopes "monkey trial" may have been a defining moment in the "science-versus-religion" war that had raged since the publication of Darwin's *On the Origin of Species* in 1859 but it was hardly the end. Skirmishes continue to this day and the war hardly seems over.[1] What this ongoing debate between "creationists" and "evolutionists" tends to obscure is that there is much more to the Christian doctrine of creation than scientific battles about origins and the age of the earth. This timely volume, which does provide a guide to the current debate but also broadens the theological discussion considerably, is a translation of Herman Bavinck's *Gereformeerde Dogmatiek* (Reformed Dogmatics), Volume II, Chapter 5, "Over de Wereld in haar Oorspronkelijke Staat" (Concerning the World in Its Original State). It is the second section of Bavinck's magisterial work to be produced by the Dutch Reformed Translation Society[2] as part of its initial project to publish the complete English translation of Bavinck's classic four-volume work from Dutch. Who was Herman Bavinck, and why is this work of theology so important?

Bavinck's *Gereformeerde Dogmatiek*, first published a hundred years ago, represents the concluding high point of some four centuries of remarkably productive Dutch Reformed theological reflection. From Bavinck's numerous citations of key Dutch Reformed theologians such as Voetius, De Moor, Vitringa, van Mastricht, Witsius, and Walaeus as well as the important Leiden *Synopsis purioris theologiae*,[3] it is clear he

1. See, for example, Phillip Johnson, *Darwin on Trial* (Washington, D.C.: Regnery, 1991).

2. The first volume was a translation of the eschatology section. See Herman Bavinck, *The Last Things: Hope for this World and the Next*, John Bolt, ed., John Vriend, trans. (Grand Rapids: Baker, 1996).

3. The Leiden *Synopsis*, first published in 1625, is a large manual of Reformed doctrine as it was defined by the Synod of Dordt. It served as a standard reference textbook for the study of Reformed theology well into the twentieth century (it is even cited by Karl Barth in his *Church Dogmatics*). As an original-source reference work of classic Dutch Reformed theology it is comparable to Heinrich Heppe's nineteenth-century more broad-

knew that tradition well and claimed it as his own. At the same time it also needs to be noted that Bavinck was not simply a chronicler of his own church's past teaching. He seriously engaged other theological traditions, notably the Roman Catholic and the modern liberal Protestant ones, effectively mined the Church Fathers and great medieval thinkers, and placed his own distinct Neo-Calvinist stamp on the *Reformed Dogmatics.*

Kampen and Leiden

To understand the distinct Bavinck flavor a brief historical orientation is necessary. Herman Bavinck was born on December 13, 1854. His father was an influential minister in the Dutch Christian Reformed Church *(Christelijke Gereformeerde Kerk)* that had seceded from the National Reformed Church in the Netherlands twenty years earlier.[4] The secession of 1834 was in the first place a protest against the state control of the Dutch Reformed Church; it also tapped into a long and rich tradition of ecclesiastical dissent on matters of doctrine, liturgy, and spirituality as well as polity. In particular, mention needs to be made here of the Dutch equivalent to English Puritanism, the so-called Second Reformation[5] *(Nadere Reformatie)*, the influential seventeenth- and early-eighteenth-century movement of experiential Reformed theology and spirituality,[6] as well as an early-nineteenth-century international, aristocratic, evangelical revival movement known as the *Réveil.*[7] Bavinck's church, his family, and his own spirituality were thus definitively shaped by strong patterns of deep pietistic Reformed spirituality. It is also important to note that though the earlier phases of Dutch pietism affirmed orthodox Reformed theology and were also nonseparat-

---

ly continental anthology, *Reformed Dogmatics* (London: Allen & Unwin, 1950). While serving as the minister of a Christian Reformed church in Franeker, Friesland, Bavinck edited the sixth and final edition of this handbook, which was published in 1881.

4. For a brief description of the background and character of the Secession church, see James D. Bratt, *Dutch Calvinism in Modern America* (Grand Rapids: Eerdmans, 1984), ch. 1, "Secession and Its Tangents."

5. See Joel R. Beeke, "The Dutch Second Reformation *(Nadere Reformatie),*" *Calvin Theological Journal* 28 (1993): 298–327.

6. The crowning theological achievement of the *Nadere Reformatie* is the devout and theologically rich work of Wilhelmus à Brakel, *Redelijke Godsdienst*, first published in 1700 and frequently thereafter (including twenty Dutch editions in the eighteenth century alone!). This work is not available in English translation: *The Christian's Reasonable Service*, trans. Bartel Elshout, 4 vols. (Ligonier, Pa.: Soli Deo Gloria, 1992–95).

7. The standard work on the *Réveil* is M. Elizabeth Kluit, *Het Protestantse Réveil in Nederland en Daarbuiten, 1815–1865* (Amsterdam: Paris, 1970). Bratt also gives a brief summary in *Dutch Calvinism in America*, 10–13.

ist in theirecclesiology, by the mid-nineteenth century the Seceder group had become significantly separatist and sectarian in outlook.[8]

The second major influence on Bavinck's thought comes from the period of his theological training at the University of Leiden. The Christian Reformed Church had its own theological seminary, the Kampen Theological School, established in 1854. Bavinck, after studying at Kampen for one year (1873–74), indicated his desire to study with the University of Leiden's theological faculty, a faculty renowned for its aggressively modernist, "scientific" approach to theology.[9] His church community, including his parents, was stunned by this decision, which Bavinck explained as a desire "to become acquainted with the modern theology firsthand" and to receive "a more scientific training than the Theological School is presently able to provide."[10] The Leiden experience gave rise to what Bavinck perceived as the tension in his life between his commitment to orthodox theology and spirituality and his desire to understand and appreciate what he could about the modern world, including its worldview and culture. A telling and poignant entry in his personal journal at the beginning of his study period at Leiden (September 23, 1874) indicates his concern about being faithful to the faith he had publicly professed in the Christian Reformed church of Zwolle in March of that same year: "Will I remain standing [in the faith]? God grant it."[11] Upon completion of his doctoral work at Leiden in 1880, Bavinck candidly acknowledged the spiritual impoverishment that Leiden had cost him: "Leiden has benefited me in many ways: I hope always to acknowledge that gratefully. But it has also greatly impoverished me, robbed me, not only of much ballast (for which I am

8. Bavinck himself called attention to this in his Kampen rectoral oration of 1888 when he complained that the Seceder emigration to America was a spiritual withdrawal and abandonment of "the Fatherland as lost to unbelief" ("The Catholicity of Christianity and the Church," trans. John Bolt, *Calvin Theological Journal* 27 [1992]: 246). Recent historical scholarship, however, suggests that this note of separatism and cultural alienation must not be exaggerated. Though clearly a marginalized community in the Netherlands, the Seceders were not indifferent to educational, social, and political responsibilities. See John Bolt, "Nineteenth- and Twentieth-Century Dutch Reformed Church and Theology: A Review Article," *Calvin Theological Journal* 28 (1993): 434–42.

9. For an overview of the major schools of Dutch Reformed theology in the nineteenth century, see James Hutton MacKay, *Religious Thought in Holland during the Nineteenth Century* (London: Hodder & Stoughton, 1911). For more detailed discussion of the "modernist" school, see K. H. Roessingh, *De Moderne Theologie in Nederland: Hare Voorbereiding en Eerste Periode* (Groningen: Van der Kamp, 1915); Eldred C. Vanderlaan, *Protestant Modernism in Holland* (London and New York: Oxford University Press, 1924).

10. R. H. Bremmer, *Herman Bavinck en Zijn Tijdgenoten* (Kampen: Kok, 1966), 20; cf. V. Hepp, *Dr. Herman Bavinck* (Amsterdam: W. Ten Have, 1921), 30.

11. R. H. Bremmer, *Tijdgenoten*, 19.

happy), but also of much that I recently, especially when I preach, recognize as vital for my own spiritual life."[12]

It is thus not unfair to characterize Bavinck as a man between two worlds. One of his contemporaries once described Bavinck as "a Secession preacher and a representative of modern culture," concluding: "That was a striking characteristic. In that duality is found Bavinck's significance. That duality is also a reflection of the tension—at times crisis—in Bavinck's life. In many respects it is a simple matter to be a preacher in the Secession Church, and, in a certain sense, it is also not that difficult to be a modern person. But in no way is it a simple matter to be the one as well as the other."[13] However, it is not necessary to rely only on the testimony of others. Bavinck summarizes this tension in his own thought clearly in an essay on the great nineteenth-century liberal Protestant theologian Albrecht Ritschl:

> Therefore, whereas salvation in Christ was formerly considered primarily a means to separate man from sin and the world, to prepare him for heavenly blessedness and to cause him to enjoy undisturbed fellowship with God there, Ritschl posits the very opposite relationship: the purpose of salvation is precisely to enable a person, once he is freed from the oppressive feeling of sin and lives in the awareness of being a child of God, to exercise his earthly vocation and fulfill his moral purpose in this world. The antithesis, therefore, is fairly sharp: on the one side, a Christian life that considers the highest goal, now and hereafter, to be the contemplation of God and fellowship with him, and for that reason (always being more or less hostile to the riches of an earthly life) is in danger of falling into monasticism and asceticism, pietism and mysticism; but on the side of Ritschl, a Christian life that considers its highest goal to be the kingdom of God, that is, the moral obligation of mankind, and for that reason (always being more or less adverse to the withdrawal into solitude and quiet communion with God), is in danger of degenerating into a cold Pelagianism and an unfeeling moralism. Personally, I do not yet see any way of combining the two points of view, but I do know that there is much that is excellent in both, and that both contain undeniable truth.[14]

12. V. Hepp, *Dr. Herman Bavinck*, 84.

13. Cited by Jan Veenhof, *Revelatie en Inspiratie* (Amsterdam: Buijten & Schipperheijn, 1968), 108. The contemporary cited is the Reformed jurist A. Anema, who was a colleague of Bavinck at the Free University of Amsterdam. A similar assessment of Bavinck as a man between two poles is given by F. H. von Meyenfeldt, "Prof. Dr. Herman Bavinck: 1854–1954, 'Christus en de Cultuur,'" *Polemious* 9 (October 15, 1954); and G. W. Brillenburg-Wurth, "Bavincks Levensstrijd," *Gereformeerde Weekblad* 10/25 (December 17, 1954).

14. H. Bavinck, "De Theologie van Albrecht Ritschol," *Theologische Studiën* 6 (1888): 397. Cited by Jan Veenhof, *Revelatie en Inspiratie*, 346–47; emphasis added by Veenhof. Kenneth Kirk contends that this tension, which he characterizes as one between "rigorism" and "humanism," is a fundamental conflict in the history of Christian ethics from the outset. See K. Kirk, *The Vision of God* (London: Longmans, Green, 1931), 7–8.

A certain tension in Bavinck's thought between the claims of modernity, particularly its this-worldly, scientific orientation, and Reformed pietist orthodoxy's tendency to stand aloof from modern culture, continues to play a role even in his mature theology expressed in the *Reformed Dogmatics*. In his eschatology Bavinck, in a highly nuanced way, still continues to speak favorably of certain emphases in a Ritschlian this-worldly perspective.[15]

In this volume on the doctrine of creation we see the tension repeatedly in Bavinck's relentless efforts to understand and, where he finds appropriate, either to affirm, correct, or repudiate modern scientific claims in light of scriptural and Christian teaching. Bavinck takes modern philosophy (Kant, Schelling, Hegel), Darwin, and the claims of geological and biological science seriously but never uncritically. His willingness as a theologian to engage modern thought and science seriously is a hallmark of his exemplary work. It goes without saying that though Bavinck's theological framework remains a valuable guide for contemporary readers, many of the specific scientific issues he addresses in this volume are dated by his own late-nineteenth-century context. As Bavinck's own work illustrates so well, today's Reformed theologians and scientists learn from his example not by repristinating his efforts but by freshly addressing new and contemporary challenges.

Grace and Nature

It is therefore too simple merely to characterize Bavinck as a man trapped between two apparently incommensurate tugs at his soul, that of other-worldly pietism and this-worldly modernism. His heart and mind sought a trinitarian synthesis of Christianity and culture, a Christian worldview that incorporated what was best and true in both pietism and modernism, while above all honoring the theological and confessional richness of the Reformed tradition dating from Calvin. After commenting on the breakdown of the great medieval synthesis and the need for contemporary Christians to acquiesce in that breakdown, Bavinck expressed his hope for a new and better synthesis: "In this situation, the hope is not unfounded that a synthesis is possible between Christianity and culture, however antagonistic they may presently stand over against each other. If God has truly come to us in Christ, and is, in this age too, the Preserver and Ruler of all things, such a synthesis is not only possible but also necessary and shall surely be effected in its own

---

15. Herman Bavinck, *The Last Things*, 161. According to Bavinck, Ritschl's this-worldliness "stands for an important truth" over against what he calls the "abstract supernaturalism of the Greek Orthodox and Roman Catholic Church."

time."[16] Bavinck found the vehicle for such an attempted synthesis in the trinitarian worldview of Dutch Neo-Calvinism and became, along with Neo-Calvinism's visionary pioneer Abraham Kuyper,[17] one of its chief and most respected spokesmen as well as its premier theologian.

Unlike Bavinck, Abraham Kuyper grew up in the National Reformed Church of the Netherlands in a congenially moderate-modernist context. Kuyper's student years, also at Leiden, confirmed him in his modernist orientation until a series of experiences, especially during his years as a parish minister, brought about a dramatic conversion to Reformed, Calvinist orthodoxy.[18] From that time Kuyper became a vigorous opponent of the modern spirit in church and society[19]—which he characterized by the siren call of the French Revolution, *"Ni Dieu! Ni maitre!"*[20]—seeking every avenue to oppose it with an alternative worldview, or as he called it, the "life-system" of Calvinism:

> From the first, therefore, I have always said to myself, "if the battle is to be fought with honor and with a hope of victory, then principle must be arrayed against principle; then it must be felt that in Modernism the vast energy of an all-embracing life-system assails us, then also it must be understood that we have to take our stand in a life-system of equally comprehensive and far-reaching power. . . . When thus taken, I found and confessed and I still hold, that this manifestation of the Christian principle is given us in Calvinism. In Calvinism my heart has found rest. From Calvinism have I drawn the inspiration firmly and resolutely to take my stand in the thick of this great conflict of principles.["]²¹

16. H. Bavinck, *Het Christendom*, in the series *Groote Godsdiensten*, vol. 2, no. 7 (Baarn: Hollandia, 1912), 60.

17. For a brief overview, see J. Bratt, *Dutch Calvinism in Modern America*, ch. 2, "Abraham Kuyper and Neo-Calvinism."

18. Kuyper chronicles these experiences in a revealing autobiographical work entitled *Confidentie* (Amsterdam: Höveker, 1873). A rich portrait of the young Abraham Kuyper is given by G. Puchinger, *Abraham Kuyper: De Jonge Kuyper (1837–1867)* (Franeker: T. Wever, 1987). See also the somewhat hagiographic biography of Kuyper by Frank Vandenberg (Grand Rapids: Eerdmans, 1960) and the more theologically and historically substantive one by Louis Praamsma, *Let Christ Be King: Reflection on the Times and Life of Abraham Kuyper* (Jordan Station, Ont.: Paideia, 1985). Brief accounts can also be found in Benjamin B. Warfield's introduction to A. Kuyper, *Principles of Sacred Theology*, trans. J. H. De Vries (Grand Rapids: Charles Scribner's, 1898), and the translator's biographical note in A. Kuyper, *To Be Near to God*, trans. J. H. De Vries (Grand Rapids: Eerdmans, 1925).

19. See especially his famous address, *Het Modernisme, een Fata Morgana op Christelijke Gebied* (Amsterdam: De Hoogh, 1871). On page 52 of this work he acknowledges that he, too, once dreamed the dreams of modernism. This important essay is now available in English translation: J. Bratt, ed., *Abraham Kuyper: A Centennial Reader* (Grand Rapids: Eerdmans, 1998), 87–124.

20. A. Kuyper, *Lectures on Calvinism* (Grand Rapids: Eerdmans, 1931), 10.

21. Ibid., 11–12.

Kuyper's aggressive, this-worldly form of Calvinism was rooted in a trinitarian theological vision. The "dominating principle" of Calvinism, he contended, "was not soteriologically, justification by faith, but in the widest sense cosmologically, *the Sovereignty of the Triune God over the whole Cosmos,* in all its spheres and kingdoms, visible and invisible."[22]

For Kuyper, this fundamental principle of divine sovereignty led to four important derivatory and related doctrines or principles: common grace, antithesis, sphere sovereignty, and the distinction between the church as institute and the church as organism. The doctrine of common grace[23] is based on the conviction that prior to and, to a certain extent, independent of the *particular* sovereignty of divine grace in redemption, there is a *universal* divine sovereignty in creation and providence, restraining the effects of sin and bestowing general gifts on all people, thus making human society and culture possible even among the unredeemed. Cultural life is rooted in creation and common grace and thus has a life of its own apart from the church.

This same insight is expressed more directly via the notion of sphere sovereignty. Kuyper was opposed to all Anabaptist and ascetic Christian versions of world-flight but was also equally opposed to the medieval Roman Catholic synthesis of culture and church. The various spheres of human activity—family, education, business, science, art—do not derive their raison d'être and the shape of their life from redemption or from the church, but from the law of God the Creator. They are thus relatively autonomous—also from the interference of the state—and are directly responsible to God.[24] In this regard Kuyper clearly distinguished two different understandings of the church: the church as institute gathered around the Word and sacraments and the church as organism diversely spread out in the manifold vocations of life. It is not explicitly as members of the institutional church but as members of the body of Christ, organized in *Christian communal* activity (schools, political parties, labor

22. Ibid., 79.
23. Kuyper's own position is developed in his *De Gemeene Gratie,* 3 vols. (Amsterdam and Pretoria: Höveker & Wormser, 1902). A thorough examination of Kuyper's views can be found in S. U. Zuidema, "Common Grace and Christian Action in Abraham Kuyper," in *Communication and Confrontation* (Toronto: Wedge, 1971), 52–105. Cf. J. Ridderbos, *De Theologische Cultuurbeschouwing van Abraham Kuyper* (Kampen: Kok, 1947). The doctrine of common grace has been much debated among conservative Dutch Reformed folk in the Netherlands and the United States, tragically leading to church divisions. For an overview of the doctrine in the Reformed tradition, see H. Kuiper, *Calvin on Common Grace* (Goes: Oostebaan & Le Cointre, 1928).
24. "In this independent character a special *higher authority* is of necessity involved and this highest authority we intentionally call—*sovereignty in the individual social sphere,* in order that it may be sharply and decidedly expressed that these different developments of social life have *nothing above themselves but God,* and that the state cannot intrude here, and has nothing to command in their domain" (*Lectures on Calvinism,* 91).

unions, institutions of mercy), that believers live out their earthly vocations. Though aggressively this-worldly, Kuyper was an avowed and ar-
ticulate opponent of the *volkskerk* tradition, which tended to merge national sociocultural identity with that of a theocratic church ideal.[25]

To state this differently: Kuyper's emphasis on common grace, used
polemically to motivate pious, orthodox Dutch Reformed Christians to
Christian social, political, and cultural activity, must never be seen in
isolation from his equally strong emphasis on the spiritual antithesis.
The regenerating work of the Holy Spirit breaks humanity in two and
creates, according to Kuyper, "two kinds of consciousness, that of the
regenerate and the unregenerate; and these two cannot be identical."
Furthermore, these "two kinds of people" will develop "two kinds of science." The conflict in the scientific enterprise is not between science and
faith but between *"two scientific systems . . . each having its own faith."*[26]

It is here in this trinitarian, world-affirming, but nonetheless reso-
lutely antithetical Calvinism that Bavinck found the resources to bring
some unity to his thought.[27] "The thoughtful person," he notes, "places
the doctrine of the Trinity in the very center of the full-orbed life of nature
and mankind. . . . The mind of the Christian is not satisfied until every
form of existence has been referred to the triune God and until the confession of the Trinity has received the place of prominence in all our life
and thought."[28] Repeatedly in his writings Bavinck defines the essence of
the Christian religion in a trinitarian, creation-affirming way. A typical
formulation: "The essence of the Christian religion consists in this, that
the creation of the Father, devastated by sin, is restored in the death of
the Son of God, and re-created by the Holy Spirit into a kingdom of
God."[29] Put more simply, the fundamental theme that shapes Bavinck's
entire theology is the trinitarian idea that *grace restores nature.*[30]

25. On Kuyper's ecclesiology, see H. Zwaanstra, "Abraham Kuyper's Conception of
the Church," *Calvin Theological Journal* 9 (1974): 149–81; on his attitude to the *volkskerk*
tradition, see H. J. Langman, *Kuyper en de Volkskerk* (Kampen: Kok, 1950).

26. A. Kuyper, *Lectures on Calvinism*, 133; cf. *Principles*, 150–82. A helpful discussion
of Kuyper's view of science is given by Del Ratzsch, "Abraham Kuyper's Philosophy of
Science," *Calvin Theological Journal* 27 (1992): 277–303.

27. The relation between Bavinck and Kuyper, including differences as well as com-
monalities, is discussed in greater detail in John Bolt, "The Imitation of Christ Theme in
the Cultural-Ethical Ideal of Herman Bavinck," unpublished Ph.D. diss., University of
St. Michael's College, Toronto, Ont., 1982, especially ch. 3: "Herman Bavinck as a Neo-
Calvinist Thinker."

28. H. Bavinck, *The Doctrine of God*, trans. W. Hendriksen (Grand Rapids: Eerdmans,
1951), 329.

29. H. Bavinck, *Gereformeerde Dogmatiek*, 4th ed. (Kampen: Kok, 1928), I, 89.

30. This is the conclusion of Jan Veenhof, *Revelatie en Inspiratie*, 346; and Eugene
Heideman, *The Relation of Revelation and Reason in E. Brunner and H. Bavinck* (Assen:
Van Gorcum, 1959), 191, 195. See *The Last Things*, 200, n. 4.

The evidence for "grace restores nature" being the fundamental defining and shaping theme of Bavinck's theology is not hard to find. In an important address on common grace, given in 1888 at the Kampen Theological School, Bavinck sought to impress on his Christian Reformed audience the importance of Christian sociocultural activity. He appealed to the doctrine of creation, insisting that its diversity is not removed by redemption but cleansed. "Grace does not remain outside or above or beside nature but rather permeates and wholly renews it. And thus nature, reborn by grace, will be brought to its highest revelation. That situation will again return in which we serve God freely and happily, without compulsion or fear, simply out of love, and in harmony with our true nature. That is the genuine *religio naturalis*." In other words: "Christianity does not introduce a single substantial foreign element into the creation. It creates no new cosmos but rather makes the cosmos new. It restores what was corrupted by sin. It atones the guilty and cures what is sick; the wounded it heals."[31]

Creation: In the Beginning

This volume, the creation section in the *Reformed Dogmatics*, also displays these distinctive characteristics of Bavinck's thought. The fundamental theme that grace does not undo nature but restores and heals means that Bavinck's doctrine of creation must be a key to understanding his theology more broadly. It is thus no surprise that Bavinck begins by telling us that the doctrine of creation is the starting point and distinguishing characteristic of true religion. Creation is the formulation of human dependence on a God who is distinct from the creature but who nonetheless in a loving, fatherly way preserves it. Creation is a distinct emphasis of the Reformed tradition, according to Bavinck, a way of affirming that God's will is its origin and God's glory its goal. In the opening chapter Bavinck demonstrates his full awareness of ancient and contemporary alternatives to creation—-of a popular as well as philosophical nature—-and insists that it is through revelation alone that we can confidently repudiate emanationist and pantheist worldviews. What Bavinck says here sounds remarkably current and relevant for today's many forms of "New Age" spirituality.

Remarkably relevant too is Bavinck's careful, biblically circumspect discussion, in the second chapter, of angels and the spiritual world. Materialist denials of the spiritual world of angels and demons destroy religion itself, he contends, because religion depends on the supernatural, on miracle and revelation. Bavinck's strong emphasis on this

---

31. H. Bavinck, "Common Grace," trans. Raymond Van Leeuwen, *Calvin Theological Journal* 24 (1989): 59–60, 61.

world as the theater of God's glory and thus on the importance of Christian cultural activity does not lead to the dualophobia of some later Neo-Calvinists who stoutly resist all "dualisms" (such as body/soul) in fear that they diminish and devalue the creational and material in favor of the spiritual.[32] Bavinck insists on a clear distinction between the spiritual and the material world though he also insists that they must never be separated in Christian thought.

Balance also characterizes Bavinck's treatment of origins and the relation between science and the Genesis accounts of creation. All religions, he notes, have "creation" stories but the biblical account is strikingly different in its orientation: Theogonic myths have no place in the Genesis accounts and the Bible simply assumes the existence of one God. Though Genesis does not give a precise scientific explanation of origins—-the earth is the *spiritual* rather than the astronomical center of the universe—it is important, according to Bavinck, to insist on the historical rather than merely mythical or visionary character of its creation account. An original unity of the human race and its historical fall into sin are essential to the biblical narrative and worldview. Creation is thus more than just a debate about the age of the earth and the evolutionary origins of humanity, important as these questions are. The solidarity of the human race, original sin, the atonement in Christ, the universality of the kingdom of God, and our responsibility to love our neighbor are all grounded in a key dimension of the doctrine of Creation, the unity of the human race created in God's own image. Creation thus is the presupposition of all religion and morality. It is especially in the fifth chapter of this volume, on the image of God, that Bavinck's characteristic understanding of the relation between nature and grace, discussed above, comes clearly into view.

That a present-day emphasis on creation does not imply a devaluation of the future life of eternal glory is clear from Bavinck's discussion of human destiny. The final state of glory for humanity, given in Christ the Second Adam, is far greater than the original state of integrity of humanity. Here again Bavinck displays no fear of "dualism" but insists that the original creation perfection was only a preparation for the final glorious consummation where God will be all in all and impart his glory to his creatures. It is in the confidence of that hope that the Christian believer trusts in the Heavenly Father's care and preservation of his creation, a believing hope that provides unspeakable comfort and consolation in the midst of this vale of tears. Here the pastoral purpose of good

32. For an example, offered in critique of this tendency, see John M. Frame, *The Doctrine of the Knowledge of God* (Phillipsburg, N.J.: Presbyterian and Reformed, 1987), 235–6.

creation theology becomes clear: Our Heavenly Father is Almighty God, the Creator of heaven and earth, who turns all things to our good.

In sum, Bavinck's Reformed dogmatics, of which this volume is a truly representative sample, is biblically and confessionally faithful, pastorally sensitive, challenging, and still relevant. Bavinck's life and thought reflect a serious effort to be pious, orthodox, and thoroughly contemporary. To pietists fearful of the modern world on the one hand and to critics of orthodoxy skeptical about its continuing relevance on the other, Bavinck's example suggests a model answer: an engaging trinitarian vision of Christian discipleship in God's world.

In conclusion, a few words about the editing decisions that govern this translated volume that is based on the second, expanded edition of the *Gereformeerde Dogmatiek*.[33] The seven chapters of this volume correspond exactly to the sections in the original, though the three major divisions ("Maker of Heaven and Earth," "The Image of God," and "God's Fatherly Care") as well as all internal chapter subdivisions and headings are new and, along with the chapter synopses, which are also not in the original, have been supplied by the editor. Bavinck's original footnotes have all been retained and brought up to contemporary bibliographic standards. Additional notes added by the editor are clearly marked. All works from the nineteenth century to the present are noted with full bibliographic information given in the first note of each chapter and with subsequent references abbreviated. Classic works produced prior to the nineteenth century (the Church Fathers, Aquinas's *Summa*, Calvin's *Institutes*, post-Reformation Protestant and Catholic works) for which there are often numerous editions are cited only by author, title, and standard notation of sections. More complete information for the original or an accessible edition for each is given in the bibliography appended at the end of this volume. Where English translations of foreign titles were available and could be consulted they have been used rather than the original. Unless indicated in the note by direct reference to a specific translation, translations of Latin, Greek, German, and French material are those of the translator taken directly from Bavinck's original text. References in the notes and bibliography that are incomplete or could not be confirmed are marked with an asterisk (*). Internal page references in the notes to other volumes of the *Gereformeerde Dogmatiek* are to the fourth edition of 1928.

---

33. The four volumes of the first edition of *Gereformeerde Dogmatiek* were published in the years 1895 through 1901. The second revised and expanded edition appeared between 1906 and 1911; the third edition, unaltered from the second, in 1918; the fourth, unaltered except for different pagination, in 1928.

The editor here gratefully acknowledges the helpful suggestions of several fellow DRTS board members and particularly the contribution of Dr. M. Eugene Osterhaven, emeritus Albertus C. Van Raalte Professor of Systematic Theology at Western Theological Seminary, Holland, Michigan, for his careful reading of the entire manuscript and his many helpful translation and stylistic suggestions as well as critical corrections.

John Bolt

1
Maker of Heaven and Earth

Creation

1

*The doctrine of creation, affirming the distinction between the Creator and his creature, is the starting point of true religion. There is no existence apart from God, and the Creator can only be known truly through revelation. Biblical religion rejects both pantheistic emanationism as well as Manichean dualism though each have had Christian and philosophical proponents. Along with materialist explanations of the universe these are not scientific in character but rather are religious worldviews masquerading as science. The sophisticated philosophical systems of Schelling, Hegel, Schopenhauer, and others fail to satisfy human religious need and are riddled with internal contradictions. To them all the Christian church confesses simply "I Believe in God the Father, Almighty, Creator of heaven and earth." This creation is properly said to be **ex nihilo**, "out of nothing," thus preserving the distinction in essence between the Creator and the world and the contingency of the world in its dependence on God. The Triune God is the author of creation rather than any intermediary. The outgoing works of God are indivisible though it is appropriate to distinguish an economy of tasks in the Godhead so that the Father is spoken of as the first cause, the Son as the one by whom all things are created, and the Holy Spirit as the immanent cause of life and movement in the universe. Scripture does relate the creation in a special way to the Son through the categories of Wisdom and Logos. The Son is the Logos by whom the Father creates all things; the whole world is the realization of an idea of God. The creation proceeds **from** the Father **through** the Son and **in** the Spirit so that, in the Spirit and through the Son it may return to the Father. Creation also means that time has a beginning; only God is eternal. As creatures we are necessarily **in time,** and speculation about pretemporal or extratemporal reality is useless speculation. The purpose and goal of creation is to be found solely in God's will and glory. It is especially in the Reformed tradition that the honor and glory of God was made the fundamental principle of all doctrine and conduct. A doctrine of creation is one of the foundational building blocks of a biblical and Christian worldview. Creation is neither to be deified nor despoiled but as the "theater of God's glory" to be delighted in and used in a stewardly manner. It is God's **good** creation.*

The realization of the counsel of God begins with creation.[1] Creation is the initial act and foundation of all divine revelation and therefore the foundation of all religious and ethical life as well. The Old Testament creation story is of a beauty so sublime that it not only has no equal, but all thinkers, including such natural scientists as Cuvier and Von Humboldt, vie with each other in extolling it. "The first page of the Mosaic document is of greater consequence than all the volumes written by natural scientists and philosophers" (Jean Paul).[2] Subsequently that [act of] creation comes to the fore again and again throughout the history of revelation.

From the very first moment, true religion distinguishes itself from all other religions by the fact that it construes the relation between God and the world, including man, as that between the Creator and his creature. The idea of an existence apart and independently from God occurs nowhere in Scripture. God is the sole, unique, and absolute cause of all that exists. He has created all things by his Word and Spirit (Gen. 1:2, 3; Pss. 33:6; 104:29, 30; 148:5; Job 26:13; 33:4; Isa. 40:13; 48:13; Zech. 12:1; John 1:3; Col. 1:16; Heb. 1:2, etc.). There was no substance or principle of any kind to oppose him; no material to tie him down; no force to circumscribe his freedom. He speaks and things spring into being (Gen. 1:3; Ps. 33:9; Rom. 4:17). He is the unrestricted owner of heaven and earth (Gen. 14:19, 22; Pss. 24:2; 89:12; 95:4, 5). There are no limits to his power; he does all he sees fit to do (Isa. 14:24, 27; 46:10; 55:10; Pss. 115:3; 135:6). From him and through him and to him are all things (Rom. 11:36; 1 Cor. 8:6; Heb. 11:3). The world is the product of his will (Ps. 33:6; Rev. 4:11); it is the revelation of his perfections (Prov. 8:22f.; Job 28:23f.; Pss. 104:1; 136:5f.; Jer. 16:12) and finds its goal in his glory (Isa. 43:17; Prov. 16:4; Rom. 11:36; 1 Cor. 8:6).

This teaching of creation, which occupies a preeminent and pivotal place in Scripture, is not, however, presented as a philosophical explanation of the problem of existence. Most certainly it also offers an answer to the question of the origin of all things. Yet its significance is first and foremost religious and ethical. No right relation to God is conceivable apart from this basis; it positions us in the proper relation to God (Exod.

---

1. *Ed. note:* The immediately preceding section of the *Reformed Dogmatics* was the concluding one on the doctrine of God and dealt with the "Counsel of God."

2. *Ed. note:* Jean Paul Friedrich Richter (1763–1825), more commonly known simply as Jean Paul after his hero Jean-Jacques Rousseau, was a popular German novelist who significantly influenced the German Romantic movement as well as the Scottish historian and writer, Thomas Carlyle (1795–1881). In view of Jean Paul's tendency toward nature-pantheism, it is rather remarkable that Bavinck cites him here at the beginning of his section on creation. For a discussion of Jean Paul as a (pre)Romantic novelist, see Alan Menhennet, *The Romantic Movement* (London: Croon Helm; Totowa, N.J.: Barnes & Noble, 1981), 172–85.

20:11; Deut. 10:12–14; 2 Kings 19:15; Neh. 9:6). It is therefore of eminent practical value, serving to bring out the greatness, the omnipotence, the majesty, and the goodness, wisdom, and love of God (Ps. 19; Job 37; Isa. 40). The teaching of creation therefore strengthens people's faith, confirms their trust in God, and is a source of consolation in their suffering (Pss. 33:6f.; 65:6f.; 89:12; 121:2; 134:5; Isa. 37:16; 40:28f.; 42:5, etc.); it inspires praise and thanksgiving (Pss. 136:3f., 148:5; Rev. 14:7); it induces humility and meekness and makes people sense their smallness and insignificance before God (Job 38:4f.; Isa. 29:16; 45:9; Jer. 18:6; Rom. 9:20).

Creation and Its Religious Alternatives: Pantheism and Materialism

The doctrine of creation is known only from revelation and is understood by faith (Heb. 11:3). Granted that Catholic teaching contends that it can also be discovered from nature by reason,[3] and the Vatican Council even elevated this doctrine to the status of a dogma.[4] But the history of religions and philosophy does not support this claim. Islam, indeed, teaches a creation from nothing but borrowed this doctrine from Judaism and Christianity.[5] Pagan cosmogonies, which are at the same time theogonies, are all polytheistic. They all assume the existence of a primordial stuff, whether it is construed as chaos, a personal principle, a cosmic egg, or something like it. Finally, they tend to be either emanationist, so that the world is an emanation from God; or evolutionistic, so that the world becomes ever more divine; or dualistic, so that the world is a product of two antagonistic principles.[6] Nor is the Chaldean Genesis, which for that matter offers striking parallels to that of the Old Testament, an exception to this rule. It is also a theogony and has Bel fashion the world from the *tiamat* that chaotically stores all things within itself.[7] Greek philosophy either, materialistically, seeks the origin of things in a material element (Ionian school; Atomists); or, pantheistically, in the one eternal immutable being (Eleatic school), or in eternal becoming

3. T. Aquinas, II *Sent.*, dist. 1, qu. 1, art. 2; idem, *Contra Gentiles*, II, 15; J. Kleutgen, *Philosophie der Vorzeit vertheidigt* (Münster: Theissing, 1863), II, 795f.; M. J. Scheeben, *Handbuch der Katholischer Dogmatik* (Freiburg i.B.: Herder, 1933), II, 5, 6; J. B. Heinrich and K. Gutberlet, *Dogmatische Theologie*, 2nd ed. (Mainz: Kircheim, 1881–1900), V, 64f.

4. "Dogmatic Constitution, *Dei Filius,* on the Catholic Faith," ch. 2, can. 2, in *Documents of Vatican Council I, 1869–1870,* selected and translated by John F. Broderich, S.J. (Collegeville, Minn.: Liturgical, 1971).

5. O. Zöckler, *Geschichte der Beziehungen zwichen Theologie und Naturwissenschaft* (Gütersloh: C. Bertelsman, 1877–99), I, 426f.

6. O. Zöckler, "Schöpfung und Erhaltung der Welt," in *Realencyklopädie für protestantische Theologie und Kirche (PRE),* 3rd ed., XVII, 681–704.

7. H. H. Kuyper, *Evolutie of Revelatie* (Amsterdam: Höveker & Wormser, 1903), pp. 37, 38, 117f.; cf. also Chapter 3 below, "Earth."

(Heraclitus, Stoa). Even Anaxagoras, Plato, and Aristotle never rose above a dualism of spirit and matter. God, to them, is not a creator but at best a fashioner of the world *(dēmiourgos)*. Though the Scholastics sometimes asserted that Plato and Aristotle taught a creation out of nothing, this view was rightly rejected by others—Bonaventure, for example.[8] The Greeks knew of a *phusis* (nature), *kosmos* (world), but not of a *ktisis* (creature). Christianity gained a victory over this pagan theogony and cosmogony in its controversy with Gnosticism which, to explain sin, predicated the existence of an inferior god alongside the supreme Deity, or an eternal *hulē* (matter). Pagan explanations of the origin of things, however, have kept surfacing also in Christian centuries. It is already stated in Wisdom of Solomon 11:17 that God's all-powerful hand "created the world out of formless matter" *(amorphos hulē)* and the same expression occurs in Justin Martyr.[9] But in this connection Justin has in mind the later so-called *creatio secunda* and in another place expressly teaches also the creation of matter.[10] Just as Gnosticism emerged in the second century, so, after the Council of Nicea, Manicheism arose, which explained sin similarly by assuming the existence of an original evil being in addition to the true God.[11] This dualism was widely disseminated in Christianity, reaching even the Priscillians in Spain, and again surfacing in the Middle Ages among the Bogomiles and Cathari.

Not only dualism but also pantheism acquired its interpreters. Under the influence of Neo-Platonism Pseudo-Dionysius taught that the ideas and archetypes of all things existed eternally in God, whose superabundant goodness moved him to confer reality on these ideas and to impart himself to his creatures.[12] In his creatures God as it were emerged from his oneness, multiplying himself and pouring himself out in them,[13] so that God is universal being,[14] the very being of all things.[15] But he adds that God nevertheless maintains his unity[16] and is all in all inasmuch as he is the cause of all.[17]

8. Bonaventure, II *Sent.*, dist. 1, p. 1, art. 1, Q. 1; cf. J. Heinrich and K. Gutberlet, *Dogmatische Theologie*, V, 29, 30.

9. Justin Martyr, *Apology*, I, 10, 59.

10. Justin Martyr, *Dialogue with Trypho*, 5; idem, *Discourse to the Greeks*, 23; K. G. Semisch, *Justin Martyr: His Life, Writings and Opinions* (Edinburgh: T. & T. Clark, 1843), II, 336.

11. See Augustine, *The Writings against the Manichaeans*, in *Nicene and Post-Nicene Fathers*, first series, vol. IV, ed. by Philip Schaff (Grand Rapids: Eerdmans, 1989 [1897]); cf. K. Kessler, "Mani, Manichaer," *PRE*[3], XII, 193–228.

12. Pseudo Dionysius, *The Divine Names*, ch. 4, 10.

13. Ibid., ch. 2, 10.

14. Ibid., ch. 5, 4.

15. Ibid., *The Celestial Hierarchy*, ch. 4, 1.

16. Ibid., *The Divine Names*, ch. 2, 11.

17. Ibid., *The Celestial Hierarchy*, ch. 5, 8.

The same ideas recur in Erigena. Though he repeatedly and expressly teaches a creation out of nothing,[18] what makes his system pantheistic is the way he relates the four natures to each other. The first nature, which creates and is not created, that is, God, by thinking brings forth out of nothing, that is, from within himself, the ideas and forms of all things in the divine Word.[19] This Word is the second nature, which is created and creates. This second nature is created nature *(natura creata)* insofar as it is brought forth by God and it is creative *(creatrix)* insofar as it is itself the cause and potency of the real world. For this second nature is not really and substantially distinct from the third nature—the phenomenal world, which is created and does not create—the former is the cause, the latter the effect but it is the same world viewed one moment in the eternity of the Word of God and the next in the temporality of the world.[20] It is God himself who first, in the ideas, creates himself, then flows down into his creatures and becomes all in all in order, finally, to return to himself in the fourth nature, which does not create and is not created.[21] And the cause of this process is the goodness of God,[22] his drive to become all things.[23]

Outside of the Christian world pantheism was propagated by the philosophers Avicenna (1036) and Averroes (1198), [among Muslims] by Sufism, which viewed the universe as an emanation of God, and among Jews by the Cabala.[24] Toward the end of the Middle Ages and at the dawn of the modern era all these pantheistic, dualistic, emanationistic ideas freely crisscrossed among mystics, theosophists, and Anabaptists, such as Floris, Amalric of Bena, the Brethren of the Free Spirit, the Libertines, Eckhardt, Tauler, Servetus, Frank, Schwenkfeld, Bruno, Paracelsus, Fludd, Weigel, and Böhme. Even Socinianism only taught a creation from formless matter *(amorphos hulē),*[25] thus abstractly positing the finite and the infinite alongside and over against each other that the former could not possibly be the effect of the latter.

Pantheism was nevertheless again restored to a position of honor in modern philosophy by Spinoza. In his view the one substance is the eternal and necessary efficient and immanent cause of the world; the

18. John Scotus Erigena, *On the Division of Nature*, Bk. III, V, 24, 33.
19. Ibid., III, 14, 17.
20. Ibid., III, 8.
21. Ibid., III, 4, 20.
22. Ibid., III, 2, 4, 9.
23. Ibid., I, 12.
24. A. Stöckl, *Philosophie des Mittelalters* (Mainz: Kircheim, 1864–66), II, 28, 92, 181, 237.
25. O. Fock, *Der Socinianismus nach seiner Stellung in der Gesammtentwicklung des christlichen Geistes* (Kiel: C. Schröder, 1847), 482.

world is the explication of the divine being and particulars are the modes by which the divine attributes of thought and extension are determined in a particular way.[26]

Toward the end of the eighteenth century this philosophy found increasing acceptance and was elevated by Schelling and Hegel to *the* system of the nineteenth century. The biblical doctrine of creation was rejected *in toto*. Fichte wrote: "the assumption of a creation is the basic error of all false metaphysics and religious teaching and particularly the arch-principle of Judaism and paganism."[27] Schelling called creation out of nothing a "cross to the intellect" and firmly opposed it.[28] In his first period he taught an absolute identity between God and the world. The two are related to each other as essence and form; they are the same, but viewed from different perspectives. God is not the cause of the All, but the All itself, and the All, accordingly, is not in process of becoming but something eternally existing, *en kai pan*.[29] But in his later period, thanks to Baader, he came under the influence of Böhme and thus under that of the Cabala and Neo-Platonism, and began to look for the world's ground in the dark nature of God. Theogony and cosmogony are most intimately connected. Just as God raises himself from his undifferentiated state, by the opposition of the *principia*, nature (*Urgrund, Ungrund*, darkness) and intellect (word, light), to the level of Spirit, love, and personality, so these three are simultaneously the potencies of the world. The dark nature in God is the principle of blind confusion, the matter and ground of the created world insofar as it is chaos and has a chaotic character. But also at work in that world is the potency of the divine intellect, which introduces light, order, and regularity into it. God meanwhile manifests himself

26. B. Spinoza, *Ethics*, Part I.

27. J. G. Fichte, *Die Anweisung zum Seligen Leben* (London: Trübner, 1873), 160. *Ed note:* A new German edition of this work was published in 1970 by Meiner in Hamburg. The essay is also found in J. G. Fichte, *Characteristics of the Present Age: The Way towards the Blessed Life: Or, the Doctrine of Religion* (Washington, D.C.: University Publications of America, 1977). For a discussion of Fichte's essay, see H. Berkhof, *Two Hundred Years of Theology* (Grand Rapids: Eerdmans, 1989), 26-28.

28. F. W. J. Schelling, *Werke*, I/2, 44f., I/8, 62f. *Ed. note:* Bavinck's references to Schelling that are to works incorporated into the new, unrevised, but abridged and repaginated *Ausgewählte Werke* (Darmstadt: Wissenschafliche Buchgesellschaft, 1968), will be cited with the full title of the work as well as Bavinck's original reference. Since this is not a complete edition of Schelling's original *Sämmtliche Werke* (Stuttgart & Augsburg: J. G. Cotta'scher, 1856–61), writings not included in the new edition will be cited as *Werke* using Bavinck's original reference.

29. F. W. J. Schelling, *Ausgewählte Werke*, III, 13f. ("Darstellung meines Systems der Philosophie," *Werke* I/4, 117f.); idem, *Werke*, I/5, 24f., 365f., 373f., idem, *Ausgewählte Werke*, III, 698f. ("System der gesammten Philosophie und der Naturphilosophie insbesondere," *Werke*, I/6, 174).

as Spirit in the spirit of mankind and achieves full personality in the spirit of mankind.[30]

Hegel, too, openly acknowledged his adherence to pantheism, not in the pantheism that regards finite things themselves as God but in the pantheism that in the finite and accidental sees the appearance of the absolute, the fossilized idea, frozen intelligence.[31] This pantheism passed from philosophy into theology. Schleiermacher rejected the distinction between creation and providence and considered the question concerning whether the world was temporal or eternal a matter of indifference, provided the absolute dependence of all things on God was upheld.[32] Similarly, in Strauss, Biedermann, Schweizer, and others, God is no more than the eternal immanent cause and ground of the world.[33]

Alongside of this pantheism there also emerged a materialism which seeks the final elements of all being in eternal (without beginning) and indestructible material atoms, and attempts to explain all phenomena of the entire universe in light of atomic processes of mechanical and chemical separation and union in accordance with fixed laws. This materialism had its roots in Greek philosophy, was reintroduced in modern times by Gassendi and Descartes, and was advocated by the British and French philosophy of the eighteenth century. It appeared in the nineteenth century, not as the fruit of scientific study but as the product of philosophical reflection in Feuerbach, who can be called the father of materialism in Germany. After 1850, as a result of a variety of incidental causes, it found acceptance at least for a time among such natural scientists as Vogt, Büchner, Moleschott, Czolbe, and Haeckel.[34]

30. F. W. J. Schelling, *Ausgewählte Werke*, IV, 303f. ("Philosophische Untersuchungen über das Wesen der menslichen Freiheit und die damit zusammenhängenden Gegenstände," *Werke*, I/7, 359f.); idem, *Werke*, II/2, 103f., II/3, 262f.

31. G. W. F. Hegel, *Sämtliche Werke*, vol. 9 (Stuttgart: F. Frommann, 1958), 49–54 (*System der Philosophie: Zweiter Teil. Die Naturphilosophie*, §§247–51, "Begriff der Natur," *Werke*, VII, 23f.). *Ed note:* When possible, references to Hegel's writings will be cited from the modern Stuttgart edition or a published English translation. The title of Hegel's work and Bavinck's original citation from Hegel's *Werke* will be given in parentheses.

32. F. Schleiermacher, *The Christian Faith*, ed. by H. R. MacIntosh and J. S. Steward (Edinburgh: T. & T. Clark, 1928), §§36, 41.

33. D. F. Strauss, *Die Christliche Glaubenslehre* (Tübingen: C. F. Osiander, 1840), I, 656f.; A. E. Biedermann, *Christliche Dogmatik* (Zürich: Füssli, 1869), §§649f.; A. Schweizer, *Die Christliche Glaubenslehre* (Leipzig: G. Hirzel, 1877), §71; O. Pfleiderer, *Grundriss der christlichen Glaubens und Sittenlehre* (Berlin: G. Reimer, 1888), §84; J. H. Scholten, *Dogmatices Christianae initia*, 2nd ed. (1858), 111; S. Hoekstra, *Wijsg. Godsd.*, II, 174. *Ed. note:* Bavinck may be referring to S. Hoekstra, *Grondslag, Wezen en Openbaring van het Godsdienstig Geloof volgens de Heilige Schrift* (Rotterdam: Altmann & Roosenburg, 1861).

34. F. A. Lange, *Geschichte des Materialismus*, 8th ed. (Leipzig: Baedekker, 1908).

It needs to be said, first of all, that neither pantheism nor materialism is the result of exact science but of philosophy, of a worldview, of systems of belief. Neither is "knowledge" in the strict sense of the word. Granted, materialism loves to pass itself off as an exact science but it can be easily demonstrated that, both historically and logically, it is the fruit of human thought, a matter of both the human heart and the human head. For the origin and end of things lie outside the boundaries of human observation and research. Science presupposes existence and rests on the foundation of what has been created. In that regard pantheism and materialism are in the same position as theism, which acknowledges the mysterious origin of things. The only question, therefore, is whether pantheism and materialism can replace this mystery with an intelligible explanation. This demand may well be made of both since they both reject the doctrine of creation on account of its incomprehensibility and view it as a "cross to the intellect." Is it indeed the case that pantheism and materialism do a better job of satisfying the intellect than theism and therefore deserve preference? Actually, in the history of humankind both systems have repeatedly made their appearance and again and again have been abandoned; they have so often been subjected to serious and effective criticism that no one can now accept them solely because they are so satisfying to the intellect. Other motives play the decisive role here. If the world did not originate by an act of creation, then certainly there must be some other explanation. And in that case—excluding dualism—here there are only two options available: either one explains matter from mind or mind from matter. Pantheism and materialism are not pure opposites; rather, they are two sides of the same coin; they constantly merge into each other and only differ in that they address the same problem from opposite directions. Thus, both run into the same objections.

Pantheism, in confronting the transition from thought to being, from idea to reality, from substance to modes, has produced nothing resembling a solution. Indeed, it has assumed various forms and described that transition by different names. It conceives the relation of God to the world as that of *en kai pan* ("one and many"), of nature bringing forth and nature already born (*natura naturans* and *naturata*), of substance and modes, of existence and appearance, of the universal and the particular, of the species and specimens, of the whole and its parts, of idea and objectivation, of the ocean and its waves, and so forth; but for all these words it has said nothing about the relation. From the pantheistic perspective it is incomprehensible how "being" emerged from "thought," how multiplicity came from unity, how matter proceeded from mind. This has become abundantly clear from the systems of Schelling and Hegel. There was certainly no lack of words in these systems [as the following characteristic phrases illustrate]: The idea assumes form, incarnates itself, objectivizes itself, passes into another mode of being; it splits off and differentiates itself; it freely decides to release and to realize itself, to turn into its opposite.[35]

This solution, however, proved so unsatisfying to both Schelling and Hegel that they frequently spoke of a "breakaway" or "defection" from the absolute by which the world originated.[36] No wonder, therefore, that Schelling in his second period and so also Schopenhauer, von Hartmann, et al., gave primacy to the will and primarily conceived the Absolute as nature, will, and drive. The pantheistic identity of thought and being proved to be in error, all the more because "Substance," the "Idea," the "All," or however pantheism may designate the Absolute, is not a fullness of being but pure potentiality, an abstraction without content, a mere nothing. And this is supposed to be the explanation of the riches of the world, the multiplicity of the existent! Let those believe it who can! Kleutgen, accordingly, is right on target when he writes: "The difference between pantheistic speculation and that of the theist . . . is this: whereas the former, starting with assumptions—as obscure as they are unprovable—about the divine being, ends in open contradictions; the latter, proceeding from a sure knowledge of finite things, gains ever-higher kinds of insights, until it encounters the Incomprehensible, not losing its grip on the fact that the One whom it recognizes as the eternal and immutable Author of all things is far above our thought processes in his essence and works."[37]

In the case of materialism the origin of things remains similarly unexplained. While pantheism pictures the universe as proceeding from one ultimate principle and therefore preferably presents itself today as

---

35. F. W. J. Schelling, *Ausgewählte Werke*, I, 386f. ("Ideen zu einer Philosophie der Natur, Einleitung," *Werke*, I/2, 62f.); idem, *Ausgewählte Werke*, III, 119f., 153f. ("Bruno oder über das göttliche und natürliche Princip der Dinge," *Werke*, I/4, 223f., 257f.); G. W. F. Hegel, *The Encyclopaedia of Logic (with the Zusätze)*, trans. by T. F. Geraets et al. (Indianapolis/Cambridge: Hackett, 1991), 306–7; idem, *Hegel's Philosophy of Nature*, trans. by M. J. Petry (London and New York: Allen Unwin, Humanities Press, 1970). *Ed. note:* Bavinck's references are to Hegel, *Werke*, VI, 413ff., VII, 23f., which comprises §§243 and following (likely through §252) of Hegel's *System der Philosophie*, found in volumes 8–10 of Hegel's *Sämtliche Werke* (Stuttgart: F. Frommann, 1958).

36. F. W. J. Schelling, *Ausgewählte Werke*, III, 614ff. ("Philosophie und Religion," *Werke*, I/6, 38f.); G. W. F. Hegel, *Lectures on the Philosophy of Religion*, trans. by E. B. Speirs and J. Burdon Sanderson (London: Kegan Paul, Trench, Trübner, 1895), II, 311–12 (*Werke*, XII, 177).

37. J. Kleutgen, *Philosophie der Vorzeit*, II, 884.

monism,[38] materialism assumes a multiplicity of "principles." But, according to materialism, these ultimate "principles" of all things are nothing other than indivisible particles of matter. Now if the proponents of this worldview remained true to this fundamental thesis of theirs, they would have no warrant for attributing to these atoms a single metaphysical and transcendent predicate. On the materialist position, rightly considered, it is not permissible to speak of "eternity," "uncreatedness," "the indestructibility of atoms," or even of "matter" and "energy." If one says that the world originated from material atoms, one should remain true to that position. Atoms, after all, since they are elements of the empirical world, can only have empirical and not metaphysical properties. The concept of atom, by definition and as such, in no way implies that it is eternal and indestructible. Those who regard atoms as the ultimate "principles" of all being cut themselves off from the road to speculation and metaphysics and must empirically explain the world solely from those empirical atoms. The materialist can only say that experience teaches that atoms do not come into being or cease to exist; he has no warrant, however, for speaking of the atoms' metaphysical nature and metaphysical properties. Natural science, to which the materialist always makes his appeal, has to do as such with the finite, the relative, with nature and its phenomena; it always starts out from nature, assumes it as a given, and cannot penetrate to what lies behind it. The moment it does this it ceases to be physics and becomes metaphysics. But materialism is not true to itself when it immediately ascribes to atoms all sorts of properties that are not part of the concept itself and are not taught by experience. Materialism, accordingly, is not an exact science, nor the fruit of rigorous scientific research, but a philosophy that is built up on the denial of all philosophy; it is inherently self-contradictory; it rejects all absolutes and makes atoms absolute; it denies God's existence and deifies matter.

One can state this in even stronger terms: if materialism wants to explain all things from matter, it lacks all warrant for speaking of atoms.

38. On pantheism, see H. Ulrici, "Pantheismus," *PRE¹*, 64–77; M. Heinze, "Pantheismus," *PRE³*, XIV, 627–41; J. I. Doedes, *Inleiding tot de Leer van God* (Utrecht: Kemink, 1870), 61f.; *C. W. Opzoomer, *Wetenschap en Wijsbegeerte* (1857), ch. 1; A. Pierson, *Bespiegeling, Gezag, en Ervaring* (Utrecht: Kemink, 1885), ch. 1; L. W. E. Rauwenhoff, *Wijsbegeerte van den Godsdienst* (Leiden: Brill & van Doesburgh, 1887), 205f.; *Hoekstra, *Wijsg. Godsd.* 11, 73ff. (*ed. note:* see note 33, above); A. Kuyper, "Pantheism's Destruction of Boundaries," *Methodist Review* 52 (1893): 520–35, 762–78; Van Dijk, *Aesthetische en Ethische Godsdienst* (1895); Hugenholtz, *Ethische Pantheisme* (Amsterdam: Van Holkema & Warendorff, 1903); Bruining, "Pantheisme of Theisme," *Teylers Theologische Tijdschrift* (1904): 433–57. *Ed. note:* Bavinck adds that this last article was opposed by De Graaf, op. cit., 165–210, which is likely a reference to the same journal, *Teylers Theologische Tijdschrift*.

Atoms have never been observed; no one has ever seen them; empirical research has never brought them to light. They are originally of a metaphysical nature and for that reason alone should be contraband to materialism. Further, as metaphysical substances they are caught up in an antinomy that has not yet been resolved by anybody. They are material and (we are told) at the same time indivisible, immutable, infinite in number, eternal, and indestructible. And in addition to all this, if matter itself—the matter that is assumed as the principle that explains the entire universe—were only known and comprehensible! But exactly the essence and nature of matter is the most mysterious thing of all. It totally eludes our cognitive grasp. It is easier for us to conceive and imagine the nature of spirit than the nature of matter. Matter is a word, a name, but we do not know what we mean by it. We face here a mystery as great in its kind as the existence of spirit which, on account of its incomprehensibility, is rejected by materialism. However, if we assume that atoms exist and that they are eternal and immutable, we have not yet done anything to explain the world by that assumption. *How* did the world originate from those atoms? If the now-existing or a preceding world had a beginning, there must be a cause by which the atoms were set in motion, and in the kind of motion that resulted in the present world. But this motion cannot be explained from matter, for all matter is by nature inert and only starts moving as the result of an impulse from without. Materialism, however, cannot accept a prime mover existing independently of matter. So the materialist has no choice but to also declare absolute and eternal (like the atom) motion, change, or, with Czolbe, even this existing world.

Materialism wraps itself in ever greater contradictions: it confuses the physical with the metaphysical, becoming with being, mutability with immutability, time with eternity, and speaks of infinite space, infinite time, and an infinite world as though it were not the most absurd self-contradiction. Finally, it has been shown, repeatedly and by various parties, that materialism remains utterly unable to explain how purely material, and therefore unconscious, inanimate, unfree, aimless atoms could produce that spiritual world of life, consciousness, purpose, religion, morality, and so on, which surely thrusts itself upon our inner consciousness with no less force than the physical world upon our senses. And it seems that little by little this criticism is beginning to have some kind of impact on the materialists themselves. The materialism that arose from pantheism in the previous century is increasingly reverting to pantheism and even incorporating a variety of mystical elements into itself. The "life force," which for a long time was rejected, once again has its defenders. Atoms are now pictured as being alive and animated. Haeckel again speaks of a "spirit in all things," of a "divine force," a "moving spirit," a "world-soul" which indwells all things. In this pantheistic monism he is looking for the connection between religion and science. But in so doing materialism is itself openly admitting its powerlessness to explain the world: in its impoverishment the mechanism of the atoms again cried out for help from the dynamic principle.[39]

Creatio ex Nihilo

Against all these movements the Christian church unitedly held fast to the confession: "I believe in God the Father, Almighty, Creator of heaven and earth." And by creation it meant that act of God through which, by his sovereign will, he brought the entire world out of nonbeing into a being that is distinct from his own being. And this is, in fact, the teaching of Holy Scripture. The word $b^{\circ}r$, originally means to split, divide, or cut (used in the piel for the clearing away of forests, Josh. 17:15, 18), and then to fashion, bring forth, create. Like the Dutch word *scheppen*, which originally means "to form" (cf. the English "to shape"), the Hebrew word by itself does not imply that something was brought into existence out of nothing, for it is frequently also used for the works of providence (Isa. 40:28; 45:7; Jer. 31:22; Amos 4:13). It is a synonym for and alternates with $hr\check{s}\ y\underline{s}r\ ^{c}\check{s}h$ (Ps. 104:30). But it differs from them in that it is always used to denote divine "making" and never with reference to human activity; in that it is never accompanied by an accusative of the matter from which something is made; and in that it therefore everywhere expresses the greatness and power of the works of God.[40] The same is true of the New Testament words *ktizein* (Mark 13:19), *poiein* (Matt. 19:4), *phemelioun* (Heb. 1:10), *katartizein* (Rom. 9:12), *kataskeuazein* (Heb. 3:4), and *plassein* (Rom. 9:20), and of the Latin word *creare*. These words also do not by themselves express creating out of nothing. The expression "to create out of nothing," accordingly, is not literally derived from Scripture but first occurs in 2 Macca-

39. On materialism, in addition to M. Heinze, "Materialismus," *PRE*³, XII, 414–24, and the literature cited there, see K. Gutberlet, *Der Mechanische Monismus: Eine Kritik der Modernen Weltanschauung* (Paderborn: F. Schöningh, 1893); W. Ostwald, *Die Ueberwindung des wissenschaftliche Materialismus* (Leipzig: Veit, 1895); J. Reinke, *Die Welt als That,* 4 vols. (Berlin: Paetel, 1905); M. Verworn, *Naturwissenschaft und Weltanschauung, eine Rede,* 2nd ed. (Leipzig: Barth, 1904); Lipps, *Naturwissenschaft und Weltanschauung* (Heidelberg: C. Winter, 1906); R. Otto, *Naturalistische und Religiöse Weltansicht* (Tübingen: H. Laupp, 1905); A. Kuyper, "Evolution," *Calvin Theological Journal* 31 (1996): 11–50; H. Bavinck, "Evolutie," in *Verzamelde Opstellen* (Kampen: Kok, 1921), 105–20. *Ed. note:* An English version of Bavinck's views on evolution can be found in his "Creation or Development," *Methodist Review* 61 (1901): 849–74.

40. Franz Delitzsch, *A New Commentary on Genesis* trans. by Sophia Taylor (Edinburgh: T. & T. Clark, 1899), 74.

bees 7:28, where it is stated that God made heaven and earth and man out of nonbeing (*ek ouk ontōn epoiēsen;* Vulg. *fecit ex nihilo*). Some scholars dispute that this expression may be understood in the strict sense and have given it a Platonic interpretation. It is nevertheless worth noting that the author does not speak of *mē onta*, that is, a nothing which could not exist *(nihilum privativum)*, a matter devoid of quality and form, but of *ouk onta*, a nothing which does not exist *(nihilum negativum)*. It is not even certain, moreover, that the author of the Book of Wisdom (11:18) taught the eternity of a formless matter; the passage can very well be understood to refer to the "secondary creation,"[41] just as this is the case in Justin Martyr.

However this may be, Scripture leaves no doubt about the matter in question. Though it does not use the term, it clearly teaches the matter. It must be granted that some scholars believe that Genesis 1:1–3, too, actually proceeded from an original, uncreated chaos. These scholars argue that because *br'št* is in the construct state, verses 1–3, to them, can be translated as follows: "In the beginning when God created heaven and earth—now the earth was a formless void, and so on—then God spoke and said: Let there be light." Therefore, according to this view, in verse 2 the existence of a formless and vacuous earth is presupposed in God's act of creating.[42] But this translation is not acceptable.[43] In the first case, the sentence thus acquires the length of a period, which is rare in Hebrew; it is not expected immediately at the beginning and in the style of Genesis 1; and puts much too strong an accent on the creation of light.[44] Furthermore, the construct state of *br'št* does not require this translation because it also occurs in the same form without suffix or genitive in Isaiah 46:10 (cf. Lev. 2:12; Deut. 33:21). In the third place, it would be strange if, while the initial clause would say that God still had to create heaven and earth, the intermediate clause already dubbed chaos with the name "earth" and made no mention whatever of the state of heaven. To this we must add that this translation, even if it were correct, in no way teaches the eternity of this desolate earth but at most leaves this issue open.

This overall view militates against the whole spirit of the creation narrative. Elohim is not presented in Genesis 1 as a cosmic sculptor who, in human fashion, with preexisting material, produces a work of art, but as

41. Augustine et al., in J. B. Heinrich and K. Gutberlet, *Dogmatische Theologie*, V, 44.

42. According to Ewald, Bunsen, Schrader, Gunkel, and others; see H. Schultz, *Alttestamentliche Theologie*, 5th ed. (Göttingen: Vandenhoeck & Ruprecht, 1896), 570f.

43. *Ed. note:* This is the translation adopted by the NRSV.

44. R. Smend, *Lehrbuch der alttestamentlichen Religionsgeschichte* (Freiburg i.B.: J. C. B. Mohr, 1893), 456; J. Wellhausen, *Prolegomena to the History of Israel* (Atlanta: Scholars, 1994 [1885]), 387, n. 1.

One who merely by speaking, by uttering a word of power, calls all things into being.[45] And with that view the whole of Scripture chimes in. God is the Almighty who is infinitely higher than all creatures and who deals with his creatures in accordance with his sovereign good pleasure. He is the absolute owner, the *qōnēh* of heaven and earth (Gen. 14:19, 22), who does whatever he pleases and to whose power there is no limit. He speaks and it comes to be, he commands and it stands forth (Gen. 1:3; Ps. 33:9; Isa. 48:13; Rom. 4:17). Further, all things in Scripture are described over and over as having been made by God and as being absolutely dependent on him. He has created all things, heaven, earth, the sea, and all that is on them and in them (Exod. 20:11; Neh. 9:6, etc.). Everything has been created by him (Col. 1:16, 17), exists only by his will (Rev. 4:11), and is of him, through him, and unto him (Rom. 11:36). Moreover, at no time or place is there even the slightest reference to an eternal formless matter. God alone is the Eternal and Imperishable One. He alone towers above processes of becoming and change. Things, by contrast, have a beginning and an end and are subject to change. [In Scripture] this is expressed in anthropomorphic language. God was there before the mountains were brought forth and his years never come to an end (Ps. 90:2; Prov. 8:25, 26); he chose and loved [his own] from the foundation of the world (Eph. 1:4; John 17:24; cf. Matt. 13:35; 25:34; Luke 11:50; John 17:5; Heb. 4:3; 9:26; 1 Pet. 1:20; Rev. 13:8; 17:8). And though in Romans 4:17 there is no express mention of creation, it does teach that God calls and summons *ta mē onta*, the things which possibly do not yet exist as if they did, *hōs onta*. Existence or nonexistence are alike to him. Hebrews 11:3 announces even more clearly that God has made the world so that what is seen is not made *ek phainomenōn*, from that which appears before our eyes. By this revelation a "formless matter" is totally ruled out; the visible world did not proceed from what is visible but rests in God who called all things into existence by his word.

This teaching of Scripture was most pointedly expressed in the words *ex nihilo* ("out of nothing") and was thus understood and passed on by Christian theology from the beginning.[46] But among Gnostics and Manichees, theosophists and naturalists, pantheists and materialists, this teaching has at all times been disputed. Especially Aristotle's dictum, *ex nihilo nihil fit* ("nothing is made from nothing"), has been advanced against it. But this polemic is entirely groundless. In the first

45. Reinke, *Die Welt als That*, 481ff., mistakenly asserts that Moses has no knowledge of a creation out of nothing and that such a creation out of nothing would in any case be at variance with the law of the constancy of energy.
46. *The Pastor of Hermas*, I, 1; *Theophilus to Autolycus*, II, 4; Tertullian, *The Prescription Against Heretics*, 13; Irenaeus, *Against Heresies*, II, 10.

place, this rule of Aristotle is not at all as simple as it looks. Every moment of the day we confront phenomena that are not reducible to present factors: history is not a simple problem of arithmetic; life is not the product solely of chemical combinations; the genius is something other and more than the child of his time and every personality is an original. But aside from these things and taken with a grain of salt, this rule of Aristotle is not unacceptable. Theology has never taught that nonbeing is the father, source, and principle of being. Perhaps redundantly, it has repeatedly added that the expression *ex nihilo* was not the description of a preexisting matter from which the world was made, but it only meant that that which exists once did not exist and that it was only called into existence by God's almighty power. Hence the expression *ex nihilo* is on a level with the term *post nihilum:* the preposition *ex* does not designate [the cause] but only excludes a material cause; the world has its cause, not in itself, but only in God.[47]

The expression *ex nihilo* was eagerly preserved in Christian theology only because it was admirably suited for cutting off all sorts of errors at the root. In the first place, it served as a defense against the paganistic notion of a formless stuff *(amorphos hulē)*, from which not even Plato and Aristotle were able to extricate themselves. In paganism a human being is bound by matter, subject to sensuality and nature worship; he cannot grasp the idea that the mind is free and above matter, and even much less that God is absolutely sovereign, defined by nothing other than his own essence. Over against this view, the doctrine of creation out of nothing teaches the absolute sovereignty of God and man's absolute dependence; if only a single particle were not created out of nothing God would not be God. In the second place, this expression rules out all emanation, every hint of an essential identity between God and the world. Granted, the Scholastics wrote repeatedly about an emanation or procession of all existence from a universal cause and also occasionally of the creature's participation in the being and life of God. But in saying this they did not mean "emanation" in the strict sense as if God's own being flowed out into his creatures and so unfolded in them, like the genus in its species. They only meant to say that God is a self-subsistent necessary being *(ens per essentiam)* but the creature is existent by participation *(ens per participationem)*. Creatures indeed have a being of their own, but this being has its efficient and exemplary cause in the being of God.[48]

47. Irenaeus, *Against Heresies*, II, 14; Augustine, *Confessions*, XI, 5; XII 7; idem, *The Literal Meaning of Genesis*, I, 1; Anselm, *Monologion*, ch. 8; T. Aquinas, *Summa Theol.*, I, qu. 45., art. 1, and so forth.
48. T. Aquinas, *Summa Theol.*, I, qu. 45, art. 1; J. Kleutgen, *Philosophie der Vorzeit*, II, 828ff., 899f.

The teaching of creation out of nothing maintains that there is a distinction in essence between God and the world. The creation does not exist as a result of a passage of the world from being in God to being outside of God, nor from being without God to being by God, but from nonexistence into existence. The world is certainly no anti-God; it has no independent existence, and remains in God as its ongoing immanent cause, as will have to be demonstrated later in the teaching of preservation, against Manicheism and Deism. But according to the teaching of Scripture the world is not a part of or emanation from the being of God. It has a being and existence of its own, one that is different and distinct from the essence of God. And that is what is expressed by the term *ex nihilo*. Nevertheless this term too has been misused by philosophy. Just as Plato understood *mē on* (nonbeing) as an eternal unformed substance, so Erigena even described God as *nihilum* insofar as he transcends all categories and limitations, all existence and being; "since, then, he is understood to be incomprehensible, he is not undeservedly called 'nihilum' on account of [his] surpassing excellence" *(dum ergo incomprehensibilis intelligitur, per excellentiam nihilum non immerito vocitatur)*. And if he brings forth everything out of nothing, that then means that he "produces essence from his own—as it were—'superessentiality,' lives from his own 'supervitality.'"[49] Even odder was the way Hegel in his *Wissenschaft der Logic* dealt with this concept when he defined "nothingness" as "nonbeing that is simultaneously a kind of being and a being that is simultaneously nonbeing," a nothingness that is at the same time everything, namely, in potentiality and nothing specific concretely.[50]

Christian theology is diametrically opposed to this conceptual confusion in philosophy. It understands "nothingness" to be purely negative and rejects all emanation. Still, even in emanation there is an element of truth which, without violating the essence of God, is especially maintained by the biblical doctrine of creation far better than in philosophy. The doctrine of creation out of nothing, in fact, gives to Christian theology a place between Gnosticism and Arianism, that is, between pantheism and Deism. Gnosticism knows no creation but only emanation and therefore makes the world into the Son, wisdom, the image of God in an antiquated sense. Arianism, on the other hand, knows nothing of emanation but only of creation and therefore makes the Son into a creature. In the former the world is deified; in the latter God is made

49. Erigena, *On the Division of Nature*, III, 19, 20.

50. G. W. F. Hegel, The Encyclopedia Logic, 139–45 (Wissenschaft der Logik, Sämtliche Werke, IV, 87–118; ed. note: Bavinck's own pagination in his note is to Werke, III, 64, 73f., when it should be Werke, III, 77–108).

mundane. But Scripture, and therefore Christian theology, knows both emanation and creation, a twofold communication of God—one within and the other outside the divine being; one to the Son who was in the beginning with God and was himself God, and another to creatures who originated in time; one from the being and another by the will of God. The former is called generation; the latter, creation. By generation, from all eternity, the full image of God is communicated to the Son; by creation only a weak and pale image of God is communicated to the creature. Still the two are connected. Without generation creation would not be possible. If in an absolute sense God could not communicate himself to the Son, he would be even less able, in a relative sense, to communicate himself to his creature. If God were not triune, creation would not be possible.[51]

The Creator Is the Triune God

Holy Scripture, accordingly, teaches that the Triune God is the author of creation. Scripture knows no intermediate beings. In the case of the plural in Genesis 1:26 the Jews thought of angels. The Gnostics saw proceeding from God a series of aeons that played a creative role. The Arians made the Son an intermediate being between Creator and creature who, though created, nevertheless himself created as well. In the Middle Ages many [scholars] were prepared to accept a cooperative role for the creature in the act of creation. They arrived at this thesis because in the church the forgiveness of sins and the dispensing of grace was inherent in [ecclesiastical] office so that a priest performing the Mass could change the bread into the body of Christ and so become "a creator of his own creator" *(creator sui creatoris)* (Biel). It is for this reason that Peter Lombard says in his doctrine of the sacraments that God could also "create some things through some person, not through him as 'author' but as minister with whom and in whom he worked."[52] Some, such as Durand, Suarez, and Bellarmine, followed him, but others, like Thomas, Scotus, Bonaventure, Richard, and so on, dissented.[53] Reformed theologians who, more than Catholic and Lutheran scholars, resisted every tendency to commingle the Creator and the creature, agreed with the latter.[54] Scripture exclusively attributes the act of creation to God

---

51. Athanasius, *Against the Arians*, I, 12; II, 56, 78.
52. P. Lombard, IV, *Sent.*, dist. 5, n. 3.
53. T. Aquinas, *Summa Theol.*, I, qu. 45, art. 3; J. Kleutgen, *Philosophie der Vorzeit*, II, 849f.; J. Heinrich and K. Gutberlet, *Dogmatische Theologie*, V, 89f.
54. G. Voetius, *Select Disp.*, I, 556f.; *Synopsis Purioris Theologiae*, X, 14; Turretin, *Institutes of Elenctic Theology*, V, qu. 2; J. H. Heidegger, *Corpus Theologiae*, VI, 14; P. van Mastricht, *Theologia*, III, 5, 20; C. Vitringa, *Doct. Christ.*, II, 81–82.

(Gen. 1:11; Isa. 40:12f.; 44:24, 45:12; Job 9:5–10; 38:2f.). It is what distinguishes him from false gods (Ps. 96:5; Isa. 37:16; Jer. 10:11, 12).

Creating is a divine work, an act of infinite power and therefore is incommunicable in either nature or grace to any creature, whatever it may be. But Christian theology all the more unanimously attributed the work of creation to all three persons in the Trinity. Scripture left no doubt on this point. God created all things through the Son (Ps. 33:6; Prov. 8:22; John 1:3; 5:17; 1 Cor. 8:6; Col. 1:15–17; Heb. 1:3) and through the Spirit (Gen. 1:2; Ps. 33:6; Job 26:13; 33:4; Ps. 104:30; Isa. 40:13; Luke 1:35). In this context the Son and the Spirit are not viewed as secondary forces but as independent agents or "principles" *(principia)*, as authors *(auctores)* who with the Father carry out the work of creation, as with him they also constitute the one true God.

This doctrine of Scripture did not immediately come into its own in the Christian church. Initially the Logos was too frequently viewed as an intermediate being who effected the linkage between God and the world while the person and work of the Holy Spirit initially fell completely into the background. But Irenaeus already pointed out that in the act of creating God needed no alien instruments, nor did he use the angels for that purpose, but had his own hands: the Logos and the Holy Spirit by whom and in whom he created all things.[55] The doctrine of creation as the work of the whole Trinity was clearly developed by Athanasius and the three Cappadocians in the East, and by Augustine in the West. No creature, says Athanasius, can be the efficient cause *(poiētikon aition)* of creation. So then, if the Son with the Father creates the world, he cannot be an extradivine created demiurge, as Arius thinks, but has to be the very own Son of the Father, the "proper offspring of his own being" *(idion gennēa tes ousias autou)*.[56] But where the Logos is, there the Spirit is also, and so "the Father through the Word and in the Spirit creates all things" *(ho pater dia tou logou en to pneumati ktizei ta panta)*.[57] Augustine puts it even more strongly: "by this supremely, equally, and immutably good Trinity all things are created" *(ab hac summe et aequaliter et immutabiliter bona trinitate creata sunt omnia)* so that the entire creation bears the stamp of the Trinity *(vestigium trinitatis)*.[58] This teaching has thus become the common property of Christian theology as a whole[59] and of the

55. Irenaeus, *Against Heresies*, IV, 20.
56. Athanasius, *Against the Arians*, II, 21f.
57. Athanasius, *Ad Serap.*, III, 5.
58. Augustine, *Enchiridion*, 10; *On the Trinity*, VI, 10; *City of God*, XI, 24; *Confessions*, XIII, 11.
59. John of Damascus, *Exposition of the Orthodox Faith*, I, 8; T. Aquinas, *Summa Theol.*, I, qu. 45, art. 6; M. Luther, *The Smalcald Articles*, I.1; J. Calvin, *Institutes*, I.xiv, xx.

various confessions as well.[60] This teaching was contradicted only
among those who also rejected the church's dogma of the Trinity and
at best believed in a creation by the Father through the Son but in no
way recognized in that creation the common work of the three divine
persons. Among the dissenters were the Arians, Socinians, Remonstrants, Rationalists and, in more recent times, Martensen, Van Oosterzee, and particularly Doedes.[61]

The two dogmas stand and fall together. The confession of the essential oneness of the three persons has as its corollary that all the outward
works of God *(opera ad extra)* are common and indivisible *(communia
et indivisa)*. Conversely, all opposition to the trinitarian work of creation is proof of deviation in the doctrine of the Trinity. The crucial
point here is that, with Scripture and church fathers, like Athanasius,
we make a sharp distinction between the Creator and the creature and
avoid all Gnostic mingling. If in Scripture the Son and the Spirit act as
independent agents *(principia)* and "authors" *(auctores)* of creation,
then they are partakers of the divine being. Furthermore, if they are
truly God, then they truly take part in the work of creation as well. The
Arian doctrine, on the other hand, wraps itself in insoluble difficulties.
It cannot be denied that Scripture teaches that creation is a work of the
Father through the Son. Now if the Son is viewed as a person outside
the divine being there is validity to the objection that no meaning can
be attached to creation by the Father through the Son. Scripture says it
but what can it mean? Did the Father charge the Son to create? But then
the Son is the real Creator. Did the Father and Son jointly create all
things? But then it is not creation by the Son.[62]

The doctrine of the Trinity provides true light here. Just as God is one
in essence and distinct in persons, so also the work of creation is one
and undivided while in its unity it is still rich in diversity. It is one God
who creates all things and for that reason the world is a unity, just as
the unity of the world demonstrates the unity of God. But in that one

60. Cf. Denzinger, *Enchiridion*, nos. 202, 227, 231, 232, 355, 367, 598; H. A. Niemeyer, *Collectio confessionum in ecclesiis reformatis publicatorum* (Leipzig: Sumptibis
Iulii Klinkhardti, 1840), 87, 331, 341. *Ed. note:* In addition, Bavinck here cites J. T.
Müller, *Die Symbolischen Bücher der Evangelisch Lutherschen Kirche*[5], 38, 299. Likely
he is referring to the Augsburg Confession, art. III, and the Smalcald Articles, art. IV,
found in *The Book of Concord: or The Symbolical Books of the Evangelical Lutheran
Church*, trans. by Henry Jacobs (Philadelphia: The United Lutheran Publication House,
1908), I, 38, 311.

61. H. Martensen, *Christian Dogmatics*, trans. by W. Urwick (Edinburgh: T. & T.
Clark, 1871), §61; J. J. van Oosterzee, *Christian Dogmatics*, trans. by J. Watson and M.
Evans (New York: Scribner, Armstrong, 1874), §56; J. I. Doedes, *De Nederlandsche
Geloofsbelijdenis* (Utrecht: Kemink & Zoon, 1880–81), 121ff.

62. J. I. Doedes, *Nederlandsche Geloofsbelijdenis*, 128.

divine being there are three persons, each of whom performs a task of
his own in that one work of creation. Not in the sense that the creation
is mainly attributable to the Father and less so to the Son and Spirit, nor
in the sense that the three persons work independently side-by-side,
supplementing each other's work and constituting three separate efficient causes of creation. The practice of speaking of three associated
causes *(tres causae sociae)* therefore encountered widespread resistance.[63] While there is cooperation, there is no division of labor. All
things originate simultaneously from the Father through the Son in the
Spirit. The Father is the first cause; the initiative for creation proceeds
from him. Accordingly, in an administrative sense, creation is specifically attributed to him. The Son is not an instrument but the personal
wisdom, the Logos, by whom everything is created; everything rests and
coheres in him (Col. 1:17) and is created for him (Col. 1:16), not as its
final goal but as the head and master of all creatures (Eph. 1:10). And
the Holy Spirit is the personal immanent cause by which all things live
and move and have their being, receive their own form and configuration, and are led to their destination, in God.[64]

Still, while the creation is a work of the whole Trinity, it cannot be
denied that in Scripture it also stands in a peculiar relation to the Son,
one that deserves independent discussion. The Old Testament repeatedly states that God created all things by his Word (Gen. 1:3; Pss. 33:6;
148:5; Isa. 48:13), that he established the earth by Wisdom and by his
understanding spread out the heavens (Ps. 104:24; Prov. 3:19; Jer.
10:12; 51:15). But that Wisdom is also represented personally as the ad-
visor and master worker of creation. God acquired and possessed it, arranged and searched it out, in order that by it as the beginning of his
way, as the first principle of his work, he might create and organize the
world. And in that way it was with him even before the creation, worked
along with him in the process of creating, and delighted in the works of
God's hands, especially in the children of men (Prov. 8:22–31; Job
28:23–27). This teaching is further elaborated in the New Testament.
There we read not only that God created all things by the Son (John 1:3;
1 Cor. 8:6; Col. 1:15–17), but there Christ is called "the firstborn of all
creation" *(prōtotokos pasēs ktiseōs,* Col. 1:15), "the origin of God's creation" *(archē tēs ktiseōs tou Theou,* Rev. 3:14), the Alpha and Omega, the

63. O. Zöckler, *Geschichte der Beziehungen zwischen Theologie und Naturwissenschaft,* 2 vols. (Gütersloh: C. Bertelsmann, 1877–79), I, 621f., 679f.
64. F. H. R. Frank, *System der christlichen Wahrheit,* 3rd rev. ed. (Erlangen and
Leipzig: A. Deichert, 1894), I, 328f.; A. Kuyper, *The Work of the Holy Spirit,* trans. by H.
De Vries (Grand Rapids: Eerdmans, 1941 [1900]), 21; cf. H. Bavinck, *The Doctrine of God,*
trans. by W. Hendriksen (Grand Rapids: Eerdmans, 1951), 319 (*Gereformeerde Dogmatiek* [Kampen: Kok, 1928], II, 285f.).

beginning and end of all things (Rev. 1:17; 21:6; 22:6), for whom all things have been created (Col. 1:16), in order to be again gathered up into him as the head (Eph. 1:10). In all these passages Christ both has soteriological and cosmological significance. He is not only the mediator of re-creation but also of creation.

The Apologists as yet did not know what to do with these ideas of Scripture. Subject as they were to Platonic influence they frequently saw little more in the Logos than the "intelligible world" *(kosmos noē-tos)*. They associated the Logos most intimately with the world, saw his generation as being motivated by creation, and inadequately distinguished the birth of the Son from the creation of the world. They still wrestled with the Gnostic idea that the Father is actually the secret and invisible Deity who is made manifest only by the Logos. Now, while this Gnostic element was banished from theology by the ancient church fathers, notably Athanasius and Augustine, it kept creeping back in. The root from which this idea springs is always a certain dualism, a more or less sharp opposition between spirit and matter, between God and the world. God is invisible, inaccessible, hidden; the world, if not anti-God, is nevertheless "ungodly," "God-less," devoid of deity. What is needed to reconcile this basic opposition is an intermediate being and that being is the Logos. In relation to God he is the cosmic idea, the image of the world, the intelligible world *(kosmos noētos);* and in relation to the world he is the actual Creator, the principle of the possibility that a world is in the making. Among the Hernhutters this notion resulted in the eclipse of the Father and the idea of Christ as the real Creator. Re-creation swallows up creation and grace nullifies nature. Various mediating theologians teach that the Logos is the world in its basic idea and that it "belongs to the very being of the Son to have his life not only in the Father but also in the world; as the heart of the Father he is simultaneously the eternal heart of the world, the eternal World-logos."[65]

This notion then automatically leads to a doctrine of incarnation apart from sin. The world as such is profane; creation is not really a divine work. For God to be able to create and for the world and mankind to be pleasing to him he must view them in Christ. God could only have willed the world in Christ and for Christ. It is only in Christ as the head and central individual of the human race that we can be pleasing to God. In this view, the incarnation is necessary for the revelation and communication of God and the God-man is the supreme goal of cre-

---

65. H. Martensen, *Christian Dogmatics*, §125; H. A. W. Meyer, *Critical and Exegetical Handbook to the Epistles to the Philippians and Colossians,* trans. by John C. Moore, rev. and ed. by William P. Dickson (Edinburgh: T. & T. Clark, 1875), 281–87 [on Col. 1:16].

ation.[66] Ultimately this train of thought culminates in the theory that the creation is necessary for God himself. Indeed God as such is nature, the Ur-ground, the depth-dimension and primal silence of the world (*būthos* and *sigē*), but for him to become personality and spirit, he needs the creation. Creation is God's own history; cosmogony is theogony.[67]

This Gnosticism can only be fundamentally overcome when all dualism between God and the world is cut off at the root. Creation as a work of God is not inferior to re-creation; nature is not of a lower order than grace; the world is not profane of itself. Consequently there was no need for an inferior divine being to enable the Father to create the world. The Christian church believes in God the Father, Almighty, Creator of heaven and earth. The creation is absolutely no more the work of the Son than of the Father. All things are from God. And concerning the Son the Christian church confesses that he is not inferior to the Father, nor closer to creatures, but of one substance with the Father and the Spirit, and that together they are one true and eternal God, Creator of heaven and earth. But it *is* true that the Son plays a role of his own in the work of creation, something especially Augustine highlighted. Although he did not equate the ideas of things with the Logos as the Apologists had done, he did feel obligated to relate them to the Logos. True: the world was not eternal but the idea of the world nevertheless was eternally in the mind of God. The Father expresses all his thoughts and his entire being in the one personal Word, and the idea of the world, consequently, is contained in the Logos. Accordingly, the Logos can be called "a certain kind of form, a form which is not itself formed but the form of all things that have been formed" *(forma quaedam, forma non formata sed forma omnium formatorum).*[68] By this line of thought the significance of the Son for the creation can be established. First there is the Father from whom the initiative for creation proceeds, who thinks the idea of the world; but all that the Father is and has and thinks he imparts to and expresses in the Son. In him the Father contemplates the idea of the world itself, not as though it were identical with the Son, but so that he envisions and meets it in the Son in whom his fullness dwells. Contained in the divine wisdom, as a part and in sum, lies also

66. I. A. Dorner, *History of the Development of the Doctrine of the Person of Christ* (Edinburgh: T. & T. Clark, 1868), III, 229–48; C. I. Nitzsch, *System der Christlichen Wahrheit,* 5th ed. (Bonn: Adolph Marcus, 1844), 195; J. P. Lange, *Christliche Dogmatik,* 3 vols. (Heidelberg: K. Winter, 1852), II, 215; and especially P. F. Keerl, *Der Gottmensch, das Ebenbild Gottes,* vol. 2 in *De Mensch, das Ebenbild Gottes* series (Basel: Bahnmeier, 1866), 1ff. *Ed. note:* Bavinck only cites the series title and volume number in his reference.
67. F. W. J. Schelling, *Werke,* II, 2, 109.
68. Augustine, *Sermon* 117; *Freedom of the Will,* III, 16, 17; *On the Trinity,* XI, 10; XV, 14; cf. Anselm, *Monologion,* 34; T. Aquinas, *Summa Theol.,* I, qu. 34, art. 3; qu. 44, art. 3.

the wisdom that will be realized in the creatures [to come]. He is the Logos by whom the Father creates all things.

The whole world is thus the realization of an idea of God; a book containing letters, large and small, from which his wisdom can be known. He is, however, not merely the "exemplary cause"; he is also the "creating agent" *(arche dēmiourgikē)*. The word which God speaks is not a sound without content; it is forceful and living [performative]. The idea of the world which the Father pronounces in the Son is a seminal word *(ratio seminalis)* a fundamental form *(forma principalis)* of the world itself. For that reason the Son is called the beginning *(archē)*, the firstborn *(prōtotokos)*, the origin of the creation *(archē tēs ktiseōs)*, the firstborn who sustains the creation, from whom it arises as its cause and example, and in whom it rests. Therefore the word which the Father utters at the creation and by which he calls the things out of nothingness into being is also effective, for it is spoken in and through the Son. And finally the Son is, in a sense, also the final cause *(causa finalis)* of the world. Because in him it has its foundation and model it is also created for him, not as its ultimate goal, but still as the head, the Lord and heir of all things (Col. 1:16; Heb. 1:2). Summed up in the Son, gathered under him as head, all creatures again return to the Father from whom all things originate. Thus the world finds its *idea*, its principle *(archē)* and its final goal *(telos)* in the triune being of God. The word that the Father pronounces in the Son is the full expression of the divine being and therefore also of all that which will exist by that word as creature outside the divine being. And the procession *(spiratio)* by which the Father and the Son are the "active basis" *(principium)* of the Spirit also contains within itself the willing of that world, the idea of which is comprehended within the divine wisdom.[69] The creation thus proceeds from the Father through the Son in the Spirit in order that, in the Spirit and through the Son, it may return to the Father.

Creation and Time

From this perspective we may also derive some insight into the difficult problem of creation and time. Scripture tells us in simple human language that all things had a beginning. It speaks of a time before the birth of mountains, before the foundation of the world, before the aeons began (Gen. 1:1; Ps. 90:2; Prov. 8:22; Matt. 13:35; 25:24; John 1:1; 17:24; Eph. 1:4; 2 Tim. 1:9; Heb. 4:3; 1 Pet. 1:20; Rev. 13:8). In our own thinking and speaking we also cannot avoid the temporal form. From this human limitation, in fact, spring all the objections which arise over and over against a creation in time. Going back in our thinking we finally come

---

69. J. Kleutgen, *Philosophie der Vorzeit*, II, 870.

to the first moment in which all things have a beginning. Before that moment there is nothing but the deep silence of eternity. But immediately a multitude of questions arise in our mind. With what images will we fill up that eternity and what kind of activity can there be if all the work of creation and providence is eliminated from consideration? The doctrines of the Trinity and the decrees offer us some hint of an answer but detached from the world they no longer furnish content to our ideas. What did God do before the act of creation—he who cannot be conceived as an idle God *(Deus otiosus)* and is always working (John 5:17)? Did he change? Did he pass from idleness to activity, from rest to labor? How can creation, the transition to the act of creating, be squared with the immutability of God? And why did he only proceed to the work of creation after an eternity had already rushed by? How is there to be found, in all that time-transcending eternity, a moment in which God passed from not-creating to creating? And why did he choose precisely that moment; why did he not begin creating the world aeons earlier?

All these questions have provoked a variety of answers. Pantheism attempted to furnish a solution by teaching that in God being and acting are one; that God did not become a Creator but that creation itself is eternal. The world had no beginning; it is the eternal self-revelation of God. Furthermore, God did not precede the world in duration, but only in a logical sense, inasmuch as he is the cause of all things. Nature bringing forth *(natura naturans)* cannot be conceived apart from nature having been brought forth *(natura naturata)*, nor substance apart from modes and attributes, or idea apart from manifestation.[70] Related to this view is Origen's solution: rejecting the eternity of matter he taught that all things were created out of nothing by the Logos but that God cannot be conceived as being idle. His omnipotence is as eternal as he is and so he also began to create from all eternity. Not that the present world is eternal, but preceding it there were countless worlds, just as following it there will also be many.[71] This view, which actually comes from the Stoa,[72] was condemned by the church at the Council of Nicea but has made numerous comebacks.[73] In this connection we

70. Erigena, *The Divine Nature*, I, 73, 74; III, 8, 9, 17; B. Spinoza, *The Principles of Descartes' Philosophy (Cogitata Metaphysica)*, trans. by Halbert Haine Briton (Chicago: Open Court, 1905), II, ch. 10; G. W. F. Hegel, *Werke*, VII, 25.

71. Origen, *On First Principles*, I, 2; II, 1; III, 5.

72. E. Zeller, *Outlines of the History of Greek Philosophy*, 13th ed., rev. by Wilhelm Nestle and trans. by L. R. Palmer (London: Routledge & Kegan Paul, 1969), §61, pp. 215–17.

73. R. Rothe, *Theologische Ethik*, 2nd rev. ed. (Wittenberg: Zimmerman, 1867–71), §§61f.; H. Ulrici, *Gott und die Natur* (Leipzig: T. O. Weigel, 1862), 671f.; H. Martensen, *Christian Dogmatics*, §§65, 66; J. A. Dorner, *History of the Development of the Doctrine of the Person of Christ* (Edinburgh: T. & T. Clark, 1868), III, 229–48; Wetzel, "Die Zeit der Weltschöpfung," *Jahrbuch für die Theologie* 1 (1875): 582f.

must also mention the question—one frequently dealt with in Scholasticism—whether the world could have been eternal. In defense of Aristotle, who taught the eternity of the world,[74] some answered this question in the affirmative.[75] But others like Bonaventure, Albertus Magnus, Henry of Ghent, Richard, Valentia, Toletus,[76] the Lutherans[77] and the Reformed,[78] firmly rejected this thesis. Only a very few considered an eternal creation a possibility.[79]

All these answers, however, fail to satisfy the mind. There is of course no difference over whether at this moment, instead of thousands of years, the world may have existed for millions of centuries. Nobody denies this in the abstract. But a very different question is whether the world could have existed eternally in the same sense as God is eternal. This, we have to say, is impossible, for eternity and time differ essentially. Kant saw an insoluble antinomy in the fact that on the one hand the world must have had a beginning because an infinitely past time is inconceivable, and on the other could not have a beginning because an empty time is similarly inconceivable.[80] The second part of the antinomy, however, is invalid: in the absence of the world there is no time, and therefore no empty time.[81] The fact that we cannot imagine this and will always need such an auxiliary notion as a time before time is irrelevant and only derives from the necessity of our thinking in a temporal form. To eliminate time from our thinking is to eliminate our thinking and hence is impossible.

This leaves us with only the first part of Kant's antinomy: namely, that the world must have had a beginning. However endlessly it is extended, time remains time and never becomes eternity. There is an essential difference between the two. The world cannot be conceived

74. E. Zeller, *Aristotle and the Earlier Peripatetics (Being a Translation from Zeller's Philosophy of the Greeks)* by B. F. C. Costello and J. H. Muirhead (London, New York, and Bombay, 1897), I, 469–77.

75. By Durandus, Occam, Biel, Cajetan, and also by Thomas Aquinas, *Summa Theol.* I, qu. 46 art. 1, 2; idem, *Contra Gentiles,* II, 31–37; according to T. Esser, *Die Lehre des heiligen. Thomas von Aquino über die Möglichkeit einer anfanglosen Schöpfung* (Münster: Aschendorff, 1895). *Rolfes, *Philos. Jahrbuch* 10 (1897), heft 1; J. Heinrich and K. Gutberlet, *Dogmatische Theologie,* V, 134f.

76. Bonaventure, I, *Sent.,* dist. 44, art. 1, qu. 4; cf. Petavius, "de Deo," III, ch. 5, 6.

77. J. Quenstedt, *Theologia,* I, 421; D. Hollaz, *Examen Theol.,* 358.

78. J. Zanchi, *Op. Theol.,* III, 22; G. Voetius, *Select. Disp.,* I, 568; M. Leydecker, *Fax. Verit.,* 140; J. Cocceius, *Summa Theol.,* ch. 15; B. De Moor, *Comm. Theol.,* II, 179; C. Vitringa, *Doctr. Christ.* II, 83; Turretin, *Institutes of Elenctic Theology,* V, qu. 3.

79. F. Burmann, *Syn. Theol.,* I, 24, 41.

80. I. Kant, *Critique of Pure Reason,* trans. by Norman Kemp Smith (New York: St. Martin's, 1965 [1929]), 396–402.

81. Irenaeus, *Against Heresies,* III, 8; Athanasius, *Against the Arians,* I, 29, 58; Tertullian, *Against Marcion,* II, 3; idem, *Against Hermogenes,* 4; Augustine, *City of God,* XI, 6.

apart from time; existence in time is the necessary form of all that is finite and created. The predicate of eternity can never, strictly speaking,
be attributable to things which exist in the form of time. Similarly, the
question whether God could not have created from all eternity is based
on the identification of eternity and time. In eternity there is no "earlier" or "later." God *did* eternally create the world; that is, in the moment in which the world came into existence God was and remained
the Eternal One and as the Eternal One created the world. Even if the
world *had* existed for an endless succession of centuries, and though
millions of worlds *had* preceded the present one, it remains temporal,
finite, limited, and therefore had a beginning. Origen's hypothesis in no
way begins to solve the problem: the question remains absolutely the
same; it is only shifted back a few million years.

Even more baseless is the question of what God did before he created. Augustine, Luther, and Calvin answered it in the spirit of Proverbs
26:5 ["Answer fools according to their folly . . ."].[82] It proceeds from the
assumption that God exists in time and that creation and providence
are for him the strenuous labor of every day. But God dwells in eternity.
He is pure actuality *(actus purissimus),* an infinite fullness of life,
blessed in himself. Without the creation he is not idle and involvement
in it does not exhaust him. "In His leisure, therefore, is no laziness, in-
dolence, inactivity; as in His work is no labour, effort, industry. He can
act while He reposes, and repose while He acts."[83]

The case is the same with pantheism. It is not, to be sure, as superficial as the Socinianism and the materialism which simply transmute
eternity into a time that is endlessly extended forward and backward
and is ignorant of the distinction between endless and infinite. It does
not maintain that God is all things and that all things are God. It makes
a distinction between "being" and "becoming," the nature that is bringing forth and the nature that has been brought forth (*natura naturans*
and *natura naturata*), between substance and its modes, the All and all
things, the idea and its manifestation, that is, between eternity and
time. But to the questions "wherein then does the difference exist?";
"what connection is there between the two?"; "how does eternity pass
into time?" pantheism has no answers. It certainly supplies enough
words and images, but they do not permit any real thought. Theism,
however, views eternity and time as two incommensurable magnitudes.
We neither may nor can neglect either one of them; both of them urge
themselves on our consciousness and powers of reflection. But we can-

82. Augustine, *Confessions,* XI, 2; J. Calvin, *Institutes,* I.xiv.1.
83. Augustine, *City of God,* XII, 17; trans. by Marcus Dods (New York: Modern Library, 1950), 400.

not clearly understand their interconnectedness. As living, thinking beings in time, we stand before the mystery of eternal uncreated being and marvel. On the one hand, it is certain that God is the Eternal One: in him there is neither past or future, neither becoming or change. All that he is is eternal: his thought, his will, his decree. Eternal, in him, is the idea of the world that he thinks and utters in the Son; eternal, in him, is also the decision to create the world; eternal, in him, is the will that created the world in time; eternal is also the act of creating as an act of God, an action both internal and immanent.[84] For God did not *become* Creator, so that first for a long time he did not create and then afterward he did create. Rather, he is the eternal Creator and as Creator he was the Eternal One and as the Eternal One he created. The creation therefore brought about no change in God; it did not emanate from him and is no part of his being. He is unchangeably the same eternal God.

On the other hand, it is certain, also to human thought, that the world had a beginning and was created in time. Augustine correctly stated that the world was not made in time but along with time,[85] as Plato and Philo and Tertullian[86] had already said before him and all theologians since have repeated. A time of idleness is inconceivable, nor was there a time before the world existed. Time is the necessary form of the existence of the finite. It is not a separate creation but something automatically given with the world, cocreated with it like space. In a sense, therefore, the world has always existed, for as long as time has existed. All change, then, occurs in it, not in God. The world is subject to time, that is, to change. It is constantly becoming, in contrast with God who is an eternal and unchangeable being. Now these two, God and the world, eternity and time, are related in such a way that the world is sustained in all its parts by God's omnipresent power and time in all its moments is pervaded by the eternal being of our God. Eternity and time are not two lines, the shorter of which for a time runs parallel to the infinitely extended one; the truth is that eternity is the immutable center which sends out its rays to the entire circumference of time. To the limited eye of the creature it successively unfolds its infinite content in the breadth of space and the length of time that that creature might understand something of the unsearchable greatness of God. But for all that, eternity and time remain distinct. All we wish to confess is that God's eternal willing can and does, without ceasing to be eternal, produce effects

84. Augustine, *City of God*, XII, 17; P. Lombard, II, *Sent.*, dist. 1, n. 2; Bonaventure, II, *Sent.*, dist. 1, art. 1, qu. 2; T. Aquinas, *Contra Gentiles*, I, 82; Petavius, "de Deo," V, 9, 9 and 13, 5; G. Voetius, *Select. Disp.* I, 565; Turretin, *Institutes of Elenctic Theology*, V, qu. 3, 16.
85. Augustine, *Confessions*, XI, 10–13; idem, *City of God*, VII, 30; XI, 4–6; XII, 15–17.
86. Tertullian, *Against Marcion*, II, 3.

in time, just as his eternal thought can have temporal objects as its content.[87] The power of God's will, which is eternally one, caused things to come into being that did not exist before, yet without bringing about any change in him. God eternally wills things that will only take place after centuries or took place centuries before. And the moment it takes place there is change in things but not in him. [As Augustine has said:]

> But when one speaks of His former repose and subsequent operation (and I know not how men can understand these things), this "former" and "subsequent" are applied only to the things created, which formerly did not exist, and subsequently came into existence. But in God the former purpose is not altered and obliterated by the subsequent and different purpose, but by one and the same eternal and unchangeable will. He effected regarding the things He created, both that formerly, so long as they were not, they should not be, and that subsequently, when they began to be, they should come into existence. And thus, perhaps, He would show in a very striking way, to those who have eyes for such things, how independent He is of what He makes and how it is of His own gratuitous goodness He creates, since from eternity He dwelt without creatures in no less perfect a blessedness.[88]

Creation's Goal

Now if this world, which originated and exists in time, is distinct in essence from the eternal and unchangeable being of God, one is all the more insistently confronted by the question as to what moved God to call this world into existence. The Scriptures continually trace all the "is-ness" and "suchness" of God's creatures back to his will (Pss. 33:6; 115:3; 135:6; Isa. 46:10; Dan. 4:35; Matt. 11:25; Rom. 9:15f.; Eph. 1:4, 9, 11; Rev. 4:11).[89] For us that is the ultimate ground, the end of all contradiction. "The will of God is the supreme law. The 'nature' of any particular created thing is precisely what the supreme Creator of the thing willed it to be."[90] To the question of why things exist and are as they are there is no other and deeper answer than that God willed it. If someone should then ask: why did God will it?, "he is asking for something that is greater than the will of God but nothing greater can be found."[91] And this has been the position of the whole Christian church and of Christian theology.

87. Thomas Aquinas, in Kleutgen, *Philosophie der Vorzeit*, II, 871.
88. Augustine, *City of God*, XII, 17; trans. by Marcus Dods (Modern Library), 400; *ed. note:* The citation included here is longer than Bavinck's original.
89. In Rev. 4:11 the preposition *dia* is followed by the accusative and hence actually means "on account of." But here and elsewhere (Rev. 12:11; John 6:57; Rom. 8:10, 20; 2 Peter 3:12) this meaning passes into that of "through" or of a dative.
90. Augustine, *City of God*, XXI, 8.
91. Augustine, *de Gen c. Manich*, I, 2.

Pantheism, however, is not satisfied with this answer and looks for a deeper ground. It then attempts especially in two ways to explain the world from the being of God. Either it presents that being as so superabundantly rich that the world automatically flows from it and, to the degree that the world distances itself from him, approaches nonbeing (the *mē on*) and solidifies into sensible matter. This is the theory of emanation which originated in the East, spread especially in Persia and India, and then, in the systems of Gnosticism and Neo-platonism, also penetrated the West. Or it attempts to explain the world from God's poverty *(penia tou Theou)*, not from his wealth *(ploutos)*. God is so needy and unblessed that he needs the world for his own development. In himself he is pure potentiality who *is* nothing but can *become* anything. He has to objectivize himself and, by contrasting himself with the world, become "spirit" or "personality" in man. In himself God is not yet the Absolute; he only achieves this status through the world-process. Being initially the implicit God *(Deus implicitus)*, he gradually becomes explicit *(Deus explicitus)*. The world, accordingly, is necessary for God; it is a necessary developmental component in his being. "Without the world God is not God." Over against this pantheism, which abolishes the personality of God and deifies the world, theism maintains the teaching that creation is an act of God's will. But that will is not to be construed as arbitrary volition. The will of God has indeed been so viewed in Islamic theology and in the thinking of Nominalists, Socinians, and Cartesians. There the world is a product of pure caprice. It exists, but it might just as well not have existed or have been very different. As a rule, however, Christian theology has avoided this extreme position and taught that, though the will of God in creation was totally free and all coercion and necessity is excluded, that divine will had its motives and God, in performing his external works, had his high and holy purposes.[92]

So there remains room for the question of what moved God to create the world; in other words: what goal did he have in mind for the creation? The answers to this question have varied. Many theologians have seen an adequate explanation for the world in God's goodness and love. Scripture, too, often speaks of the fact that God is good, that his goodness is manifest in all his works, that he loves all his creatures and wills their salvation. Furthermore, God could not be conceived as needing anything; he could not have created the world to receive something from it but only to give and communicate himself. His goodness, therefore, was the reason for creation. Plato, Philo, and Seneca already spoke along that line,[93] and Christian theologians often said as well that God

---

92. Cf. H. Bavinck, *The Doctrine of God*, 232–41 (*Gereformeerde Dogmatiek*, II, 207–15).
93. Plato, *Timaeus*, 29 D; Seneca, *Letters*, 95; for Philo, see Zöckler, art. *PRE*[3], XI, 643.

did not create the world out of need but out of goodness, not for himself but for human beings. "God made the world not for himself but for man."[94] "If he were not able to make good things, he would possess no power at all; if, however, he were able but did not, there would be great blame."[95] But the God of all is good and excellent by nature. For a good being would be envious of no one, so he envies nobody's existence but rather wishes everyone to exist in order to exercise his kindness.[96]

These pronouncements repeatedly alternated, however, with other statements in which God himself and his honor were designated as the cause and purpose of the creation. But humanism placed man in the foreground. Socinianism did not look for man's essence in communion with God but in his dominion over the earth. The doctrine of natural law, natural morality, and natural religion made man autonomous and independent from God. Leibnitz taught that by his goodness, wisdom, and power God was morally bound to choose the best of the many possible worlds and to bring that into being. Kant, on grounds of practical reason, only appealed to God for help in supplying to man in the hereafter the eternal life to which his virtue entitled him. And thus, in the rationalism of the eighteenth century, man became the most interesting of creatures: everything else existed for him and was subservient to his perfection. Man was his own end *(Selbstzweck)* and all else, God included, only a means.[97] And even today many thinkers teach that God must impart reality to the idea of the world which he deems necessary, for otherwise he would be selfish and not the highest love. Because he is good, he does not want to be blessed by himself alone, but establishes a kingdom of love and pursues the blessedness of his creatures, which for him is the ultimate goal.[98]

94. Tertullian, *Against Marcion*, I, 43; *Against Praxeas*, 5.

95. Augustine, *The Literal Meaning of Genesis*, IV, 16.

96. Athanasius, *Contra Gentes*, 41; John of Damascus, *Exposition of the Orthodox Faith*, II, 2; T. Aquinas, *Summa Theol.*, I, qu. 19, art. 2; G. Voetius, *Select. Disp.*, I, 558.

97. K. G. Bretschneider, *Systematische Entwicklung aller in der Dogmatik* (Leipzig: J. A. Barth, 1841), 442f.; idem, *Handbuch der Dogmatik* (Leipzig: J. A. Barth, 1838), I, 669; J. A. L. Wegschneider, *Institutiones theologiae christianae dogmaticae* (Halle: Gebauer, 1819), §95.

98. R. Rothe, *Theologische Ethik*, §49; I. Dorner, *Christian Faith*, I, II, 29–34; H. Martensen, *Christian Dogmatics*, §59; J. C. C. Von Hofmann, *Der Schriftbeweis*, 2nd ed., I, 205f.; F. A. Kahnis, *Die Luthersche Dogmatik* (Leipzig: Dorfflung & Francke, 1861–68), I, 428; J. Müller, *Die Christliche Leher von der Sunde* (Bremen: C. Ed. Muller, 1889), II, 187f.; L. Schöberlein, *Prinzip und System der Dogmatik* (Heidelberg: C. Winter, 1881), 628; G. Thomasius, *Christi Person und Werk* (Erlangen: A. Deichert, 1888), I, 44; James Orr, *The Christian View of God and the World*, 7th ed. (Edinbugh: A. Elliot, 1904), 155; A. Ritschl, *The Christian Doctrine of Justification and Reconciliation*, trans. and ed. by H. R. MacIntosh and A. B. MacCaulay (Edinburgh: T. & T. Clark, 1900), 290–96; also Hermes and Günther, according to Kleutgen, *Theologie der Vorzeit*, I, 642.

From a Christian viewpoint, however, this doctrine of man as *Selbstz-weck* is unacceptable. Of course God's goodness also becomes manifest in creation, as Scripture repeatedly asserts. Still it is not correct to say that God's goodness requires the creation or else God would be selfish. Remember, God is the all-good Being, perfect love, total blessedness within himself, and therefore does not need the world to bring his goodness or love to maturity, any more than he needs it to achieve self-consciousness and personality. It is in the nature of the case, moreover, that God does not exist for the sake of man and that man exists for the sake of God. For although man may in a sense be called *Selbstzweck* insofar as he, as a rational, moral being, may never be degraded into a "will-less" instrument, he is nevertheless fundamentally dependent on God and possesses nothing he has not received. God alone is Creator; man is a created being and for that reason alone he cannot be the goal of creation. Inasmuch as he has his origin in God, he can also have his destiny only in God. And, finally, the theory that creation is grounded in God's goodness and has for its final end the salvation of man is also at variance with reality. The universe is not, certainly, exhausted by its service to humanity and must therefore have some goal other than utility to man. The pedestrian utilitarianism and the self-centered teleology of the eighteenth century have been sufficiently refuted. The suffering and pain which is the daily lot of humanity cannot be explained in terms only of God's goodness. And the final outcome of world history, which speaks to us not only of the salvation of the elect but also of an eternal triumph over the ungodly, reveals attributes of God entirely different from his goodness and love.

Scripture, accordingly, takes another position and points to a higher goal. It says that all of nature is a revelation of God's attributes and a proclaimer of his praise (Ps. 19:1; Rom. 1:19). God created man after his image and for his glory (Gen. 1:26; Isa. 43:7). He glorified himself in the Pharaoh of the Exodus (Exod. 14:17), in the man born blind (John 9:3), and made the wicked for the day of trouble (Prov. 16:4; Rom. 9:22). Christ came to glorify God (John 17:4) and he bestows all the benefits of grace for his name's sake: redemption, forgiveness, sanctification, and so forth (Pss. 105:8; 78:9; Isa. 43:25; 48:11; 60:21; 61:3; Rom. 9:23; Eph. 1:6f.). God gives his glory to no other (Isa. 42:8). The final goal is that all kingdoms will be subjected to him and every creature will yield to him (Dan. 7:27; Isa. 2:3–13; Mal. 1:11; 1 Cor. 15:24f.). Even on earth already he is given glory by all his people (Ps. 115:1; Matt. 6:13). Some day God alone will be great (Isa. 2:3–13) and receive glory from all his creatures (Rev. 4:11; 19:6). He is the First and the Last, the Alpha and the Omega (Isa. 44:6; 48:12; Rev. 1:8; 22:13). Of him, through him, and to him are all things (Rom. 11:36). On this basis Christian theology almost unanimously teaches that the glory of God is the final goal of all God's works. Although in its early years especially the goodness of God was featured as the motive for creation, still the honor of God as the final end of all things is not lacking. Athenagoras, for example, writes that it was "for his own sake and for the purpose of showing that his goodness and wisdom had been advanced in all his works that God made man."[99] Tertullian says that God created the world "for the embellishment of his majesty."[100] This [emphasis on the] "glory of God" increasingly came into its own, especially in the medieval theology of Anselm, who made the honor of God the fundamental principle of his doctrine of the incarnation and the atonement,[101] but also in Lombard, Thomas, Bonaventure, and others.[102] And we find the same teaching in the thought of later Roman Catholic theologians,[103] in that of the Lutherans,[104] and finally and particularly in the theology of the Reformed.[105] The difference between the Reformed on the one hand and the Lutherans and Roman Catholics on the other is not that the former posited the honor of God, while the latter chose man as the final end of creation. It is rather that the Reformed tradition made the honor of God the fundamental principle of all doctrine and conduct, of dogmatics and morality, of the family, society, and the state, of science and art. Nowhere was this principle of the glory of God more universally applied than among the confessors of the Reformed religion.

But a twofold objection has been registered against God's glory as the final goal of all creatures. First, on this view God is made self-centered, self-seeking, devaluing his creatures, specifically human beings, into means. We already confronted this objection earlier and demonstrated that as the perfect good God can rest in nothing other than himself and cannot be satisfied in anything less than himself. He has no alternative but to seek his own honor. Just as a father in his family and a ruler in

99. Athenagoras, *The Resurrection of the Dead*, 12.

100. Tertullian, *Apology*, 17.

101. Anselm, *Cur Deus Homo*, 11.

102. P. Lombard, II, *Sent.* dist. I; T. Aquinas, *Summa Theol.*, I, qu. 44, art. 4, qu. 66, art. 2, qu. 103, art. 2; idem, *Contra Gentiles*, III, 17, 18; idem, II, *Sent.*, dist. 1, qu. 2, art. 2; Bonaventure, II, *Sent.*, dist. 1, 2.

103. M. J. Scheeben, *Handbuch der Katholischen Dogmatik* (Freiburg i.B.: Herder, 1933), II, 31f.; H. Th. Simar, *Lehrbuch der Dogmatik* (Freiburg i.B.: Herder, 1879–80), 234f.; Kleutgen, *Theologie der Vorzeit*, I, 640–92; Schwetz, *Theol. Dogm.* I, 396f.; J. B. Heinrich and K. Gutberlet, *Dogmatische Theologie*, V, 151f.; G. M. Jansen, *Praelectiones Theologiae Fundamentalis* (Utrecht, 1875–77), II, 319f.

104. J. Gerhard, *Loci. Theol.*, V, ch. 5; J. Quenstedt, *Theologia*, I, 418; D. Hollaz, *Ex. Theol.*, 360.

105. For example, Jonathan Edwards, "Dissertation Concerning the End for Which God Created the World," in Paul Ramsey, ed., *Ethical Writings*, vol. 8, *The Works of Jonathan Edwards* (New Haven, Conn.: Yale University Press, 1989), 399–536.

his kingdom must seek and demand the honor due to him in that capacity, so it is with the Lord our God. Now a human being can only ask for the honor that is due to him in the name of God and for the sake of the office to which God has called him, but God asks for and seeks that honor in his own name and for his own being. Inasmuch as he is the supreme and only good, perfection itself, it is the highest kind of justice that in all creatures he seek his own honor. And so little does this pursuit of his own honor have anything in common with human egotistical self-interest that, where it is wrongfully withheld from him, God will, in the way of law and justice, even more urgently claim that honor. Voluntarily or involuntarily, every creature will someday bow his knee before him. Obedience in love or subjection by force is the final destiny of all creatures.

Another objection is that, in seeking his honor, God does need his creature after all. Since the world serves as an instrument of his glorification there is something lacking in his perfection and blessedness. Creation meets a need in God and contributes to his perfection.[106] This objection seems irrefutable, though in all kinds of human labor there is an analogy which can clarify God's creative activity for us. At a lower level humans labor, because they have to; they are impelled to work by need or force. But the more refined the work becomes, the less room there is for need or coercion. An artist creates his work of art not out of need or coercion but impelled by the free impulses of his genius. "I pour out my heart like a little finch in the poplars; I sing and know no other goal" (Bilderdijk). A devout person serves God, not out of coercion or in hope of reward, but out of freeflowing love. So there is also a delight in God which is infinitely superior to need or force, to poverty or riches, which embodies his artistic ideas in creation and finds intense pleasure in it. Indeed, what in the case of man is merely a weak analogy is present in God in absolute originality. A creature, like the creation of an artist, has no independence apart from and in opposition to God. God, therefore, never seeks out a creature as if that creature were able to give him something he lacks or could take from him something he possesses. He does not seek the creature [as an end in itself] but through the creature he seeks himself. He is and always remains his own end. His striving is always—also in and through his creatures—total self-enjoyment, perfect bliss. The world, accordingly, did not arise from a need in God, from his poverty and lack of bliss, for what he seeks in a creature is not that creature but himself. Nor is its origination due to an uncontrollable fullness *(pleroma)* in God, for God uses all creatures for his

---

106. D. F. Strauss, *Christian Faith*, I, 633; E. Von Hartmann, *Gesammelte Studien und Aufsätze* (Leipzig: Friedrich, 1891), 715.

own glorification and makes them serviceable to the proclamation of his perfections.

A Creation-Based Worldview

From this perspective arises a very particular worldview. The word "creation" can denote either the act or the product of creation. From one's understanding of the act flows one's view of the product. Pantheism attempts to explain the world dynamically; materialism attempts to do so mechanically. But both strive to see the whole as governed by a single principle. In the former the world may be a living organism *(zōon),* of which God is the soul; in the latter it is a mechanism which is brought about by the union and separation of atoms. But in both systems an unconscious blind fate is elevated to the throne of the universe. Both fail to appreciate the riches and diversity of the world, erase the boundaries between heaven and earth, matter and spirit, soul and body, man and animal, intellect and will, time and eternity, Creator and creature, being and nonbeing, and dissolve all distinctions in a bath of deadly uniformity. Both deny the existence of a conscious purpose and cannot point to a cause or a destiny for the existence of the world and its history.

Scripture's worldview is radically different. From the beginning heaven and earth have been distinct. Everything was created with a nature of its own and rests in ordinances established by God. Sun, moon, and stars have their own unique task; plants, animals, and humans are distinct in nature. There is the most profuse diversity and yet, in that diversity, there is also a superlative kind of unity. The foundation of both diversity and unity is in God. It is he who created all things in accordance with his unsearchable wisdom, who continually upholds them in their distinctive natures, who guides and governs them in keeping with their own increated energies and laws, and who, as the supreme good and ultimate goal of all things, is pursued and desired by all things in their measure and manner. Here is a unity that does not destroy but rather maintains diversity, and a diversity that does not come at the expense of unity but rather unfolds it in its riches. In virtue of this unity the world can, metaphorically, be called an organism in which all the parts are connected with each other and influence each other reciprocally. Heaven and earth, man and animal, soul and body, truth and life, art and science, religion and morality, state and church, family and society, and so on, though they are all distinct, are not separated. There is a wide range of connections between them; an organic, or, if you will, an ethical bond holds them all together.

Scripture clearly points [to this bond] when it not only sums up the universe under the name of heaven and earth but also calls it ʿwlm, that is, a hidden, invisible, indefinite time in the past or future, aeon, eternity, the world (Eccles. 1:4; 3:11); and in the New Testament *kosmos* (John 1:10); *ta panta* (1 Cor. 8:6; 15:25f.); *ktisis* (Mark 10:16); *aiōnes* (Heb. 1:2), duration, lifetime, age, world (cf. *seculum* in connection with *sexus*), a human lifetime, world, and our word "world" [ME *weorld*, fr. OE *weoruld, worold* human existence, age or lifetime]. The words ʿwlm and *aiōnes* assume the idea that the world has duration, or age, that a history takes place in it which culminates in a specific goal. The Greek word *kosmos* and the Latin *mundus*, on the other hand, stress the beauty and harmony of the world. And in fact the world is both. Just as Paul simultaneously compares the church to a body and a building and speaks of a growing temple (Eph. 2:21) and Peter calls believers living stones (1 Pet. 2:5), so also the world is both a history and a work of art. It is a body that grows and a building that is erected. It extends itself in the "breadth" of space and perpetuates itself in the "length" of time. Neither the mechanical principle of materialism, nor the dynamic principle of pantheism is sufficient to explain it. But whatever is valid in both is recognized in the doctrine of the world as the Scriptures teach it. It is to be regarded both horizontally and vertically. From the lowest forms of life it strives upward to where the light and life of God is, and at the same time it moves forward to a God-glorifying end. In that way it displays the attributes and perfections of God, in principle already at the outset, to an increasing degree as it develops, and perfectly at the end of the ages.

Augustine, the church father who most deeply understood these ideas, also presented the most elaborate account of them. In *The City of God (de civitate Dei)* he offers a Christian philosophy of history, demonstrates how the Christian worldview finds its truth and proof in history, and sketches the origin and essence of the heavenly city *(civitas coelestis)*, both in its development and relation to the earthly city *(civitas terrena)*, in its end as well as its goal.[107] But at the same time he includes in it an account of the universe as a splendid harmony. In Augustine the world is a unity: the universe derives its name from the word "unity."[108] Nevertheless that unity is not a uniformity but an infinitely varied diversity.[109] For God is the supreme being: supremely true, supremely good, and supremely beautiful. For that reason he created many creatures who in varying degrees partake of his being, truth, goodness, and beauty. "To some things he gave more of being and to others less and in this way arranged an order of natures in a hierarchy of being."[110] Ap-

107. J. Biegler, *Die Civitas Dei des heiligen Augustinus* (Paderborn: Junfermann, 1894).
108. Augustine, *de Gen. Contr. Manich.*, I, 21.
109. Augustine, *City of God*, XI, 10.
110. Ibid., XII, 2.

pealing to the Book of Wisdom ("you have arranged all things by measure and number and weight," 11:20), Augustine states that all things are distinct in mode, species, number, degree, and order. And precisely by these qualities they bring about that world, that universe, in which God, in his good pleasure, distributes good things, and which on that account is a manifestation of his perfections.[111] For all that diversity can only be attributed to God, not to the merits of his creatures. "There is no nature even among the least and lowest of beasts that he did not fashion . . . the properties without which nothing can either be or be conceived."[112]

This worldview has been that of Christian theology in its entirety. The world is one body with many members. In the works of the church fathers, the unity, order, and harmony exhibited in the world is a powerful proof for the existence and unity of God.[113] God is the center and all creatures are grouped in concentric circles and a hierarchical order around him.[114] Thomas compares the world to perfectly keyed string music whose harmonies interpret for us the glory and blessedness of the divine life. "Its parts are found to have been arranged just like the parts of a whole animal, which serve each other reciprocally."[115] "There is no spot in the universe," says Calvin, "wherein you cannot discern at least some sparks of his glory."[116] "Nothing in the whole world is more excellent, more noble, more beautiful, more useful, and more divine than the diversity of its many elements, the distinction and that order in which one is more noble than another and one depends on another, one is subject to another, and one receives obedience from another. Hence comes the adornment, beauty, and excellence of the whole world. Hence arise its many uses, its usefulness and benefits for us. Hence the very goodness, glory, wisdom, and power of God shines forth and is revealed more brilliantly."[117] And for all of them the world is a theater, a "splendidly clear mirror of his divine glory."[118]

111. Augustine, *de diversis quaestionibus octoginta*, qu. 41; idem, *Divine Providence and the Problem of Evil*, I, 19; idem, *The Literal Meaning of Genesis*, I, 9; II, 13; idem, *Confessions*, XII, 9; idem, *City of God*, XI, 33.

112. Augustine, *City of God*, XI, 15; cf. *Scipio, *Des Aurelius Augustinus Metaphysik* (Leipzig: Breitkopf und Hartel, 1886), 31–80.

113. Athanasius, *Against the Arians*, II, 28, 48; idem, *Against the Heathen*, ch. 39.

114. Pseudo Dionysius, in his writings, *Celestial Hierarchies* and *Ecclesiastical Hierarchies*.

115. T. Aquinas, *Summa Theol.*, I, qu. 25, art. 6; idem, II *Sent.*, dist. 1, qu. 1, art. 1.

116. J. Calvin, *Institutes*, I.v.1.9. *Ed note:* Translation is from the Battles/McNeill edition (Philadelphia: Westminster, 1960).

117. J. Zanchius, *Opera*, III, 45.

118. Cf. also Armin Reiche, *Die künsterlichen Element in der Weltund Lebensanschauung des Gregor von Nyssa* (Jena: A. Kámpte, 1897), 221f.; Otto Gierke, *Johannes Althusius* (Breslau: W. Koebner, 1880), 60f.; Pesch, *Die Welträthsel*, I, 135f.; M. Scheeben, *Dogmatik*, II, 94f.; J. Heinrich and K. Gutberlet, *Dogmatik*, V, 173f.

As a result of this worldview Christianity has overcome both the contempt of nature and its deification. In paganism a human being does not stand in the right relationship to God and therefore not to the world either.[119] Similarly, in pantheism and materialism the relation of human beings to nature is fundamentally corrupted. One moment man considers himself infinitely superior to nature and believes that it no longer has any secrets for him. The next moment he experiences nature as a dark and mysterious power that he does not understand, whose riddles he cannot solve, and from whose power he cannot free himself. Intellectualism and mysticism alternate. Unbelief makes way for superstition and materialism turns into occultism. But the Christian looks upward and confesses God as the Creator of heaven and earth. In nature and history he observes the unfathomability of the ways of God and the unsearchability of his judgments but he does not despair, for all things are subject to the government of an omnipotent God and a gracious Father and will therefore work together for good to those who love God. Here, accordingly, there is room for love and admiration of nature, but all deification is excluded. Here a human being is placed in the right relation to the world because he has been put in the right relation to God. For that reason also creation is the fundamental dogma: throughout Scripture it is in the foreground and is the foundation stone on which the Old and New Covenants rest.

Finally, this doctrine rules out an egoistic theology and a false optimism. Certainly there is an element of truth in the view that all things exist for the sake of man, or rather for the sake of humanity, the church of Christ (1 Cor. 3:21–23; Rom. 8:28). But that humanity has its ultimate purpose, along with all other creatures, in the glorification of God. To that end all things are subordinate. To that end all things, even sin and suffering, work together. And with a view to this end the world is functionally well organized. In Scholasticism the question was sometimes asked whether God could make anything better than he actually made it. Abelard said no, because the goodness of God required that he always had to will the best, or else he would be selfish[120] and Leibnitz later reasoned along the same line. But in God we cannot posit any uncertainty or choice. He did not choose the best out of many possible worlds. His will is fixed from eternity. A creature can always as such be

119. R. Smend, *Alttestamentlichen Religionsgeschichte,* 458: "The Hebrew man faces the world and nature in sovereign self-awareness. He has no fear of the world. But that posture is wedded to the strongest possible sense of responsibility. As God's deputy, but only as such, he is in charge of the world. He may not follow his own arbitrary impulses but only the revealed will of God. Paganism, on the other hand, oscillates between presumptuous misuse of the world and a childish terror before its powers."

120. Abelard, *Introduction to Theology,* III, ch. 5.

conceived as better, larger, or more beautiful than it actually is, because a creature is contingent and capable of development and improvement. And even the universe as a contingent entity can be conceived differently and better for us human beings. Thomas indeed said: "the universe cannot be better on account of the ideal order attributed to these things by God in whom the good of the universe consists; if some one of these things were better, the proportion of the order would be ruined just as when one string is overplayed, the melody of the cither is ruined." But he also added: "God could nevertheless make other things or add other things to the things that have been made and that other universe would be better.[121] The nature of a creature is such that both in its "isness" and "suchness" it can only be thought as contingent. But to God this question does not exist. This world is good because it answers to the purpose he has set for it. It is neither the best nor the worst but it is good because God called it so. It is good because it is serviceable, not to the individual human being, but to the revelation of God's perfections. And to the person who regards it so, it is also good, because it makes known to him the God whom to know is eternal life. Lactantius, accordingly, spoke truly when he said: "The world was made for this reason that we should be born. We are born, therefore, that we should know the Maker of the world and our God. We know Him that we may worship Him. We worship Him that we may gain immortality as a reward for our labors, since the worship of God rests on very great labors. Therefore, we are rewarded with immortality that, made like the angels, we may serve the Father and Lord Most High forever and be an everlasting kingdom for God. This is the sum of everything; this the secret of God; this the mystery of the world."[122]

121. T. Aquinas, *Summa Theol.*, I, qu. 25, art. 6, ad. 3; cf. P. Lombard, I, *Sent.*, dist. 44; Bonaventure, I, *Sent.*, qu. 44, art. 1, qu. 1–3; Hugh of St. Victor, *On the Sacraments*, II, ch. 22; G. Voetius, *Select. Disp.*, I, 553; P. Van Mastricht, *Theologia*, III, 6, 11; J. H. Heidegger, *Corpus Theologiae*, VI, 21.
122. Lactantius, *The Divine Institutes*, VII, 6; translation by Sister Mary Francis McDonald, O.P., vol. 49, *The Fathers of the Church* (Washington, D.C.: Catholic University Press, 1964), 488.

Heaven: The Spiritual World   2

The Bible joins all the world's religions in acknowledging a spiritual, non-material, invisible realm. While some (Sadducees, modernists) deny the existence of angels, excessive, unhealthy interest in spirits or speculation about them is a greater problem. Belief in a spiritual world cannot be demonstrated philosophically; it is rooted in and profoundly expresses the truth of revelation. Humans cannot bridge the boundary between this world and the one beyond; only God can make it known to us, and he has in Scripture. The world of angels is as richly varied as is the material world, and they exist in distinct kinds and classes. Scripture also teaches that among angels there are distinctions of rank and status, of dignity and ministry, of office and honor. The elaborate hierarchical classification of Pseudo-Dionysius, however, far exceeds what is known from revelation. Speculation about the number of angels or the time of their creation is unhelpful. While we do not know exact details about their nature, Scripture does indicate that, unlike God himself, angels are not simple, omnipresent, or eternal. This has led some to conclude that angels—in their own ethereal way—are corporeal, bounded in time and space. But though angels always appear to humans in visible corporeal form and are symbolically represented in this way, it is best not to ascribe corporeality to angels so as to avoid all forms of pantheistic identity-philosophy that mixes heaven and earth, matter and spirit, and erases the distinction between them. Though they are finite creatures, angels do relate more freely to time and space than humans do. Modern analogies of light and electricity help us here. There is a unity among the angels: like humans, they are all created, spiritual, rational, moral beings; but only humans are God's image-bearers, joined in a common humanity, and constituting the church. The extraordinary ministry of angels is to accompany the history of redemption at its cardinal points; their ordinary ministry is to praise God day and night. Though angels are used by God to watch over believers, there is no ground for believing in individual or national guardian angels. Care must be taken to avoid veneration and worship of angels; only God is to be worshiped.

According to Holy Scripture, creation is divided into a spiritual and a material realm, into heaven and earth, into "things in heaven and things on earth, things visible and things invisible" (Col. 1:16). The existence of such a spiritual realm is recognized in all religions. In addition to the actual gods, also a variety of demigods or heroes, demons, genii, spirits, souls, and so on, have been the objects of religious veneration. Especially in Parsism there was a vigorous development in the doctrine of angels. In it a host of good angels, called *Jazada*, surrounds Ahuramazda, the God of light, just as Ahriman, the God of darkness, is surrounded by a number of evil angels, called *Dewas*.[1] According to Kuenen,[2] as well as many other scholars, the Jews derived their view of angels especially from the Persians after the Babylonian exile. But this hypothesis is grossly exaggerated. In the first place, even Kuenen recognizes that belief in the existence and activity of superior beings was present in [preexilic] ancient Israel. In the second place, there is a big difference between the angelology of the canonical writings and that of Jewish folk religion. And finally there is still so much uncertainty about the interrelationship between Judaism and Parsism that James Darmesteter in his work about the Zendavesta (1893) claimed in opposition to the prevailing theory that the Persian doctrine of angels was derived from Judaism.[3]

This opinion, to be sure, did not meet with much acceptance, but Schürer was still able to write only a few years later: "A carefully detailed study, especially of the influence of Parsism, has not yet been furnished up until now. Scholars will probably have to reduce the extent of this influence to a relatively small measure."[4] But according to Acts 23:8, the existence of angels was denied by the Sadducees who, therefore, probably considered the angel appearances in the Pentateuch to be momentary theophanies. Josephus leaves several angel appearances unmen-

---

1. According to Lehmann, in P. D. Chantepie de la Saussaye, *Lehrbuch der Religionsgeschichte* (Tübingen: J. C. B. Mohr [Paul Siebeck], 1905), II, 188–99. *Ed. note:* The section on Persian religion in de la Saussaye's handbook was written by Dr. Edv. Lehmann.

2. Abraham Kuenen, *The Religion of Israel to the Fall of the Jewish State*, trans. by Alfred Heath May (Edinburgh: Williams & Norgate, 1883), III, 37–44.

3. Cf. W. Geesink, "De Bijbel en het Avesta," *De Heraut* 830 (November 1893); contrary to Darmesteter, C. P. Tiele, "Iets over de oudheid van het Avesta," *Verslagen en Mededeelingen der Koninklijke Akademie van Wetenschappen* (1895): 364–83; Lehmann, in de la Saussaye, *Lehrbuch*, 190.

4. *Ed. Note:* The sentence cited by Bavinck comes from the third German edition of Shürer's *Geschichte des jüdischen Volkes im Zeitalter Jesu Christi*. The revised English edition (1979), incorporating insights from the Qumran discoveries and therefore focusing on the Essene sect's angelology, reads as follows:

In the circumstances, the issue of foreign influences which so greatly exercised pre-Qumran scholarship, becomes quite secondary. Buddhist and Indian borrowings must now be considered most unlikely. Persian impact on Essene dualism and angelology is probable but derives no doubt from Iranian influences on Judaism as such, rather than directly on the sect itself.

(Emil Schürer, *The History of the Jewish People in the Age of Jesus Christ [175 B.C.–A.D. 135]*, rev. and ed. by Geza Vermes, Fergus Millar, and Matthew Black [Edinburgh: T. & T. Clark, 1979], II, 589.) Bavinck also adds, cf. Erik Stave, *Über den Einfluss des Parsismus auf das Judentum* (Haarlem: E. F. Bohn, 1898); B. Lindner, "Parsismus," *Realenencyclopädie für protestantische Theologie und Kirche*, 3rd ed. (*PRE³*), XIV, 699–705.

tioned and attempts to explain others naturally.[5] According to Justin,[6] the angels were held by some to be temporary emanations from the divine being, who, upon completing their task, again returned into God. In a later time the existence of the angels was denied by the followers of David Joris,[7] by the Libertines,[8] by Spinoza[9] and by Hobbes,[10] who simply regarded them as revelations and workings of God. Balthazar Bekker, in his *Enchanted World (Betoverde Werelt)*, did not go that far but did limit the activity of angels, in many cases considering them to be humans. Like Spinoza, he taught that in their doctrine of angels Christ and his apostles accommodated themselves to the beliefs of their contemporaries.[11] Leibnitz, Wolff, Bonnet, Euler, and the supranaturalists attempted to maintain their existence especially on rational grounds, asserting that beginning from human beings there could be no break *(vacuum formarum)* either upward or downward in the ascending scale of creatures.[12] Even Kant did not rule out the existence of thinking beings other than humans.[13] The eighteenth century erased the distinction between angels and humans, as did the nineteenth century between humans and animals. Swedenborg, for example, had learned from the angels themselves that they were really humans; the inner core of a human being is an angel and man is destined to become angelic.[14]

In modern theology, however, only little is left of angels. Rationalists like Wegschneider, while they do not deny the existence of angels, do deny their manifestation.[15] Marheineke, in the second edition of his dogmatics, omitted the section on angels. Strauss figured that the worldview of modernity had robbed the angels of their dwellingplace: they owe

5. F. Josephus, *Antiquities*, VIII, 13, 17.

6. Justin Martyr, *Dialogue with Trypho*, 128.

7. According to J. Hoornbeek, *Summa Contr.* 413.

8. John Calvin, *Treatises against the Anabaptists and against the Libertines*, ed. and trans. by Benjamin Wirt Farley (Grand Rapids: Baker, 1982), 230–33.

9. Baruch Spinoza, *Tractatus Theologico-Politicus*, II, 56.

10. Thomas Hobbes, *Leviathan*, ed. A. R. Waller (Cambridge: Cambridge University Press, 1935), 285–96 (III, 34).

11. Balthasar Bekker, *De Betoverde Wereld* (Amsterdam: D. van den Dalen, 1691), II, 6–15.

12. Franz V. Reinhard, *Grundriss der Dogmatik* (Munich: Seidel, 1802), 184; K. G. Bretschneider, *Handbuch der Dogmatik* (Leipzig: J. A. Barth, 1838), I, 746f.

13. Otto Zöckler, *Geschichte der Beziehungen zwischen Theologie und Naturwissenschaft* (Gutersloh: C. Bertelsman, 1877–99), II, 69, 249.

14. Emanuel Swedenborg, *The True Christian Religion Containing the Universal Theology of the New Church* (New York: Swedenborg Foundation, 1952), 29 (n. 20), 176 (n. 115), 179 (n. 118), 183 (n. 121). *Ed. note:* These are the passages where Swedenborg deals with humans and angels as spiritual beings; Bavinck cites the second German edition (1873), pp. 42, 178.

15. Julius A. L. Wegschneider, *Institutiones theologiae christianae dogmaticae* (Halle: Gebauer, 1819), 102.

their existence solely to folk sagas, to the desire for balancing the mass of matter in the world with a greater quantity of spirit.[16] In the thinking of Lipsius they are merely "graphic illustrations of the vital workings of divine providence" and belong solely to the domain of religious symbolism.[17] Schleiermacher, too, though he did not rule out the possibility of their existence, judged that Christ and his apostles had not taught anything positive about angels, since they had accommodated themselves to the popular imagination and spoke of angels as we do of fairies and elves; and that angels had no theological or religious significance for us.[18] Furthermore, those who upheld the existence of angels frequently altered their nature. Schelling, for example, held the good angels to be potentialities which, on account of the fall, had not become realities and are now no more than the idea or power of an individual or people.[19]

Others transformed angels into inhabitants of the planets. At an early stage—it already occurs in Xenophanes and some of the Stoics—we encounter the opinion that the planets were inhabited. After modern astronomy had abandoned the geocentric position and acquired a vague notion of the staggering spaces of the universe, the idea that planets other than the earth were also inhabited again found acceptance with Descartes, Wittichius, Allinga, Wilkins, Harvey, Leibnitz, Wolff, Bonnet, Kant, Reinhard, Bretschneider, Swedenborg,[20] and many others right into our own times.[21] Some theologians also united this view with

16. David F. Strauss, *Die Christliche Glaubenslehre in ihrer geschichtlichen Entwicklung und im Kampfe mit der moderne Wissenschaft,* 2 vols. (Tübingen: C. F. Osiander, 1840–41), I, 671f.

17. Richard A. Lipsius, *Lehrbuch der evangelisch-protestantischen Dogmatik* (Braunschweig: C. A. Schwetschke, 1893), §518f.; A. E. Biedermann, *Christliche Dogmatik.*[2] (Berlin: Reimer, 1884–85), II, 550f.

18. F. Schleiermacher, *The Christian Faith,* ed. by H. R. MacIntosh and J. S. Steward (Edinburgh: T. & T. Clark, 1928), §42; cf. J. Bovon, *Dogmatique Chrétienne,* 2 vols. (Lausanne: Georges Bridel, 1895–96), I, 297.

19. F. W. J. Schelling, *Werke,* II, 4, 284; cf. H. L. Martensen, *Christian Dogmatics,* trans. by W. Urwick. (Edinburgh: T. & T. Clark, 1871), §§68–69.

20. O. Zöckler, *Geschichte der Beziehungen,* II, 55f.; F. A. Lange, *Geschichte des Materialismus und Kritik seiner Bedeutung in der Gegenwart,* 8th ed. (Leipzig: Baedekker, 1908), 431; David F. Strauss, *The Old Faith and the New,* trans. by Mathilde Blind (New York: Holt, 1873), 189–92.

21. *C. Du Prel, *Die Planetenbewohner;* C. Flammarion, *La Pluralite des Mondes Habités* (Paris: Didier, 1875); L. Büchner, *Kraft und Stoff* (Leipzig: Theod. Thomas, 1902), 80–88; E. Haeckel, *The Riddle of the Universe,* trans. by Joseph McCabe (New York and London: Harper & Brothers, 1900), 368–72; O. Liebmann, *Zur Analysis der Wirklichkeit: Eine Erörterung der Grundprobleme der Philosophie,* 3rd ed. (Strassburg: K. J. Trübner, 1900); F. Bettex, *Het Lied der Schepping* (Rotterdam: Wenk & Birkhoff, 1901), 227f.; C. Snijders, "De Bewoonbaarheid der Hemellichamen," *Tijdspiegel* (February 1898): 182–204; Pohle in *Der Katholiek* (1884 and 1886), cited by J. B. Heinrich and K. Gutberlet, *Dogmatische Theologie,* 2nd ed., 10 vols. (Mainz: Kircheim, 1881–1900), V, 236.

the idea that the inhabitants of the stars were angels.[22] In addition, in opposition to materialism, around the middle of the nineteenth century there arose a reaction in the form of spiritism which not only acknowledges the existence of deceased spirits but also admits the possibility of communion between them and human beings on earth. By its sensational seances and extensive literature spiritism has won thousands upon thousands of adherents.[23]

Reaching Beyond the Boundary

Philosophically the existence of angels is not demonstrable. The argument of Leibnitz that beginning with man, both downward and upward, on the scale of existence, there have to be all kinds of creatures, so that there should be no *vacuum formarum* (a vacuum of forms), nor a leap of nature, is not acceptable because it would by implication erase the distinction between the Creator and the creature and lead to Gnostic pantheism. Even much less, however, can philosophy advance any argument against the possibility of such an existence. For as long as we ourselves are psychic beings and cannot explain the life of the soul from metabolism but have to predicate an underlying spiritual substance for that life, a life that even continues after death, so long also the existence of a spiritual world is not inconsistent with any argument of reason or any fact of experience. Not only Leibnitz and Wolff but also Schleiermacher and Kant have roundly acknowledged the possibility. The universality of belief in such a spiritual world proves, moreover, that inherent in such an acknowledgment there is something other and something more than caprice and chance. Strauss's observation that the world of angels is a compensation for the quantity of matter in creation, though it implies the admission that a materialistic worldview is not satisfactory to the human mind, is inadequate as an explanation of the belief in angels. Insufficient to that end is also the reasoning of Daub that human beings, situated as they are between good and evil, [imaginatively] created symbolic types in two directions, thus arriving at the idea of angels as well as devils.[24]

22. J. H. Kurtz, *The Bible and Astronomy: An Exposition of the Biblical Cosmology and Its Relations to Natural Science*, trans. by Thomas Davis Simonton (Philadelphia: Lindsay & Blakiston, 1857), 222–28, 456–61.; K. Keerl, *Der Mensch das Ebenbild Gottes* (Basel: Bahnmeier, 1866), I, 278f.; F. J. Splittgerber, *Tod, Fortleben und Auferstehung*, 5th ed. (Halle: Fricke, 1879), 150; J. H. Lange, *Christliche Dogmatik*, 3 vols. (Heidelberg: K. Winter, 1849–52), II, 362f.; K. Keerl, "Die Fixsterne und die Engel," *Beweis des Glaubens* 32 (June 1896): 230–47.

23. H. N. De Fremery, *Handleiding tot de Kennis van het Spiritisme* (Bussum, 1904); idem, *Een Spiritistische Levensbeschouwing* (Bussum, 1907).

24. I. A. Dorner, *A System of Christian Doctrine*, trans. by A. Cave and J. S. Banks (Edinburgh: T. & T. Clark, 1891), II, 98.

Belief in a spiritual world is not philosophical, but religious in nature. It is intimately linked with revelation and miracle. Religion is inconceivable apart from revelation, and revelation cannot occur apart from the existence of a spiritual world above and behind this visible world, a spiritual world in communion with the visible world. In all religions, angels are not factors in the life of religion and ethics itself so much as in the revelation on which this life is built. Given with the fact of religion is the very belief that its deepest causes do not lie within the circle of visible things. Good and evil, both in a religious and an ethical sense, are rooted in a world other than that which appears to our senses. Belief in angels gives expression to that other world. While it does not constitute the essence and center of religion, belief in angels is connected with it. The transcendence of God, belief in revelation and miracle, the essence of religion—all this automatically carries with it belief in spiritual beings. The world that is present to our senses does not satisfy human beings. Ever and again we thirst for another world that is no less rich than this one. By way of a reaction to it, materialism evokes spiritualism. But the spiritism in which this spiritualism today manifests itself in the lives of many people is nothing other than a new form of superstition. It is hard to prove whether there is any reality underlying it. For not only is the history of spiritism rife with all sorts of deceptions and unmaskings, but there is no way to check whether the spirits that are said to appear are really the persons they claim to be. There always remains a huge distinction, therefore, between the strange and marvelous phenomena to which spiritism appeals and the explanation it gives for those phenomena. Many of these phenomena can be adequately explained in terms of psychology; but concerning the remainder it is absolutely not certain whether they must be attributed to the workings of deceased humans, or of demonic spirits, or of the hidden powers of nature.[25]

One thing is certain: in numerous cases spiritism has a very injurious effect on the psychic and physical health of its practitioners,[26] and it follows a path that is prohibited by Scripture (Deut. 18:11f.). Between this world and the world beyond there is a gap that humans cannot bridge. If they nevertheless attempt to cross it, they lapse into superstition and become prey to the very spirits they have conjured up.

And just as between the world on this side of the grave and that on the other side there is a boundary which humans must respect, so also

25. O. Zöckler, "Spiritismus," *PRE*[3], XVIII, 654–66; Traub, "Der Spiritismus," in Ernst Kalb, *Kirchen und Sekten der Gegenwart* (Stuttgart: Buchhandlung der Evangische Gesellschaft, 1907), 485–549.
26. Zeehandelaar, "Het spiritistisch Gevaar," *Gids* (August 1907): 306–37.

we humans here on earth have no knowledge of what takes place on other planets. Under the influence of the Copernican worldview, some people, thinking that the earth had lost its central significance for the universe, took pleasure in populating other planets not only with organic, intelligent beings but with superhuman creatures as well. But others are now also pulling back from these fantastic speculations. Some years ago the well-known British scientist Alfred R. Wallace demonstrated that no planet is inhabitable.[27] He based his arguments not on philosophical reasoning but on facts advanced by recent astronomy, physics, chemistry, and biology, and simply poses the question of what these facts tell us about the inhabitability of the planets and, if they do not yield absolute proof one way or the other, what they suggest is the greatest likelihood. Now spectral analysis has shown that the visible universe consists of the same chemical components as the earth, that the same laws of nature prevail everywhere, and, accordingly, that also the development of animate beings is most probably bound to the same universal laws. Animate beings, though they may differ in kind among themselves, do nevertheless have many things in common: all need nitrogen, oxygen, hydrogen, and carbon, moderate temperatures, and the alternation of day and night. Countless conditions must therefore be met before the planets can be considered habitable by animate beings.

Now Wallace demonstrates at great length how these conditions are met only on earth. The moon is not inhabitable since it has neither water nor atmosphere; the sun is not, because it is largely a gaseous body; Jupiter, Saturn, Uranus, and Neptune are not, because they are still in a seething state; Mercury and Venus are not, because they do not rotate and are therefore intolerably hot in one hemisphere and intolerably cold in the other. This leaves only Mars. This planet does indeed have day and night, summer and winter, good weather and bad, fog and snow, but the atmosphere there is as rare as the atmosphere on earth is at 12,500 meters above sea level, while water is scarce and seas presumably nonexistent. So while Mars is not exactly uninhabitable, conditions there can hardly be considered favorable for animate beings. Granted, outside our solar system there are additionally numerous dark and light stars, but also concerning them it cannot be proved that they meet the conditions under which organic life is possible. Wallace thus comes to the conclusion that the earth is a highly privileged celestial body. According to him the stellar world in its totality is not infinitely

27. Alfred R. Wallace, *Man's Place in the Universe: A Study of the Results of Scientific Research in Relation to the Unity or Plurality of Worlds* (New York: McClure, Phillips, 1903); cf. H. H. Kuyper, *De Heraut* (October 1904), and subsequent issues; idem, "'s-Menschen Plaats in het Heelal," *Wetenschappelijke Bladen* (April 1904): 67–78.

large but has the shape of a sphere and is surrounded by a belt, the
Milky Way, which is thickest in the middle, thus, in conjunction with
the sphere, forming a spheroid. In that Milky Way there are still storms
and disturbances but within the sphere things are relatively quiet and
conditions prevail which make the earth inhabitable and existence possible for animate beings, specifically also human beings. Even if it is
true that the stellar world in its totality does not constitute a unity but
that, as Prof. Kapstein contends, there are two distinct "universes of
stellar systems,"[28] or that the present uninhabitability of the stars still
does not rule out their inhabitability in an earlier or later time,[29] nevertheless this much is certain: belief in the existence of animate rational
beings on planets other than the earth belongs totally to the realm of
conjecture and is contradicted rather than confirmed by present-day
science.

As a result of this pronouncement of science the doctrine of angels
as Scripture presents it to us gains in value and significance. Philosophically there is nothing that can be advanced against it. The idea of the
existence of other and higher rational beings than humans has more in
its favor than against it. In the religions, belief in such higher beings is
a more than accidental component. And revelation involving this belief
gains in reality and liveliness. But while in the various religions and in
spiritistic theories this doctrine of angels is distorted, the boundary between God and his creatures erased, and the distinction between revelation and religion denied, in Scripture this doctrine again surfaces in
a way that does not rob God of his honor and leaves the purity of religion untouched. For the Christian the revelation given in Scripture is
the sure foundation also of belief in angels. In an earlier time people
sought to prove the existence of good and especially of bad angels historically, that is, from oracles, appearances, ghosts, the demon-
possessed, and so on.[30] But these proofs were no more convincing than
those based on reason. In Scripture, on the other hand, the existence of
angels is taught very clearly. Spinoza and Schleiermacher, to be sure,
advanced against this teaching that Christ and the apostles spoke about
angels from a stance of accommodation to folk belief and did not themselves teach anything positive about them. But Jesus and the apostles
themselves openly and repeatedly expressed their belief in angels (e.g.,
Matt. 11:10; 13:39; 16:27; 18:10; 24:36; 26:53; Luke 20:36; 1 Cor. 6:3;

28. H. H. Turner, "Man's Place in the Universe," *Fortnightly Review* (April 1907): 600–
610.
29. Alfred H. Kellogg, "The Incarnation and Other Worlds," *Princeton Theological Review* 3 (April 1905): 177–79.
30. T. Aquinas, *Summa Theol.*, I, qu. 50, art. 1; J. Zanchi, *Op. Theol.* II, 2; G. J. Vossius,
De orig. et prog. idol. I, 6; G. Voetius, *Select. Disp.*, I, 985–1017.

Heb. 12:22; 1 Pet. 1:12, etc.). When we speak of elves and fairies everybody knows this is meant figuratively; but in Jesus' time belief in angels was universal. When Jesus and the apostles spoke of angels, everyone within earshot had to think they themselves believed in them. The ultimate ground for our belief in angels, accordingly, lies also in revelation. Christian experience as such does not teach us anything on this subject. The object of true faith is the grace of God in Christ. Angels are not factors in our religious life, neither are they objects of our trust or our worship. Nowhere in Scripture are they such objects, and therefore they may not be that for us either. In the Protestant confessions there is therefore very little mention of angels.[31] Especially the Reformed tended in this connection to sin more by defect than by excess. In Reformed Catholicism, angelology occupies a much larger place, but there too the subject distorts the religion and obscures the glory of God. In short, though angels are not a factor or an object in our religion, in the history of revelation they are nevertheless of great importance and especially from this fact they derive their value for the religious life.

The Angels in Scripture

The name "angel," under which we usually subsume the entire class of higher spiritual beings, is not a name deriving from their nature *(nomen naturae)* but from their office *(nomen officii)*. The Hebrew *ml'k* simply means "messenger," "envoy," and can also mean a human being sent either by other humans (Job 1:14; 1 Sam. 11:3, etc.) or by God (Hag. 1:13; Mal. 2:7; 3:1). The same thing is true of *angelos,* which is repeatedly used to denote humans (Matt. 11:10; Mark 1:2; Luke 7:24, 27; 9:52; Gal. 4:14; James 2:15). In some translations it is erroneously reproduced by "angel" instead of "messenger" (e.g., Gal. 4:14; Rev. 1:20 in the KJV). In Scripture there is no common distinguishing name for the entire class of spiritual beings, though they are frequently called "sons of God" (Job 1:6; 2:1; 38:7; Pss. 29:1; 89:7); "spirits" (1 Kings 22:19; Heb. 1:14); "holy ones" (Ps. 89:5, 7; Zech. 14:5; Job 5:1; 15:15; Dan. 8:13); "watchers" (Dan. 4:13, 17, 23).

There are distinct kinds and classes of angels, each of which has a name of its own. The world of angels is as richly varied as the material world, and just as in the material world there is a wide assortment of creatures which nevertheless jointly form a single whole, so it is in the

---

31. *Belgic Confession,* art. 12; *Heidelberg Catechism,* Lord's Day, 49 (*ed. note:* Bavinck's own reference is to questions 112, 117; the former has reference to the devil, but the latter none to spiritual beings); H. A. Niemeyer, *Collectio confessium in ecclesiis reformatis publicatorum* (Leipzig: Klinkhardt, 1840), 315, 316, 476.

world of spirits. First to be mentioned in Scripture are the *cherubim*. In Genesis 3:24 they act as guards to protect the garden. In the tabernacle and temple they are depicted with faces that are turned to the mercy seat and with wings that cover the mercy seat (Exod. 25:18ff.; 37:8, 9; 1 Chron. 28:18; 2 Chron. 3:14; Heb. 9:5), between which the Lord sits enthroned (Pss. 80:2; 90:1; Isa. 37:16). When God comes down to earth he is represented as riding the cherubim (2 Sam. 22:11; Ps. 18:10 or Ps. 104:4; Isa. 66:15; Heb. 1:7). In Ezekiel 1 and 10 they appear under the name of "living creatures," four in number, in the form of humans, each with four wings and four faces, namely, that of a human, a lion, an ox and an eagle, while in Revelation 4:6f., as the four living creatures *(zōa)*, each with one face and six wings, they surround the throne of God and sing the "thrice-holy" night and day. The name *kĕrbîm* is variously derived, sometimes from *keb* and *rôb* meaning "many" (Hengstenberg), then from *rkyb* meaning "wagon," or also from *krb* (Arab.), meaning "to frighten," hence "horrible beings," but mostly from a stem that means "to seize," "to hold onto" (cf. *grups*[32]).

There is similar disagreement about the nature of the cherubim. Some exegetes consider them to be mythical beings, others as symbolic figures, still others as divine forces in creation, or as the original term for thunderclouds or storms.[33] But in Genesis 3:24, Ezekiel 1, and Revelation 4 they are clearly represented as animate personal beings. Even the human form in them is predominant (Ezek. 1:5). But inasmuch as they are beings of extraordinary human strength and glory, Scripture uses symbolic representation to give us some idea of their spiritual nature. They are pictured as "living beings" *(zōa)* in whom God's power and strength come to expression with greater vividness than in a frail human being. They have the power of an ox, the majesty of a lion, the speed of an eagle, and on top of this, the intelligence of a human being. The wings with which they fly and the sword with which they guard the garden point to the same attributes. From this representation, which is not a depiction but a symbol, we learn that among the angels the cherubim are also highly positioned beings who more than any other creatures reveal the power, majesty, and glory of God and are therefore charged with the task of guarding the holiness of God in the garden of Eden, in the tabernacle and temple, and also in God's descent to earth.[34]

32. F. Delitzsch, *A New Commentary on Genesis*, trans. by Sophia Taylor (Edinburgh: T. & T. Clark, 1899), I, 73–76 (on Gen. 3:24); idem, *Biblical Commentary on the Psalms*, trans. by Francis Bolton (Edinburgh: T. & T. Clark, 1871), I, 256–57 (on Ps. 18:11).
33. R. Smend, *Lehrbuch der alttestamentlichen Religiongeschichte* (Freiburg i.B.: J. C. B. Mohr, 1893), 21ff.
34. *Johannes Nikel, *Die Lehre des A.T. über die Cherubim und Seraphim* (Breslau, 1890).

Then, in Isaiah 6, there is mention of the *seraphim (šĕrampîm),* a word that is probably derived from the Arabic stem *sarufa* ("it was no-ble"). In this passage they are also symbolically represented in human form, but with six wings, two of them to cover the face, two to cover the feet, and two for the swift execution of God's commands. In distinction from the cherubim, they stand as servants around the king who is seated on his throne, acclaim his glory and await his commands. Seraphim are the noble ones, cherubim the powerful, among the angels. The former guard the holiness of God; the latter serve at the altar and effect atone-ment. Finally, in Daniel we further encounter two angels with proper names: Gabriel (8:16; 9:21) and Michael (10:13, 21; 12:1). Contrary to the opinion of many earlier and later interpreters, like the Van den Hon-erts, Burman, Witsius, Hengstenberg, Zahn (et al.), they are to be con-sidered created angels and must not be identified with the Son of God.[35]

According to the New Testament, there are various classes of angels. The angel Gabriel appears in Luke 1:19, 26. Michael occurs in Jude 9, Revelation 12:7, and 1 Thessalonians 4:16. Included among the angels there are also principalities and powers (Eph. 3:10; Col. 2:10); domin-ions (Eph. 1:21; Col. 1:16); thrones (Col. 1:16), powers (Eph. 1:21; 1 Pet. 3:22), all of them terms that point to a distinction in rank and dignity among the angels, while in John's Apocalypse, finally, seven angels re-peatedly and clearly come into the foreground (8:2, 6; 15:1, etc.). Add to this that the number of angels is very high. This is indicated by the words Sabaoth [hosts] and Mahanaim [camps] (Gen. 32:1, 2), legions (Matt. 26:53), host (Luke 2:13), and the numbers of a thousand times a thousand (Deut. 33:2; Ps. 68:17; Dan. 7:10; Jude 14; Rev. 5:11; 19:14).

Such large numbers naturally call for distinction in order and rank— all the more because angels, unlike humans, are not related by family and are therefore much more alike in many respects. Scripture, accord-ingly, clearly teaches that among angels there are all kinds of distinc-tions of rank and status, of dignity and ministry, of office and honor, even of class and kind. This splendid idea of diversity in unity may not be abandoned, despite its having been elaborated on a fantastic scale by Jews and Catholics. The Jews made all sorts of distinctions among the angels.[36] Initially, in the early church, people were content with the data of Scripture.[37] Augustine still maintained he did not know how the soci-ety of angels was organized.[38] But Pseudo-Dionysius, in his *The Celestial*

35. *W. Leuken, *Michael, eine Darstellung und Vegeleichung der jüd. und der morgentl.-christl. Tradition* (Göttingen, 1898).

36. F. W. Weber, *System der altsynagogalen palastinischen Theologie* (Leipzig: Dörf-flung & Franke, 1880), 161f.

37. Irenaeus, *Against Heresies,* II, 54; Origen, *On Principles*, I, 5.

38. Augustine, *Enchiridion*, 58.

Hierarchy and *The Ecclesiastical Hierarchy*, offered a schematic division.
Proceeding from the idea that at the creation God as it were left his oneness behind and entered into multiplicity, he teaches that all things proceed from God in an ever-descending series and so again successively return to him. God is the center and creatures gather peripherally around
him. There is a twofold hierarchy of things, one celestial and the other
ecclesiastical. The celestial hierarchy is formed by three classes of angels. The first and highest class exclusively serves God; it embraces the
seraphim, who unceasingly behold the being of God; the cherubim, who
ponder his decrees; and the thrones, who adore his judgments. The second class serves the visible and invisible creation; it embraces the do-
minions who order the things that must happen according to God's will;
the powers who execute the things decreed, and the authorities who
complete the task. The third class serves the earth, both individuals and
peoples; it embraces the principalities who foster the general well-being
of human beings; the archangels who guide particular nations; and the
angels who watch over individual persons. Of that celestial hierarchy
the ecclesiastical hierarchy is a mirror: in its mysteries (baptism, the Eu-
charist, ordination), its functionaries (bishop, priest, deacon), and its
laity (catechumens, Christians, monks). This hierarchy as a whole has
its origin and head in Christ, the incarnate Son of God, and its goal in
deification. This classification of Pseudo-Dionysius, which divulges the
celestial and earthly hierarchy as an intimate idea of the Roman Catholic system, found fertile soil and was generally accepted.[39]

Now Scripture also clearly teaches the distinction and ranking of angels. Some scholars erroneously think that, though different names are
used, the reference is always to the same angels, only viewed each time
from a different angle.[40] It must even be acknowledged that this ranking has not sufficiently come into its own in Protestant theology. There
is order and rank among those thousands of beings. God is a God of
order in all the churches (1 Cor. 14:33, 40). The realm of spirits is no
less rich and splendid than the realm of material beings. But the hierarchy of Roman Catholic doctrine far exceeds the revelation of God in
his Word. It was therefore unanimously repudiated by the Protestants.[41] Similarly all calculations concerning the number of the angels

39. John of Damascus, *Exposition of the Orthodox Faith*, II, 3; P. Lombard, II *Sent.*,
dist. 9; T. Aquinas, *Summa Theol.*, I, qu. 108; Petavius, "de angelis," II; J. H. Oswald, *Angelologie* (Paderborn: Ferdinand Schöningh, 1883), 57f.
40. J. C. C. Von Hofmann, *Der Schriftbeweis*, 3 vols. (Nördlingen: Beck, 1857–60), I, 301.
41. J. Calvin, *Commentaries on the Epistles of Paul the Apostle to the Galatians, Ephesians, Philippians and Colossians*, trans. by T. H. L. Parker, ed. by David W. Torrance and
Thomas F. Torrance (Grand Rapids: Eerdmans, 1965), 137 [commentary on Eph. 1:21];
G. Voetius, *Select. Disp.*, I, 882f.; A. Rivetus, *Op. Theol.*, III, 248f.; J. Quenstedt, *Theologia*,
I, 443, 450; J. Gerhard, *Loci Theol.*, V, 4, 9.

were considered futile and unfruitful, as, for example, those of Augustine, who supplemented the number of the angels, after the fall of some, with the number of predestined humans;[42] or of Gregory, who believed that the number of people who were saved would be equal to the number of angels who remained faithful;[43] or of William of Paris, who called the number of angels infinite; or of Hilary and many others, who, on the basis of Matthew 18:12, thought that the ratio of the number of humans to that of angels was 1 to 99;[44] or of G. Schott, who put the number of the angels at a thousand billion.[45] Nor were they much interested in the question of whether the angels among themselves were differentiated in essence and species. Thomas was very firm on this teaching,[46] but most of the church fathers were of a different mind.[47] However many distinctions there may have been among the angels, Scripture does not discuss them and offers only scant information. In relation to us humans their unity comes to the fore much more than their diversity: they all have a spiritual nature, they are all called "ministering spirits," and they all find their primary activity in the glorification of God.

Angelic Nature: Unity and Corporeality

That unity comes out, in the first place, in the fact that they are all created beings. Schelling may say that the good angels, as pure potencies, are uncreated,[48] but the creation of angels is clearly stated in Colossians 1:16 and implied in the creation of all things (Gen. 1:4; Ps. 33:6; Neh. 9:6; John 1:3; Rom. 11:36; Eph. 3:9; Heb. 1:2). About the *time* of their creation, however, little can be said with certainty. Many church fathers, appealing to Job 38:7, believed that the angels were created before all [other] things.[49] The Socinians[50] and the Remonstrants[51] agreed and in this manner weakened the distinction between the Logos and the angels. But this idea has no support in Scripture. Nothing is an-

42. Augustine, *Enchiridion*, 29; idem, *City of God*, XXII, 1; Anselm, *Cur Deus Homo*, I, 18.
43. P. Lombard, II *Sent.*, 9.
44. D. Petavius, *Theol. Dogm.*, "de angelis," I, 14.
45. C. Busken Huet, *Het Land van Rembrandt*, 2nd rev. ed., 2 vols. (Haarlem: H. D. Tjeenk Willink, 1886), II, 2, 37.
46. T. Aquinas, *Summa Theol.*, I, qu. 50, art. 4.
47. John of Damascus, *Exposition of the Orthodox Faith*, II, 3; Petavious, "de angelis," I, 14; G. Voetius, *Select. Disp.*, V, 261.
48. F. W. J. Schelling, *Werke*, II, 4, 284.
49. Origen, *Homily on Genesis 1;* Basil, *Hexaemeron*, homily 1; Gregory of Nazianzen, *Orations*, 38; John of Damascus, *Exposition of the Orthodox Faith*, II, 3; Dionysius, *The Divine Names*, 5.
50. J. Crell, *Opera Omnia*, "liber de deo," 1, 18.
51. S. Episcopius, *Inst. Theol.*, IV, 3, 1; P. Van Limborch, *Theol. Christ.*, II, 210, 4.

terior to the creation of heaven and earth, of which Genesis 1:1 speaks. Job 38:7 indeed teaches that, like the stars, they were present at the time of creation but not that they already existed before the beginning of creation. On the other hand, it is certain that the angels were created before the seventh day when heaven and earth and all the host of them were finished and God rested from his labor (Gen. 1:31; 2:1, 2). As for the rest, we are in the dark. It may, however, be considered likely that, just as in Genesis 1:1 the earth was created as such but still had to be further prepared and adorned, so also heaven was not completed at a single stroke. The word "heaven" in verse 1 is proleptic. Only later in the history of revelation does it become evident what is implied in it.[52] Scripture sometimes speaks of heaven as the sky with its clouds (Gen. 1:8, 20; 7:11; Matt. 6:26); then as the stellar heavens (Deut. 4:19; Ps. 8:4; Matt. 24:29); and finally as the abode of God and his angels (Pss. 115:16; 2:4; 1 Kings 8:27; 2 Chron. 6:18; Matt. 6:19–21; Heb. 4:14; 7:26; 8:1, 2; 9:2f., etc.). Now just as the heavens of the clouds and of the stars only came into being in the course of six days, it is possible and even likely that also the third heaven with its inhabitants was formed in stages. To the extent that we think of that spiritual realm as being more fully furnished and populated, even far surpassing the material world in diversity, it is all the more plausible to posit a certain interval of time for the preparation of that heaven as well, even though the creation story does not breathe a word about it.

Second, the unity of angels is evident from the fact that they are all spiritual beings. On this subject, however, there was at all times much difference of opinion. The Jews attributed to them bodies that were airy or fiery in nature,[53] and were followed in this respect by most of the church fathers.[54] At the Second Council of Nicea (787), the patriarch Tarasius read a dialogue composed by a certain John of Thessalonica in which the latter asserted that the angels had delicate, refined bodies and might therefore be depicted, adding that they were spatially defined and had appeared in human form and were therefore depictable. The synod registered its agreement with this view.[55] But gradually, as the line between spirit and matter was drawn more sharply, many authors attributed to angels a purely spiritual nature.[56] The Fourth Lat-

52. *Gebhardt, "Der Himmel im N.T.," *Zeitschrift fur Kirchliche Wissenschaft und Kirchliche Leben*, 1886; Cremer, "Himmel," *PRE*³, VIII, 80–84.

53. F. W. Weber, *System der altsynagogalen palastinischen Theologie*, 161f.

54. Justin Martyr, *Dialogue with Trypho*, 57; Origen, *On First Principles*, I, 6; Basil, *On the Holy Spirit*, 16; Tertullian, *On the Flesh of Christ*, 6; Augustine, *On the Trinity*, II, 7.

55. J. Schwane, *Dogmengeschichte*, 4 vols. (Freiburg i.B.: Herder, 1882–95), II, 235.

56. John of Damascus, *Exposition of the Orthodox Faith*, II, 3; T. Aquinas, *Summa Theol.*, I, qu. 50, art. 1., qu. 51, art. 1.

eran Council in 1215 called the nature of angels "spiritual"[57] and most Catholic and Protestant theologians concurred in this judgment. Nevertheless also later a certain corporeality of angels was taught from time to time by Catholics, such as Cajetan, Eugubinus, Bannez, as well as by such Reformed theologians as Zanchius and Vossius;[58] and by Episcopius, Vorstius, Poiret, Böhme, Leibnitz, Wolff, Bonnet, Reinhard, and so on; in modern times by Kurtz, Beck, Lange, Kahnis, Vilmar, and others.[59] The chief reason for this opinion is that the concept of a purely spiritual, incorporeal nature is metaphysically inconceivable as well as incompatible with the concept of "creature." God is purely Spirit but he is also simple, omnipresent, eternal. But angels are bounded in relation to time and space; if they really move from one place to another they have to be—in their own way—corporeal. Similarly, angels are not simple like God but composed of matter and form. Also for that reason a certain material—finely ethereal, to be sure—corporeality has to be attributed to them. Added to this line of thought was the exegesis which in considering the "sons of God" in Genesis 6 saw them as angels. This exegesis of Philo, Josephus, the Jews, the LXX, was taken over by many church fathers,[60] Justin, Irenaeus, Clemens, Tertullian, Lactantius, Cyprian, Ambrose (et al.), adopted also by Luther and again defended in modern times by Ewald, Baumgarten, Hofmann, Kurtz, Delitzsch, Hengstenberg, Köhler, and Kübel (et al.). In addition, in arguing for the corporeality of angels, people appeal to their appearances, to certain special texts in holy Scripture, like Psalm 104:4; Matthew 22:30; Luke 20:35; 1 Corinthians 11:10; and sometimes also to the fact that as inhabitants of the stars they certainly have to be corporeal.

Over against all these arguments, however, stands the clear pronouncement of Holy Scripture that the angels are spirits (*pneumata;* Matt. 8:16; 12:45; Luke 7:21; 8:2; 11:26; Acts 19:12; Eph. 6:12; Heb. 1:14), who do not marry (Matt. 22:30), are immortal (Luke 20:35, 36) and invisible (Col. 1:16), may be "legion" in a restricted space (Luke 8:30), and, like spirits, have no flesh and bones (Luke 24:39). Moreover, the conception that the "sons of God" *(bĕnĕ-hāĕlōhîm)* in Genesis 6:2 are angels and not men is untenable. Though this designation is used

---

57. Denzinger, *Enchiridion*, 355.

58. J. Zanchi, *Op. Theol.*, 69; G. J. Vossius, *de idol.* I, 2, 6.

59. J. H. Kurtz, *The Bible and Astronomy*, 191–207; *Beck, *Lehrewissenschaft*, I, 176; P. Lange, *Christliche Dogmatik*, II, 578; F. A. Kahnis, *Die Luthersche Dogmatik* (Leipzig: Dorfflung & Francke, 1861–68), I, 443; A. F. C. Vilmar, *Handbuch der evangelischen Dogmatik* (Gütersloh: Bertelsmann, 1895), I, 306; K. Keerl, "Die Fixstern und die Engel," 235–47; cf. F. Delitzsch, *A System of Biblical Psychology*, 2nd ed. (Edinburgh: T. & T. Clark, 1875), 78–87.

60. Justin Martyr, *Second Apology*, 5 [ed. note. Bavinck erroneously cites *Apol.* I, 1 here.]; Irenaeus, *Against Heresies*, IV, 16, 2; V, 29, 2.

repeatedly for angels (Job 1:6; 2:1; 38:7), it can also very well denote humans (Deut. 32:5; Hos. 2:1; Pss. 80:16; 73:15), and is in any case inapplicable to bad angels, who must have committed their sin on earth. Moreover, the expression "took to wife" *lqh ʾšh* in Genesis 6:2 is always used with reference to a lawful marriage and never to fornication. Finally, the punishment of the sin is imposed only on humans, for they are the guilty party and there is no mention of angels (Gen. 6:3, 5–7). Neither do the other Scripture passages prove the corporeality of angels. Psalm 104:4 (cf. Heb. 1:7) only says that God uses his angels as ministers, just as wind and fire serve to carry out his commands, but absolutely not that the angels are changed into wind or fire. Matthew 22:30 asserts that after the resurrection believers will be like the angels in that they will not marry, but says nothing about the corporeality of angels. And when 1 Corinthians 11:10 says that wives, as a sign of their subordination to their husbands, should cover their heads in church in order not to displease the good angels who are present in the church, there is no reason here to think of bad angels who would otherwise be seduced by the women. As to angel appearances, it is indeed certain that they always occurred in visible corporeal form, just as symbolic representations always show angels in visible forms as well. But this still does not imply anything in favor of their corporeality. God, remember, is spirit and is nevertheless envisioned by Isaiah (ch. 6) as a King sitting on his throne. Christ appeared in the flesh and is still truly God. Both in their appearances and in symbolism the angels continually assume different forms. The representations of the cherubim in Genesis 3:24, above the ark of the covenant, in Ezekiel and the Apocalypse, are all different; and the forms in which they appear are far from identical (Gen. 18; Judg. 6:11, 12; 13:6; Dan. 10:11; Matt. 28:3; Luke 2:9; Rev. 22:8). How these bodies are to be conceived is another question. One cannot say with certainty whether they were real or only apparently real bodies.[61]

The strongest proof for the corporeality of angels, as stated above, is derived from philosophy. But in this connection a variety of misunderstandings plays a role. If corporeality only meant that the angels are limited in both time and space, and are not simple like God, in whom all attributes are identical with his essence, then a certain type of corporeality would have to be attributed to the angels. But usually corporeality does entail a certain materiality, even if it were of a more refined nature than in the case of man and animals. And in that sense there can and may be no ascription of a body to angels. Matter and spirit are mu-

61. John of Damascus, *Expositon of the Orthodox Faith*, II, 3; T. Aquinas, *Summa Theol.*, I, qu. 51, arts. 1–3; F. Turretin, *Institutes of Elenctic Theology*, VII, 6, 5.

tually exclusive (Luke 24:39). It is a form of pantheistic identity-philosophy to mix the two and to erase the distinction between them. And Scripture always maintains the distinction between heaven and earth, angels and humans, the spiritual and the material, invisible and visible things (Col. 1:16). If, then, angels are to be conceived as spirits, they relate differently—more freely—to time and space than humans. On the one hand, they do not transcend all space and time as God does, for they are creatures and therefore finite and limited. Theirs is not a space that is completely filled *(ubi repletivum)*, they are not omnipresent or eternal. Nor do they occupy a circumscribed space *(ubi circumscriptivum)* like our bodies, for the angels are spirits and therefore have no dimensions of length and breadth, hence no extension or diffusion through space. It was usually said, therefore, that theirs was a defined or definite space *(ubi definitivum)*. That is, as finite and limited beings, they are always somewhere. They cannot be in two places at once. Their presence is not extensive but punctual; and they are spatially so free that they can move at lightning speed and cannot be obstructed by material objects; their translocation is immediate. Of course, such speed of movement and such temporal and spatial freedom that nevertheless is not atemporal or nonspatial is inconceivable to us. But Scripture clearly refers to it; and in the speed of thought and imagination, of light and electricity, we have analogies that are not to be despised.[62]

The unity of angels is further manifest in the fact that they are all rational beings, endowed with intellect and will. Both of these faculties are repeatedly attributed in Scripture to both good and bad angels (Job 1:6f.; Zech. 3:1f.; Matt. 24:36; Matt. 8:29; 18:10; 2 Cor. 11:3; Eph. 6:11, etc.). All sorts of personal attributes and activities occur in their existence, such as self-consciousness and speech (Luke 1:19), desire (1 Pet. 1:12), rejoicing (Luke 15:10), prayer (Heb. 1:6), believing (James 2:19), lying (John 8:44), sinning (1 John 3:8, etc.). In addition, great power is ascribed to them; the angels are not timid beings but an army of mighty heroes (Ps. 103:20; Luke 11:21; Col. 1:16; Eph. 1:21; 3:10; 2 Thess. 1:7; Acts 5:19; Heb. 1:14). On this ground it is incorrect, with Schelling and others, to view angels as qualities or forces. Still it is desirable, in our description of the personality of angels, to stick with the simplicity of Holy Scripture. Augustine distinguished two kinds of knowledge in angels: one which they acquired as it were at the dawn of creation, apriori, via the vision of God, and another which they acquired, as it were, in

---

62. Augustine, *City of God*, XI, 9; John of Damascus, *Exposition of the Orthodox Faith*, II, 3; T. Aquinas, *Summa Theol.*, I, qus. 52–53; G. Voetius, *Select. Disp.*, V, 252f.: F. A. Phillipi, *Kirchliche Glaubenslehre* (Gütersloh: Bertelsmann, 1902), II, 302; J. H. Oswald, *Angelologie*, 23–43.

the evening of creation, aposteriori, from their contemplation of creatures.[63] The Scholastics not only adopted this distinction but tried to
define the nature and extent of that knowledge more precisely. That
knowledge is not, as in the case of God, identical with their being and
substance. Nor is their knowledge acquired by sense perception. The
distinction between potential and active understanding does not apply
to them. Their power to understand is never purely a faculty, never at
rest but always active. They cannot *be* without knowing: they know
themselves, their own being, by themselves, completely and immutably. They know created things, not from their appearance, but via innate ideas, not by abstraction and discursively, but intuitively and intel-
lectually. And while the angels do not know [things] immediately
through their natural powers, but by having the form stamped upon
them *(per speciem impressam)* through and simultaneously with their
own being, still, in the supernatural order to which the angels have been
elevated, they know God by immediate vision.[64] Some even taught—in
the interest of defending prayer addressed to the angels and to the
saints—that angels, seeing God who sees all things, saw all things in
him and therefore knew all our afflictions and needs.[65]

Protestants, on the other hand, were more cautious, warning people
to be modest. In the way in which we humans arrive at knowledge there
is so much that is mysterious. How much more would that be true of
angels![66] One can only say that they are more richly endowed with
knowledge than we here on earth (Matt. 18:10; 24:36). They acquire
their knowledge from their own nature (John 8:44), from the contemplation of God's works (Eph. 3:10; 1 Tim. 3:16; 1 Pet. 1:12), and from
revelations imparted to them by God (Dan. 8:9; Rev. 1:1). Nevertheless
they are bound to objects (Eph. 3:10; 1 Pet. 1:12). They do not know either the secret thoughts of our hearts or those of each other (1 Kings
8:39; Ps. 139:2, 4; Acts 1:24), so that also among themselves they need a
language for communicating their thoughts (1 Cor. 13:2) and in general
to be able, in their own way and in accordance with their own nature,
to glorify God in speech and song.[67] They do not know the future, nor
future contingencies, but can only conjecture (Isa. 41:22, 23). They do

63. Augustine, *The Literal Meaning of Genesis*, V, 18; idem, *City of God*, XI, 29.
64. T. Aquinas, *Suma Theol.*, I, qus. 54–58; idem, *Summa Contra Gentiles*, II, 96–101,
II, 49; Bonaventure, II *Sent.*, dist. 3, art. 4 and dist. 4, art. 3; Petavius, "de angelis," *Op.
Theol.*, I, 6–9; Kleutgen, *Philosophie der Vorzeit*, I, 196f.; Oswald, *Angelologie*, 43–51.
65. Gregory the Great, *Moralia in Iob.*, 12, 13; T. Aquinas, *Summa Theol.*, II, 2, qu. 83,
art. 4; III, qu. 10, art. 2; Bellarmine, "de sanct. beat.," *Controversiis*, 1, 26.
66. J. Zanchi, *Op. Theol.*, III, 108f.; G. Voetius, *Select. Disp.*, V, 267; J. Gerhard, *Loci
Theol.*, V, 4, 5.
67. Petavius, *Opera Omnia*, "de angelis," 1, 12.

not know the day of judgment (Mark 13:12). And their knowledge is capable of expansion (Eph. 3:10). To this we may certainly add that the knowledge and power of angels vary greatly among themselves. Also in this respect there is variety and order. From the few angelic names that occur in Scripture, we may even infer that angels are not only members of distinct classes but are also distinct as persons. Each angel as such has an individuality of its own, even though we must reject the opinion of some Scholastics that every angel constitutes a particular species.[68]

Finally, the angels are unified by the fact that they are all moral beings. This is evident from the good angels who serve God night and day, as well as from the bad angels who did not remain in the truth. About the original state of angels Scripture says very little. It only testifies that at the end of the work of creation God saw all things and, behold, it was very good (Gen. 1:31). In John 8:44, Jude 6, and 2 Peter 2:4, moreover, the state of integrity of all angels is assumed. The same view is demanded by the theism of Scripture which utterly rules out all Manicheism. Imagination and reasoning had ample play, however, precisely because Scripture reveals so little. Augustine believed that at the very moment of their creation some of the angels had fallen and others had remained standing. To the latter, therefore, God granted the grace of perseverance along with their nature, "simultaneously constituting their nature and lavishing grace on them."[69] To this view Scholasticism later appealed for its doctrine of the superadded gifts, also in the case of angels. According to Bonaventure,[70] Alexander of Hales, Peter Lombard, Duns Scotus (et al.), the angels first existed for a time as pure natures and later received the assistance of actual grace. But Thomas along with others believed that the distinction between nature and grace could only be understood logically and that the grace to remain standing was granted to the different angels in various measure.[71] Equipped with that grace, the angels could merit the supreme, inadmissible blessedness that consists in the vision of God.[72] In the locus on man the doctrine of the superadded gifts will call for our special attention. Here we have to confine ourselves to pointing out that at least in the case of angels this doctrine lacks all basis in Scripture. Protestant theology, accordingly, rejected it unanimously. It was content to say that the angels who remained standing were confirmed in the good. And, along with August-

68. Bonaventure, II *Sent.*, dist. 4, art. 2; T. Aquinas, *Summa Contra Gentiles*, II, 52.
69. Augustine, *City of God*, XII, 9; cf. idem, *On Rebuke and Grace*, 11, 32.
70. Bonaventure, II *Sent.*, dist. 4, art. 1, qu. 2.
71. T. Aquinas, *Summa Theol.*, I, qu. 62, arts. 3, 6.
72. Petavius, *Opera Omnia*, "de angelis," I, 16; Becanus, *Theol. Schol.*, "de angelis," 2, 3; *Theologia Wirceburgensis*, III (1880): 466f.; C. Pesch, *Praelectiones Dogmaticae*, 9 vols. (Freiburg: Herder, 1902–10), III, 204f.; Oswald, *Angelologie*, 81f.; Jansen, *Prael.*, II, 361f.

ine and the Scholastics, it maintained this position against Origen,[73] and against the Remonstrants who considered the will of the good angels as still mutable. Indeed, in Holy Scripture the good angels are always presented to us as a faithful company that invariably does the will of the Lord. They are called "angels of the Lord" (Pss. 103:20; 104:4); "elect" (1 Tim. 5:21); "holy ones" (Deut. 33:2; Matt. 25:31); "angels of light" (Luke 9:26; Acts 10:22; 2 Cor. 11:14; Rev. 14:10). They daily behold God's face (Matt. 18:10), are held up to us as examples (Matt. 6:10), and someday believers will become like them (Luke 20:36).

Angels, Humanity, and Christ

In all these qualities of createdness, spirituality, rationality, and morality angels are similar to humans. Now precisely because in Scripture the unity of the angels is highlighted and their diversity recedes into the background there is a danger that we will neglect the difference between angels and humans. Their similarity seems far to surpass the difference between them. Both humans and angels are personal, rational, moral beings; both were originally created in knowledge, righteousness, and holiness; both were given dominion, immortality, and blessedness. In Scripture both are called the sons of God (Job 1:6; Luke 3:38). Still the difference between them is most rigorously maintained in Scripture by the fact that humans *are,* but the angels are *never,* said to be created in the image of God. In theology this distinction is largely neglected. According to Origen the angels and the souls of humans are of the same species; the union of the soul with the body is a punishment for sin and therefore really accidental. Origen arrived at this position because he taught that all dissimilarity originated with the creature. In the beginning God created all things alike; that is, he only created rational beings and all of these, angels and souls, the same. Dissimilarity originated among them by free will. Some remained standing and received a reward; others fell and received punishment. Souls were specifically united to bodies. Hence the entire material world and all the diversity present in it is due to sin and to the different degrees of sin. It does not exist to display God's goodness but to punish sin.[74] Now the church rejected this teaching of Origen and theology maintained the specific difference between humans and angels.[75] Nevertheless, to a degree the idea persists that the angels, since they are exclusively spiri-

73. Origen, *On First Principles*, 1, 5, and 3, 4.
74. T. Aquinas, *Summa Theol.*, I, qu. 47, art. 2; J. B. Heinrich and K. Gutberlet, *Dogmatische Theologie*, 10 vols., 2nd ed. (Mainz: Kircheim, 1881–1900), V, 177.
75. T. Aquinas, *Summa Theol.*, I, qu. 75, art. 7.

tual, are superior to humans and therefore have at least as much or even more right to be called "image-bearers of God."[76] In the hierarchy of creatures the angels, as purely spiritual beings, are the closest to God. "You were and nothing was there besides out of which you made heaven and earth; things were of two kinds: one near you and the other near to nothing; one to which you alone would be superior; the other to which nothing would be inferior."[77] "Necessarily, then, he [God] brought forth not only the nature which is at the greatest distance from him—the physical—but also the one very close to him, the intellectual and incorporeal."[78] But Lutheran and Reformed theologians also often have lost sight of this distinction between humans and angels, and called the angels "image-bearers of God."[79] Only a handful, such as Theodoret, Macarius, Methodius, Tertullian (et al.), opposed this confusion.[80] Augustine expressly states: "God gave to no other creature than man the privilege of being after his own image."[81]

However great the resemblance between humans and angels may be, the difference is no less great. Indeed, various traits belonging to the image of God do exist in angels but man alone *is* the image of God. That image does not just reside in what humans and angels have in common, but in what distinguishes them. The principal points of difference are these: first, an angel is spirit and as spirit the angel is complete; man, on the other hand, is a combination of soul and body; the soul without the body is incomplete. Man, accordingly, is a rational but also a sensuous being. By the body man is bound to the earth, is part of the earth, and the earth is part of man. And of that earth man is head and master. After the angels had already been created, God said that he planned to create man and to give him dominion over the earth (Gen. 1:26). Dominion over the earth is integral to being human, a part of the image of God, and is therefore restored by Christ to his own, whom he not only ordains as prophets and priests, but also as kings. But an angel, however strong and mighty he may be, is a servant in God's creation, not a master over the earth (Heb. 1:14).

---

76. John of Damascus, *Exposition of the Orthodox Faith,* II, 3; T. Aquinas, *Summa Theol.,* I, qu. 93, art. 3; idem, *Commentary on* II *Sent.,* dist. 16; Oswald, *Angelologie,* 25.
   77. Augustine, *Confessions,* XII, 7.
   78. Bonaventure, *Breviloquiam,* II, 6.
   79. John Calvin, *Institutes,* I.xiv.3; A. Polanus, *Syn. Theol.,* V, 10; *Synopsis Purioris Theologiae,* XII, 7 and XIII, 17; A. Comrie and N. Holtius, *Examen van het Ontwerp van Tolerantie,* vol. 9, *Over de staat des rechtschapen Mensch* (Amsterdam: Nicolaas Byl, 1757), 187; B. De Moor, *Comm. Theol.,* II, 335; J. Gerhard, *Loci Theol.,* V, 4, 5; F. Delitzsch, *A System of Biblical Psychology,* 78.
   80. D. Petavius, *Opera Omnia,* "de sex dierum opif.," II, 3, §§4–8.
   81. Cited by T. Aquinas, *Summa Theol.,* I, qu. 93, art. 3; cf. S. Maresius, *Syst. Theol.,* V, 37.

Second, as purely spiritual beings, the angels are not bound to each other by ties of blood. There is among them no father–son relationship, no physical bond, no common blood, no consanguinity. However intimately they may share an ethical bond, they are disconnected beings, so that when many fell, the others could remain standing. In man, on the other hand, there is an adumbration of the divine being, in which there are also persons, united not only in will and affection, but also in essence and nature.

Third, there is consequently something called "humanity" but no "angelity" in that sense. In one man all humans fell, but the human race is also saved in one person. In humanity there could be an Adam and therefore also a Christ. The angels are witnesses, but humans are objects, of God's most marvelous deeds, the works of his grace. The earth is the stage of God's miraculous acts: here the war is fought, here the victory of God's kingdom is won, and angels turn their faces to the earth, longing to look into the mysteries of salvation (Eph. 3:10; 1 Pet. 1:12).

Fourth, angels may be the mightier spirits but humans are the richer of the two. In intellect and power angels far surpass humans. But in virtue of the marvelously rich relationships in which humans stand to God, the world, and humanity, they are psychologically deeper and mentally richer. The relations that sexuality and family life, life in the family, state, and society, life devoted to labor, art, and science brings with it make every human a microcosm, which in multifacetedness, in depth, and in richness far surpasses the personality of angels. Consequently also the richest and most glorious attributes of God are knowable and enjoyable only by humans. Angels experience God's power, wisdom, goodness, holiness, and majesty; but the depths of God's compassions only disclose themselves to humans. The full image of God, therefore, is only unfolded in creaturely fashion in humans—better still, in *humanity*.

Finally, let me add that the angels therefore also stand in a totally different relation to Christ. That there exists a relation between Christ and the angels cannot be doubted. In the first place, various Scripture passages teach that all things (Ps. 33:6; Prov. 8:22f., John 1:3; 1 Cor. 8:6; Eph. 3:9; Heb. 1:2) and specifically also the angels (Col. 1:16) were created by the Son, and thus he is the "mediator of union" of all that was created. But, in the second place, Ephesians 1:10 and Colossians 1:19, 20 contain the profound idea that all things also stand in relation to Christ as the mediator of reconciliation. For God reconciled all things to himself by Christ and gathers them all under him as head. Granted—it is not that the relation consists, as many people have thought, in that Christ has acquired grace and glory for the good angels,[82] nor, as others judged, that the angels could be called members of the church.[83] But it consists in the fact that all things, which have been disturbed and ripped apart by sin, are again united in Christ, restored in their original relationship, and are gathered up under him as head. Thus, while Christ is indeed the Lord and head, he is not the Reconciler and Savior of the angels. All things have been created by him and therefore they are also created unto him that he may return them, reconciled and restored, to the Father. But humans alone constitute the church of Christ; it alone is his bride, the temple of the Holy Spirit, the dwellingplace of God.

The Ministry of Angels

Corresponding to this angelic nature is their ministry and activity. In this connection Scripture makes a distinction between the extraordinary ministry and the ordinary ministry of angels. The extraordinary ministry does not begin until after the fall, having been necessitated by sin. It is an important component in special revelation. We first see the angels play a role in guarding Eden (Gen. 3:24); but then they appear to convey revelations, acting to bless or to punish in the history of the patriarchs and prophets and throughout the entire Old Testament. They appear to Abraham (Gen. 18), to Lot (Gen. 19), to Jacob (Gen. 28:12; 32:1); they function in the giving of the law (Heb. 2:2; Gal. 3:19; Acts 7:53); they take part in Israel's war (2 Kings 19:35; Dan. 10:13, 20); they announce the counsel of God to Elijah and Elisha, to Ezekiel, Daniel, and Zechariah. As if to prove that they are not remnants of polytheism and do not belong to a prehistoric age, their extraordinary ministry even broadens in the days of the New Testament. They are present at the birth of Jesus (Luke 1:13; 2:10) and at his temptation (Matt. 4:11); they accompany him throughout his entire earthly life (John 1:51) and appear especially at the time of his suffering (Luke 22:43), resurrection (Matt. 28), and ascension (Acts 1:10). Subsequently they reappear from time to time in the history of the apostles (Acts 5:19; 12:7, 13; 8:26; 27:23; Rev. 1:1); then they cease their extraordinary ministry and will only resume a public role at the return of Christ (Matt. 16:27; 25:31; Mark 8:38; Luke 9:26; 2 Thess. 1:7; Jude 14; Rev. 5:2, etc.), when they will do battle against God's enemies (Rev. 12:7; 1 Thess. 4:16; Jude 9), gather the elect (Matt. 24:31), and cast the ungodly into the fire (Matt. 13:41, 49).

---

82. Cf. G. Voetius, *Select. Disp.*, II, 262f.; J. Gerhard, *Loci Theol.*, 4, §42; and later in our discussion of the consummation (*ed. note:* see Herman Bavinck, *The Last Things: Hope for This World and the Next*, ed. by John Bolt, trans. by John Vriend [Grand Rapids: Baker, 1996], 142).
83. J. Gerhard, *Loci Theol.*, XXII, 6, 9.

Accordingly, the extraordinary ministry of the angels consists in accompanying the history of redemption at its cardinal points. They themselves do not bring about salvation but they do participate in its history. They transmit revelations, protect God's people, oppose his enemies, and perform an array of services in the kingdom of God. Always, in this connection, they are active in the area of the church. Also where they receive power over the forces of nature (Rev. 14:18; 16:5), or intervene in the fortunes of nations, this activity occurs in the interest of the church. In this ministry they never push aside the sovereignty of God, nor are they the mediators of God's fellowship with humans. But they are ministering spirits in the service of those who will inherit salvation. They especially serve God in the realm of grace, even though the realm of nature is not totally excluded in the process. Consequently, this extraordinary ministry automatically ceased with the completion of revelation. Whereas earlier they constantly had to transmit special revelations and descend to earth, now they rather serve as examples to us and we rise toward them. As long as special revelation was not yet completed, heaven approached the earth and God's Son descended to us. Now Christ has appeared and the Word of God has been fully revealed to us. Consequently the angels now look to the earth to learn from the church the manifold wisdom of God. What could the angels still give us now that God himself gave us his own Son?

But Scripture also speaks of an ordinary ministry of angels. The primary feature of that ministry is that they praise God day and night (Job 38:7; Isa. 6; Pss. 103:20; 148:2; Rev. 5:11). Scripture conveys the impression that they do this in audible sounds, even though we cannot imagine what their speech and songs are like. But part of this ordinary ministry is also the fact that they rejoice over the conversion of a sinner (Luke 15:10), watch over believers (Pss. 34:8; 91:11), protect the little ones (Matt. 18:10), are present in the church (1 Cor. 11:10; 1 Tim. 5:21), follow it on its journeys through history (Eph. 3:10), allow themselves to be taught by it (Eph. 3:10; 1 Pet. 1:12), and carry believers into Abraham's bosom (Luke 16:22). They are also active "by standing in the presence of God, assisting devout humans, and resisting devils and evil people."[84]

Scripture usually confines itself to this general description of the ordinary ministry of angels and does not go into detail. But theology was not content to stop there. In all kinds of ways it has elaborated this account, especially in the doctrine of guardian angels. The Greeks and Romans had something similar in view when they spoke of *daimones* (semidivine beings) and *genii*. They not only attributed to every human a

---

84. D. Hollaz, *Examen theologicum acroamaticum,* 390.

good or evil genius but also spoke of the *genii* of houses, families, associations, cities, countries, peoples of the earth, sea, world, and so on. The Jews, appealing to Deuteronomy 32:8 and Daniel 10:13, assumed the existence of seventy angels of nations and further assigned a companion angel to every Israelite.[85] Christian theology soon adopted this view. The Shepherd of Hermas assigned to every human two angels, "one for righteousness and the other for evil," and further placed the whole creation and the whole formation of the church under the guardianship of angels.[86] Origen had a special fondness for developing this doctrine of guardian angels. Sometimes—in his writings—every human has a good and a bad angel; sometimes he adds that only the good angels of baptized Christians see the face of God; sometimes he also says that only Christians and virtuous people have a guardian angel and that, depending on their merit, they receive either a lower-ranking or higher-ranking angel as their guardian. But he also assumes there are special angels for churches, countries, peoples, the arts and sciences, plants, and animals. Raphael, for example, is the angel of healing; Gabriel, the angel of war; Michael, the angel of prayer, and so on.[87]

In substance, all the church fathers taught this, though there were differences of opinion concerning whether all humans or only Christians had a guardian angel; whether every human had only a good angel or also a bad angel; when the guardian angel was given to a human, at birth or at baptism; when he was taken from him or her, on attaining perfection or only at death. All were convinced that there were guardian angels for humans not only but also for countries, peoples, churches, dioceses, provinces, and so on.[88] In part this angelic protection was later restricted and in part it was expanded. It was restricted insofar as some of them, following Pseudo-Dionysius,[89] taught that the three top classes of angels (cherubim, seraphim, and thrones) only served God in heaven,[90] and expanded insofar as Scholasticism figured that God's entire providence in nature and history, particularly in the movement of the stars, was mediated by angels.[91] Guardian angels for humans were universally accepted by Roman Catholic theologians and also recognized in the *Roman Catechism* IV, ch. 9, qu. 4 and 5. But for the rest there is much difference of opinion among them on all the above

85. F. W. Weber, *System der altsynagoalen palastinischen Theologie,* 161f.
86. Pastor of Hermas, *Commandments,* VI, 2; *Visions,* III, 4.
87. Origen, *On First Principles,* I, 8, III, 3; idem, *Against Celsus,* V, 29; VIII, 31.
88. J. Schwane, *Dogmengeschichte,* II, 244.
89. Dionysius, *The Celestial Hierarchies,* 13.
90. T. Aquinas, *Summa Theol.,* I, qu. 112.
91. T. Aquinas, *Summa Theol.,* I, qu. 70, art. 3, qu. 110, art. 1; idem, *Summa Contra Gentiles,* III, 78f.; Bonaventure, II *Sent.,* dist. 14, p. 1, art. 3, qu. 2.

points.[92] We find the same teaching in Luther,[93] but Lutheran theologians were usually more cautious.[94] Calvin rejected the notion of guardian angels[95] and most Reformed scholars followed him;[96] only a few of them assumed the existence of guardian angels for humans.[97] In modern times the doctrine of guardian angels again found support in Hahn, Weiss, Ebrard, Vilmar, Martensen, and others.[98] The ordinary ministry of angels was further refined in the view that with their intercession on behalf of believers on earth they were active for good in heaven. This, too, had already been taught by the Jews as well as by Philo, taken over by Origen[99] and the church fathers, and laid down in the Roman Catholic symbols.[100] The Lutheran confessional writings,[101] as well as Lutheran dogmaticians, still speak of this intercession as well.[102] In contrast, it is unanimously rejected by the Reformed.

For this special ministry of angelic protection and intercession an appeal is made to a number of Scripture passages, especially Deuteronomy 32:8; Daniel 10:13, 20; Matthew 18:10; Acts 12:15; Hebrews 1:14; Revelation 1:20; 2:1; and so on; Job 33:23; Zechariah 1:12; Luke 15:7; Revelation 18:3 and especially to Tobit 12:12–15. By itself this doctrine of the protection and intercession of angels is not objectionable. That God often and even regularly employs angels, in special as well as in general revelation, is not impossible. Nor is it absurd to think that angels send up prayers to God on behalf of humans, inasmuch as they are

92. Cf. D. Petavius, *Opera Omnia*, "de angelis," II, 608; Becanus, *Theol. Schol.*, "de angelis," *Tr.*, 6; *Theol. Wirceburgensis* (1880), III, 480; C. Pesch, *Prael. Dogm.*, III, 210; Oswald, *Angelologie*, 120f.

93. J. Köstlin, *The Theology of Luther in Its Historical Development and Inner Harmony*, trans. by Charles E. Hay, 2 vols. (Philadelphia: Lutheran Publication Society, 1897), II, 345.

94. J. Gerhard, *Loci Theol.*, V, 4, 15; J. Quenstedt, *Theologia*, 1450; D. Hollaz, *Syst. Theol.*, 390.

95. J. Calvin, *Institutes*, I.xiv.7; *Commentary on Psalm 91*; *Commentary on Matthew 18:10*.

96. G. Voetius, *Select. Disp.*, I, 897.

97. J. Zanchi, *Op. Theol.*, III, 142; G. Bucanus, *Inst. Theol.*, VI, 28; Maccovius, *Loci. Comm.*, 394; A. Rivetus, *Op. Theol.*, II, 250; cf. H. Heppe, *Reformed Dogmatics*, rev. and ed. by Ernst Bizer, trans. by G. T. Thompson (London: George Allen & Unwin, 1950), 212–13; C. Vitringa, *Doctr. Christ.*, II, 117.

98. *J. Weiss, *Bibl. Theol. des. N.T.*, 594; J. H. A. Ebrard, *Christliche Dogmatik*, 2nd. ed., 2 vols. (Königsberg: A. W. Unzer, 1862–63), §239; A. F. C. Vilmar, *Handbuch der evangelischen Dogmatik* (Gütersloh: C. Bertelsmann, 1895), I, 310; H. Martensen, *Christian Dogmatics*, trans. by W. Urwick (Edinburgh: T. & T. Clark, 1871), §69; Abraham Kuyper, *De Engelen Gods* (Amsterdam: Höveker & Wormser, n.d.) 279; Cremer, "Engel," *PRE*[3], V, 364–72.

99. Origen, *Against Celsus*, VIII, 64.

100. *Roman Catechism*, ch. 12, q. 5, no. 2.

101. *Apol. Conf.*, art. 21; *Schmalkald Articles*, II/2.

102. F. Philippi, *Kirchliche Glaubenslehre* (Gütersloh: Bertelsmann, 1902), II, 324.

interested in their fate and the progress of the kingdom of God in the history of humankind. But, however unobjectionable these teachings may be as such, in relation to the protection and intercession of angels Scripture observes a sobriety that must also be normative for us. In Deuteronomy 32:8, 9 we read that God, in apportioning the nations and dividing humankind, already thought of his people Israel and determined their dwelling "according to the number of the children of Israel" *(lĕmisppar bĕnĕ᾽ yiśrāēl)* so that Israel would receive an inheritance sufficient to accommodate its numbers. The LXX, however, translated these words by "according to the number of angels" *(kata arithmon angelōn)* and thereby occasioned the doctrine of "the angels of nations." The original text, meanwhile, does not say a word about this and therefore totally loses its function as proof text. The case is somewhat different with Daniel 10:13, 20. There we read that the figure who appeared to Daniel in verse 5 opposed the prince of Persia and, aided by Michael who is called "one of the chief princes" (v. 13), the "great prince" and protector of the children of Israel (12:1; 10:21), drove away that prince of Persia and took his place among the kings of Persia. Calvin and Reformed exegetes after him usually identified that prince of Persia with the Persian kings. But it seems we must interpret that prince to be someone else, namely, the guardian spirit of Persia. For, first, there can be no doubt that Israel has such a guardian angel in Michael, who is called "your prince" (10:13; 12:1). Second, the kings of Persia are clearly distinguished in 10:13 from that prince. And third, the analogy requires that the spiritual power on the one side should fight against a spiritual power on the other. The Book of Daniel, accordingly, really conveys a picture in which the war between the kingdom of God and the kingdoms of the world is not only conducted down here on earth but also in the realm of spirits between angels. And that is all we may infer from it. There is absolutely no claim here that every country and people has its own angel. But in the colossal struggle waged between Israel and Persia, that is, between the kingdom of God and that of Satan, there are on both sides angels who take part in the struggle and support the [opposing] peoples. Even less can we deduce from Revelation 1:20 (etc.) that every church has its angel, for the "angels" of the seven churches are nothing other than their ministers: they are totally viewed as the representatives of the churches. It is their works that are praised or blamed. It is to them the letters are addressed.

Most support for the doctrine of guardian angels comes from Matthew 18:10, a text which undoubtedly implies that a certain class of angels is charged with the task of protecting "the little ones." However there is here not even a hint that every elect person is assigned his or her own angel. This idea is found only in the apocryphal Book of Tobit.

But by that very fact this doctrine of guardian angels also betrays its origin. The doctrine is essentially of pagan origin and leads to all kinds of clever questions and futile issues. We do not know whether an angel is assigned to every human, and even to the anti-Christ, as Thomas thought,[103] or only to the elect, nor whether only a good or a bad angel accompanies everyone. Nor do we know when such an angel is given to a person or is taken away; or what the angel's precise ministry is. Consequently all we can say is that certain classes of angels are charged with the promotion of certain interests on earth. It is the same with the intercession of angels that is taught in Tobit 12:16 but does not occur in Scripture. In Job 33:23, there is a reference to the "uncreated Angel." Luke 15:7 also teaches that the angels rejoice over the repentance of one sinner, which indeed presupposes that the angels desire that repentance, but does not speak of intercession in the strict sense of the word. And while in Revelation 8:3 an angel indeed receives a censer with incense to make the—inherently sinful—prayers of the saints lovely and pleasing to the Lord, the text does not breathe a word about intercession. The angel is simply a servant; he does not build the altar; he does not himself prepare the incense but receives it and only lets the prayers, along with the fragrance of the incense, rise to God. The ministry he performs is like that of the seraphim in Isaiah 6:6, 7.

Veneration of Angels

This doctrine of guardian angels and their intercession, finally, also had the disadvantage that in practice it soon led to a veneration and worship of angels. Colossians 2:18 tells us that such "worship of angels" *(threskeia tōn angelōn)* already occurred in apostolic times. In his commentary on this passage Theodoret comments that in his day such angel worship was still being practiced in Phyrgia and that the Synod of Laodicea had prohibited it, lest God be abandoned.[104] Many church fathers cautioned against the veneration and adoration of angels.[105] At that time the conviction that only God may be worshiped and that angels are only entitled to "civil honor" was still universal. "We honor them with our love, not our servitude."[106] They are "rather to be imitated than called upon."[107] In his commentary on the Song of Solomon

103. T. Aquinas, *Summa Theol.*, I, qu. 113, art. 4.
104. J. Schwane, *Dogmengeschichte*, III, 245.
105. Irenaeus, *Against Heresies*, II, 32; Origen, *Against Celsus*, V, 4, 5;. VIII, 13; Athanasius, *Against the Arians*, II, 23; Augustine, *On True Religion*, 55; idem, *Confessions*, X, 42; *City of God*, VIII, 25.
106. Augustine, *On True Religion*, 55.
107. Augustine, *The City of God*, X, 26.

8, Gregory the Great still says that, since Christ has come on earth, "the church is honored even by those very angels." In the Old Testament dispensation Joshua worshiped the angel (Josh. 5:14) but in the New Testament the angel rejected John's worship (Rev. 19:10; 22:9) because angels, though higher in rank, are nevertheless "fellow servants." Still, these warnings do serve as proof that in practice the boundaries between the worship of God and the respect due to angels were being wiped out. The invocation of angels was first clearly mentioned by Ambrose: "We to whom the angels have been given for assistance and protection ought to entreat them."[108]

Eusebius already made the distinction between the "veneration" *(timan)* which is fitting for us to offer to angels, and the "worship" *(sebein)* to which only God is entitled.[109] Augustine adopted it as a strategy for preventing the religious veneration of angels.[110] But before long that distinction was used to sanction the invocation of angels. This already occurred at the [Second] Council of Nicea (787) and then also among the Scholastics.[111] The Council of Trent called such invocation "good and profitable" (Sess. 25). *The Roman Catechism* (III, ch. 2, qu. 4, no. 3) found warrant for it in the ground that the angels always behold the face of God and have taken upon themselves "the sponsorship of our salvation" *(patrocinium salutis nostrae).* The Roman Breviary incorporated prayers [addressed to angels] in the Feast of the Angels and Roman Catholic dogmaticians unanimously defend it,[112] although later they usually treat it under the heading of "the veneration of saints" *(cultus sanctorum).*

Lutheran and Reformed people and virtually all Protestants were on solid ground, however, when they rejected the religious veneration of angels along with that of the saints.[113] For in the first place, there is not a single example of it in Scripture. True, Roman Catholics do base their position on certain Old Testament passages like Genesis 18:2; 32:26; 48:16; Exodus 23:20; Numbers 22:31; Joshua 5:14; Judges 13:17, but in all these passages we are dealing, not with a created angel, but with "the angel of the Lord," and in the New Testament there is not even a sem-

108. Ambrose, *De Viduis,* ch. 9, §55.
109. Eusebius, *Praep. Ev.;* Origen, *Against Celsus,* VIII, 13, 57.
110. Augustine, *The City of God,* V, 15; VII, 32; X, 1.
111. P. Lombard, III *Sent.,* dist. 9; T. Aquinas.
112. Bellarmine, *Controversiis,* "de sanct. beat.," I, 11–20; D. Petavius, *Opera Omnia,* "de angelis," II, 9, 10.
113. Luther, according to J. Kösten, *The Theology of Luther,* II, 23ff.; U. Zwingli, *Opera,* I, 268f.; 280f., III, 135.; J. Calvin, *Institutes,* I. xiv.10–12; cf. III.xx.20–24; J. Gerhard, *Loci Theol.,* XXXVI, §§370–480 (on angels, esp. §427); J. Quenstedt, *Theologia,* I, 486; F. Turretin, *Institutes of Elenctic Theology,* VII, qu. 9; idem, *De Necessaria secessione nostra ab ecclesia Romana* (Geneva, 1692), disp. 2–4, "de idolatria Romana," 33–109.

blance of proof for it. But that is not all: the veneration of angels is not
only devoid of precept or example in Scripture, so that Rome might be
able to say with some semblance of reason that the veneration of angels
and saints is not prohibited in Scripture and therefore permitted and
therefore that it does not actually impose and require it but only per-
mits it and regards it as profitable.[114] The fact is that Scripture clearly
prohibits it (Deut. 6:13; 10:20; Matt. 4:10; Col. 2:18, 19; Rev. 19:10;
22:9). According to Scripture, religious honor may be accorded only to
God and no creature is entitled to it. Roman Catholics have not had the
courage to deny this altogether but, by the distinction between worship
(latria) and homage *(dulia)*, they have nevertheless sought to justify the
veneration of angels. Now in Catholicism this is not a distinction between religious and civil honor, which might be considered reasonable;
no: in Catholicism the veneration of angels and saints definitely has a
religious character, though it is relative. The *dulia* is religious worship.
But thus understood it is condemned by both Scripture and practice.
Scripture knows no twofold religious veneration, one of a lower, the
other of a higher kind. Roman Catholics, accordingly, admit that worship *(latria)* and homage *(dulia)* are not distinguished in Scripture as
they distinguish them, and also that these words furnish no etymologi-
cal support for the way they are used. The Hebrew word *ʿbr* is sometimes rendered by *douleia,* sometimes by *latreia* (cf. Deut. 6:13 and
1 Sam. 7:3; 1 Sam. 12:20 and Deut. 10:12); and Israel is commanded to
abstain both from *douleuein* and *latreuein* of other gods (Exod. 20:5;
Jer. 22:9). Similarly the Hebrew word *šrt* is translated by both Greek
words (Exod. 20:32; Isa. 56:6). Repeatedly *douleuein* is used with reference to God (Matt. 6:24; Rom. 7:6; 14:18; 16:18; Gal. 4:9; Eph. 6:7; Col.
3:24; 1 Thess. 1:9); and *latreuein* is also used of service rendered to humans. Neither etymologically nor scripturally do the two words carry
the distinctions Catholicism teaches. The entire distinction is arbitrary.

   In any case, the implication of monotheism is that there is and can
only be one kind of religious veneration. All veneration of creatures is
either exclusively civil or it violates monotheism and attributes divine
character to creatures. This reality comes through loud and clear in
practice. Even though we are regularly told that angels and saints are
only intermediaries; that they themselves are not being directly invoked but that God is being invoked in them; that, by our invoking
them, God's honor is not diminished but increased—all this is immate-
rial, for experience shows all too clearly that Roman Catholic Christians put their trust in creatures. Moreover, even if the distinction per
se were correct, it still could not serve as warrant for the religious ven-

114. Jansen, *Prael.,* III, 1008.

eration of angels. For if this reasoning were a sufficient defense of the practice, no idolatry and no image worship could any longer be condemned. The Gentiles, praying to animals and images, knew very well that these animals and images were not identical with the gods themselves (Rom. 1:23). The Jews did not equate the golden calf with YHWH himself (Exod. 32:4, 5; 1 Kings 12:28). When Satan tempted Christ he certainly did not demand that Christ should regard him as God (Matt. 4:9). And John by no means believed that the angel who appeared to him was God (Rev. 19:10). Nevertheless Jesus still answered: "You shall worship the Lord your God and him only shall you serve." This *only* is exclusive, just as the only Mediator Christ Jesus excludes all other angels or humans as mediators. But this is precisely the point that Roman Catholicism denies. Just as Matthew 19:17; 23:8; John 9:5; 1 Timothy 2:5; 6:16, and the like do not rule out that also humans can be called "good," "master," "light," "mediator," and "immortal," so also—says Rome—Matthew 4:10 does not prove that God alone may be worshiped. Angels and saints, according to Roman Catholic teaching, participate in the very nature of God. The supernatural gifts, though given and derived, are of the same nature as the divine being itself. And therein, according to the teaching of Rome, lies the deepest ground for the worship of saints and angels. In supernatural righteousness *(justitia supernaturalis)* God imparts his own essence to creatures; and for that reason they may also be accorded religious veneration. The controlling idea of Catholicism here is: "there are as many species of adoration as there are species of excellence."[115]

By the rejection of the religious veneration of angels Protestantism has acknowledged that the angels are not an indispensable element in the religious life of Christians. They are not the effective agents of our salvation, neither are they the ground of our trust nor the object of our veneration. It is not with them but with God that we enter into communion. They do not even appear to us any more today and all special revelation by means of angels has ceased. In Protestant churches and confessions angels cannot and may not occupy the place assigned to them in Roman Catholic churches and creeds. Still, this is not to deny the significance for religion of the world of angels. This significance is, first of all, anchored in the fact that God, in his working in the sphere of grace, chooses to make use of the ministry of angels. The angels are of extraordinary significance for the kingdom of God and its history. We meet them at all the great turning points in its history: they are the

---

115. T. Aquinas, *Summa Theol.*, II, 2, qu. 103, art. 3; Bellarmine, *Controversiis*, "de sanct. beat.," I, 12; D. Petavius, *Prael Theol.*, III, 1017; J. A. Möhler, *Symbolik* (Regensberg: G. J. Manz, 1871), 52, 53.

mediators of the resurrection and witnesses of God's mighty deeds. Their significance is much more of an objective than a subjective nature. In our religious experience we know nothing of communion with the world of angels. Neither on our religious nor on our moral life do the angels have an influence that can be clearly verbalized. Influences and operations of angels do, of course, impact us, but since they no longer appear to us visibly, we cannot trace those operations specifically to concrete rules. Their value lies in the history of revelations, as Scripture makes them known to us.

In the second place, therefore, the angels cannot be the object of the respectful homage that we pay to humans. Most certainly there is a civil honor that we are obligated to accord to them. But this is nevertheless again different from the honor we accord to humans whom we know and have met personally. Roman Catholics undergird the veneration of angels especially with the argument that as envoys of the Most High they are entitled to our homage, as in honoring the ambassadors of rulers we honor the rulers themselves. And as such this is perfectly appropriate. If an angel were to appear to us, it would be entirely fitting for us to welcome him with deeply reverent homage. And this is precisely what happened when angels appeared to humans in the days of revelation. Only such appearances no longer occur. In our case there cannot be the kind of homage that the patriarchs, prophets, and apostles accorded the angels who appeared to them. It is simply not possible to offer them such reverence and homage.

Nevertheless there is, in the third place, a kind of honor that we are obligated to show to angels. But that honor is in no respect religious but only civil in nature; it is essentially the same kind of honor we accord to humans or other creatures. This civil honor *(honor civilis)* consists in our thinking and speaking of them with respect; in not despising them in our little ones (Matt. 18:10); in being mindful of their presence (1 Cor. 4:9; 11:10); in proclaiming to them the manifold wisdom of God (Eph. 3:10); in giving them insight into the mysteries of salvation (1 Tim. 5:21); in giving them joy by our repentance (Luke 15:10); in imitating them in the observance of God's will (Matt. 6:10); in feeling ourselves to be one with them and living in the expectation of joining them (Heb. 12:22); in forming with them and all other creatures a choir for the glorification of the name of the Lord (Ps. 103:20, 21). In these things lies the true veneration of angels.

And if these things are correctly understood, then, in the fourth place, the doctrine of angels can also serve us as consolation and encouragement. God has revealed also this teaching to us that he may strengthen us in our weakness and lift us up from our despondency. We are not alone in our spiritual struggle. We are connected with a great cloud of witnesses present all around us. There is still another, a better world than this one, one in which God is served in perfection. This world is for us a model, a stimulus, a source of encouragement; at the same time it awakens our nostalgia and arouses our awareness of the final goal. Just as in revelation the world of angels has come down to us, so in Christ the church rises up to greet that world. We shall be like the angels and daily see the face of our Father who is in heaven.[116]

116. P. Van Mastricht, *Theologia*, III, 7, 25; Love, *Theol. Practica*, 205; Philippi, *Kirchliche Glaubenslehre*, II, 320f.; Frank, *Christliche Wahrheit*, I, 353. J. Van Oosterzee, *Christian Dogmatics*, trans. by J. Watson and M. Evans, 2 vols. (New York: Scribner, Armstrong, 1874), §57, 10.

Earth: The Material World   3

A theological perspective on the material world differs from but should not be isolated from a philosophic/scientific one. All religions have creation stories; all scientific systems are rooted in religious beliefs. Every effort to base the biblical story of creation on foreign sources such as Babylonian myths do not stand up under close scrutiny. The creation narrative in Genesis is utterly unique; it is devoid of theogony and is rigorously monotheistic. The interpretation of Genesis 1–2 has a rich and diverse history. To understand the "week" and the "days" of creation, it is important to distinguish the first act of creation—as immediate bringing forth of heaven and earth out of nothing—-from the secondary separation and formation of the six days which begins God's preservation and government of the world. The six-day period is best divided into three parts: creation, separation, adornment. The Christian church is not confessionally tied to a specific worldview so the shift away from an Aristotelian and Ptolemaic cosmology is not a problem for Christian theology. The Bible does not provide us with a scientific cosmology—using the language of ordinary experience—but, spiritually and ethically, the earth (with humanity) is the center of the universe. The data of natural science must be taken seriously by Christians as general revelation, but only special, biblical revelation can describe the true state of the world. The biblical chronology and order of creation seem, on the face of it, at odds with the accounts given by geology and paleontology, and various attempts to harmonize them achieve only modest and not finally satisfying results. It is important, however, to insist on the historical rather than merely mythical or visionary character of the creation story in Genesis. The science of geology is still young and faces many unanswered questions. The reality of a cataclysmic flood bringing immense changes in the world—a story tradition found virtually among all peoples—complicates matters considerably. Theology should neither fear the sure results of science nor, in immoderate anxiety, make premature concessions to opinions of the day. As the science of divine and eternal things, it should uphold its confessional convictions with dignity and honor and in patience.

Besides the spiritual there also exists a material world. But while the existence and being of the angels are known only from revelation and are hidden from reason and science, the material world is visible to all and comes up for consideration in philosophy as well as in theology; in religion as well as in science. On this score, therefore, differences and clashes are possible at all times. It is true that philosophy and theology speak about the material world in different ways. The former investigates the origin and nature of all things but the latter starts with God and traces all things back to him. Theology deals with creatures only insofar as they are the works of God and reveal something of his attributes. Hence also where it deals with creatures it is and always remains theology.[1] Even though there is an important distinction between the two, theology and philosophy nevertheless deal with the same world. To avoid a clash between them, people have often proposed a division of labor. Science, they said, should study the things that are visible, and leave to religion and theology nothing but the world of ethics and religion; or, even more rigorously, all that exists should be for science to explore and only in the matter of value judgments should religion be allowed to speak. But, theoretically as well as practically, such a division is impossible. Just as every scientific system is ultimately rooted in religious convictions, so there is not a single religion that does not bring with it a certain view of the created world. All religions have their cosmogonies, cosmogonies that did not arise from intellectual reasoning but are at least in part based on tradition and represent a religious interest. Even the creation story in Genesis 1 does not pretend to be a philosophical worldview but presents itself as a historical narrative that is based on tradition and in some respects agrees with the cosmogonies of other religions but in many ways again exhibits remarkable differences from them.

In recent times it is especially the kinship between the biblical and Babylonian creation stories that has attracted attention. This story, which had earlier been known from fragments of Berossus,[2] was rediscovered and published in 1875 by George Smith. It again broke into prominence when excavations in Assyria and the discovery of the Tell-el Amarna letters placed in bold relief the great culture-historical significance that Babylonia possessed in antiquity. Considering the high level of civilization found in Babylonia centuries before the emergence of the people of Israel, many scholars wondered whether all that was uniquely Israelitish could not be explained in terms of Babylon. For years critics assumed that the cultural impact of Babylon on the Jews occurred shortly before, during, and after the exile. But this picture of the situation could not be maintained: the excavations made it clear as day that

---

1. T. Aquinas, *Summa Contra Gentiles*, II, 2ff.; A. Polanus, *Syn. Theol.*, V, 7.
2. *Ed. note:* Berossus (b. 340 B.C.), was author of a three-volume Greek history of Babylon.

all the surrounding peoples in antiquity had been dominated by the culture of Babylonia. In Canaan, thanks to the Canaanites, or even much earlier in the patriarchal age, also the Israelites became familiar with it and took over a variety of things from it which they later refashioned along the lines of their own Yahwistic outlook. Many scholars believe that all that is peculiarly Israelitish, as for example the name YHWH, monotheism, the stories of creation, fall, flood, building a tower, the seven-day week, the Sabbath, and so on, has its origin in Babylonia. But this is not all. The facts and ideas of Christianity, the preexistence, supernatural birth, miracles, atoning death, and suffering of Christ, the resurrection, ascension, and return of Christ; the idea of Mary as the mother of God; the doctrine of the Holy Spirit as comforter, and of the Trinity—this and much more are all said to be rooted in the astral worldview which from ancient times was the characteristic possession of the Babylonians.[3] According to Jensen, the entire history of the gospel is interwoven with sagas, so that there is no reason to consider anything said about Jesus to be historical; the Jesus-saga is an "Israelitish Gilgamesh-saga" and as such "a sister-saga to numerous, that is, the majority of Old Testament sagas."[4]

The derivation of the creation story from the land of the Tigris and Euphrates, therefore, is only a small part of this pan-Babylonianism. What we are dealing with here is not an isolated instance but a general intellectual trend which, after the literary-critical school had displayed its impotence, attempted to explain the problem of the Bible along religious-historical lines. The sorting out and splitting up of the documents is of no advantage if religion itself remains standing behind them as an enigmatic sphinx. It therefore seemed a godsend when the East began to unveil its treasures. From the East light seemed to dawn over Israel's religion and over the whole phenomenon of Christianity. But even now further investigation is showing and will increasingly bring to light the vanity of this attempt at interpretation. In the case of the creation story in Genesis the assertion that it originated in Babylon is primarily based on the traces of mythological origin which, we are told, can still be found in the biblical story despite the editing process: (1) the portrayal of chaos under the ancient terms of *tĕhôm* and *tōhû wābōhû* and the notion that God formed the present world out of chaos; (2) the reference to the brooding of the Spirit upon the waters, which implies that the world is here, as in many mythologies, conceived as an egg; (3) the hia-

3. P. Biesterveld, *De Jongste Methode voor de Verklaring van het Nieuwe Testament* (Kampen: Bos, 1905); cf. H. Bavinck, *Gereformeerde Dogmatiek*, I, 148.

4. P. C. A. Jensen, *Das Gilgamesch-Epos in der Weltliteratur* (Strassburg: Trubner, 1906); cf. H. Schmidt, *Theologische Rundschau* (1907): 189ff.

tus that exists in Genesis 1 between verses 2 and 3 and that was for-merly filled with the theogony; (4) the feature that the darkness was not created by God nor called "good," whereas, in the Israelitish teaching, God is the creator of light and darkness (Isa. 45:7); (5) the saying that the sun, moon, and stars were set [in the firmament] to "rule" the day and the night; (6) the plural form in which God speaks of himself at the creation of man; the idea that man is the image of God and bears his likeness and that, upon the completion of the creation week, God rests on the Sabbath.[5]

Of all these comments only the first has some significance because the *těhôm* in Genesis 1:2 indeed corresponds to the Babylonian *tiamat,* and elsewhere in the Old Testament as well we encounter the idea that God from ancient times waged a struggle against a natural power. In some texts there is mention of *Rahab* (Job 9:13; 26:12; Pss. 40:5; 87:4; 89:10f.; Isa. 30:7; 51:9f.); *Leviathan* (Job 3:8; 40:25f.; Pss. 74:12f.; 104:26; Isa. 27:1); the dragon *Tannin* (Job 7:12; Isa. 27:1; 51:9; Ezek. 29:3; 32:2); the serpent *Nahash* (Job 26:13; Isa. 27:1; Amos 9:2)—all of them powers that were opposed and overcome by God. But upon a care-ful reading none of these passages yields virtually any ground for the as-sertion that belief in creation in Israel still in many respects bears a mythological character. For, in the first place, it cannot be denied that these representations serve to describe very different things. In Job 9:13; 26:12, 13, Rahab is indeed a sea monster, but in Psalms 87:4; 89:11; Isaiah 30:7; 51:10 it is undoubtedly a metaphor for Egypt. In Job 7:12 and Isaiah 51:9 Tannin is a sea dragon but in Isaiah 27:1 it serves as a symbol of a *future* power that will be overcome by God, and in Ezekiel 29:3; 32:2 it is used as a metaphor for Egypt. In Job 3:8 Levia-than is the celestial dragon that devours the light of the sun and stars, as does Nahash in Job 26:12, but in Isaiah 27:1 the prophet employs both of these images to depict *future* world powers. All this is proof that the words *Rahab,* and so forth, whatever may have been their meaning originally, are used as images for different things.

Second, when these words are used as descriptions of natural powers, they never in Scripture refer to the natural power that the Babylonian creation story introduces as *Tiamat,* but to various natural powers that either were in the past, especially in the salvation of Israel from Egypt and the passage through the Red Sea (Pss. 74:13, 14; 89:11; Isa. 51:9, 10), or are still in the present (Job 3:8; 9:13; 26:12, 13) opposed and overcome

5. H. Gunkel, *Die Genesis übersetzt und erklärt* (Göttingen: Vandenhoeck und Rupre-cht, 1902), 109 (Eng. trans. *Genesis,* trans. by Mark E. Biddle [Macon, Ga.: Mercer Uni-versity Press, 1997]); cf. V. Zapletal, *Der Schöpfungsbericht der Genesis,* 2nd ed. (Regensburg: G. J. Manz, 1911), 62–63.

by God. But we are nowhere told that at the creation there was a natural power opposed to God which he had to overcome. There is absolutely no proof for the identification of Rahab, Leviathan, and so on, with the Babylonian *Tiamat*. Third, the notion that God subdues and overcomes the natural powers is a poetic description that can in no way serve as support for the assertion that Israel's poets and prophets gave credence to pagan mythology. It is indeed possible that in some cases the terms "Tannin" and "Leviathan" (Pss. 74:13, 14; 104:26; Job 7:12; 40:20) refer to real sea monsters. But even where this is not the case, and some natural power, as, for example, the darkness which devours the light, is represented as a Rahab or Leviathan or Nahash (Job 3:8; 9:13; 26:12, 13), Hebrew poetry is employing an image in the same way in which we in our day still speak of the Zodiac, the Great Bear (Ursa major) and the Little Bear (Ursa minor), the Cancer or Crab (the fourth sign of the zodiac) and Scorpio (the eighth sign of the zodiac), or Minerva and Venus. Such use of mythological images in no way constitutes proof of belief in their reality. This is even more evidently the case because the Old Testament very often pictures the sea as an enormous natural power that is rebuked by God (Job 12:26; 38:11; Pss. 18:16; 65:8; 93:4; Jer. 5:22; Nah. 1:4). Finally, the word *těhôm* as such proves nothing. For even if this is identical with the Babylonian *tiamat*, one cannot infer anything from it for the identity of the ideas that are associated with these words in the Babylonian creation story and in Scripture. However, these ideas are in fact not the same but, on the contrary, very far removed from each other. For while the *Tiamat* is the only existing chaos whose existence precedes the creation of the gods and subsequently rebels against the gods, the *těhôm* in Genesis 1:2 is simply the designation of the formless state in which the earth originally existed, just as the phrase *tōhû wābōhû* serves this purpose without any mythological associations.

Actually the creation stories in Genesis and that of Babylon are very different on all points. According to Genesis, the existence of God is anterior to all things; in the Babylonian creation story the gods are born after, and out of, the chaos. In Scripture heaven and earth are called into being by a divine word of power, and thereafter the Spirit of God moves over the face of the waters; in Babylonian mythology chaos originally existed by itself and from it, in an incomprehensible manner, the gods came forth, against whom the chaos then rebels. In the Bible, after the mention of the formless state of the earth there first follows the creation of light, but the latter is completely lacking in the Babylonian story. In the former the preparation of the earth in regular order is completed in six days; in the latter such an order is absolutely nonexistent. The only resemblance between them actually consists in this, that in both stories a chaos precedes the formation of heaven and earth. To construe from this parallel a common identity or common origin for the two stories is premature and unfounded. The creation narrative in Genesis is utterly unique; it is devoid of any trace of a theogony, is rigorously monotheistic, teaches a creation out of nothing, and knows nothing of primary matter. It therefore is unbelievable that the Jews, in exile or even earlier in Canaan, borrowed this story from the Babylonians. In the first place, the creation was known to the Israelites even before the exile. This was also true of the seven-day week, which is based on the days of creation. It is unlikely, further, that the Jews should have taken over such an important piece of their doctrine from Babylonians or Canaanites. And, finally, the pagan cosmogonies were so thoroughly polytheistic that they had to repel rather than attract the monotheistic people of Israel; they were therefore unsuited to being easily transformed into a beautiful monotheistic narrative like that of Genesis 1. Everything rather argues for the assumption that in Genesis 1 we have a tradition that derives from the most ancient times, was gradually adulterated in the case of the other peoples, and preserved in its purity by Israel.[6]

The Week of Creation

In the narrative of Genesis 1 the first verse needs to be read as the account of an independent fact. In verse 2 the earth already exists, be it in a disordered and vacuous state. And verse 1 reports the origin of that earth; from the very start it was created by God as earth. After a brief initial reference to heaven in verse 1, verse 2 immediately starts speaking about the earth: cosmogony becomes geogony. And from the very first moment that earth is *earth:* not *hulē* (matter) in an Aristotelian sense, nor prime matter, nor chaos in the sense of the pagan cosmogonies. "A created chaos is an absurdity" (Dillmann). True: the earth is now described to us as *tōhû wābōhû*, as a *tĕhôm*, which the darkness covered. But this means something very different from what is usually understood by chaos. The word *tĕhôm* occurs repeatedly, especially in Isaiah, and consistently prompts us to think of empty space (cf. Isa. 45:18), an area in which everything is trackless and undeveloped. The word *bōhû* is also found in Isaiah 34:10 and Jeremiah 4:23, both times in conjunction with *tōhû*, and expresses the same idea. The state of the earth in Genesis 1:2 is not that of a positive destruction but of a not-yet-having-been shaped. There is no light, no life, no organic creature, no form and configuration in things. It is further explained by the fact that

6. F. Delitzsch, *A New Commentary on Genesis,* trans. by Sophia Taylor (Edinburgh: T. & T. Clark, 1899), 60–61; H. H. Kuyper, *Evolutie of Revelatie* (Amsterdam: Höveker & Wormser, 1903), esp. 117–23.

it was a *tĕhôm*, a seething watery mass that is wrapped in darkness. The earth was formed "out of water and by means of water" (2 Pet. 3:5; Ps. 104:5, 6). This unformed, undeveloped state, according to Genesis, certainly lasted for some time, however short. There is no description here of a purely logical assumption but rather of a factual state. Only in that case the question arises how long this state lasted. And this question is again completely dependent on whether the creation of heaven and earth of which Genesis 1:1 speaks occurred before or within the span of the first day. Genesis leaves no other impression but that the creation of heaven and earth in verse 1 and the unformed state of the earth in verse 2 are anterior to the first day. In verse 2, after all, darkness still prevails and there is no light. Now it is the case that the day is not darkness and does not begin with darkness but with light. It is only the creation of light (v. 3) which makes the day possible. God, accordingly, does not call the darkness "day" but the light, and the darkness he called "night" (v. 5). The alternation of light and darkness could only begin with the creation of light. Only after it had been light could it again be evening and thereupon morning, and with this morning the first day ended, for Genesis 1 calculates the day from morning to morning. Hence the work of the first day did not consist in the creation of heaven and earth, nor in the perpetuation of the unformed state, but in the creation of light and the separation of light and darkness.

Now there would be absolutely no objection to this exegesis did we not read elsewhere that God created heaven and earth in six days (Exod. 20:11; 31:17). This can only be understood, however, of the second creation *(creatio secunda)*. Indeed, in both of these texts the emphasis does not fall on the fact that God brought forth all things out of nothing but on the fact that he was occupied for six days with the formation of heaven and earth, and this is offered to us as a paradigm. There is clearly a distinction between what God did "in the beginning" (Gen. 1:1; cf. John 1:1) and what he did "by the words of his mouth" in six days (Gen. 1:3ff.). The unformed state of Genesis 1:2 separates the two. The first creation *(creatio prima)* is immediate, an act of bringing forth heaven and earth out of nothing. It absolutely does not presuppose the existence of available material but occurred "with time" *(cum tempore)*. But the second creation which starts with verse 3 is not direct and immediate; it presupposes the material created in verse 1 and links up with it. It occurs specifically "in time" *(in tempore)* and that in six days. Hence this second creation already anticipates the works of preservation and government. In part it is already preservation and no longer merely creation. For that matter, the very moment when heaven and earth were created by God they were also preserved by him. Creation immediately and instantly passes into preservation and government.

Nevertheless the work of the six days (Gen. 1:3ff.) must still be counted as belonging to creation. For, according to Genesis, all the creatures which were brought forth in those six days (light, firmament, sun, moon, stars, plant, animal, man) did not emerge by immanent forces in accordance with fixed laws from the available matter in the manner of evolution. That matter was in itself powerless to produce all this solely in the way of natural progression by immanent development. In itself it did not have the capacity for it; it only possessed a capacity for obedience *(potentia obedientialis)*. From the primary matter of Genesis 1:1, God, by speaking and creating, brought forth the entire cosmos. While in every new act of formation he linked up with what already existed, the higher phase did not solely proceed by an immanent force from the lower. At every stage a creating word of God's omnipotence was needed.

The Six Days of Creation

Herder and others divided the work of creation into two ternaries, so that the works of the second ternary corresponded to those of the first. There is indeed a correspondence between the work of the first and that of the fourth day; but the second and the fifth days, similarly the third and sixth days, do not exactly fit this parallel pattern. On the fifth day, after all, not only the birds in the firmament but also the fish and aquatic animals were created, which rather fits with the work of the third day. In the works of creation we do, however, observe a clear progression from a lower to a higher level, from the general conditions for organic life to this organic life itself in its various forms. Therefore, the old division of the overall work of creation into three parts is preferable: *creation* (Gen. 1:1, 2); *separation* on the first three days between light and darkness, heaven and earth, land and sea; and *adornment* on the fourth to the sixth days, the population of the prepared earth with all kinds of living entities.[7] Still, even this division is not intended as a sharp demarcation either since the plants, created on the third day, also serve as ornamentation.[8] The *separation* and *adornment* mark the can-

7. T. Aquinas, *Summa Theol.*, I, qu. 74.
8. V. Zapletal, *Der Schöpfungsbericht*, 107ff. therefore chooses a different division and bases this on Gen. 2:1. There we read that heaven and earth were completed and all their multitude (hosts). Thus a distinction is made between heaven and earth, the dwelling place, on one hand, and the multitudes that inhabit heaven and earth on the other. There is therefore a distinction between *productio regionum* and a *productio excercituum*. The former occurs in the first three days, the latter in the second. Sun, moon, and stars are the multitudes (hosts) of heaven; fish and birds of water and air; animals and man of the earth. For this reason, the creation of plants takes place on the third day—plants do not belong to the multitudes (hosts) of the earth, but to the earth as dwelling place and are the necessary condition for the life of animals and man.

cellation of the *tōhû* condition of the earth. The unformed and undeveloped state of the earth referred to in verse 2 may not for a moment, however, be thought of as passive. For however long or short a period it may have existed, there were powers and energies at work in it. We read, after all, of the Spirit of God moving over the waters. The verb *rht* means "to hover over" (cf. Deut. 32:11) and the use of this word proves that in the case of *rûaḥ ĕlōhîm* we must not think of the wind but more specifically of the Spirit of God to whom elsewhere too the work of creation is attributed (Pss. 33:6; 104:30). The Spirit of God, as the principle of creaturely being and life, impacts the watery mass of the earth in a formative, vivifying way and so anticipates the creative words of God which in six days, following up on the already existent condition of the earth, called into being the various orders of creatures.

The work of the first day consists in the creation of light, in the separation of light and darkness, in the alternation of day and night, hence also in movement, change, becoming. Light—according to the most widely accepted hypothesis today—is not a substance, nor enormously rapid undulation, as Huygens, Young, and Fresnel assumed, but consists, according to the theory of Maxwell, later confirmed by Hertz, Lorentz, and Zeeman, in electrical vibrations and is therefore an electrical phenomenon.[9] It is to be distinguished, accordingly, from emitters of light, sun, moon, and stars, and according to Genesis precedes them. Light is also the most general prerequisite for all life and development. Whereas the alternation of day and night is only necessary for animals and humans, light also meets a requirement of the world of plants. In addition, it gives form, shape, and color to all things. On the second day a separation is made between the firmament, the sky and the clouds, which in its appearance to our eyes is often presented as a tent (Ps. 104:2), a curtain (Isa. 40:22), a pavement of sapphire stone (Exod. 24:10; Ezek. 1:22), a molten mirror (Job. 37:18), a roof or dome extended over the earth (Gen. 7:11; Deut. 11:17; 28:12; Ps. 78:23, etc.),[10] and the earth with its waters (Pss. 24:2; 136:6). The work of separation and demarcation begun on the first day is continued on the second. The distinction between light and darkness, of day and night, is now made subservient to the separation of heaven and earth, of the air and the clouds above and the earth and water beneath. At the end of the second day we do not read that God saw that it was good. From this omission some readers have concluded that the number two was an ominous number or that hell was created on that day, but the reason is likely that the work of the second day is very intimately bound up with that of the

9. J. D. van der Waals, "Het Zeeman-verschijnsel," *De Gids* 67 (March 1903): 493–512.
10. Cf. G. V. Schiaparelli, *Astronomy in the Old Testament* (Oxford: Clarendon, 1905).

third day and was only completed in the separation of the waters. Divine approval follows at the end of the third day, for on that day the separation between earth and water, land and sea, is completed and earth becomes a cosmos with continents and seas, mountains and valleys, fields and streams. Undoubtedly all these formations occurred under the impact of the colossal mechanical and chemical processes inherent in nature. These processes were aroused by the divine word of power and the animation of the Spirit and have given the earth its cosmic shape and appearance. From this point on also other forces, that is organic ones, make their appearance. The earth is still naked and featureless. For that reason this day does not end until the earth is clothed in green with vegetation that is divided into two kinds, herbs and trees, each of them having seed of their own and thus propagating themselves. This world of vegetation could do without the sun but not without light.

But that is not true of the animal and human world. Before they are created, the fourth day must come and sun, moon and stars have to be readied. This does not imply that the masses of matter of which the planets are composed were only then called into being, but only that all these planets would on this day become what they would henceforth be to the earth. Together they would assume the role of light and be signs of wind and weather, of events and judgments, for the earth. They would serve to regulate the seasons for agriculture, the shipping industry, annual feast days, the life of man and animal, and finally provide a basis for the calculation of days, months, and years. The fourth day, therefore, recounts the appearance of the starry skies in relation to the earth. From now on day and night, and so forth, are regulated by the sun; the earth becomes an integrated part of the universe; it is positioned in harmony with all other planets. Now the earth has been readied as the abode of animated living beings, of animals and humans.

On the fifth day, by a divine word of power, the waters themselves bring forth all aquatic animals, and the sky is filled with an assortment of bird species. Of both kinds of animals a massive number of all kinds are created. Next, on the sixth day, follows the creation of land animals who at God's command come forth from the earth—specifically in three kinds: wild animals, cattle, and creeping things; and finally also the creation of man who, after a specific counsel of God, was formed from the earth as to his body and as to his soul was directly created by God. Thus the whole creation was completed. God saw all that he had made and indeed it was very good. He took great delight in his own work and for that reason rested on the seventh day. This rest is a consequence of God's satisfaction with and delight in his works, which are now completed as the works of creation. At the same time it is a positive act of blessing and sanctifying the seventh day so that the creation, in its continued existence on the seventh day, having been blessed with all kinds of forces and consecrated by God to his service and honor, would henceforth develop under the providential care of the Lord and answer to its destiny.

Christian theology has always treated this six-day period with special fondness. The literature on the subject is astonishingly rich but has been almost exhaustively processed in the work of Zöckler on the history of the relations between theology and natural science.[11] The most ancient Christian interpretation of the six-day period has been preserved in the second book of Theophilus's *Ad Autolycum* (chs. 9–38). It is also more or less extensively treated in the work of Tertullian and Origen, but especially by Basil, Gregory of Nyssa, and John of Damascus in the East,[12] and in the West by Lactantius, Ambrose, and Augustine.[13] These works were utilized by Isodore, Beda, Alcuin, and others and continue to serve as the basis for the discussion of the six-day period in Scholasticism by Lombard, Thomas, Bonaventure, and others.

The same worldview and the same view of the six-day period, in both Roman Catholic and Protestant theology, is maintained after the Reformation. From the side of Catholicism the most important treatments are those of Cajetan in his commentary on Genesis, Eugubinus in his *Cosmopoeia* (1535), Catharinus in his commentary on the first five chapters of Genesis, Pererius in his four-part work on the first book of Moses, Lapide in his well-known commentary, Molina in his treatise *De opere sex dierum*, Suarez in his commentary on the first part of the *Summa*, Petavius, Becanus, and others. From the side of Lutheranism the following deserve to be listed: Luther's commentary on Genesis, Melanchthon's annotations on Genesis 1–6, and the discussions of Chemnitz, Quenstedt, Hollaz, and others in their systematics. Even richer is the literature produced on the subject by Reformed scholars. This material is considered in the commentaries of Calvin, Zwingli, Oecolampad, Musculus, Martyr, Piscator, de Dieu, Coccejus, and others; in dogmatic works like those of Polanus, Gomarus, Heidegger, Mastricht, Maresius, De Moor; but in addition to commentaries and systematic reflections also numerous separate treatises are devoted to

11. O. Zöckler, *Geschichte der Beziehungen zwischen Theologie und Naturwissenschaften mit besonderes Rucksicht auf die Schöpfungsgeschichte*, 2 vols. (Gütersloh: C. Bertelsmann, 1877–79); cf. idem, "Schöpfung und Erhaltung der Welt," *PRE³*, XVII, 681–704.

12. Tertullian, *Against Hermogenes*, 19ff.; Origen, in his homily about the hexaëmeron at the beginning of his seventeen homilies on Genesis; Basil, *On the Hexaëmeron hom.*, IX; Gregory of Nyssa, *Apology in Hexaëmeron;* John of Damascus, *Exposition of the Orthodox Faith*, II.

13. Lactantius, *The Divine Institutes*, II, 8–12; Ambrose, *Hexaëmeron*, VI; Augustine, *The Literal Meaning of Genesis*, 1, XII; idem, *The City of God*, XI, 4; idem, *Confessions*, XI–XII.

the subject, like those of Capito, Danaeus, Voetius, Rivet, Hottinger, and so forth.[14]

All these works arise from an Aristotelian-Ptolemaic worldview. The earth sits motionless at the center of the universe; all the stars and the whole expanse of the heavens rotate around it. The authors could not conceive of those stars as moving freely in space, but pictured every star as being fixed in a particular sphere. They therefore had to assume the existence of as many celestial spheres as they observed stars of dissimilar movement and rotational time. To them it was not the stars but the spheres that moved, carrying their stars with them. The vault of the heavens, then, consisted of a system of eight or more tightly telescoped concentric spheres. The outermost sphere is that of the fixed stars, the "first heaven," as Aristotle called it. The earth was pictured as a bullet or a disc surrounded by water. Only a few of the authors assumed that there could be antipodes and that there was land also on the other side of the ocean. As a rule both of these positions were rejected.

Of course, this Ptolemaic worldview also influenced the exegesis of the six-day period. In this respect one can clearly discern two distinct schools of thought. The one rejects the temporal character of the six days, for the most part ascribes visionary significance to them, sees the entire world as being created simultaneously at a single stroke, and frequently arrives at a variety of allegorical interpretations. It was already represented by Philo and later, in the Christian church, by Clement, Origen, Athanasius, Augustine, Erigena, Abelard, Cajetan, Canus, Gonzales, and others, as well as by Moses Maimonides.[15] The other school adheres to the literal sense of the creation narrative, including that of the six days. It was followed by Tertullian, Basil, Gregory of Nyssa, Ephraem, John of Damascus. Later on it achieved almost exclusive dominance in Scholasticism, in Roman Catholic as well as Protestant theology, although the alternative exegesis of Augustine was consistently discussed with respect and never branded heretical.[16]

Despite this important disagreement in exegesis, however, there was perfect agreement in the matter of worldview. The Ptolemaic system held firm even into modern times long after Copernicus had come on the scene with his explanation of the movement of heavenly bodies. It was absolutely not the church and orthodoxy as such which opposed the newer worldview, as people love to portray the situation.[17] Instead

14. In addition to O. Zöckler, also see J. G. Walch, *Bibliotheca Theologica selecta*, 4 vols. (Jenae: Croecker, 1757–65), I, 242; C. Vitringa, *Doctr. Christ.*, II, 93.

15. M. Maimonides, *More Nebochim* (Warsaw: Goldman, 1872), II, 30.

16. P. Lombard, *Sentences*, II, dist. 15, 5; T. Aquinas, *Summa Theol.*, I, qu. 74, art. 2.

17. Cf., e.g., J. W. Draper, *History of the Conflict between Religion and Science* (New York: D. Appleton, 1897).

it was Aristotelianism which in every domain, both that of science and that of religion, that of art and that of the church, sought to maintain itself in the face of modernity.[18] That is the reason why the Christian church and Christian theology, although today they have generally exchanged the Ptolemaic for the Copernican hypothesis, have continued to exist to this day and are by no means dead even in this century. This is proof that the church and theology are not so tightly bound up with these worldviews that they must stand or fall with them. Indeed, it is not at all obvious that the Copernican hypothesis, if in fact it adequately explains the astronomical phenomena, would as such have to be rejected by Christian theology. For Scripture indeed always speaks geocentrically and also explains the origin of things from a geocentric viewpoint, but in this matter it uses the same language of ordinary daily experience as that in which we still speak today, even though we have a very different picture of the movement of the heavenly bodies from that which generally prevailed in the time when the Bible books were written. It can even also be roundly admitted that the Bible writers had no other worldview than that which was universally assumed in their day. There is a difference after all between historical authority (*auctoritas historiae:* "descriptive") and normative authority (*auctoritas normae:* "prescriptive").[19] From the perspective of this language employed by Scripture we can explain how the miracle narrated in Joshua 10:12, 13; 2 Kings 20:9; and Isaiah 38:8 is described in terms of the sun standing still and its shadow turning back on the dial. It is by no means established by this account that the miracle itself consisted in an objective "standing still" of the sun and a "turning back" of its shadow. The miracle can be and has in fact been interpreted in various ways by scholars[20] who did not rationalistically exegete it into oblivion. Even we today would describe the same phenomena in the same manner: Scripture reports the miracle as a fact; it does not tell us how it came about.

But we must state the matter still stronger: even if, in an astronomic sense, the earth is no longer central to us, it is definitely still central in a religious and an ethical sense, and thus remains central to all people

18. E. Dennert, *Die Religion der Naturforscher,* 4th ed. (Berlin: Buchhandlung der Berliner Stadtmission, 1901), 13; R. Schmid, *Das Naturwiss. Glaubensbekenntnis eines Theologen* (Stuttgart: n.p., 1906), 38–42 (*The Scientific Creed of a Theologian,* trans. by J. W. Stoughton, 2nd ed. [New York: A. C. Armstrong, 1906]).

19. Cf. H. Bavinck, *Gereformeerde Dogmatiek,* I, 427.

20. F. W. J. Dilloo, *Das Wunder an den Stufen des Achas* (Amsterdam: Hoveker, 1885); G. F. Wright, *Wetensch. Bijdragen tot Bevest. der Oud-Test. Geschiedenis,* trans. by C. Oranje (Rotterdam: D. A. Daamen, 1907), 63ff. (*Scientific Confirmations of Old Testament History* [Oberlin: O. Bibliotheca Sacra, 1906]).

without distinction, and there is not a thing science can do to change that. Man, in a sense, is the weakest of all creatures; the power of nature, the power of many an animal, far surpasses his. Still man is king of the earth, the crown of creation. He may be frail as a reed, but he is a *thinking* reed *(roseau pensant)*. The earth may be a thousand times smaller than many other planets; in an ethical sense it is and remains the center of the universe. It is the only planet fit to be the dwelling place for higher beings.[21] Here the kingdom of God has been established; here the struggle between light and darkness is being waged; here, in the church, God is preparing for himself an eternal dwelling. From this earth, therefore, we will continue to look up from where, both in a physical and an ethical sense, the rain and the sunshine and the increase will have to come, without imagining that we are thereby determining the place of heaven in an astronomic sense or know its precise location in the universe. To say, however, that scientific investigation has robbed God and the angels of their place of residence is absurdly superficial. For though Lalande presumed to say that he had searched through the entire universe and had not found God, the truth is that, to our limited vision, the universe with its measureless spaces is still one vast mystery; and one who does not find God in his or her immediate presence, in his or her heart and conscience, in the word and the Christian community, will not find him in the universe either, even though he equips himself with the best telescope that money can buy.[22]

The Hypotheses of the Natural Sciences

Christian theology, then, has no objections to the Copernican worldview. The situation is very different, however, with the hypotheses assumed nowadays by science with respect to the genesis of our solar system and the earth. With respect to the first, Kant and Laplace posed the hypothesis that our solar system and actually even the whole universe was originally one vast blob of gaseous chaos, marked by an extremely

21. Cf. Alfred R. Wallace, *Man's Place in the Universe* (New York: McClure, Phillips, 1903).

22. J. H. A. Ebrard, *Der Glaube an die H. Schrift und die Ergebnisse der Naturforschung,* trans. by A. v. d. Linde (Amsterdam: n.p., 1862); *P. Wigand, *Die Erde der Mittelpunkt der Welt,* Heft 144 of *Zeitfragen des Christlichen Volkslebens;* H. Schell, *Der Gottesglaube und die Naturwissenschaftliche Welterkenntniss*[2] (Bamberg: Schmidt, 1904) writes: "As a result of the Copernican worldview the *earth* has become small, but not *man:* For whereas the magnitude of the earth consists in its massive materiality, that of humankind consists in its *spirit*" (p. 12); Also cf. R. Schmid, *Das Naturwissenschaftliche Glaubensbekenntnis eines Theologen* (Stuttgart, 1906), 42. (English translation, *The Scientific Creed of a Theologian,* trans. by J. W. Stoughton [London: Hodder & Stoughton, 1906]).

high temperature and turning on its own axis from west to east. This rotation moved with such force that parts of this gaseous mass broke away and, since they continued to move in the same direction, took on a spherical shape.[23]

Now we must note first of all that this hypothesis, however deistically conceived, was absolutely not intended by Kant to eliminate God. It was his judgment, however, that this chaotic condition of all matter was the most elementary state which could follow on nothingness and that these materials themselves were all so shaped by God as the first cause that by immanent forces and in accordance with fixed laws they could produce the present world system without any miraculous intervention by God. But, in our opinion, this hypothesis is insufficient to explain the origin of the universe, of motion, and of organic beings. In general it needs to be said that, however primitive and chaotic that first state of all matter may be thought to be and however many millions of years it may be projected back, it does not provide rest for our thinking. For one will *either* have to recognize with Kant that this original state of the creation depends in its totality immediately on God and follows upon nothingness, *or* one will have to view that chaotic state not only as the beginning of the present world system but also as the end and the destruction of a preceding world and so on *ad infinitum* and thus *eternalize* matter and motion.[24] Furthermore this hypothesis is open to many objections and does not explain the phenomena. These need not all be discussed here: we can, for example, overlook the objection that there are also heavenly bodies that make a retrograde movement and do not turn from west to east but from east to west. The above objections are so weighty, however, that even Haeckel recognizes them. And we do want to point out that, given this gaseous nebula and given the mechanical motion, this hypothesis is by no means capable of explaining this world system. For motion and matter by themselves are not enough to explain it. There has to be direction in that motion, and aside from matter there also has to be still something else to explain the world of spiritual and mental phenomena. Why did our present world

23. E. Haeckel, *Naturliche Schöpfungs-Geschichte*[5] (1874), 285ff. (9th ed. [Berlin: G. Reimer, 1898]); E. Haeckel, *The Riddle of the Universe at the Close of the Nineteenth Century*, trans. by Joseph McCabe (New York: Harper & Brothers, 1900), 239–40; L. Büchner, *Kraft und Stoff*, 17c A. (1888), 130ff. (*Force and Matter*, 4th ed. trans. from the 15th German ed. [New York: P. Eckler, 1891]); F. Pfaff, *Schöpfungsgeschichte*[3] (Heidelberg: C. Winter, 1881), 190ff.; O. Liebmann, *Zur Analysis der Wirklichkeit*[3] (Strassburg: K. J. Trübner, 1900), 389ff.

24. F. A. Lange, *Geschichte des Materialismus und Kritik seiner Bedeutung in der Gegenwart*, 8th ed. (Leipzig: Baedekker, 1908), II, 522; D. F. Strauss, *Der alte und der neue Glaube* (Leipzig: Hirzel, 1872), 225; Büchner, *Kraft und Stoff*, 133 [*Force and Matter*]; Haeckel, *The Riddle of the Universe*, 249–50.

system, which everywhere exhibits order and harmony and would implode or collapse at the least deviation from that order, arise from this nebulous mass? How could an unconscious, purposeless movement of atoms result in the formation of the universe? The chance of such an ordered whole originating from such a chaotic state is highly improbable and actually quite impossible. "It is just as simple to regard the creation as a playful vagary of chance as to explain a Beethoven symphony from marks and dots that have accidentally appeared on a piece of paper."[25]

Add to this that this hypothesis, even if it did explain the phenomena, would still be no more than a hypothesis. For what conclusion can be drawn for reality from a possibility? The consequences do not validate the movement from possibility to existence *(A posse ad esse non valet consequentia)*. What proof can be cited that the world system not only *could* but actually *did* originate in that manner? There is a big difference between a logical assumption and an actual state of affairs which may at one time have existed. When natural science investigates the phenomena, it attempts to trace them to their simplest form. Consequently it finally assumes the existence of extremely primitive and simple elements such as atoms, dynamisms, energies, ether, chaos, and so on. But these are logical assumptions at which it arrives. The idea that such atoms at one time existed as pure atoms in a primordial state, one that followed upon a state of nothingness, is by no means proved by such assumptions. Like the original elements of things (atoms, dynamisms, monads), so also the primordial states which scientists posit as having preceded the process of becoming are nothing but constructs, not reality. Their status is like the a-religious state that is currently assumed in research inquiring into the origin of religion, or like Rousseau's state of nature from which, by way of a social contract, the state is supposed to have originated. Perhaps all such hypotheses can be of some use as constructs, like construction lines in mathematics, but this doesn't yet make them into actual explanations of existing reality.

What no natural science can teach us, finally, is given us by revelation, which is further confirmed by the tradition of all peoples. It teaches us that it has pleased God, in forming the world, to proceed from the imperfect to the perfect, from the simple to the complex, from the lower to the higher. There is an element of truth in the theory of evolution that is recognized in Scripture, as Genesis 1:2 clearly shows. But there the state of creation is real; there is no chaos in the true sense, no

25. Oswald Heer, according to E. Dennert, *Moses oder Darwin?*[2] (Stuttgart: Kielman, 1907), 50.

hulē (matter) in the Aristotelian sense, no primal matter without form, no inconceivable mass of pure atoms, but a state of cosmic formlessness that existed for a time, over which the Spirit of God hovered and upon which that Spirit brooded. It simply will not do, with many Christian apologists, to adopt the Kant–Laplace hypothesis without any form of criticism and then to be grateful that they have so beautifully managed to fit it into Genesis 1:2. The truth is rather that Scripture tells us the story of an actual state, while natural science is offering us assumptions that are not scientifically tenable.[26]

In recent years this hypothesis has, accordingly, been abandoned by many scientists and exchanged for Lockyer's "meteorite"-hypothesis. Thus Sir G. H. Darwin, son of the famed naturalist, at a meeting of the British Association held at Johannesburg on August 30, 1905, delivered a lecture in which he spoke about the results of his studies concerning the so-called nebular theory of the origin of the world and expressed his grave doubts about the correctness of this theory. The main "evidence" for this theory was the observation that all planets, both large and small, moved in the same direction around the sun and its satellites. But in recent years astronomers have discovered a satellite of Jupiter and a new satellite of Saturn whose movement is not congruent with that of their planets. It also seems doubtful whether one of the two recently discovered moons of Jupiter is really moving in the same direction as the other. But even if one accepts the postulates of Laplace, there are mathematical reasons for doubting whether from the postulated primordial state a system of planets and satellites had to arise rather than a swarm of asteroids or even smaller celestial bodies. Prof. Darwin is therefore attempting to replace the Kant–Laplace hypothesis by another. If one pictures a planet spinning around a sun and inserts into this system a series of smaller meteoric bodies, then these meteors (assuming they are so small that their mutual gravitational pull can be neglected) will describe extraordinarily complicated courses. But after a longer or shorter period the majority of them will either have come to

26. F. Pfaff, *Schöpfungsgeschichte* (Frankfurt a.M.: Heyder & Zimmer, 1877), 731ff.; H. Ulrici, *Gott und die Natur* (Leipzig: T. O. Weigel, 1862), 334–53; F. H. Reusch, *Nature and Bible*, trans. by Kathleen Lyttelton from 4th German ed., 2 vols. (Edinburgh: T. & T. Clark, 1886), II, 31; T. Pesch, *Die Grossen Welträthsel*, 2nd ed., 2 vols. (Freiburg i.B.: Herder, 1892), II, 326–52; D. G. Braun, "Die Kant-Laplace'sche Weltbildungstheorie," *Neue Kirchliche Zeitschrift* 3 (September 1903): 672–704; E. G. Steude, *Christentum und Naturwiss Wissenschaft* (Gütersloh: n.p., 1895), 142ff.; P. Schanz, *Uber neue Versuche der Apologetik Gegeneuber dem Natural. und Spiritual.* (Regensburg: Nat. Verl-Anst., 1897), 211ff.; C. Gutberlet, *Der Mechanische Monismus* (Paderborn: F. Schöningh, 1893), 28ff.; W. Hahn, *Die Entstehung der Weltkörper* (Regensburg: Pustet, 1895), 6ff.; A. Dippe, *Naturphilosophie* (München: C. H. Beck, O. Beck, 1907), 238; W. H. Nieuwhuis, *Twee Vragen des Tijds* (Kampen: Kok, 1907), 73.

rest in the sun or a planet and only a few, which from the beginning enjoyed the most favorable conditions of speed and direction, would have preserved their original independent existence and increased in size. Hence, if one accepts an already existent sun and a planet, Darwin's theory only assumes a sufficient quantity of meteoric matter to explain the present solar system. But the theory says nothing about the origination of the sun and the first planet.[27]

The Formation of the Earth

A similar difference like the one we encountered in connection with the formation of our solar system occurs also in connection with the history of the development of the earth. Geology, basing itself on the strata of the earth's crust and the fossils of plants, animals, and humans found in those strata, has formed a hypothesis about the different periods of the earth's development. According to that hypothesis the oldest period is the Azoic,[28] or that of the Primeval-formation, in which especially the eruptive types of rock were formed and not a trace of organic life is found. Next followed the Paleozoic Era or that of the primary formation in which, besides various types of rock, especially also coal was formed and even plants of the simplest kind and all classes of animals except birds and mammals are found. In the third, the Mesozoic Era or that of the secondary formation, there occurred limestone formation (among other things) and different kinds of plants and animals, including the first oviparous and mammalian animals, are found. The next-following Tertiary or Cenozoic Era runs from the formation of limestone to the Ice Age, and, aside from plants, land and freshwater animals, witnessed especially the rise of predators and many of the now-extinct mammals. According to some scholars,[29] in the Tertiary Period humans already lived side by side with these animals as well, but according to the majority, humans did not appear on the scene until the end of this era, after the Ice Age, in the Quaternary

27. *Handelsblad*, November 17, 1905. Darwin's lecture entitled "Cosmic Evolution" has been included in *Wetenschappelijke Bladen* (June 1906): 406–34. A similar judgment has been expressed by Fr. Ratzel in E. Dennert, *Glauben und Wissen* (September, 1906): 304; and by Riem, *Glauben und Wissen* (1905): 228; cf. also E. Dennert, *Die Weltanschauung des Modernen Naturforschers* (Stuttgart: M. Rielmann, 1907), 64; R. Schmid, *Das Naturwissenschaftliche Glaubensbekenntnis*, 49, 50 [*The Scientific Creed*]; Stölzle, "Newtons Kosmogonie," *Philosophisches Jahrbuch* 20 (1907): 54.

28. *Trans. note:* The term "Azoic" is no longer current today; it is roughly equivalent to the Precambrian.

29. For example, H. Burmeister, *Geschichte der Schöpfung*, 7th ed. (Leipzig: C. G. Giebel, 1872), 612; L. Reinhardt, *Der Mensch zur Eiszeit in Europa und Seine kulturentwicklung bis zum Ende der Steinzeit* (München: Ernst Reinhardt, 1913), 1ff.

Period.[30] There is no doubt that this theory of geological periods is much more firmly grounded than the Kantian hypothesis; it is based on data yielded by the study of the strata of the earth's crust. Here, therefore, the conflict between revelation and science has a much more serious character. On many points there is difference and contradiction, first of all, in the *time* and, second, in the *order* in which the various creatures originated.

As to the *time*, the difference is very striking. We know that the chronology of the LXX differs substantially from that of the Hebrew text. The church fathers, who frequently followed the Greek translation, calculated the time between the creation of the world and the capture of Rome by the Goths at 5611 years.[31] In later times, especially after the Reformation, scholars gave preference to the chronology of the Hebrew text and on that basis calculated that the creation of the world took place in 3950 B.C. (Scaliger), 3984 (Kepler, Petavius), 3943 (Bengel), or 4004 (Ussher). The Jews currently count the years 5689.[32] But some sought an even more precise calculation. There was serious controversy over whether the creation took place in the spring or in the fall of the year. The former was the opinion of Cyril, Basil, Beda, Cajetan, Molina, Lapide, Luther, Melanchthon, Gerhard, Alsted, Polanus, G. J. Vossius, and others; the latter was defended by Petavius, Calvisius, Calov, Danaeus, Zanchius, Voetius, Maresius, Heidegger, Turretin among others. Sometimes the date was even determined more exactly: on March 25 or October 26.[33] In contrast, the geologists and natural scientists of our day posit calculations based on the rotation of the earth in connection with the flattening of its poles, the constant drop in the earth's temperature at the surface, the formation of the deltas of the Nile and the Mississippi, the formation of the earth's strata, the various kinds of rock, especially coal, and so forth. The figures assumed for the age of the earth are fabulous—as among some pagan peoples: Cotta speaks of an unlimited space of time, Lyell of 560 million, Klein of 2000

30. F. Pfaff, *Schöpfungsgeschichte*, 485ff.; Ulrici, *Gott und die Natur*, 353ff.; Reusch, *Nature and Bible*, 265ff.; K. A. von Zittel, *Aus der Urzeit*, 2nd ed. (Munchen: R. Oldenbourg, 1875), 537.

31. Augustine, *The City of God*, XII, 10.

32. O. Zöckler, *Die Lehre vom Urstand des Menschen* (Gütersloh: C. Bertelsmann, 1870), 289ff.; P. Schanz, *Das Alter des Menschengeschlechts nach der Heiligen Schrift, der Profangeschichte und der Vorgeschichte* (Freiburg i.B.: Herder, 1896), 1ff.

33. G. Voetius, *Select. Disp.*, I, 587; K. R. Hagenbach, *Lehrbuch der Dogmengeschichte* (Leipzig: Hirzel, 1888), 630 note. A parallel to such credulity in modern times occurs in Sigmund Wellisch who, in his *Das Alter der Welt und des Menschen* (Vienna: Hartleben, 1899), assures us that the earth is 9,108,300 years old, the moon 8,824,500, man in his animal state 1,028,000, and man as a cultural being 66,000 years; cf. *Der Beweis des Glaubens* (May 1900): 164.

million, Helmholtz of 80 million, and even Pfaff of at least 20 million years.[34]

But, in the second place, there is also a very great difference between the creation story in Genesis and the opinion of many scholars with respect to the *order* in which created beings originated. To mention just a few points: according to Scripture the light was indeed created on the first day, but our solar system did not come into being until the fourth day, after the earth had been readied on the second and third days and covered with luxuriant plant growth. According to geologists, however, the order is precisely the reverse. According to Genesis, the plant kingdom was created on the third day, but animals were not created until the fifth; geology, however, tells us that in the primary or Paleozoic Era animals of the lower kind and fish occurred as well. Genesis relates that all aquatic animals and all birds were created on the fifth day and all land animals plus humans appeared on the sixth day, but according to geology certain mammals occur already in the secondary or Mesozoic Era. Hence on many significant points there are clear differences between Scripture and science.

Harmonizing Science with Scripture

Naturally various attempts at reconciliation have been made. There is, first of all, the *ideal* theory, so called because it only adheres to the idea and not to the letter of the creation story. It does not view Genesis 1 as a historical account but as a poetic description of the creating acts of God. The six days are not seen as chronologically ordered periods of longer or shorter duration but only different perspectives from which the one created world can be viewed each time in order to give the limited human eye a better overview of the whole. It is therefore completely left to paleontology to determine the time, the manner, and the order of the origination of the different periods. It can be acknowledged that this theory had its forerunner in the allegorical exegesis which from ancient times had been followed in the Christian church with respect to Genesis 1. Following the example of Philo and appealing to Sirach 18:1 ("God created all things *at once*"), Origen, Augustine, and many others taught that God had created all things at once and simultaneously; the six days are not actually successive periods but only refer

34. F. Pfaff, *Schöpfungsgeschichte*, 640–66; F. Pfaff, "Das Alter der Erde," *Zeitfragen des Christlichen Volkslebens*, VII; O. Peschel, *Abhandlungen zur Erd und Völkerkunde*[5] (Leipzig: Duncker & Humboldt, 1878), 42–52; E. Haeckel, *Natürliche Schöpfungsgeschichte* (Berlin: G. Reimer, 1889), 340ff. [English trans. by E. Ray Lankester, *The History of Creation, or, The Development of the Earth and Its Inhabitants by the Action of Natural Causes* (London: Henry S. King, 1876)].

to the causal connection and logical order of created beings and describe how in successive stages the angels gained knowledge of the whole of creation. And even among those who clung to the literal sense of the creation story, allegory nevertheless still played a large role. Chaos, light, the term "one day" instead of the first day, the absence of divine approval at the end of the second day, paradise, the creation of Eve, and so forth—all gave rise to ingenious spiritualizations. Similar allegorizing, mythologizing, and rationalizing interpretations of the creation story flourished especially after the awakening of natural science and were applied by Hobbes, Spinoza, Beverland, Burnet, Bekker, Tindal, Edelmann, J. L. Schmidt, Reimarus, and others. Herder regarded Genesis 1 as a splendid poem of the most ancient humanity which, proceeding from the dawning day, hymned the praises of the seven-day week.[35] Modern philosophy and theology has gone farther down this road, rejecting even the concept of creation along with the story of creation and regarding Genesis 1 as a myth which at best has a religious core. Christian theologians have not gone as far, but, in the interest of reconciling religion and science, have frequently returned to the ideal conception of Augustine and abandoned the literal and historical interpretation of Genesis 1.[36] Closely related to this ideal theory is the *visionary* theory which was composed by Kurtz and was later, after other attempts at reconciliation (see below) failed to bring about a satisfactory solution, taken over by many others. According to this hypothesis we are dealing in the creation story with prophetic historical tableaux that God showed the first human being in a vision, the same way

35. J. G. Herder, *Aelteste Urkunde des Menschengeschlechts* (Riga: Hartknoch, 1774–76); Bishop W. Clifford also held Genesis 1 to be a hymn to the seven-day week; V. Zapletal, *Der Schöpfungsbericht*, 88; J. B. Heinrich, and C. Gutberlet, *Dogmatische Theologie*, 10 vols., 2nd ed. (Mainz: Kircheim, 1881–1900), V, 206; cf. the view—which is related to Clifford's theory—of Prof. de Grijse in P. Mannens, *Theologiae Dogmaticae Institutiones*, II, 239.

36. F. Michelis, *Entwicklung der beiden ersten Kapitel der Genesis* (Münster: Theissing, 1845) and in various essays in his journal *Natur und Offenbarung*, 1855ff.; Reusch, *Nature and Bible*, I, 348–75; P. Schanz, *Apologie des Christenthums*, 3 vols. (Freiburg i.B.: Herder, 1887–88), I, 293ff. [English trans. by Rev. Michael F. Glancey and Rev. Victor J. Schobel, *A Christian Apology*, 4th rev. ed. (Ratisbon: F. Pustet, 1891)]; M. J. Scheeben, *Handbuch der Katholischer Dogmatik*, 4 vols. (Freiburg i.B.: Herder, 1933), II, 105ff.; Heinrich and Gutberlet, *Dogmatische Theologie*, V, 234ff.; H. Lüken, *Die Stiftungsurkunde des Menschengeschlechts* (Freiburg i.B.: Herder, 1876); C. Güttler, *Naturforschung und Bibel in ihrer Stellung zur Schöpfung* (Freiburg i.B.: Herder, 1877); F. Hettinger, *Apologie des Christenthums*, 4 vols., 7th ed. prepared by Eugen Muller (Freiburg i.B.: Herder, 1895–98), III, 206. Belonging to this school on the Protestant side are T. Zollmann, *Bibel und Natur in der Harmonie ihrer Offenbarungen* (Hamburg: n.p., 1869), 52ff.; G. Riehm, *Christentum und Naturwissenschaft*, 2nd ed. (Leipzig: J. C. Hinrichs, 1896); Steude, *Christentum und Naturwissenschaft* (Gütersloh: C. Bertelsmann, 1875); A. Dillmann, *Genesis* (Edinburgh: T. & T. Clark, 1897); Vuilleumier, "La première page de la Bible," *Revue de théologie et de philosophie* (1896): 362ff., 393ff.

in which the latter was instructed about the creation of woman in a vision, which he later passed down in a regular story. In that case Genesis 1 is not real history but "a backward-looking prophecy in the form of a visionary presentation" that bears a revelatory character insofar as it leads toward the history of salvation.[37]

A second attempt at reconciliation is the so-called *restitution* theory. It attempts to bring about agreement between revelation and science as follows: It makes a separation between Genesis 1:2 and 1:3, and inserts all the events and phenomena that geology has taught us into the period before the chaos mentioned in verse 2. It does not view the *tōhû wābōhû* as the description of a purely negative, still unformed state, but as the term describing a destruction caused by the preceding great catastrophes. The six-day unit that begins with verse 3 then recounts the restoration of that state of destruction and the preparation of the earth as a dwellingplace for humanity. The proponents of this theory believe that by it they can resolve every conceivable conflict between the Bible and geology and maintain the literal and historical meaning of the work of the six days of creation.

Whereas the first-mentioned theory could appeal to the example of church fathers, the emergence of this second theory only occurred considerably later. The Remonstrants Episcopius and Limborch had already posited a longer time space between Genesis 1:1 and 2 to make room for the fall of the angels.[38] In the eighteenth century the restitution theory was advocated by J. G. Rosenmuller, J. D. Michaelis, and Reinhard; the theosophists Oetinger, Hahn, St. Martin, von Baader, Schelling, Fr. von Meyer, Steffens, Schubert, Keerl, Kurtz, Delitzsch, and others, linked it with the idea that the first earth, created in Genesis 1:1, was actually the abode of the angels and catastrophically ruined by their fall.[39] Without this theosophic association it was also accepted by Chambers, Buckland, Cardinal Wisemann, and a few others, but found little acceptance.[40]

---

37. J. H. Kurtz, *The Bible and Astronomy*, trans. by T. D. Simonton, 3rd ed. (Philadelphia: Lindsay & Blakiston, 1857) 112–17; O. Zöckler, art. *Geschichte der Beziehungen zwischen Theologie und Naturwissen schaften mit besonderes Rucksicht auf die Schöpfungs geschichte*, 2 vols. (Gütersloh: C. Bertelsmann, 1879); Dennert, *Moses oder Darwin*, 9ff.; F. Hümmelauer, *Der biblische Schöpfungsbericht ein exegetischer Versuch* (Freiburg i.B.: Herder, 1877); idem, *Nochmals der biblische Schöpfungsbericht* (Freiburg i.B.: Herder, 1898); B. Schäfer, *Bibel und Wissenschaft* (Münster: Theissing, 1881); M. Gander, *Naturwissenschaft und Glaube. Benzigers Naturwissenschaftliche Bibliothek* (New York: Benziger Bros., 1905), 117.

38. S. Episcopius, *Instit. Theol.*, IV, sect. 3, 3; P. van Limborch, *Theol. Christ.* (Amsterdam: n.p., 1735), II, 19–21.

39. Cf. below in connection with the fall of the angels.

40. N. Wisemann, *Zusammenhang zwischen Wissenschaft und Offenbarung* (Regensberg: Manz, 1866), 263ff.

A third theory, the so-called concordistic theory, seeks to achieve harmony between Scripture and science by viewing the days of creation as periods of longer duration. Already early in Christian history, the exegesis of the six days raised problems. The sun, moon, and stars were not created until the fourth day; the three preceding days in any case had to be different therefore from the second set of three days. Basil's explanation was that God effected the first three days by the emission and contraction of the light created on the first day.[41] But this explanation was not satisfactory to everyone, not to Augustine, for example, who at times deviated from his own simultaneity theory.[42] In addition there was further disagreement over whether each day's work of creation was completed in a single moment or successively spread out over the entire course of the day. Descartes, after all, had said that the purely natural things *(res pure naturales)* could have emerged from the existing chaos without any act of divine creation. This suggested the idea of natural development. A few Cartesian theologians, such as Wittichius, Allinga, and Braun, therefore theorized that each work of creation took a full day to complete.[43] And Whiston already said that the days had to be viewed as years, a theory also adopted by others. But the father of the concordistic theory is the abbot of Jerusalem. It was taken over by natural scientists such as de Luc, Cuvier, Hugh Miller, Pfaff, and the like; by theologians such as Lange, Delitzsch, Lougemont, Godet, Ebrard, Luthardt, Zöckler, and others,[44] as well as by Catholics like Heinrich, Palmieri, Simar, Pesch, and so forth.[45] Many scholars combined this view with the restitution theory and contented themselves even then with agreement in essentials. Hugh Miller, for example, had the Azoic period coincide with Genesis 1:3; the Paleozoic with Genesis 1:6–13; the Mesozoic with Genesis 1:14–23; the Cenozoic with Genesis 1:24.[46]

41. D. F. Strauss, *Chr. Dogm.*, I, 621.

42. Augustine, *The Literal Meaning of Genesis*, I, 16.

43. Cf. C. Vitringa, *Doctr. Christ.*, II, 95; B. de Moor, *Comm. Theol.*, II, 212.

44. J. Ebrard, *Der Glaube an die H. Schrift und die Ergeb. der Naturforsch.*, trans. by A. v. d. Linde (Amsterdam: n.p., 1861); C. E. Luthardt, *Apologetische Vorträge uber die Grundwahrheiten des Christenthums*[8] (Leipzig: Dörffling und Franke, 1878); O. Zöckler, "Schöpfung," in PRE[2], XIII, 647; Brandt, *Der Beweis des Glaubens* (1876): 339ff.; E. W. Hengstenberg, "Biblischen Kosmogenie und Kosmogenischen Wissenschaft," *Beweis des Glaubens* 3 (1867): 400–18; cf. G. F. Wright, *Wetenschappelijke Bijdragen*, 304ff. (English original: *Scientific Confirmations of Old Testament History* [Oberlin, Ohio: Bibliotheca Sacra, 1907]).

45. Heinrich and Gutberlet, *Dogmatische Theologie*, V, 234, 256; H. Th. Simar, *Lehrbuch der Dogmatik*, 2 vols. (Freiburg i.B.: Herder, 1879–80), 249; C. Pesch, *Praelectiones Dogmaticae* (Freiburg i.B.: Herder, 1916–25), III, 40; P. Mannens, *Theologiae Dogmaticae Institutiones*, II, 233.

46. O. Zöckler, *Geschichte der Beziehungen zwischen Theologie und Naturwissenschaft*, 544.

Finally, the fourth theory, the one sometimes called the "antigeo-logical" theory, continues to hold the literal and historical view of Genesis 1, and tries to place the results of geology in part in the six creation days, in part also in the period between Adam and Noah, and especially in the time of the flood. From ancient times already the flood was regarded as very important in this connection. Exegetes argued about a partial versus a universal flood—an issue that has always been in discussion—about the construction of the ark, and about the height of the flood.[47] But the flood acquired geological significance only after Newton. In 1682 Thomas Burnet published his *Theoria sacra telluris* and in it postulated a very large difference between the time before and the time after the flood. To him the flood becomes the end of an old world and the birth of an entirely new world. It was a tremendous catastrophe that altered the entire surface of the earth, created oceans and mountains, put an end to the prevailing mild spring climate, the luxuriant fecundity, and the extraordinary longevity of the people who lived before that time and especially changed the earth's axis, which was formerly parallel with that of the sun, so that it was now positioned obliquely in relation to the earth's orbit. This wholly new theory, while it was vehemently opposed, among others by Spanheim and Leydecker, was nevertheless further developed by Whiston, Clüver, and many others.[48] Toward the end of the eighteenth century, this diluvial theory was increasingly abandoned but continued to be held in honor among many orthodox Catholic and Protestant theologians.[49]

The proponents of this attempt at reconciliation continued to equate the biblical flood with the diluvium or the Ice Age of geology and in that connection judged that the flood was universal and therefore extended over the entire earth. In recent times most geologists and theologians, such as Sedgwick, Greenough, Buckland, Hitchcock, Hugh Miller, Barry, Dawson, Diestel, Dillmann, Pfaff, Kurtz, Michelis, Reusch, and Guttler,[50] believe that the biblical flood was very different from the diluvium of geology and therefore also has to be viewed as partial. It can only be called universal insofar as the entire human race perished as a result of it, although this point is again denied by some, such as Cuvier. Others have also expressed doubts about the reality of such an enormous flood, be it universal or partial, but then had to face

47. Ibid., II, 122ff.
48. Ibid., II, 143–92.
49. C. F. Keil and F. Delitzsch, *Commentary on Genesis*, vol. 1 (Edinburgh: T. & T. Clark, 1864–1901) and others by Zöckler, *Geschichte der Beziehungen*, II, 420–82, 288.
50. Cf. also A. Kuyper, *De Heraut*, 929 (13 October 1895): 1; 930 (20 October 1895): 1; 962 (31 May 1896): 1.

the question whether in the flood stories they were dealing with sagas or myths, whether the underlying premise was fact or idea. The Viennese geologist Suess assumed that a horrendous inundation of the valleys of the Euphrates and the Tigris constituted the core of the story.[51] Although this hypothesis at first found wide acceptance, it was later strongly opposed, among other things, with the argument that flood stories are found not only in Babylonia and Israel but also in Egypt and throughout the world, among the Eskimos, the various peoples of the South Sea Islands, and so forth. This distribution of evidence seemed not to be explained by memories of a great flood in Babylonia.[52] For that reason others started to collect, compare, order, and sort out the various flood stories[53] and came to think either again of a certain historical fact, such as for example a flood in Mongolia,[54] or of various inundations in different countries,[55] or of a myth in which the birth and ascendancy of a light-god was narrated.[56] As is clear from this brief survey, the debate on this important and difficult issue is far from over, and the most recent studies seem rather to argue for the old diluvial view of the flood. G. F. Wright considers it a disaster in Central Asia that concluded a series of disasters in the Ice Age and which, except for Noah's family, destroyed the members of the human race still remaining there.[57]

51. E. Suess, *Die Sintfluth* (Leipzig: G. Freitag, 1883).

52. On the comparison of the biblical with the Babylonian flood story one can consult *(inter alia)* the following: Kosters, "De Bijbelsche Zondvloedverhalen met de Babyl. vergeleken," *Theol. Tijdschr.* (1885): 161ff., 321ff.; J. S. Nikel, *Genesis und Keilschriftforschung* (Freiburg i.B.: Herder, 1903), 173ff.; H. H. Kuyper, *Evolutie of Revelatie* (Amsterdam: Höveker & Wormser, 1903), 123ff.

53. R. Andree, *Die Flutsagen, ethnographisch betrachtet* (Braunschweig: F. Vieweg, 1891); F. v. Schwarz, *Sintfluth und Völkerwanderungen* (Stuttgart: Enke, 1894); H. Usener, *Die Sintflutsagen,* vol. 3 of *Religionsgeschichtliche Untersuchungen* (Bonn: Cohen, 1899); Winternitz, *Die Flutsagen des Altertums und der Naturvölker* (Wien, 1901).

54. Thus Schwarz, *Sintfluth und Völkerwanderungen.*

55. *Winternitz, *Die Flutsagen des Altertums,* also held this view, as did also L. von Ranke.

56. So H. Usener, *Die Sintflutsagen;* Winternitz, *Die Flutsagen des Altertum.*

57. Further cf. Diestel, "Die Sintflut," *Deutsche Zeit und Streitvragen,* vr. 137; Reusch, *Bibel und Natur⁴,* 289ff. [*Nature and Bible*]; P. Schanz, *Apologie des Christentums,* I, 341ff. [*A Christian Apology*]; F. G. Vigouroux, *Les Livres Saints,* 4 vols. (Paris: A. Roger & F. Chernoviz, 1886–90), IV, 239; Jürgens, "War die Sintflut eine Erdbebenwelle?" *Stimmen aus Maria-Laach* (1884); H. H. Howorth, *The Mammoth and the Flood* (London: S. Low, Marston, Searle, & Rivingon, 1887); R. Girard, *Etudes de Géologie Biblique,* I (Freiburg: Fragnière, 1893); C. Schmidt, *Das Naturereignis der Sintflut* (Bazel: n.p., 1895); *O. Zöckler, *Neue Jahrb. f. d. Theol.,* 3–4 (1895); M. Gander, *Die Sündflut in ihrer Bedeutung für die Erdgeschichte* (Münster: Aschendorff, 1896); A. Trissl, *Sündflut oder Gletscher?* (Regensburg: G. J. Manz, 1894); Th. Schneider, *Was ist's mit der Sintflut?* (Wiesbaden, 1903); J. Riem, *Die Sintflut in Sage und Wissenschaft* (Hamburg: Rauhe Haus, 1925); G. F. Wright, *Wetensch. Bijdragen,* 164, 287 [*Scientific Confirmations*].

The Six-Day Week of Creation

These four attempts to harmonize Scripture and science are not in every respect opposed to each other. Even in the ideal theory listed above there is an element of truth. Every one agrees, after all, that Scripture does not speak the language of science but that of daily experience; that also in telling the story of creation it assumes a geocentric or anthropocentric viewpoint; and that in this connection it is not attempting to give a lesson in geology or any other science but, also in the story of the genesis of all creatures, remains the book of religion, revelation, and the knowledge of God. "We do not read in the Gospel that the Lord said: 'I will send to you a Paraclete who will teach you about the course of the sun and the moon! For he wanted to make Christians, not mathematicians."[58] "Moses, accommodating himself to uneducated people, followed the things which appear to the senses."[59] "Scripture intentionally does not treat the things we know in philosophy."[60] But when Scripture, from its own perspective precisely as the book of religion, comes in contact with other sciences and also sheds its light on them, it does not all at once cease to be the Word of God but remains that Word. Even when it speaks about the genesis of heaven and earth, it does not present saga or myth or poetic fantasy but offers, in accordance with its own clear intent, history, the history that deserves credence and trust. And for that reason Christian theology, with only a few exceptions, continued to hold onto the literal historical view of the creation story.

It is nevertheless remarkable that not a single confession made a fixed pronouncement about the six-day continuum and that in theology as well a variety of interpretations were allowed to exist side by side. Augustine already urged believers not too quickly to consider a theory to be in conflict with Scripture, to enter the discussion on these difficult subjects only after serious study, and not to make themselves ridiculous by their ignorance in the eyes of unbelieving science.[61] This warning has not always been faithfully taken to heart by theologians. Geology, it must be said, may render excellent service to us in the interpretation of the creation story. Just as the Copernican worldview has pressed theology to give another and better interpretation of the sun's "standing still" in Joshua 10; as Assyriology and Egyptology form precious sources of information for the interpretation of Scripture; and as history frequently finally enables us to understand a prophecy in its true signifi-

---

58. Augustine, *Proceedings Against Felix the Manichee*, I, 10.

59. T. Aquinas, *Summa Theol.*, I, qu. 70, art 4.

60. J. Alsted, *Theol.*, I–II, 181; cf. G. Voetius, *Select. Disp.*, V, 131; Hettinger, *Apologie des Christenthums*, III, 196.

61. Augustine, *The Literal Meaning of Genesis*, I, 18, 19, 20, 21; cf. T. Aquinas, *Summa Theol.*, I, qu. 68, art. 1.

cance, so also geological and paleontological investigations help us in this century to gain a better understanding of the creation story. We must remember that the creation and preparation of heaven and earth is a divine work par excellence, a miracle in the absolute sense of the word, full of mysteries and secrets. Genesis nevertheless tells the story of this work in such a simple and sober manner that there almost seems to be a contradiction between the fact itself and its description. Behind every feature in the creation story lies a world of marvels and mighty deeds of God which geology has displayed before our eyes in a virtually endless series of phenomena. Accordingly, Scripture and theology have nothing to fear from the *facts* brought to light by geology and paleontology. The world, too, is a book whose pages have been inscribed by God's almighty hand. Conflict arises only because both the text of the book of Scripture and the text of the book of nature are often so badly read and poorly understood. In this connection the theologians are not without blame as they have frequently condemned science, not in the name of Scripture but of their own incorrect views. Natural scientists have repeatedly interpreted the facts and phenomena they discovered in a manner, and in support of a worldview, which were justified neither by Scripture nor by science. For the time being it would seem advisable for geology—which is a relatively young science and, though it has already accomplished a lot, has still a vast amount of work to do— to restrict itself to the gathering of material and to abstain from forming conclusions and framing hypotheses. It is still utterly incapable of doing the latter and must still practice patience for a long time before it will be competent and equipped to do it.

Now if these provisional remarks have been taken to heart, I would say that it is probable, in the first place, that the creation of heaven and earth in Genesis 1:1 preceded the work of the six days in verses 3ff. by a shorter or longer period. The restitution theory certainly erred when it located the fall of the angels and the devastation of the earth in Genesis 1:2. There is nothing in this verse that supports this position. The text does not say that the earth *became* waste and void but that it was so and was so created. The trackless void by no means implies that the earth had been devastated, but only that though it was already earth, it was still unformed, without configuration or form. For the rest, it is true that the creation of heaven and earth and the trackless and vacuous state of the earth cannot be placed within the boundaries of the first day. The latter only began, and could in the nature of the case only begin, with the creation of the light. The first day was not formed by a combination of original darkness and subsequently created light, but it was formed by the first alternation of evening and morning which was initiated after the creation of the light. The darkness mentioned in Genesis 1:2 was not the first evening;

only after the creation of light was there an evening and then a morning. And that morning brought to completion the first day which had begun with the creation of light. A day in Genesis begins and ends with the morning.[62] Augustine, Lombard, Thomas, Petavius, and many others rightly judged therefore that the creation of heaven and earth, and the *tōhû wābōhû* state of the earth, occurred before any day existed *(ante omnem diem)*.[63] Only in this way can one do justice to the fact that the creation in Genesis 1:1 is simply recounted as a fact without any further description but that the preparation of the earth (Gen. 1:3ff.) is recounted at length. Genesis 1:1 only states that God is the Creator of all things but it does not tell us that God created them by his Word and Spirit. Of course, this latter point is not denied, but neither is it stated, nor are we told in how much time and in what manner God created heaven and earth or how long the unformed state of the earth lasted. It is only when the six-day work begins that we are told that also that unformed earth is maintained and made fruitful by the Spirit of God (Gen. 1:2) and that all things on and in that earth have been brought into being by the Word of God (Gen. 1:3ff.). In the ordering and adornment of the earth during the six days God's wisdom is manifest.[64] But even if, with a view to Exodus 20:11; 31:17, one wanted to include the story of Genesis 1:1 and 2 in the first day, that would only have resulted in the first day's becoming most unusual. It would then have started at the moment of creation and would initially have been dark for a time and have begun with a long night (Gen. 1:2), a situation that is hard to square with Genesis 1:3–5.

Something similar is true of the days in which the earth was formed and made into an abode for humans. At all times people have entertained different opinions on that matter, and Thomas rightly affirms that in the things which do not belong to the necessity of faith various opinions are permitted.[65] Augustine believed that God created all things simultaneously in a single instant, so that the days of which Genesis 1 speaks make known to us not the temporal but only the causal order in which the parts of the work of creation stand to each other. And in obscure matters, he warned believers against taking such a firm stand in favor of a certain interpretation of Scripture that, when a clearer light should dawn over a passage, we would rather shine in defending our own opinion than fight for the meaning of Holy Scripture.[66] This has

62. Cf. *Comm. on Genesis* by C. F. Keil and F. Delitzsch.

63. Augustine, *Confessions*, XII, 8; P. Lombard, *Sent.*, II, dist. 12, 1, 2; T. Aquinas, *Summa Theol.*, I, qu. 74, art. 2; D. Petavius, *Opera Omnia*, "De sex dier. opif.," I, 9, n. 2; W. G. T. Shedd, *Dogmatic Theology*, 2 vols. (New York: Charles Scribner's Sons, 1888–89), I, 474.

64. J. Calvin, *Commentary on Genesis*, 1:3.

65. T. Aquinas, *Sent.*, II, dist. 2, qu. 1, art. 3.

66. Augustine, *The Literal Meaning of Genesis*, book 1, chapter 18, in vol. 41 of *Ancient Christian Writers* (New York: Newman, 1982), 41: "In matters that are obscure and far be-

happened, for example, when in an earlier time the Copernican world-view was deemed to be in conflict with Joshua 10:12 and hence rejected on the basis of an incorrect exegesis. But Augustine's warning applies to the left as well as to the right. A few years ago the concordistic theory mentioned above was widely accepted because it seemed to bring agreement between the biblical creation story and the periods of geology. But very serious objections have been raised against this theory too, two of which deserve attention in particular. In the first place, as regards their order and duration, the geological periods, as will appear later, are not so invulnerable to objection that in them we are dealing with an established result of science. And even if that were the case, harmony between geology and Scripture is still not achieved by the concordistic theory because various points of difference remain. The main purpose for which it was proposed and recommended, namely, agreement between Scripture and natural science, could not be achieved by it and consequently this theory increasingly declined in significance and influence.

An additional objection, namely, that the days in Genesis 1 are not periods in which there occur repeated daily alternations of light and darkness but days which in each case are formed by one single alternation of darkness and light and defined by [one] evening and morning. And although despite this objection the concordistic theory is still being advocated by many scholars,[67] others have completely abandoned it, not indeed to return to the historical view accepted earlier, but on the contrary to move on to the ideal, visionary, or even mystical theory.[68] Augustine's opinion, which he himself for that matter presented only as

yond our vision, even in such as we may find treated in Holy Scripture, different interpretations are sometimes possible without prejudice to the faith we have received. In such a case, we should not rush in headlong and so firmly take our stand on one side that, if further progress in the search of truth justly undermines this position, we too fall with it. That would be to battle not for the teaching of Holy Scripture but for our own, wishing its teaching to conform to ours, whereas we ought to wish ours to conform to that of Sacred Scripture." Cf. T. Aquinas, *Summa Theol.*, I, qu. 68, art. 1.

67. E.g., Heinrich and Gutberlet, *Dogmatische Theologie*, V, 256; F. P. Kaulen, *Der biblische Schöpfungsbericht* (Freiburg i.B.: Herder, 1902); P. Mannens, *Theologiae Dogmaticae Institutiones*, II, 233; F. Bettex, in various works; A. Gnandt, *Der mosaische Schöpfungsbericht in seinem Verhältnis zur modernen Wissenschaft* (Graz, 1906); G. F. Wright, *Wetensch. Bijdragen*, 332ff. [*Scientific Confirmations*].

68. E.g., O. Zöckler, *Beweis des Glaubens* (1900): 32–39 and art. "Schöpfung" in PRE³; Bachmann, "Der Schöpfungsbericht und die Inspiration," *Neue Kirchliche Zeitschrift* (May 1906): 383–405, Cf. also *Neue Kirchliche Zeitschrift* (October 1907): 743–762; Urdritz, *Neue Kirchliche Zeitschrift* (October 1899): 837–52; Schmid, *Das Naturwiss. Glaubens.*, 26ff. [*The Scientific Creed*]; J. Reinke, *Die Welt als That: Umrisse Einer Weltansicht auf Naturwissenschaftlicher Grundlage*, 4 vols. (Berlin: Gebruder Paetel, 1905), 481ff.; C. Holzhey, *Schöpfung, Bibel und Inspiration* (Mergentheim: Carl Ohlinger, 1902); F. Hümmelauer, *Nochmals der bibischen. Schöpfungsbegriff;* M. Gander, *Naturwissenschaft und Glaube* (New York: Benziger Bros., 1905): 117.

a possible, not as an undoubted, interpretation,[69] was usually discussed by theologians with appreciation but nevertheless quite generally rejected because it seemed to do violence to the text of Holy Scripture. And this is even much more the case with respect to the visionary and mythical theory. Granted: revelation can exploit all kinds and genres of literature, even the fable;[70] but whether a given section of Holy Scripture contains a poetic description, a parable, or a fable, is not for us to determine arbitrarily but must be clear from the text itself. The first chapter of Genesis, however, hardly contains any ground for the opinion that we are dealing here with a vision or myth. It clearly bears a historical character and forms the introduction to a book which presents itself from beginning to end as history. Nor is it possible to separate the facts (the religious content) from the manner in which they are expressed. For if with Lagrange, for example, the creation itself is regarded as a fact but the days of creation as form and mode of expression, then the entire order in which the creation came into being collapses and we have removed the foundation for the institution of the week and the Sabbath which, according to Exodus 20:11, is most decidedly grounded in the six-day period of creation and the subsequent Sabbath of God.

So, although for the above reasons the days of Genesis 1 are to be considered days and not to be identified with the periods of geology, they nevertheless—like the work of creation as a whole—have an extraordinary character. This is evident from the following. In the first place, it will not do, as already stated earlier, to pack the "first creation" (Gen. 1:1) and the unformed state of the earth (Gen. 1:2) into the first day. For the first evening (Gen. 1:5), which does not coincide with the darkness of Genesis 1:2, began and could only begin after the light was created and had shone for a time. Hence the first day began with the creation of light; after it had shone for a time, evening fell and the morning came. At that point the first day was over: Genesis calculates the day from morning to morning. In the second place, the first triduum of the "second creation" is formed and calculated in the biblical story in a way that differs from the second triduum. The essence of a day and night does not consist in their duration (shorter or longer) but in the alternation of light and darkness, as Genesis 1:4 and 5a clearly teaches. In the case of the first triduum this alternation was not effected by the sun, which only made its appearance on the fourth day, but came about in a different way: by the emission and contraction of the light created in verse 3. If this is the case, the first three days, however much they

69. Augustine, *The Literal Meaning of Genesis*, IV, 28.
70. Cf. H. Bavinck, *Gereformeerde Dogmatiek*, I, 418–20.

may resemble our days, also differ significantly from them and hence were extraordinary cosmic days. In the third place, it is not impossible that the second triduum still shared in this extraordinary character as well. For while it is true that the sun and the moon and the stars were created on the fourth day, and it is conceivable therefore that the second triduum was determined by the rotation of the earth in relation to the sun, it does not follow from the formation of the sun, the moon, and the stars on the fourth day that astronomical and terrestrial relations were the same then as they are now. Scripture itself shows us that as a result of the fall and the flood cataclysmic changes occurred, not only in the human and animal world, but also in the earth and its atmosphere;[71] and the period of creation in the nature of the case existed in very different circumstances from those which prevailed after the completion of creation. In the fourth place, it is very difficult for us to find room on the sixth day for everything Genesis 1–2 has occur in it if that day was in all respects like our days. For occurring on that day are the creation of the animals (Gen. 1:24, 25), the formation of Adam (Gen. 1:26; 2:7), the planting of the garden (Gen. 2:8–14), the announcement of the probationary command (Gen. 2:16, 17), the conducting of the animals to and their naming by Adam (Gen. 2:18–20), Adam's deep sleep and the creation of Eve (Gen. 2:21–23).

Now, it may be possible for all these things to have taken place within the span of a few hours, but it is not likely. In the fifth place, much more took place on each day of creation than the sober words of Genesis would lead us to suspect. The creation was a series of awesome miracles that the biblical story, which is both sublime and simple, portrays to us each time with a single brushstroke without giving details. Just as in the decalogue one single sin represents many other sins, so in the creation story of each day only the most prominent item is featured: that which was most important and necessary for man as lord of the earth and image of God. Natural science, accordingly, reveals to us all sorts of creatures about which nothing is said in Genesis. A wide assortment of components of celestial bodies, numerous minerals, plants, and animal species are left unreported in Genesis. They must have been created, however, and taken their place among the works of creation of the six days. Each day's work of creation must certainly have been much grander and more richly textured than Genesis summarily reports in its sublime narrative. For all these reasons, "day," in the first chapter of the Bible, denotes the time in which God was at work creating. With every morning he brought into being a new world; evening began when he

71. Cf. A. Kuyper, *De Gemeene Gratie in Wetenschap en Kunst* (Amsterdam: Höveker & Wormser, 1905), I, 10ff., 84ff.

finished it. The creation days are the workdays of God. By a labor, resumed and renewed six times, he prepared the whole earth and transformed the chaos into a cosmos. In the Sabbath command this pattern is prescribed to us as well. As they did for God, so for man too six days of labor are followed by a day of rest. In Israel the divisions of the liturgical calendar were all based on that time of creation. And for the whole world it remains a symbol of the eons of this dispensation that will some day culminate in eternal rest, the cosmic Sabbath (Heb. 4).

Facts and Interpretations

Now that we have basically come to know the content of the biblical creation story it is of some importance to also focus our minds for a moment on the facts and phenomena that have been brought to light by geological research. No one has any objection, no one *can* have any objection, to the facts advanced by geology.[72] These facts are just as much words of God as the content of Holy Scripture and must therefore be believingly accepted by everyone. But these facts must be rigorously distinguished from the exegesis of these facts that geologists present. The phenomena that the earth exhibits are one thing; the combinations, hypotheses, and conclusions that the students of earth science connect with these phenomena are quite another. Regardless now of the absolutely nonimaginary possibility that also the observation, identification, and description of the geological facts and phenomena are sometimes decidedly colored by an a priori worldview, contemporary geology agrees that the earth's crust is composed of different layers, all of which clearly show the marks of having been deposited in water; that these layers, wherever and in as far as they are present, always occur in a certain order, so that, say, a lower formation never occurs in between higher ones; and, finally, that these earth layers contain a large mass of fossils which again are not indiscriminately scattered throughout all the layers but occur in the lower sediments to the degree that they are lower in kind. These are the facts, and on that basis geologists have constructed all those protracted geological periods we listed earlier.

But very serious objections exist precisely to these long periods. In the first place, the fact that geology is a young science deserves consideration. It is not yet a hundred years old. In the first half of its existence, in the case of men like von Buch, de Saussure, and so forth, it was absolutely not hostile to Scripture. It was only when Lyell and others harnessed it to the doctrine of evolution that it became a weapon in the war

72. So already Augustine, *The Literal Meaning of Genesis*, I, 21.

against the biblical creation story. This consideration alone tells us to be cautious; as geological science becomes older and richer, it will probably review itself on this point.

Second, one can call geology the archaeology of the earth. It acquaints us with the conditions in which the earth existed in earlier times. But, of course, it tells us virtually nothing about the cause, the origin, the duration, and so forth, of these conditions. The wish to reconstruct the history of the earth from the phenomena of the earth seems a priori as precarious an undertaking as the wish to compose the history of a people from its archaeological artifacts. As an auxiliary science archaeology can be very useful, but it cannot replace history. Geology offers important data, but in the nature of the case it can never produce a history of creation. Anyone attempting to write such a history must continually resort to conjectures. All birth, said Schelling, is from darkness into light. All origins are wrapped in obscurity. If no one tells us who our parents and grandparents are or were, we do not know it. Absent a creation story, the history of the earth is and remains unknown to us.

Third, geology, therefore, can never rise to the level of the creation story; it operates on the foundation of what has been created and does not come near to the level of Genesis 1. It can identify what it observes but only conjecture about its origins. The geologist Ritter von Holger very correctly and beautifully observes: "We have to contend with the unpleasant fact that we arrived at the theater only after the curtain had already fallen. We must attempt to guess the play that was presented from the decorations, set pieces, weapons, and so forth, that have been left behind on the stage (they are the paleontological discoveries or fossilizations); hence it is entirely excusable if we make mistakes."[73]

Fourth, although the earth layers, wherever and insofar as they occur in a given location, are situated in a certain order, it is equally true that they nowhere occur all together and completely, since some are found in one place and others elsewhere. "We nowhere possess a complete copy of the book of the earth; what we have, scattered over the face of it, is a huge mass of defective copies of the most diverse size and format and on very different materials."[74] The series and order of the earth layers and hence also of the geological periods based on them are therefore not immediately conveyed to us by the facts, but they rest on a combination of facts which is open to all sorts of conjectures and errors. As

73. In A. Trissl, *Das Biblische Sechstagewerk vom Standpunkle der Katholischen Exegese und vom Standpunkte der Naturwissenschaften,* 2nd ed. (Regensburg: G. J. Manz, 1894), 73.
74. F. Pfaff, *Schöpfungsgeschichte,* 5.

the geologists themselves acknowledge, it takes a lot of patience and painstaking effort to establish the true order of the earth layers.[75]

Fifth, only a very small part of the earth's surface has so far been investigated, notably England, Germany, and France. Very little is known about the other parts of Europe, virtually nothing about the greatest percentage of Asia, Africa, and Australia, and so on. Even Haeckel admits that barely a thousandth part of the earth's surface has been paleontologically examined.[76] And this estimate is certainly not too low. Hence later investigations may still bring to light an assortment of other facts. In any case, the hypotheses and conclusions of geology have been constructed on too slim a factual foundation.

Sixth, it is a fact, one that is increasingly acknowledged from the side of geology itself, that the time of the formation of the earth layers can absolutely not be determined from the nature and quality of those layers. "The composition of the layers," writes Pfaff[77] "usually does not yield any clue on which to base a conclusion concerning the time of its formation." Under the influence of Darwinism, which has sought to explain everything in terms of infinitely small changes over infinitely long timespans, scientists have spoken of millions of years. But those are not more than mythological figures that lack all basis in fact.[78] Geologists absolutely do not know whether in earlier time the same, or different, circumstances prevailed. And even when circumstances are identical, everything grows much more rapidly and vigorously in youth than in later years. Furthermore, all the grounds on which geologists have so far based their figures have proved untenable. The delta formations, the risings and fallings of the landmasses, the coal formations, and so forth, have all again been abandoned as a base for calculation. Level-headed natural scientists, accordingly, speak a very different language today. "We lack any precise standard for the calculation of prehistoric events or processes."[79]

75. A. S. Geikie, *Geology* (New York: D. Appleton, 1880), 74–82; F. Pfaff, *Schöpfungsgeschichte*, 5.

76. Haeckel, *Naturliche Schöpfungsgeschichte*, 355.

77. Pfaff, *Schöpfungsgeschichte*, 5.

78. Cf. already F. W. J. Schelling, *Werke*, II, 1, 229.

79. A. Zittel, *Aus der Urzeit: Bilder aus der Schöpfungsgeschichte* (München: R. Oldenburg, 1875), 556. Also Sir G. H. Darwin, in the lecture cited above, said that we can neither use the nebular nor the meteorite hypothesis to estimate the time needed for the development of the solar system. He does believe that geologists with their calculations suggesting a time between 50 million and a billion years are closer to the truth than the physicists with their shorter time (as a rule) of about 20 million years. But, he continues, in recent times a new element has been added: radioactivity. A small percentage of radium in the sun would be sufficient to explain its present radiation. This branch of science is still young but we can learn from it how dangerous it is to decide from our lofty positions what is possible and what is not. The duration of the geological periods remains unknown to us (*Wetenschappelijke Bladen* [June 1906]: 425ff.).

Seventh, even the order in which the earth layers occur cannot be a standard for calculating the time and duration of their formation. Naturally, at a given place the lowest layer is older than the top layer, but all warrant is missing for combining the different earth layers of different places and thus forming a patterned series of formations and periods. "Just as in our lakes limestone deposits build up at certain locations today while at the same time, in other locations, layers of sand or clay are deposited, so also in earlier times differing layers simultaneously built up at different locations, and similar layers at different times."[80] The layers dating back to so-called different periods are not consistently different and those which are held to be equally old are not always qualitatively identical.[81] In the same time period, in different parts of the earth, similar formations may have occurred, as it still frequently happens today.

Eighth, the time of the formation of earth layers and the order of their position, therefore, is almost exclusively determined in terms of the fossils found in them. Geology has become dependent on paleontology and the latter is almost completely captive to the theory of evolution today. It is a priori assumed as a proven fact that organic beings have developed from the lower to the higher; and on this basis, then, the order and duration of sediment formations is determined. Conversely, scientists then use the order of the sedimentations as proof for the theory of evolution, thus following a vicious circle. The truth is that paleontology tends to contradict rather than to favor the theory of evolution, inasmuch as in the different layers different fossils of plants and animals occur, not just a few specimens and species, but large numbers. At each layer geology is all at once confronted by an incalculably rich realm of organic life, differentiated in kinds but not augmented by transitional forms. Fossils of plants and animals are found which have since become extinct, surpass all later formations in size and strength, and as it were reveal nature in its primal creative power and luxuriant fecundity.[82]

Ninth, now it is true that the fossils are not scattered indiscriminately over all layers and that in certain layers usually also fossils of cer-

80. F. Pfaff, *Schöpfungsgeschichte*, 5.
81. A. Trissl, *Das Biblische Sechstagewerk*, 61.
82. F. Pfaff, *Schöpfungsgeschichte*, 667–709. According to *Glauben und Wissen* (March 1906): 104–5, G. H. Darwin in his South African lecture also stated the following: "We can compare the facts on which theories of evolution are based with a mixed and colorful heap of glass beads from which an astute person in search of truth picks out a few which he than arranges on a string, incidentally noticing that these beads look somewhat alike . . . but the problem of introducing order in that pile of beads will probably always put the astuteness of the researcher to shame. . . . the immeasurable magnitude of the undiscovered will be forever there to humble the pride of humans."

tain plants and animals occur. But from this state of affairs, too, nothing can be inferred with certainty, either for the theory of evolution or for the geological periods. The different plant and animal species, after all, were and are distributed over the earth's surface in accordance with their nature and the corresponding conditions of life. They lived in different places and zones and therefore also had to petrify in the different sediments that were formed in various places. Accordingly, the fossils are not the representatives of the time in which these organic beings originated but of the higher or deeper zones in which they lived. Suppose that plants and animals now living throughout the world were suddenly buried in earth layers and had petrified. In that case no decision could be made with respect to the time of their origin either from the various kinds of fossils which emerged or from the different layers in which they occurred. Add to this the factors which make the division and dating of the geological periods virtually impossible. Examples are that in the earliest times the different species of plants and animals were not so widely distributed over the earth as they were later; that of any number of plants and animals no fossils have been preserved in the various layers; that a wide range of causes may have brought certain plants and animals into places and zones in which they were not indigenous; that the same earth layers, indeed as a rule but far from always, contained the same species of fossils, and that therefore earth layers which are qualitatively the same and were at one time placed in the same period were later identified as belonging to another period because new and different fossils were found in them.

Finally, geologists themselves frequently admit that the geological periods cannot be clearly distinguished. This is especially evident in the case of the Tertiary and Quaternary periods. Here virtually everything is still uncertain. Uncertainty applies to the boundaries, the beginning and the end, of those two periods as well as to the cause, extent, and duration of the so-called Ice Age. There is disagreement over whether we must assume one or more Ice Ages. Even the occurrence of any Ice Age at all is still subject to serious doubt. There is uncertainty about the cause by which as well as the time and manner in which the large prehistoric animals perished, animals whose fossils have in some cases been preserved fully intact. There is uncertainty about the debut of man, before or after the Ice Age, in the Tertiary or Quaternary period, simultaneously with or after the mammoth, the mastodon, and rhinoceros. Uncertainty applies to the cause of the diluvial formations and their distribution over the globe. Scientists are uncertain about the cause and the time of the formation of mountains and glaciers. In this connection the fact that the displacement of glaciers from the north to the center of Europe would require a height of

44,000 meters for the mountains of Scandinavia yields a virtually insurmountable objection.

The Flood Factor

Added to all this, finally, is the fact that Scripture and the unanimous tradition of virtually all peoples recount the story of a cataclysmic flood which brought about immense changes in the entire state of the earth. According to Scripture, a whole new state of affairs for humanity and the earth set in after the flood. Before the flood, humankind was distinguished by great intellect, a vigorous enterprising spirit, titanic courage, greatly extended life expectancy, strong physiques, and appalling wickedness. And undoubtedly nature, the plant-and-animal kingdom, was in accord with that humanity. But in the flood almost all people perished, numerous plant and animal species became extinct, nature was curbed, and a gentler dispensation was inaugurated, the one in which we live. These testimonies of Scripture are currently being confirmed from every direction by geology. No human remains have as yet been found from the Tertiary period; and it is not likely that such remains will ever be found. Before the flood humanity was probably not yet spread out over the earth. The flood itself explains why no fossils remain of humans before that time. Human skulls and bones found here and there all originated in the Quaternary period and do not differ from our own. Geology further teaches clearly that humans were contemporaneous with the mammoths, the Hebrew "behemoth" (Job 40:10), and that the mammoths therefore belong in historic time. The universality of the diluvial formations proves that the flood must have been extended over the whole earth. Mountains, in large part, originated in historic time. The causes of the Ice Age, if it ever existed, are totally unknown and may therefore very well be traced to the flood and the subsequent lowering of the temperature. It is only by and after the diluvium that the earth acquired its present form.[83] There is actually only one serious objection to the identification of the diluvium with the flood, and that is time. Geology usually places the Ice Age and the diluvium several thousands of years before Christ. But against this objection it may be remarked, on the one hand, that the chronology of Scripture has as yet by no means been established either. One need not go as far as de Sacy, who wrote "there is no biblical chronology," to still argue with Voetius who stated: "No exact computation can be derived from Holy Scripture."[84] It cannot be ruled out that at times some generations

---

83. For the literature on the flood, cf. notes 37–53, above.
84. G. Voetius, *Select. Disp*, V, 153; cf. p. 113, n. 33 above.

have been skipped and that personal names are intended as the collective names of peoples. And, on the other hand, as we said above, the calculations of geology are also much too uncertain to derive from them a solid objection against the view stated above.

If we now summarize the above and take everything into account, we can say that from the moment of creation in Genesis 1:1 to the flood, Scripture offers a time span that can readily accommodate all the facts and phenomena that geology and paleontology have brought to light in this century. It is hard to see why they could not all be placed in that time frame. This is all theology has to do at this point. It does not have to involve itself in the issue of what has caused these phenomena. Let geology explain the facts! But, in that connection, Scripture can perhaps render more service than the natural sciences usually suspect. It does, after all, point out that the creation is a divine work *par excellence*. In the origination and formation of things forces have been at work, up until the flood conditions have existed, and in that flood a catastrophe has occurred, such as has never been seen since. The genesis of things is always controlled by other laws than their subsequent development. The laws issued by the creature are not the rule of creation, still less that of the Creator. Further, theology will be well advised to stick only to the indisputable facts that geology has uncovered, and to be on its guard against the hypotheses and conclusions that geology has added to the mix. For that reason theology should refrain from making any attempt to equate the so-called geological periods with the six creation days. It is no more than an undemonstrable opinion, after all, that these periods has unfolded successively and in that order. This is not to deny that, say, the Azoic formations began to occur already from the moment of creation. Everything rather points to the thesis that, in response to the operation of all kinds of mechanical and chemical forces, these formations then began to occur. But geology can in no way know whether these formations did not occur also later in conjunction with Paleozoic, and so on, formations and only guesses about the causes and manner of their origination. The same is true of all the other periods. It is very probable that the so-called Tertiary period extends to the flood and that diluvium and Ice Age coincide with this catastrophe. Further, nothing is settled in the so-called Paleozoic period by the simultaneous occurrence of plant and animal fossils with respect to the order in which these species originated. For geology does not know the first thing about the origination of these organic beings; it finds them but cannot penetrate the mystery of their origin. And it too must assume that the plant kingdom originated before the animal kingdom, for the simple reason that animals live from plants. In so far as geology can say a word about the origin of things it is in perfect agreement with Scripture. First there was the inorganic creation; then came the organic creation, beginning with the plant kingdom; next followed the animal kingdom, and this again in the same order, first the aquatic, then the land animals, and among them especially the mammals.[85]

So as Christians and as theologians we await with some confidence the *certain* results of the natural sciences. Theology has nothing to fear from thorough, multifaceted research. It only needs to be on its guard against attaching too much value to a study that is still completely new, imprecise, and incomplete, and is therefore constantly being augmented with conjectures and suspicions. It needs to be on its guard against making premature concessions to, and to seek agreement with, the so-called scientific results which can at any time be knocked down and exposed in their untenability by more thorough research. As the science of divine and eternal things, theology must be patient until the science that contradicts it has made a deeper and broader study of its field and, as happens in most cases, corrects itself. In that manner theology upholds its dignity and honor more effectively than by constantly yielding and adapting itself to the opinions of the day.[86]

85. F. Pfaff, *Schöpfungsgeschichte*, 742; G. F. Wright, *Wetensch. Bijdragen*, 304ff. enz. [*Scientific Confirmations*].

86. Cf. Howorth, *The Mammoth and the Flood;* idem, *The Glacial Nightmare and the Flood* (London: S. Low, Marson, 1893).

II
The Image of God

Human Origins 4

Humanity, where the spiritual and material world are joined together, is the crowning culmination of creation. This is affirmed by the two creation accounts in Genesis 1 and 2. Of the many alternative conjectures about human origins that have been ventured outside of scriptural revelation, the hypothesis of Darwinian evolutionism through natural selection is dominant in the contemporary world. The Christian objection is not to the idea of development as such, which goes back to Greek philosophy, but to the naturalism and materialism of the Darwinian hypothesis. This theory has been seriously opposed, not only by Bible-believers but also by natural scientists and philosophers more broadly. As naturalism and materialism demonstrated its spiritual bankruptcy, a new mystical and even pantheistic spirituality attracted many, further discrediting Darwinism. The arguments against Darwinism in general are weighty, with the problem of human origins and transitions from one species to another particularly insoluble. The theory of evolution also clashes with Scripture in regard to the age, the unity, and the original abode of humanity. Above all, it is essential to maintain the fundamental unity of the human race; this conviction is the presupposition of religion and morality. The solidarity of the human race, original sin, the atonement in Christ, the universality of the kingdom of God, the catholicity of the church, and the love of neighbor are all grounded in it.

Creation culminates in humanity where the spiritual and material world are joined together. According to the creation story in Genesis 1, "man," the man and the woman, was created on the sixth day (Gen. 1:26f.), following the creation of the land animals. By this arrangement Scripture, too, teaches the existence of close kinship between man and animal. Both were created on the same day; both were formed from the dust of the earth. But along with this kinship there is also a big difference. At God's command the animals were brought forth by the earth (Gen. 1:24); man, however, was created, after divine deliberation, in the image of God, to be master over all things. These brief descriptions are clarified and expanded in the second chapter of

Genesis.[1] The first chapter offers a general history of creation which has its goal and end in humanity, while the second deals especially with the human creation and with the relation in which other creatures stand to man. In the first report, man is the end of nature; in the second, man is the beginning of history. The first account shows how all other creatures prepare the advent of humanity; the second introduces the history of the temptation and the fall and to that end describes especially the human original state. In the first chapter, therefore, the story of the creation of all other things (heaven, earth, firmament, etc.) is told at some length and in a regular order, but the creation of humanity is reported succinctly; the second chapter presupposes the creation of heaven and earth, follows no chronological but only a topical order, and does not say when the plants and animals are created but only describes the relation in which they basically stand to human beings. Genesis 2:4b–9 does not imply that the plants were formed after human creation, but only that the garden of Eden was planted after that event. The author undoubtedly thought of the creation of plants as occurring between verses 6 and 7. Similarly in Genesis 2:18f., though the creation of animals is in fact recounted after that of man, the idea is not thereby to describe the objective course of creational events but only to show that a helper for man was not to be found among the animals but only in a being like himself. The account of the creation of the woman, finally, is by no means in conflict with that in Genesis 1 but only a further explication of it.[2]

Creation and Evolution: Darwinism

This divine origin of man has never been questioned in the Christian church and in Christian theology. But outside special revelation all

1. According to some exegetes, the so-called second creation story begins at Gen. 2:4; according to others, at Gen. 2:4b; and according to still others at Gen. 2:5. H. Gunkel inclines to the view that Gen. 2:4a originally preceded Gen. 1:1 (H. Gunkel, *Genesis*, trans. by Mark E. Biddle [Macon, Ga.: Mercer University Press, 1997], 103); V. Zapletal (*Der Schöpfungsbericht der Genesis* [Regensburg: G. J. Manz, 1911]) considers Gen. 2:4 an interpolation. In the opinion of many scholars, Gen. 2:4b cannot be a postscript to the preceding story since *toledoth* refers not to the origin, but to the ancestry and procreation of creatures; and according to others it cannot be the title of the following story inasmuch as the Yahwist never uses this formula. Still, Gen. 2:4b is probably intended as a transition to and title of the following in the sense that what follows contains the developmental history of heaven and earth, specifically that of the earth, for in v. 4b it is mentioned before heaven.

2. Cf. E. W. Hengstenberg, *Authenthie des Pentateuchs* in *Beiträge zur Einleitung in Alte Testament*, 2 vols. (Berlin: Oehmigke, 1836–39), I, 306ff. *Ed. note:* English trans. by J. E. Ryland, 2 vols. *Dissertations on the Genuineness of the Pentateuch* (Edinburgh: John D. Lowe, 1847); G. F. Oehler, *Theology of the Old Testament*, trans. by Ellen D. Smith and Sophia Taylor (Edinburgh: T. & T. Clark, 1892–93) §18; *Köhler, *Lehrbuch d. Bibl. Gesch. d. A. T.*, I, 24; Chr. E. Baumstark, *Christliche Apologetiek*, II (Frankfurt a.m., 1872), 458ff.; H. van Eyck van Heslinga, *De Eenheid van het Scheppingsverhaal* (Leiden, 1896).

sorts of conjectures have been ventured with respect to human origins. Many pagan sagas attribute human creation to the gods or the demi-gods.[3] Philosophy also, especially that of Socrates, Plato, and Aristotle, usually recognized, in its assessment of man as a being made from the dust of the earth, a rational principle that derived from the gods. In both religion and philosophy, however, very different ideas about man's origin have frequently been entertained as well. Sometimes man is viewed as having emerged autochthonously from the earth; then again as having evolved from some other animal, or as the fruit of some tree, and so forth[4] The idea of development or evolution, accordingly, is not a product of modernity but occurred already among the Greek philosophers. We find it among the Ionian philosophers of nature, especially in Anaximenes, elaborated in a pantheistic sense by Heraclitus, and presented in materialistic form by the Atomists. Aristotle, too, incorporated it in his system but attributed an organic and teleological character to it: in the way of development potentiality turns into actuality. From the Christian position there is not the least objection to the notion of evolution or development as conceived by Aristotle; on the contrary, it is creation alone which makes such evolution possible.[5] But in the eighteenth century evolution was torn from its basis in theism and creation and made serviceable to a pantheistic or materialistic system. Some French Encyclopedists attempted to explain humanity completely—also psychologically—in terms of matter. Bodin, Hobbes, Montesquieu, Rousseau, Voltaire, Kant, Schiller, Goethe, and Hegel all promoted this trend insofar as they reversed the order generally accepted earlier and thought of humanity as starting in an animal state. Nevertheless man was still viewed as being in a class by himself, produced, not by a gradual evolution from an animal, but by the creative omnipotence of nature. Evolution was still conceived as organic and teleological. But step by step this evolutionary theory was so refashioned that it led to the descent of humanity from animal ancestry. Lamarck (1744–1829), Saint Hilaire (1772–1844), Oken (1779–1851), Von Baer (1836), H. Spencer (1852), Schaafhausen (1855), Huxley (1859), Nägeli (1859) had already taken this position before the appearance on the world stage of Charles Darwin. It was his claim to fame, however, that he made an enormous number of observations which related to the life of humanity and animals and brought to light the kinship between

3. Hesiod, *Works and Days*, I, 23–25; Ovid, *Metamorphoses*, I, 82ff., 363ff.

4. Cf. A. Lang, *Onderzoek naar de Ontwikkeling van Godsdienst, Kultus en Mythologie*, I, trans. by L. Knappert (Haarlem: F. Bohn, 1893), 143, 275.

5. Cf. M. Heinze, "Evolutionismus," *PRE*[3], V, 672–81; and H. Bavinck, "Creation or Development," *The Methodist Review* 60 (1901): 849–74; idem, "Evolutie," in *Pro en Contra* (Baarn: Hollandia, 1907).

them. He managed to combine them in an unusual way and to make them serviceable to a hypothesis that was already dominant, and showed a way in which human descent from animal ancestors seemed to have been made possible.[6] A legion of scholars including Lyell, Owen, Lubbock, Tylor, Hooker, Tyndall, Huxley, Moleschott, Haeckel, Hellwald, Büchner, Vogt, Bölsche, and others believed that the earlier hypothesis was virtually proven by Darwin's research, and passed it off as the incontrovertible result of natural science.[7]

Now then, by Darwinism we must understand the theory that the species in which organic entities used to be divided possess no constant properties but are mutable; that the higher organic beings have evolved from the lower and that man in particular has gradually evolved, in the course of centuries, from an extinct genus of ape; that the organic, in turn, emerged from the inorganic, and that evolution is therefore the way in which, under the sway of purely mechanical and chemical laws, the present world has come into being. That's the thesis, or rather, the hypothesis. Darwin tries to render this theory of evolution plausible by the following considerations: first, nature everywhere evinces a struggle for life in which every being participates, and by which it is forced to develop and to perfect itself or else to perish; second, from countless plants, animals, and people nature selects those for survival and reproduction ("natural selection") which are best organized; this natural selection is reinforced by sexual selection, a process in which every female gives preference to the best-organized male; third, the favorable properties acquired in the way of struggle and selection pass from parents to children or even to grandchildren (atavism) and by incremental mutations increasingly perfect the organism. These are not proofs, of course, but assumptions and interpretations of how, according to Darwin, evolution is possible. Proofs for the hypothesis are actually derived exclusively from the kinship which can be observed between organic entities and which, both physically and psychologically, exist also between animal and man; from the mutation and transmission of properties which we observe over and over in the world of humans and animals; from the rudimentary organs which remain in humans from their earlier animal state; from embryology, according to which the higher organisms recapitulate, as embryos, the degrees of development of the lower organisms; from paleontology, which studies fossilized bones

6. C. Darwin, *On the Origin of Species by Means of Natural Selection* (London: J. Murray, 1859); idem, *The Descent of Man* (New York: D. Appleton, 1871).

7. E. Haeckel, for example, writes: "The monophyletic or single-stock origin of the entire class of mammals is therefore now considered a firmly established fact by all well-formed scholars in the field" (*Der Kampf um den Entwickelungs-Gedanken* [Berlin: G. Reimer, 1905], 56, 70).

and skulls and seeks to infer from them the big difference between the earlier and present-day humans; from mimicry according to which some animals assume the form, the build, or the color of some other object in nature in order thereby to protect themselves from their enemies; from the blood relationship which according to transfusion tests, especially those of H. Friedenthal, is alleged to have existed between humans and the higher apes.[8]

Now then, with however much authority this theory of descent has suddenly come upon us, from the beginning it encountered very serious contradiction, not only among theologians and philosophers,[9] but also among natural scientists;[10] and that contradiction, so far from having been muted over the years, has made itself heard with increasing volume and vigor. At almost every annual conference of natural scientists, Virchov repeated his protest against those who passed off Darwinism as

8. G. J. Romanes, *The Scientific Evidences of Organic Evolution* (London: Macmillan, 1882). On the mimicry, cf. C. Gutberlet, *Der Mensch* (Paderborn: Schöningh, 1903), 106ff. On the blood-relation of man and ape, see E. Wasmann, *Biology and the Theory of Evolution*, trans. by A. M. Buchanan, 3rd ed. (St. Louis: B. Herder, 1923) 456–61; E. Dennert, *Die Weltanschauung des modernen Naturforschers* (Stuttgart: M. Rielmann, 1907), 21ff.

9. In addition to the titles by the following, listed in the bibliography—H. Lüken, J. S. Nikel, H. Lotze, A. R. Gordon, B. Platz, O. Zöckler, Pressensé, J. Buibert, C. Hodge, D. Gath, Whitley, J. Orr, Geesink—also see the Genesis commentaries of F. Delitzsch, H. Gunkel, et al.; cf. H. Ulrici, *Gott und die Natur* (Leipzig: T. O. Weigel, 1862); idem, *Gott und der Mensch* (Leipzig: T. O. Weigel, 1874); ed. von Hartmann, *Wahrheit und Irrthum im Darwinismus* (Berlin: C. Duncker, 1875) reprinted in *Philos. des Unbew.* 11th ed., III (1904); B. Carneri, *Sittlichkeit und Darwinismus* (Wien: W. Braumüller, 1903); G. P. Weygoldt, *Darwinismus, Religion, Sittlichkeit* (Leiden: E. J. Brill, 1878); E. G. Steude, *Christentum und Naturwissenschaft* (Gütersloh: C. Bertelsmann, 1895), 148ff. (*Ed. note:* cf. E. Gustav Steude, *Der Beweis für die Wahrheit des Christentums* [Gütersloh: C. Bertelsmann, 1899]); T. Pesch, *Die Grossen Welträthsel*, 2 vols., 2nd ed. (Freiburg i.B.: Herder, 1892), II, 147–71ff.; F. H. Reusch, *Nature and the Bible: Lectures on the Mosaic History of Creation in Its Relation to Natural Science*, trans. by Kathleen Lyttelton, vol. II, 4th ed. (Edinburgh: T. & T. Clark: 1886) 32–120; R. Otto, *Naturalistische und Religiose Weltansicht* (Tübingen: H. Laupp, 1905) enz.

10. L. Agassiz, *Essay on Classification*, ed. by Edward Lurie (Cambridge: Belknap Press of Harvard University Press, 1962); J. W. Dawson, *Nature and the Bible* (New York: Wilbur B. Ketcham, 1875); Dana (cf. F. Wright, *Wetenschappelijke Bijdragen tot Bevestiging der Oud-Testamentische Geschiedenis*, enz. 306 [*Scientific Confirmations of Old Testament History* (Oberlin: O. Bibliotheca Sacra, 1906)]); C. Nägeli, *Entstehung und Begriff der Naturhistorischen* (Müchen: Köningliche Akademie, 1865); C. Nägeli, *A Mechanico-physiological Theory of Organic Evolution* (Chicago: Open Court, 1898); A. Wigand, *Der Darwinismus und die Naturforschung Newtons und Cuviers*, 3 vols. (Braunschweig: F. Vieweg und Sohn, 1874–77); J. Ranke, *Der Mensch*, 2nd ed. (Leipzig: Bibliographisches Institut, 1894); *G. Beck, *Der Urmensch* (Basel: A. Gaering, 1899); F. Bettex, *Naturstudie en Christendom*, 4th ed. (Kampen: J. H. Kok, 1908); J. Reinke, *Die Welt als That*, 4 vols., 3rd ed. (Berlin: Gebruder Paetel, 1905); J. Reinke, *Die Natur und Wir* (Berlin: Gebruder Paetel, 1908); E. Dennert, *At the Deathbed of Darwinism*, trans. by E. V. O'Harra and John H. Peschges (Burlington, Iowa: German Literary Board, 1904); E. Dennert, *Die Weltanschauung des modernen Naturforschers* (Stuttgart: M. Rielmann, 1907); A. Dippe, *Naturphilosophie* (München: C. H. Beck, O. Beck, 1907); E. Wasmann, *Modern Biology*.

established dogma. Dubois Reymond spoke in 1880 of seven world mysteries that could not be solved by natural science and a few years before his death in December of 1896 wrote: "the only option left, it seems, is to cast oneself into the arms of supernaturalism."[11] In 1890 Renan reconsidered the great expectations which he had cherished for science in his earlier years.[12] In 1895 Brunetière spoke of science's bankruptcy and, though he was not thereby denying its discoveries, attempted to show that it was not the only means by which humanity could improve its lot.[13] Romanes, who was a resolute Darwinist, died in 1895, having reconciled himself with the faith of the Anglican Church.[14] At the end of the nineteenth century the intellectual life of people underwent a remarkable change. Although an array of brilliant results had been achieved in the natural sciences, in culture, and in technology, the human heart had been left unsatisfied, and so people turned from intellectualism to mysticism, from exact science to philosophy, from mechanicism to dynamism, from dead matter to the vital force, from atheism back to pantheism. Materialism, upon continued scrutiny, proved completely untenable. The concept of atom, which was its premise, could not withstand the test of a logical critique. Physics was compelled to abandon the concept of action-at-a-distance and to conceive all of space as being filled with a cosmic ether. The discovery of X-rays led to a heretofore unsuspected divisibility of matter. Monistic thought came to acknowledge that even materialism with its matter and force had not overcome dualism, and philosophical idealism yielded the insight that matter and all of nature are only given us in the form of an idea. All these considerations paved the way for the pantheism of Spinoza or Hegel and exerted such influence that even Haeckel could not escape it, prompting him to elevate his materialistic monism to the level of a new religion.[15]

This change of mood also undermined belief in the truth of Darwinism. In this connection a distinction has to be made, however, between Darwinism in a more restricted sense and Darwinism in a broader sense. Darwinism in a broader sense, that is, the opinion that the higher organisms evolved from the lower organisms and that the human species therefore gradually evolved from animal ancestry, still enjoys as much agreement as it did earlier. Darwinism in the more restricted

    11. Cf. D. Reymond, *Beweis des Glaubens* 31 (February 1895): 77–78.
    12. E. Renan, *L'avenir de la science* (Paris: Calmann-Levy, 1890).
    13. F. Brunetière, *La Science et la Religion* (Paris: Firmin-Didot, 1895).
    14. G. J. Romanes, *Thoughts on Religion*, ed. by Charles Gore, 6th ed. (Chicago: Open Court, 1911).
    15. E. Haeckel, *Der Monismus als Band zwischen Religion und Wissenschaft*, 6th ed. (Leipzig: A. Kroner, 1908); idem, *The Riddle of the Universe at the Close of the Nineteenth Century*, trans. by Joseph McCabe (New York: Harper & Brothers, 1900), 331–46.

sense, that is, the peculiar explanation which Darwin, with his theory of natural selection, offered for the origin of species, fell into disrepute with many people or was even completely abandoned. Nevertheless the Darwinism of the one sense is bound up with the Darwinism of the other. For Darwin himself the truth of his theory of descent depended on the possibility of explaining it;[16] when the explanation attempted proves not to be sound, the theory also begins to totter and sinks to the level of an assumption which has as much or as little right to exist as any other. In fact, then, also the arguments which can be advanced against the theory of human descent are of no less force and weight than those which are directed against Darwin's explanation.

Critique of Darwinism

Those arguments are, in the main, the following: in the first place, until now the theory of descent has proven completely unable to make the origin of life somewhat understandable.[17] Initially scientists resorted to the notion of an "ambiguous generation" *(generatio aequivoca)*, that is, the idea of the origination of organic entities by an accidental combination of inorganic materials. When Pasteur's researches had proved its untenability, they latched onto the assumption that the protoplasms or life germs had been brought to the earth by meteorites from other planets (Helmholtz, Thomson).[18] When this hypothesis too proved to be little more than a brain wave, they announced the theory that the cells and life germs had always existed alongside the inorganic and therefore, like matter, force, and movement, were eternal. But by saying this the proponents of evolutionary theory themselves acknowledged the inadequacy of it: those who make "matter," "movement," and "life" eternal do not solve the riddle but despair of a solution.[19] Many

---

16. Cf. J. Orr, *God's Image in Man and Its Defacement in the Light of Modern Denials* (London: Hodder & Stoughton, 1906), 99.

17. O. Hertwig, *Die Entwicklung der Biologie im neunzehnten Jahrhundert,* 2nd ed. (Jena: G. Fischer, 1908); E. Von Hartmann, "Mechanismus und Vitalismus in der mod. Biologie." *Archiv für Systematische Philosophie* (1903): 139–78, 331–77; R. Otto, "Die mechanist. Lebenstheorie und die Theologie," *Zeitschrift fur Theologie und Kirche* (1903): 179–213; idem, *Naturalistische und religiöse Weltansicht,* 2nd ed. (Tübingen: J. C. B. Mohr [Paul Siebeck], 1909), 145ff.; English trans. by J. Arthur Thomson and Margaret R. Thomson (London: Williams & Norgate; New York: Putnam, 1907); R. P. Mees, *De Mechanische Verklaring der Levensverschijnselen* ('s Gravenhage, 1899); J. Grasset, *Les limites de la biologie* (Paris: Alcan, 1902).

18. Cf. also *Mac Gillavry, *De Continuïteit van het Doode en het Levende in de Natuur* (Leiden, 1898).

19. In an essay ("Geist oder Instinkt," *Neue Kirchliche Zeitschrift* [1907]: 39) Hoppe correctly comments: "Darwinism has ceased to produce an explanation of the theory of evolution; in its place has come the spiritualization of matter and voila! evolution has been rescued."

natural scientists, including Rindfleisch, Bunge, Neumeister, Merkel, and others, have therefore returned to vitalism.

In the second place, Darwinism has also proved incapable of explaining the further development of organic entities. Scripture, on the one hand, recognizes the truth that inheres in evolution when it has plants and animals come forth from the earth at God's command (Gen. 1:11, 20, 24). On the other hand, however, it says that the earth could only bring forth these organic entities by a word of divine omnipotence and that these organic entities existed side by side from the beginning as distinct species, each with its own nature (Gen. 1:11, 21). It cannot be ruled out, therefore, that within the species all sorts of changes could occur, nor has the freedom of science to further define the boundaries of these species been curtailed. It is not even absolutely necessary to view all the species now listed by botany and zoology as original creations. The notion of species is far from being sharply and clearly defined.[20] But it is equally certain that the essential diversity and dissimilarity of creatures is rooted in God's creative omnipotence. It is he who makes the difference between light and darkness, day and night, heaven and earth, plant and animal, angel and human.[21] And in Darwinism this diversity and dissimilarity of creatures, specifically of organic entities, remains a riddle. If humans descended from the animals, precisely the huge difference which exists between them and which is manifest in the entire organism would remain an insoluble riddle. Today it is almost universally recognized that the numerous species of plants and animals cannot be inferred from one single organism or even from four or five original organisms.[22] Both morphologically and physiologically the species are much too divergent. Natural and sexual selection are insufficient to make possible such changes in the species and have accordingly already been significantly limited and modified by Darwin himself.[23]

In addition to this, transitions from one species into another have never been observed, either in the past or in the present. The same species of plants and animals we now know also existed thousands of years ago and appeared suddenly in large numbers. Transitional forms which

20. Cf. E. Wasmann, *Modern Biology*, 296–305, 427–29.
21. T. Aquinas, *Summa Theol.*, I, qu. 47.
22. "There is no evidence at all in support of a monophyletic phylogeny" (E. Wasmann, *Modern Biology*, 291).
23. Darwin's theory that the species originated as a result of minute incremental changes over an endless series of years has yielded, in the work of Hugo de Vries, to the theory of abrupt salutatory mutations. *Species and Varieties; Their Origin by Mutation*, ed. by Daniel Trembly MacDougal, 2nd ed., corrected and rev. (Chicago: Open Court). But in this connection the question whether the resulting new organisms are species or varieties remains unanswered.

would bring now-existing species closer together have nowhere been found. Paleontology does not demonstrate a slow, gradual, rectilinear ascent of organic entities from the lower to the higher but shows that all kinds of species existed side by side from the beginning. But such transitional forms should be available in large numbers because the morphological changes occurred so slowly over thousands of years and were each time only of minute significance. It is inconceivable that all of them were all accidentally destroyed by catastrophes; even more so, because right up to the present all the lower organisms have continued to exist alongside the higher ones despite their imperfection and unfitness for the struggle to survive. Add to this that especially August Weismann, but also others, have on good grounds defended the thesis that precisely the acquired properties are not transmitted by heredity, so that on this subject and on heredity in general there are enormous differences of opinion.[24] Totally contrary to Darwin's theory, morphological properties are the most variable. If morphological changes proceeded at such a slow rate and were each time of so little significance, they would be absolutely of no advantage in the struggle for life. In the time of transition they would be more a handicap than a help. For as long as breathing through gills changed into breathing by lungs, the process was more a hindrance than an advantage in the struggle for existence. For all these reasons the natural scientist, whose science must rest on facts, would do well to refrain from making judgments in this matter. Materialism and Darwinism, [we should note], are both historically and logically the result of philosophy, not of experimental science. Darwin himself, in any case, states that many of the views he presented were highly speculative.[25] According to Haeckel, Darwin did not discover any new facts; what he did was combine and utilize the facts in a unique way.[26] The profound kinship between humans and animals has always been recognized, a fact that comes through in the concept of "rational animal."[27] But in earlier times this fact was not yet combined with the monistic philosophy which says that from a pure potency, which *is* nothing, like such things as atoms, chaos, or cells, everything can nevertheless evolve.

24. O. Hertwig, *Biological Problems of Today: Preformation or Epigenesis?* (New York: Macmillan, 1900); H. H. Kuyper, *Evolutie of Revelatie* (Amsterdam: Höveker & Wormser, 1903).
25. C. Darwin, *The Descent of Man,* 620.
26. E. Haeckel, *Natürliche Schöpfungs-Geschichte* (1874) 25 [9th ed. (Berlin: G. Reimer) 1898].
27. E. Wasmann, *Instinkt und Intelligenz im Thierreich,* 8th ed. (Freiburg i.B.: Herder, 1905); W. M. Wundt, *Vorlesungen über die Menschen- und Thierseele,* 2 vols. (Leipzig: L. Voss, 1863).

In the third place, in Darwinism the origin of humanity is an insoluble problem. Positive proofs of human descent from animal ancestry do not really exist. Haeckel's ontogeny can no longer be considered as proof after the refutation by Bischoff and others.[28] Arguments based on a variety of human bones and skulls found in caves, most recently in the Dutch East Indies, have been abandoned in turn in case after case.[29] Study, on the one hand, of anthropoid species of apes and, on the other, of an assortment of bones, skulls, abnormal humans, microcephalics, dwarves, and so forth, ended in the observation that the difference between animals and humans is essential and has always existed.[30] It is generally recognized, accordingly, that no species of ape, as it exists today or has existed in the past, can be the ancestral stock of the human race.[31] The most ardent defenders of Darwinism admit that some sort of transitional species has to be assumed, a species of which up until now not a trace has been found. At a conference of natural scientists in 1894, Virchov commented: "Until now no ape has as yet been found which can be considered the true ancestor of humans, nor any semi-ape. This question is no longer on the forefront of research."[32]

In the fourth place, Darwinism above all fails to provide an explanation of humanness in terms of its psychic dimension. Darwin began with the attempt to derive all the mental phenomena to be found in humans (consciousness, language, religion, morality, etc.) from phenomena occurring in animals,[33] and many others have followed him in this regard. But up until now these attempts have not been successful either. Like the essence of energy and matter, the origin of movement, the origination of life, and teleology, so also human consciousness, lan-

28. Also cf. O. Hertwig, "Das biogenetische Grundgesetz nach dem heutigen Stande der Biologie," *Internationale Wochenschrift* 1 (1907), n. 2.3.

29. Hubrecht, *Gids*, June 1896. As Virchov did earlier, so Dr. Bumuller of Augsburg, at the congress of anthropologists held in September 1899 at Lindau, asserted that the *Pithecanthropus erectus* of Dubois was a gibbon (in *Beweis des Glaubens* [1900]: 80), cf. E. Wasmann, *Modern Biology*, 465–80.

30. F. Pfaff, *Schöpfungsgeschichte*, 3rd ed. (Heidelberg: C. Winter, 1881), 721; cf. E. Wasmann in *Modern Biology*.

31. E. Haeckel, *Der Kampf um den Entwickelungsgedanken*, 58.

32. In F. Hettinger, *Apologie des Christenthums*, 5 vols., 7th ed. (Freiburg i.B.: Herder, 1895–98), III, 297 (*ed. note:* Selections from Hettinger's *Apologie* were translated into a one-volume edition by Henry Sebastion Bowden, *Natural Religion*, 2nd ed. [London: Burns & Oates, 1892]); J. Reinke, *Die Entwicklung der Naturwissenschaften insbesondere der Biologie im neunzehnten Jahrhundert* (Kiel: Universitäts-Buchhandlung [P. Toeche], 1900), 19, 20, therefore wrote: "We must unreservedly acknowledge that there is not a single completely unobjectionable proof for its (man's animal ancestry) correctness." Also cf. Branco, in E. Wasmann, *Modern Biology*, 407–79, and Wasmann himself, 456–83.

33. Ch. Darwin, *Descent of Man*, chs. 3–4, and *The Expression of Emotions in Man and Animals* (London: John Murray, 1872).

guage, freedom of the will, religion, and morality still belong to the enigmas of the world that await resolution. Ideas, which are entirely mental, relate to the brain in a very different way from the way bile relates to the liver and urine to the kidneys. In the words of Max Müller language is and remains the Rubicon between us and the animal world. The psychological explanation of religion is untenable. And the derivation of morality from human social instincts fails to do justice to the authority of the moral law, to the categorical character of the moral imperative, to the "imperatives" of the good, to conscience, responsibility, the sense of sin, repentance, remorse, and punishment. Indeed, although Darwinism as such is not wholly identical with materialism, it nevertheless tends in that direction, finds there its most significant support, and thus also paves the way for the subversion of religion and morality and the destruction of our humanness. There is no advantage for people to say that it is better to be a highly developed animal than a fallen human. The theory of the animal ancestry of humans violates the image of God in man and degrades the human into an image of the orangutan and chimpanzee. From the standpoint of evolution humanity as the image of God cannot be maintained. The theory of evolution forces us to return to creation as Scripture presents it to us.

The Age of Humanity

In connection with the theory of the origin of man the doctrine of evolution also tends to conflict with Scripture in regard to the age, the unity, and the original abode of the human race. Great age was attributed to the human race by many peoples, including the Japanese, the East Indians, the Babylonians, the Egyptians, the Greeks, and the Romans, who spoke of several world ages and of myriads and hundreds of thousands of years. Modern anthropology has from time to time returned to these fabulous figures but is no more consistent than pagan mythology; it ranges between 10,000 and 500,000 years and more.[34]

In recent years there is a general tendency to observe greater moderation in calculating the age of the earth and humanity. Darwin, of course, demanded an incalculable number of years to allow for the origination of species by minute changes, for if evolution never proceeded faster than it does now, the origin of life and of every type of organism required an extraordinarily long time. When scientists began to compute, consistently with this theory of evolution, how long it would take for the human eye to develop from a tiny spot of pigment and for the

34. A. R. Wallace, for example, speaks of a half million years, according to J. Orr, *God's Image in Man,* 166.

brains of mammals to develop from an original ganglion, they automatically arrived at immensely long times, which had to be multiplied a number of times for the duration of all of life on earth. Some of them, along with Darwin himself in the first edition of his *Origin of Species*, therefore came to a figure of 300 million years for the age of life on earth and the majority used even higher figures.[35]

But gradually physicists and geologists began to register objections to these figures. They themselves began to calculate, attempting in various ways and by various methods to estimate the age of the earth, the ocean, the moon, and the sun. And although they differed among themselves over millions of years, still the time they assumed for that age was generally much shorter than that demanded by biologists. They spoke at most of 80 or 100 million, and sometimes went down as low as 10 or 20 million years. Now if the age of the earth requires no more than a figure between 10 to 100 million years—and, as is clear from this difference, the calculation is again highly uncertain and subject to modification at a moment's notice—[36] it is self-evident that the origin of life and of humanity is again much less remote. On this question, accordingly, there is a wide spread of opinion. Some scientists, such as Bourgeois, Delaunay, de Mortillet, Quatrefages, and others, assume that man already occurs in the Tertiary period. Others, on the other hand, such as Virchov, Mor. Wagner, Oskar Schmidt, Zittel, Cathaillac, John Evans, Joseph Prestwich, Hughes, Branco, Wasmann, Dawson, Haynes, and so forth, are of the opinion that humanity did not make a debut until the Quaternary period.[37] The decision is also difficult because the boundaries between the two periods cannot be clearly drawn and these periods may very well have existed side by side in different regions of the earth. But even if the human species existed in the Tertiary period and man was a contemporary of the mammoth, it does not follow that this establishes the age of humanity; one can equally well infer from this that this period is much more recent than was initially believed. As a matter of fact, in calculating the dates of the Ice Age, scientists have returned to a more modest number. In recent years there is even considerable agreement on this point. Most experts, such as

35. H. de Vries, *Species and Varieties*, 14; F. Wright, *Wetenschappelijke Bijdragen*, 176 [*Scientific Confirmations*]; J. Orr, *God's Image in Man*, 176.
36. J. Orr, *God's Image in Man*, 168.
37. Ibid., 174, 306; J. Guibert, *In the Beginning*, trans. by G. S. Whitmarsh (London: Kegan Paul, Trench, Trubner, 1900), 264–97; Gutberlet, *Der Mensch*, 265ff.; E. Wasmann, *Modern Biology*, 477. According to Wasmann, no traces of tertiary humans have as yet been found and the signs of human activity that are thought to have been found in the Tertiary Period are extremely doubtful. In contrast, there are many diluvial human remains left, all of which prove that at that time man was already a "complete *Homo sapiens*."

G. F. Wright, Salisbury, Winchell, and others, have arrived at the conclusion that the Ice Age in America, and therefore roughly also that in Europe, is no more than eight or ten thousand years behind us.[38] In this connection one must always bear in mind that the calculations based on the pile dwellings found in Switzerland and elsewhere; on bones and skulls that have been encountered in caves near Liège, Amiens, Dusseldorf, and in many other places; on the delta formations of the Nile and Mississippi; on the formation of the falls at Niagara and of St. Anthony near Minneapolis; on the duration of the Stone, Bronze, and Iron Age, and so on—that all these calculations rest on a hypothetical foundation and are far from being absolutely certain. In this connection, even more than in that of the age of the earth, it is the case that though scientists can mention numbers, they do not have the material for a history over so long a period.

Of more value for the determination of the age of the human race are the chronological data that are furnished us by the history and monuments of different peoples. The history of India and China does not provide a firm basis for a chronology, arising as it does only a few centuries before Christ. But the situation is somewhat different with the history of Egypt and Babylonia. Here we undoubtedly have an ancient civilization; it already existed as far as we can go back in history. Scripture itself, too, clearly teaches this. But the chronology is nevertheless still so uncertain that one cannot base much on it. This uncertainty is illustrated by the fact that according to Champollion the rule of the Egyptian king Menes started in 5867 B.C.; according to Boeckh in 5702; according to Unger in 5613; according to Brugsch in 4455; according to Lauth in 4157; according to Lepsius in 3892; according to Bunsen in 3623; according to Edward Meyer in 3180; according to Wilkinson in 2320—a spread of more than 3500 years; and also by the fact that Bunsen has Babylon's historical period begin in 3784, Von Gutschmid in 2447, Brandis in 2458, Oppert in 3540, and so on.[39]

Every student of ancient history has his own chronology. It is a labyrinth without a thread to guide the inquirer. Only in the case of the

---

38. J. Orr, *God's Image in Man*, 306; F. Wright, *Wetenschappelijke Bijdragen*, 201–7 [*Scientific Confirmations*]; Upham, "Die Zeitdauer der geologischen Epochen," *Gaea* 30 (1894): 621ff. cites various scholars who situate the Ice Age approximately seven or eight thousand years before Christ.

39. F. Hettinger, *Apologie des Christenthums*, III, 258ff.; A. Baumgartner, *Geschichte der Weltliteratur*, I (Freiburg i.B.: Herder, 1897), 89; H. H. Kuyper, *Evolutie of Revelatie*, 76, 90. The most recent excavations in Egypt have led to the thesis that there a prehistoric civilization preceded historical time. The bearer of that prehistoric civilization was an ancient indigenous race; cf. the article: "Egypte vóór den tijd der Piramiden," *Wetensch. Bladen* (August 1907): 274–93, (September 1907): 436–53; J. Orr, *God's Image in Man*, 179, 306.

people of Israel can we actually speak of a history and a chronology. Fritz Hommel is therefore right in saying that the chronology for the first thousand years before Christ is fairly well established, sometimes down to the details; that in the second thousand years before Christ we seem to have been given only a few fixed reference points; and that in the third thousand years, that is, before 2000 B.C., everything is uncertain.[40] As a matter of fact, there are other reasons as well why the human race cannot have existed many thousands of years before Christ. If it had, the world's population at the time of Christ would have been much larger and much more widely distributed. A thousand years before Christ, after all, the largest part of the globe was still uninhabited; this applies to what we now call Northern Asia, Central and Northern Europe, Africa south of the Sahara, Australia, the South Sea Islands, America. Even at the time of Christ—aside from Asia—humanity lived primarily around the Mediterranean Sea. If humanity were as old as it is claimed, many more ruins of cities and human remnants would have been found; as it is, they are now very scarce and limited to a part of the earth. The most reliable figures, accordingly, do not rise beyond from five to seven thousand years before Christ.[41] If in this connection we remember that scholars are far from having reached agreement about the chronology of the Bible,[42] then on this point too there is no significant disagreement between Scripture and science. But even if according to the usual calculation the Flood occurred in 2348 B.C., there was a period of 450 years to the calling of Abraham in 1900 B.C.; this period is sufficiently long to allow for quite powerful empires to develop along the Euphrates and the Nile. In fourteen generations of 33 years

40. F. Hommel, *Geschichte des alten Morgenlandes* (Leipzig: Göschen, 1895), 38.

41. F. Pfaff, *Schöpfungsgeschichte*, 710–28; M. Gander, *Die Sündflut in ihrer Bedeutung für die Erdgeschichte* (Münster: Aschendorff, 1896), 78–90; P. Schanz, *Das Alter des Menschengeschlechts nach der Heiligen Schrift der Prophangeschichte und der Vorgeschichte* (Freiburg i.B.: Herder, 1896).

42. Various attempts have been made to extend the chronology of the Bible and so to bring it into harmony with that of natural science and history. The chronology of the Hebrew text of the Old Testament is different from that of the Greek translation. The genealogies of Genesis 5 and 10 perhaps skip generations and, while they establish the family line, they do not fix the duration of the generations. So, for example, W. H. Green and F. Wright, *Wetenschappelijke Bijdragen*, 37 [*Scientific Confirmations*]; J. Urquhart, *How Old Is Man? Some Misunderstood Chapters in Scripture Chronology* (London: Nisbet, 1904), is of the same opinion and calculates the time from Adam to Christ at 8,167 years. Also cf. N. Howard, *Neue Berechnungen über die Chronologie des Alten Testaments und ihr Verhältnis zu der Altertumskunde*, foreword by V. E. Rupprecht (Bonn: 1904); *Totheringham, *The Chronology of the Old Testament* (Cambridge, 1906); A. Bosse, *Untersuchungen zum chronologischen Schema des Alten Testament* (Cothen, 1906); Herders, art. "Bibl. Chronologie," *Kirchenlexicon*; J. B. Heinrich and K. Gutberlet, *Dogmatische Theologie*, VI, 2nd ed. (Mainz: Kircheim, 1881–1900), 272; cf. above pages 123, 131.

each, that is in 462 years, Noah and his three sons (at 6 children per marriage) could have more than 12 million descendants.[43]

The Unity of the Human Race

The unity of the human race is a certainty in Holy Scripture (Gen. 1:26; 6:3; 7:21; 10:32; Matt. 19:4; Acts 17:26; Rom. 5:12f.; 1 Cor. 15:21f., 45f.) but has almost never been acknowledged by the peoples who lived outside the circle of revelation. The Greeks considered themselves autochthonous and proudly looked down on "barbarians." This contrast is found virtually in all nations. In India there gradually came into being even a sharp division between four castes of people, for each of which a distinct origin was assumed. The Stoa was the first school of thought to assert that all human beings formed one single body *(sustēma politikon)* of which everyone was a member, and hence proclaimed universal justice and love of men.[44] Following the Renaissance the idea of various origins of the human race again surfaced. This idea sometimes occurred in the form of true polygeneticism, as in Caesalpinus, Blount, and other deists; in part as co-adamitism, that is, the descent of different races from different ancestors, in Paracelsus and others; in part (in Zanini and especially in Isaac de la Peyrère) as preadamitism, that is, the descent of savage peoples who were dark in color from an ancestor before Adam, while in that case Adam was only the ancestor of the Jews or also of white humanity.

In 1655 de la Peyrère published (without indicating the name of the author, the printer, or the place) a small work entitled *Praeadamitae* and the subtitle *Systema theologiae ex praeadamitarum hypothesi*. In this booklet the assertion is made (with an appeal to Gen. 4:14, 16, 17; 6:2–4) that people had existed long before Adam. These people descended from the first pair whose creation is reported in Genesis 1. In Genesis 2, however, we find the story of the creation of Adam and Eve, who are the ancestors of the Jews. These two broke the law given them in paradise and fell into even greater sins than the peoples descended from the first man, for the latter did not, as Paul puts it (Rom. 5:12–14),

43. For further material on the age of the earth, cf. O. Zöckler, *Geschichte der Beziehungen zwischen Theologie und Naturwissenschaft* (Gütersloh: C. Bertelsmans, 1877–99), II, 755ff.; idem, *Die Lehre vom Urstand des Menschen* (Gütersloh: C. Bertelsmann, 1879), 87ff.; O. Zöckler, art. "Mensch" in *PRE*³, XII, 624; P. Schanz, *Apologie des Christentums*, 3 vols. (Freiburg i.B.: Herder, 1887–88), I, 333ff. [*A Christian Apology*, trans. by Michael F. Glancey, Victor J. Schobel, 4th rev. ed. (Ratisbon: F. Pustet, 1891)]; F. Hettinger, *Apologie des Christenthums*, III, 281–310; F. G. Vigouroux, *Les Livres Saints*, 4 vols. (Paris: A. Roger & F. Chernoviz, 1886–90), III, 452ff.; B. Platz, *Der Mensch* (Würzburg and Leipzig: Woerls Rusenbucher-verlag, 1898), 385ff.
44. E. Zeller, *Philosophie der Greichen*, IV, 287ff.

sin in the likeness of Adam's sin. They did not violate a positive law; they committed natural sins but no sins against law. For a time this theory gained wide acceptance and also provoked opposition from all sides.[45] But it soon fell into oblivion. Only a few authors, such as Bayle, Arnold, and Swedenborg, thought it had some merit. Especially when in the eighteenth century knowledge of the peoples of the world gained more currency and people began to realize the great diversity in color, hair, build, customs (etc.) among them, many scholars again came up with the idea of different ancestors: Sullivan (1795), Crüger (1784), Ballenstedt (1818), Stanhope Smith (1790), Cordonnière (1814), Gobineau (1853–55), and others. By some it was made serviceable to the defense of slavery, as was the case with Dobbs in Ireland against Wilberforce, by Morton Nott, Glidon, Knox, Agassiz, and others. Another kind of polygenesis was taught by Schelling.[46] He too assumed the existence of many races of people before Adam, but these had so elevated and developed themselves from their inferior animal status that finally they brought forth *him* in whom humanness first manifested itself and could therefore bear the name of *the human* ("ha-adam") with good warrant. Similarly a certain preadamitism was propagated by Oken, Carus, Baumgartner, Perty, and Bunsen.[47] After 1860 there was added to these views the Darwinism which on account of its theory of variability could very well be monogenetic but among many of its adherents nevertheless became polygenetic. The development from animal to man took place at various times and places and gave rise to different races, according to Haeckel, Schaafhausen, Caspari, Vogt, Büchner, and others.[48] On the position of Darwinism, however, the question concerning the origin and age of humanity cannot be answered; the transition from animal to man occurred so slowly that there really was no first man. Against this polygeneticism, monogeneticism was again defended by von Humboldt, Blumenbach, St. Hilaire,

---

45. F. Spanheim, *Opera*, III, 1249ff.; F. Turretin, *Institutes of Elenctic Theology*, trans. by George Musgrove Giger, ed. by James T. Dennison, 3 vols. (Phillipsburg, N.J.: Presbyterian & Reformed, 1992–), V, qu. 8; J. Marckius, *Historia Paradisi* (Amsterdam: Gerardus Borstius, 1705), II, 2 §3ff.; B. de Moor, *Comm. Theol.*, II, 1001–5; C. Vitringa, *Doctr. Christ.*, II, 127; cf. J. I. Doedes, "Nieuwe Merkwaardigheden uit den Oude-boeken-schat," ed. by W. Moll and J. G. De Hoop Scheffer, *Studien en Bijdragen* (Amsterdam: G. L. Funke, 1880), IV, 238–42; O. Zöckler, *Geschichte der Beziehungen*, I, 545ff., II, 768ff.; idem, *Die Lehre vom Urstand*, 231ff.

46. F. W. Schelling, *Werke*, II, I, 500–515.

47. Also cf. W. Bilderdijk, *Opstellen van Godgeleerden en Zedekundigen Inhoud* (Amsterdam: Immerzeel, 1883), II, 75; D. F. Strauss, *Christliche Dogmatik*, I, 680; G. A. Schwalbe, *Studien zur Vorgeschichte des Menschen* (Stuttgart: Schweizerbart, 1906).

48. Cf. L. Gumplovicz, *Grundriss der Sociologie*, 2nd ed. (Wien: Manzsche Buchhandlung, 1905), who ardently promotes polygeneticism and bases his sociology on it (138ff.).

von Baer, von Meyer, Wagner, Quatrefages, Darwin, Peschel, Ranke; Virchov, too, allowed for the possibility.[49]

Now the existence of various peoples and races within humanity is most certainly an important issue whose solution we are not even close to finding. The differences in color, hair, skull, language, ideas, religion, mores, customs, and so on, are so great and the expansion of the one human race over the globe—for example, to the South Sea Islands and America—so unknown that the idea of the different origins of peoples can hardly surprise us. In Genesis 11, Scripture, accordingly, traces the origination of languages and of peoples to a single act of God by which he intervened in the development of humanity.[50] The origination of distinct peoples has a deep religious-ethical meaning and speaks of intellectual and spiritual decline. The more savage and rough humanity becomes, the more languages, ideas, and so forth, will take different tracks. The more people live in isolation, the more language differences increase. The confusion of languages is the result of confusion in ideas, in the mind, and in life.

Still in all that division and brokenness unity has been preserved. The science of linguistics has discovered kinship and unity of origin even where in the past it was not even remotely suspected. While the existence of races and peoples is a fact, the determination of their boundaries is nevertheless so difficult that it generates immense disputes. Kant assumed there were four different races, Blumenbach five, Buffon six; Peschel seven, Agassiz eight, Haeckel twelve, Morton even twenty-two.[51] Within and between all races there are again transitional forms which seem to mock all attempts at classification. Genesis 10, accordingly, maintains the unity of the race in the face of all diversity and Johann von Müller with good reason said, "all history must start with this capital."

Now against this unity Darwinism cannot really raise any objections. The difference between man and animal is in any case always much greater than that between humans. If man could evolve from an animal, it is hard to see why the idea of a common origin of mankind should as such encounter objection. Darwinism indeed furnishes the conceptual means of explaining the possibility of a wide assortment of changes

49. Cf. C. Darwin himself, *Descent,* ch. 7, and further F. Hettinger, *Apologie des Christenthums,* III, 224.

50. F. W. Schelling, *Werke,* II, I, 94–118; H. Lüken, *Die Traditionen des Menschengeschlechts* (Munster: Aschendorff, 1869), 278ff.; C. A. Auberlen, *The Divine Revelation,* I (Edinburgh: T. & T. Clark, 1867); F. Kaulen, *Die Sprachenverwirrung zu Babel* (Mainz: F. Kirchheim, 1861); Strodl, *Die Entstehung der Völker Schaffhausen* (Schaffhausen, 1868).

51. O. Peschel, *Abhandlungen zur Erd und Völkerkunde,* 5th ed. (Leipzig: Duncker & Humboldt, 1878), 316ff.; H. Schurtz, *Katechismus der Völkerkunde* (Leipzig: J. J. Weber, 1893); J. Guibert, *In the Beginning,* 212–53.

within a given species as a result of various climatic and lifestyle influences. To that extent, it renders excellent service to the defense of truth. For, however great the difference between the races may be, upon deeper investigation the unity and kinship of all people nevertheless emerges all the more clearly.[52] It is also evident from the fact that parents of the most diverse races can mate and produce fertile children; that every class of humans can inhabit every zone on earth and live there and that peoples who have never been in contact nevertheless have various attributes and practices in common, such as gestures, the decimal system, skin painting, tattooing, circumcision, couvade, and so forth. Furthermore, numerous physiological phenomena are the same in all races, such as the erect posture, the shape of the skull, the average weight of the brain, the number and length of teeth, the duration of pregnancy, the average number of pulse beats, the interior structure of the organism, the hand, the foot (etc.), average age, body temperature, monthly periods, susceptibility to diseases, and so forth. Finally, in intellectual, religious, moral, social, and political respects human beings have a wide range of things in common: language, intellect, reason, memory, knowledge of God, conscience, sense of sin, repentance, sacrifice, fasting, prayer, traditions about a golden age, a flood, and so forth. The unity of the human race, as Scripture teaches, is powerfully confirmed by all this. It is, finally, not a matter of indifference, as is sometimes claimed, but on the contrary of the utmost importance: it is the presupposition of religion and morality. The solidarity of the human race, original sin, the atonement in Christ, the universality of the kingdom of God, the catholicity of the church, and the love of neighbor are all grounded in it.[53]

52. The significance of the races is alternately exaggerated, as it is by Ammon, Driesmann, H. St. Chamberlain, Dühring, Gumplovicz, Nietzsche, Marx, and so on, and underestimated, as it is by Jentsch, Hertz, Colajanni, esp. Finot; cf. Snijders, "Het ontstaan en de verbreiding der menschenrassen," *Tijdsp.* (April 1897); S. R. Steinmetz, "De rassenkwestie," *Gids* 71 (January 1907): 104–39; H. Kern, *Rassen, Volken, Staten* (Haarlem: Bohn, 1904). "Oud en Nieuw over de menschenrassen," *Wetenschappelijke Bladen* (June 1904): 337–57.
53. On the unity of the human race, cf. further: O. Zöckler, "Die einheitliche Abstammung des Menschengeschlechts," *Jahrbuch für die Theologie* (1863): 51–90; idem, *Geschichte der Beziehungen,* II, 768ff.; idem, *Die Lehre vom Urstand,* 231ff.; idem, in *PRE³*, XII, 621; Rauch, *Die Einheit des Menschengeschlechts* (Augsburg, 1873); Th. Waitz, *Ueber die Einheit des Menschengeschlechts und den Naturzustand des Menschen* (Leipzig: Fleischer, 1859); H. Ulrici, *Gott und der Mensch,* I, 2, 146ff.; H. Lotze, *Mircrocosmus,* trans. by Elizabeth Hamilton and E. E. Constance Jones (New York: Scribner & Welford, 1866), 173–92; O. Peschel, *Abhandlungen zur Erd und Völkerkunde,* 14ff.; F. H. Reusch, *Nature and Bible,* II, 181–245; P. Schanz, *Apologie des Christenthums,* I, 318–33 [*A Christian Apology*]; F. G. Vigouroux, *Les Livres Saints,* IV, 1–120; F. Delitzsch, *A New Commentary on Genesis,* trans. by Sophia Taylor (Edinburgh: T. & T. Clark, 1899) 190; F. Hettinger, *Apologie des Christenthums,* III, 223–80; J. H. A. Ebrard, *Apologetics,* trans. by William Stuart and John Macpherson, 2nd ed., 3 vols. (Edinburgh: T. & T. Clark, 1886–87), I, 262–302.

The Original Abode of Humanity

Finally, there is the difference over the original abode of man. Genesis relates that God, after he had created Adam, planted a garden in Eden. ᶜ*ēden* (delight, land of delight) is therefore not identical with paradise but a region in which the garden (LXX *paradeisos;* according to Spiegel from the Persian word *pairi-daēza,* enclosure) was planted. This paradise is then called the garden of Eden (Gen. 2:15; 3:23), the garden of God (Ezek. 31:8, 9), the garden of the Lord (Isa. 51:3), and is sometimes equated with Eden (Isa. 51:3; Ezek. 28:13; 31:9). God, further, planted that garden in Eden "eastward," "away to the east," that is, from the point of view of the author. A river flowed out of Eden to water the garden; and from there, that is, from that garden, as it flowed from the garden, it divided itself in four heads or branches which are named Pishon, Gibon, Hiddekel, and Phrath. The last two rivers are the Tigris and the Euphrates; but about the first two there has always been disagreement. The church fathers, like Josephus, usually associated the Pishon with the Ganges and the Gihon with the Nile. But they never undertook a careful study of the location of paradise. For them paradise on earth often flowed together with the heavenly paradise and was interpreted allegorically. Augustine says there were three views on paradise.[54] Some viewed it as an earthly, others as a heavenly paradise, and still others combined the two. Those who regarded it as an earthly paradise believed it was situated on a very high level between heaven and earth, that it even extended to the moon, or that at one time the entire earth had been paradise, or that it was situated on the other side of the ocean. According to some exegetes, paradise was completely destroyed after the fall, especially by the flood; according to others, it still existed but had been rendered inaccessible by mountains and seas; and still others thought it had been incorporated in heaven. The first person who attempted to pin down the geographic location of paradise was Augustine Steuchus of Gubbio, hence Eugubinus (d. 1550). In his work *Kosmopoiia,* which was published in Lyons in 1535, he developed the so-called Pasitigris hypothesis, according to which the four rivers are the estuaries of one vast river, the so-called Tigris-Euphrates, and paradise is therefore situated near the present city of Corna. This hypothesis was warmly accepted by Catholics like Pererius, Jansen, Lapide, Petavius, Mersenna; by Reformed scholars such as Calvin and Marck; also by several Lutherans, and was adopted, in modified form, by Pressel.[55]

---

54. Augustine, *The Literal Meaning of Genesis,* VIII, 1.
55. J. J. Herzog, art. "Paradise," in *Schaff-Herzog;* "Paradies" in *PRE*[1].

In addition, around the middle of the seventeenth century, there arose the so-called Armenia hypothesis, the groundwork for which had already been laid by Rupert of Deutz, Pellican, and Fournier, and which had been developed especially by Reland, professor at Utrecht (d. 1706). Its thesis is that Pishon is the Phasis, Gihon the Araxes, Havilah the Colchis, Cush the land of the *Kossioi* between Media and Susiana, and hence looked for paradise in a much more northernly area, namely, way up in Armenia, approximately between Erzerum and Tiflis. It found more acceptance than the Pasitigris hypothesis and was still defended in our own time by von Raumer, Kurtz, Baumgarten, Keil, Lange, Delitzsch, Rougement, and others. In contrast, Friedrich Delitzsch in his work, *Wo lag das Paradies?* (Leipzig, 1881), looked for the location of paradise in a more southern direction: in the landscape of Babylon, which on account of its beauty was called "the garden of the God Dunias" by Babylonians and Assyrians. Hence the river from Eden was the Euphrates in its upper reaches; Pishon and Gihon were two auxiliary canals. Other scholars, however, have gone much further and view the paradise story as a saga that has gradually traveled from east to west and in which Pishon and Gihon originally denote the Indus and the Oxus (J. D. Michaelis, Knobel, Bunsen, Ewald, and others). Others regard it as a myth in which Havilah represents the golden land of the saga and the Gihon is the Ganges or the Nile (Paulus, Eichhorn, Gesenius, Tuch, Bertheau, Schrader, and others).[56]

Most anthropologists and linguists no longer take any account of Genesis 2 at all and mention very different countries as the original abode of humanity. But they are far from unanimous and have bestowed this honor practically on all countries. Romanes, Klaproth, de Gobineau, and George Browne refer to America; Spiller thought of Greenland, because, after the cooling down of the earth, the polar regions were the first to be inhabitable. Wagner considered Europe the continent where the ape had first evolved into a human. Unger specified Styria, L. Geiger Germany, Cuno and Spiegel southern Russia, Poesche the region between the Dniepr and the Njemen, Benfey and Whitney central Europe, Warren the North Pole. Others, such as Darwin, Huxley, Peschel, and others favored Africa because they deemed the gorilla and the chimpanzee to be man's closest relatives. And Link, Häckel, Hellwald, Schmidt invented a certain country called "Lemuria," where the apes had first become humans, and which was situated between Af-

---

56. Cf. also H. Zimmern, *Biblische und Babylonische Urgeschichte*, 2 vols. (Leipzig: J. C. Hinrichs, 1901) *(ed. note:* Bavinck erroneously cites this as *Bibl. und parad. Urgeschichte); H. Gunkel and H. Zimmern, *Schöpfung und Chaos*, 2nd ed. (Göttingen: Vandenhoeck und Ruprecht, 1921), and his commentary on Genesis.

rica and Australia, but at the end of the Tertiary period had accidentally sunk into the depths of the sea. In this connection many scholars assume, not just one single original abode of man, but believe that the evolution from animal to man occurred in various parts of the earth, thus combining Darwinism with polygeneticism (Haeckel, Vogt, Schaafhausen, Caspari, Fr. Muller, and others).

Even this spectacular disagreement among anthropologists illustrates that up until now natural science has not been able to say anything with certainty on this point. It loses itself in conjectures but knows nothing about the origin and abode of the first humans. There is not a single fact, therefore, which compels us to abandon the stipulation of Holy Scripture concerning Eden. Ethnology, linguistics, history, and the natural sciences furnish us data that make plausible the choice of Asia as the original abode of man. Neither Africa, nor Europe, nor America, and much less a country like "Lemuria," can match the claim of Asia to this distinction. Here we find the most ancient peoples, the most ancient civilization, the most ancient languages; all of ancient history points us to this continent. From within this part of the earth Europe, Africa, Australia but also America have been populated. Granted, in this connection many questions arise to which we do not yet know the answers. It is especially uncertain how and when America was populated.[57] But these objections by no means overthrow the teaching of Scripture that Asia is the cradle of humanity. About the location of paradise and Eden there may be different opinions, so that it is alternately placed in the center, or east or south, of Asia; the geography may no longer lie within our capacity to determine, but Scripture and science unite in the witness that it is in Asia that we must look for the original abode of man.[58]

57. O. Zöckler, *Geschichte der Beziehungen*, I, 542ff.; O. Peschel, *Abhandlungen zur Erd und Völkerkunde*, 402ff.; F. G. Vigouroux, *Les Livres Saints*, IV, 98ff.; *E. Schmidt, *Die Aeltesten Spuren des Menschen in N. Amerika*, nos. 38 and 39 *Deutsche Zeit- und Streitfragen; *Wetenschappelyke Bladen* (1895).

58. O. Peschel, *Abhandlungen zur Erd und Völkerkunde*, 35–41; O. Zöckler, *Geschichte der Beziehungen*, passim, esp. I, 128ff., 170ff., 395ff., 654ff., II, 779ff.; idem, *Die Lehre vom Urstand*, 216ff.; F. H. Reusch, *Nature and Bible*, II, 181–245; *O. Zöckler, *Biblische und Kirchenhistorische. Studien* (München: 1893), V, 1–38; F. Delitzsch, *A New Commentary on Genesis*, 114–46; Volck, art. "Eden" in *PRE*³, V, 158–62; W. Engelkemper, *Die Paradiesesflüsse* (Münster, 1901); B. Poertner, *Das biblische Paradies* (Mainz: Kirchheim, 1901); *Fr. Coelestinus, *Het Aardsche Paradijs,* Tilburg and so forth.

Human Nature   5

To be human is to be an image-bearer of God, created in his likeness and originally righteous and holy. The whole person is the image of the whole deity. There has been extensive debate in the Christian church about the image of God in humanity. Some sought it essentially in human rationality, others in dominion over creation, others in freedom of the will or moral qualities such as love or justice. Pelagian and Socinian rationalist naturalism identified the image with a formal human freedom of moral choice, opening the door to an evolutionary view that sees the essence of humanity in an endless process of self-willed improvement. This view is diametrically contrary to Scripture, which does not consider a primitive animal state as an early stage in human history. Science provides no evidence for this hypothesis either and it faces numerous philosophical and theological objections. Over against the naturalist view of human nature the Roman Catholic tradition posits a supernatural one that sees infused grace as the means by which human beings achieve and merit their true and supernatural end, the vision of God. Grace elevates nature. Protestant theology rejected key elements of this dualistic understanding, especially the meritorious character of natural elevation. The Reformers judged that the Roman Catholic position also weakened the view of original sin. But among the Protestants too there were differences. Lutherans tended to identify the image with the original gifts of righteousness while the Reformed incorporated the whole human essence in the image, though they do speak of a narrow and broad sense of the image. Yet it is important to insist that the whole person is the image of the whole, that is, Triune, God. The human soul, all the human faculties, the virtues of knowledge, righteousness, and holiness, and even the human body images God. The incarnation of our Lord is definitive proof that humans, not angels, are created in the image of God, and that the human body is an essential component of that image. From the beginning creation was arranged and human nature was immediately so created that it was amenable to, and fit for, the highest degree of conformity to God and for the most intimate indwelling of God.

The essence of human nature is its being [created in] the image of God. The entire world is a revelation of God, a mirror of his attributes and perfections. Every creature in its own way and degree is the embodiment of a divine thought. But among creatures only man is the image of God, God's highest and richest self-revelation and consequently the head and crown of the whole creation, image of God and the epitome of nature, both *mikrotheos* (microgod) and *mikrokosmos* (microcosm). Even pagans have recognized this reality and called man the image of God. Pythagoras, Plato, Ovid, Cicero, Seneca, and others distinctly state that man, or at least the soul of man, was created as God's image, that he is God's kin and offspring.[1]

Not only that, but virtually all peoples have traditions of a golden age. Among the Chinese, the people of India, Iranians, Egyptians, Babylonians, Greeks, Romans, and others, one finds stories of an earlier time when humans lived in innocence and bliss and in communion with the gods. These stories were celebrated in song by the poets Hesiod, Ovid, and Virgil, and acknowledged by the philosophers in their truth.[2] Only Scripture, however, sheds a full and true light on this doctrine of man's divine likeness. The first creation narrative has it that, after intentional deliberation, God created man in his image and likeness (*běṣalmēnû kidmûtinû, kat eichona ēmeteran kai kath homoiōsin, ad imaginem et similitudinem nostram*, Gen. 1:26, 27). In Genesis 5:1 and 9:6 it is further repeated that God created man in the likeness of God *(bidmût ĕlōhîm)* and in the image of God *(běṣelem ĕlōhîm)*. Psalm 8 sings of man as the master of all creation, and Ecclesiastes 7:29 reminds us that God made man upright *(yšr)*. For the rest, the Old Testament says little of the original state of integrity *(status integratis)*. More than any other people, Israel was a people of hope; she focused on the future, not on the past. Even the New Testament says relatively little about the image of God in which humanity was originally created. There is direct mention of it only in 1 Corinthians 11:7, where the man is called "the image and glory of God," and in James 3:9, where it said of humans that they "are made in the likeness of God." Luke 3:38 also calls Adam "the son of God" and Paul quotes a pagan poet to the effect that "we are indeed his offspring" (Acts 17:28). Indirectly, however, also Ephesians 4:24 and Colossians 3:10 are of great importance here. In

1. T. Pfanner, *Syst. theol. gent.*, 189ff.

2. J. G. Friderici, *De Aurea Aetate Quam Poëtae Finxerunt* (Leipzig, 1736); H. Lüken, *Die Traditionen des Menschengeschlechts* (Freiburg i.B.: Herder, 1876); O. Zöckler, *Die Lehre vom Urstand des Menschen* (Gütersloh: C. Bertelsmann, 1879), 84ff.; J. H. Oswald, *Religioese Urgeschichte der Menschheit* (Paderborn: Schöningh, 1887), 37ff.; E. L. Fischer, *Heidenthum und Offenbarung* (Mainz: Kirchheim, 1878); O. Zöckler, *Biblische und Kirchenhistorische. Studien* (München: C. H. Beck, 1893), V, 1ff.; O. Willmann, *Geschichte des Idealismus* (1894), I, 1–136 [(Braunschweig: F. Vieweg und Sohn, 1907)]; C. P. Tiele, *Inleiding tot de Godsdienstwetenschap* (Amsterdam: P. N. van Kampen, 1897–99), II, 93ff., 197.

these verses we read of the "new man" which believers must "put on," and of this new man it is said that it was created "after the likeness of God in true righteousness and holiness," and "renewed in knowledge after the image of its creator." Here it is implied that the new man, which believers put on, was created by God, in conformity with God and his image, and that this conformity specifically emerges in the righteousness and holiness which is the fruit of appropriated truth. This, however, refers to the original creation insofar as the words that Paul employs are clearly derived from the [Genesis] creation account; insofar as the second creation—as the whole of Scripture teaches—is not a "creation from nothing," but a renewal of all that existed; and insofar as the *anakainousthai* (Col. 3:10) of the believer clearly describes this creation as a renewal. Underlying Ephesians 4:24 and Colossians 3:10, therefore, is the idea that man was originally created in God's image and in the re-creation is renewed on that model.

Scripture, however, not only recounts the fact of man's creation in God's image but also explains its meaning. While the two words "image" and "likeness" (*šlm* and *dmwt*, *eikōn* and *homoiōsis*) are certainly not identical, there is no essential material distinction to be made between them either. They are used interchangeably, and alternate for no specific reason. Both occur in Genesis 1:26 (cf. 5:3); in 1:27 and 9:6 (cf. Col. 3:10) only the image is referred to and in Genesis 5:1, James 3:9 only the likeness. The distinction between them comes down to this: *šlm* means "image," both archetype *(Urbild)* and ectype *(Abbild)*; *dmwt* means "likeness, both example *(Vorbild)* and copy *(Nachbild)*. The concept of "image" is more rigid, that of "likeness" more fluid and more "spiritual," so to speak; in the former the idea of a prototype predominates, in the latter the notion of an ideal.[3] The likeness is a further qualification, an intensification and complement of the image. "Likeness" as such is weaker and broader than "image"; an animal has some features in common with man (likeness) but is not the image of man. "Image" tells us that God is the archetype, man the ectype; "likeness" adds the notion that the image corresponds in all parts to the original.[4] Just as there is little distinction between these two concepts, so there is little difference between the prepositions "in" *(b)* and "after" *(k)* used in this connection. These two are also used alternatively: in Genesis 5:1 we have *b* by *děmût* similarly in verse 3, and also *k* by *šelem;* the New Tes-

---

3. F. Delitzsch, *A New Commentary on Genesis*, trans. by Sophia Taylor (Edinburgh: T. & T. Clark, 1899), 98–100, on Gen. 1:26; cf. also W. Riedel, *Alttestamentliche Untersuchungen* (Leipzig: A. Deichert [George Böhe], 1902), 42–47.

4. Augustine, *De diversis quaestionibus octginta tribus liber*, qu. 74; T. Aquinas, *Summa Theol.*, I., qu. 93, art. 9; J. Gerhard, *Loci Theol.*, VIII, § 18; A. Polanus, *Syn. Theol.*, V, 10 enz.

tament has *kata* by *eikōn* (Col. 3:10) but also in the case of *homoiōsis* (James 3:9). Hence nothing can be constructed on this basis; all we can say, with Delitzsch, is that in the case of *b* one thinks of the prototype as a cast metal mold, in the case of *k* as a model held before us. There is therefore no reason, with Böhl, to derive from the preposition *b* the conclusion that the image of God is an atmosphere and element in which man was created.[5]

In addition to these words, Scripture offers the following data for the image of God. First, it is clear that the words "image" and "likeness" do not refer to anything in God but to something in man, not to the uncreated archetype, but to the created ectype. The idea is not that man has been created after something in God which is called "image" or "likeness," so that it could, for example, be a reference to the Son, but that man has been created after God in such a way that he is his image and likeness. Further, this creation in God's image is in no way restricted, either on the side of the archetype or on the side of the ectype. It is not stated that man was created only in terms of some attributes, or in terms of only one person in the divine being, nor that man bears God's image and likeness only in part, say, only in the soul, or the intellect, or in holiness. The case is rather that the whole human person is the image of the whole Deity. Third, the meaning of the image of God is further explicated to us by the Son, who in an entirely unique sense is called the Word *(logos)*, the Son *(huios)*, the image *(eikōn)*, or imprint of God *(charaktēr tou theou)* (John 1:1, 14; 2 Cor. 4:4; Col. 1:15; Heb. 1:3) and to whom we must be conformed (Rom. 1:29; 1 Cor. 15:49; Phil. 3:21; Eph. 4:23f.; 1 John 3:2). The Son already bears these names now because he is "God of God" and "light of light," having the same attributes as the Father. He is so called not on account of some part of his being but because his nature absolutely conforms to that of God. This, in turn, applies also to man. Like the Son, so man as such is altogether the image of God. He does not just bear but *is* the image of God. There is this difference, of course, that what the Son is in an absolute sense, man only is in a relative sense. The former is the eternal only begotten Son; the latter the created son of God. The former is the image of God *within*, the latter *outside* of the divine being. The one is the image of God in a divine manner, the other is that in a creaturely manner. But thus, then, and within his limits, man is the image and likeness of God. Finally, Scripture here and there tells us in what ways that image reveals and manifests itself openly. The full content of that image of God

5. E. Böhl, *Dogmatik* (Amsterdam: Scheffer, 1887), 154ff.; cf. in opposition A. Kuyper, *De Vleeschwording des Woords* (Amsterdam: Wormser, 1887), viiiff.; *Daubanton, *Theol. Stud.* (1887), 429–44.

is nowhere unfolded. But Genesis 1:26 clearly indicates that the image of God manifests itself in man's dominion over all of the created world (cf. Ps. 8; 1 Cor. 11:7). The portrayal of the paradisal state in Genesis 1 and 2 demonstrates that the image of God includes conformity to the will of God (cf. Eccl. 7:29). And re-creation in conformity to the image of God or Christ primarily consists in putting on the new man which, among other things, consists in righteousness and holiness of truth.

Defining the Image

On the content of the image of God there was initially a wide range of opinion in the Christian church. At times it was located in the human body, then in rationality, or in the freedom of the will, then again in dominion over the created world, or also in other moral qualities such as love, justice, and the like.[6] But gradually two views came to the fore side by side or as opposites, both of them appealing to the distinction between image *(ślm)* and likeness *(dmwt)*. Some, like Clement of Alexandria, Origen, and others, noted that Genesis 1:26 indeed says that God planned to create man after his image and likeness, but that, according to verse 27, he only created him in his image, that is, as a rational being, in order that man himself would acquire likeness with God in the way of obedience and receive it in the end as his reward from God's hand.[7] Others, on the other hand, believed that along with the image, that is, a rational nature, man also immediately received the likeness as a gift and that, having lost that gift by sin, he would regain it through Christ.[8] The first view, which one might call the naturalistic one, found support in the doctrine of the freedom of the will. Consequently, its adherents could not conceive holiness as a divine gift bestowed on humanity at the outset, but only as a good that he had to achieve by his own moral efforts.[9] Many theologians, accordingly, taught that humanity was created in a state, not of positive holiness, but of childlike innocence.[10]

6. Cf. J. C. Suicerus, *s.v.* "εἰκων," in *Thesaurus Ecclesiasticus* (Amsterdam: J. H. Wetsten, 1682); Petavius, *Opera Omnia,* "de sex dier. opif.," II, 2; W. Münscher, *Lehrbuch des Christlichen Dogmengeschichte,* ed. by Daniel von Coelln, 3rd ed. (Cassel: J. C. Krieger, 1832–38), I, 339ff.; K. R. Hagenbach, *Lehrburch der Dogmengeschichte* (Leipzig: Hirzel, 1888), §56.
7. Clement of Alexandria, *Stromateis,* II, 22; Origen, *On First Principles,* III, 6.
8. Irenaeus, *Against Heresies,* V, 16, 2; Athanasius, *Against the Arians,* II, 59; idem, *Against the Heathens,* 2; idem, *On the Incarnation,* 3.
9. A. Harnack, *History of Dogma,* 7 vols., trans. by N. Buchanan, J. Millar, E. B. Speirs, and W. McGilchrist, ed. by A. B. Bruce (London: Williams & Norgate, 1896–99), II, 128–48.
10. Tertullian, *Treatise on the Soul,* 38; Theophilus, *To Autolycus,* II, 24, 27; Irenaeus, *Against Heresies,* IV, 38.

Naturalism

It was to such pronouncements that Pelagius later appealed when he identified the essence and original state of man with moral indifference, with nothing but a formal freedom of moral choice. The image of God, Pelagius taught, consists only in a natural God-given possibility of perfection which cannot be lost and is therefore still a part of every human being. God bestows the ability *(posse)* but the will *(velle)* is up to us.[11] Later this view found acceptance among the Socinians who located the image of God solely in human dominion over nature;[12] among the Anabaptists who said that as a finite earthly creature man was not yet the image of God but could only realize that status by a rebirth;[13] among the Remonstrants,[14] the Rationalists and Supernaturalists,[15] and numerous modern theologians,[16] all of whom saw the state of integrity as a state of childlike innocence. As a rule these theologians still hold to the historical reality of such an original state. But in their view of the image of God in the first humans they materially agree totally with those who, detaching the idea from the fact, deny the reality of a state of integrity and locate the image of God

11. Augustine, *On the Grace of Christ*, I, 3ff.

12. O. Fock, *Der Socinianismus* (Kiel: C. Schröder, 1847), 484.

13. *Ed. note:* Bavinck here lists Menno Simons, *Werken*, 125, 126, 180. He is likely referring to Simons' *A Fundamental Doctrine from the Word of the Lord* of 1556 or *The True Christian Faith which Converts, Changes, Makes Pious, Sincere, New, Peaceful, Joyful and Blessed the Human Heart* of 1556, both of which deal with the "new birth." These two treatises can be found in *The Complete Works of Menno Simon* (Elkhart: John F. Funk & Brother, 1871), I, 165–78, 103–63; cf. H. W. Erbkam, *Geschichte der Protestantischen Sekten* (Hamburg and Gotha: F. & A. Perthes, 1848), 461; J. Cloppenburg, *Op. Theol.*, II, 144ff.

14. *Conf. Remonstr.*, V, 5; S. Episcopius, *Apologia pro Confessiones;* idem, *Instit. theol.*, IV, 3, 7; P. van Limborch, *Theol. Christ.*, II, 24, 5.

15. J. A. L. Wegscheider, *Institutiones theologiae christianae dogmaticae* (Halle: Gebauer, 1819), §99; K. G. Bretschneider, *Handbuch der Dogmatik* (Leipzig: J. A. Barth, 1838), §§115, 116; F. V. Reinhard, *Grundriss der Dogmatik* (Munich: Seidel, 1802), §70.

16. I. A. Dorner, *A System of Christian Doctrine*, trans. by Alfred Cave and J. S. Banks, 4 vols., rev. ed. (Edinburgh: T. & T. Clark, 1888), II, 77–84; J. P. Lange, *Christliche Dogmatik*, 3 vols. (Heidelberg: K. Winter, 1849–52), II, 298ff.; J. Müller, *Die christliche Lehre von der Sünde*, 2 vols. (Breslau: J. Mar, 1844), II, 457ff. [*The Christian Doctrine of Sin*, trans. by Wm. Urwick, 5th ed. (Edinburgh: T. & T. Clark, 1868)]; G. Beck, *Lehrw.*, I, 186ff.; Beck, *Chr. Glauben.*, II, 328; H. Martensen, *Dogm.*, 139 [*Christian Dogmatics*, trans. by William Urwick (Edinburgh: T & T. Clark, 1871); F. A. Kahnis, *Die Luthersche Dogmatik* (Leipzig: Dorffling & Francke, 1861–68)], I, 432; O. Zöckler, *Die Lehre vom Urstand*, 40ff., 333; Grétillat, *Theol. syst.*, III, 464ff.; P. Hofstede de Groot, *De Groninger Godgeleerdheid in Hunne Eigenaardigheid* (Groningen: Scholtens, 1855), 89ff.; J. I. Doedes, *De Leer der Zaligheid Volgens het Evangelie in de Schriften des Nieuwen Verbonds Voorgesteld* (Utrecht: Kemink, 1876), §24; J. I. Doedes, *De Nederlandsche Geloofsbelijdenis* (Utrecht: Kemink & Zoon, 1880–81), 145; J. I. Doedes, *De Heidelbergsche Catechismus* (Utrecht: Kemink & Zoon, 1881), 69.

solely in man's free personality, his rational or moral nature, in a religious-ethical bent, in man's vocation to enter communion with God.[17] This view then unwittingly prompts them to accept the theory of evolution, according to which the essence of man is situated not in what he was or is but in what he, in an endless process of development and by his own exertions, may become. Paradise lies ahead, not behind us. An evolved ape deserves preference over a fallen human. Originally bearing the image of an orangutan and chimpanzee, man gradually pulled himself up from a state of raw brutishness to that of a noble humanity.

It hardly needs saying that Holy Scripture is diametrically opposed to this theory of evolution. Christian churches, accordingly, almost unanimously rejected the naturalistic Pelagian view of the image of God and man's original state. Aside from the arguments for the Darwinian hypothesis, which we already rebutted earlier, there are actually no direct historical proofs for the animal state of man as pictured by evolutionary theorists. The bones and skulls that have been found all prove, on closer scrutiny, to derive from beings wholly like ourselves. As far as we can go back into history we find a condition of relatively high levels of civilization in China, India, Babylonia, and Egypt. All proof that the peoples of those areas evolved from an animal state is lacking. The appeal to so-called primitive people, who for that matter are not completely devoid of culture either, has no cogency, for it cannot be proven that they are closer than the civilized peoples to the original state of humanity. There is greater reason to believe that, being isolated from humanity, they gradually declined into a state of barbarism. They all bear the character of degenerates who, like branches off a tree, were torn

---

17. I. Kant, *Religion Within the Limits of Reason Alone*, trans. by Theodore M. Greene and Hoyt H. Hudson (New York: Harper & Brothers, 1934), 21–23; J. G. Fichte, *The Vocation of Man*, trans. by William Smith, 2nd ed. (Chicago: Open Court, 1910); G. W. F. Hegel, *Sämtliche Werke* (Stuttgart: Fr. Frommann, 1959), vol. 15, 199ff. ("Vorlesung über die Philosophie der Religion, Erster Band," *Werke*, XI, 183ff.); F. Schleiermacher, *The Christian Faith*, ed. by H. R. MacIntosh and J. S. Steward (Edinburgh: T. & T. Clark, 1928); D. F. Strauss, *Der alte und der neue Glaube* (Leipzig: Hirzel, 1872), II, 72; A. E. Biedermann, *Christliche Dogmatik* (Zurich: Füssli, 1869), II, 562; Lipsius, *Dogm.*, §§420, 440; A. Ritschl, *Die Christliche Lehre von der Rechfertigung und Versöhnung*, 4th ed. (Bonn: A. Marcus, 1895–1903), III, 314; C. E. Nitzsch, *Lehrbuch der Evangelische Dogmatik*, 3rd ed. prepared by Horst Stephan (Tübingen: J. C. B. Mohr, 1902), 306ff; J. Kaftan, *Dogmatik* (Tübingen: J. C. B. Mohr, 1901), §39; Th. Häring, *Der Christliche Glaube*, 2nd ed. (Calw: Verlag der Vereinsbuchhandlung, 1912), 248ff. (Engl. trans. by John Dickie and George Ferries, *The Christian Faith: A System of Dogmatics*, 2 vols. [London & New York: Hodder & Stoughton, 1913]); J. Bovon, *Dogmatique chrétienne*, 2 vols. (Lausanne: Georges Bridel, 1895–96), I, 132, 139; J. H. Scholten, *De Leer der Hervormde Kerk*, 2 vols., 2nd ed. (Leyden: P. Engels, 1850–51), I, 304ff., II, 67ff.

from the main stock, and, not receiving fresh vitalities from without, died away and disappeared.[18]

The question pertaining to the primitive state of humans, accordingly, is not really historical but philosophical, since that state by definition precedes all historical evidence. The answer given to that question is determined by the idea one has of human nature. The more one thinks about this being, the more impossible it becomes to imagine human history as starting with a barbaric or animal state. Life, consciousness, language, religion, the difference between truth and untruth, and so forth, cannot be explained from the perspective of evolution but presuppose an origin of their own, a creation *ex nihilo*. Even in the theology of modernists this is evident. They indeed deny the creation of man in God's image and hence the state of integrity, but the idea of creation suddenly appears again at the most critical point. Either consciousness is something specifically human; or at least religion has its own original principle in humans. Or, if evolution has been accepted as interpretive principle also at this point, a halt is called in the case of the ethical dimension and this theology insists on its independence; the moral life and the moral disposition is unique *(sui generis)* and has its own origin *(sui originis)*.[19] But this intermediate position between creation and evolution is untenable. It was repeatedly held by a variety of Pelagian schools of thought because their adherents objected to both creation and evolution and hence looked for a mediating theory. The first human was neither an animal nor a perfect holy human being but an innocent child. He was neither positively good, nor positively evil, but stood somewhere in between; he was morally indifferent, could do one thing as well as another. In actual fact he was nothing; potentially he was everything, pious and wicked, holy and unholy, good and evil. The disposition and ability *(posse)* originated by creation, but all that was constructed on that foundation of potentiality developed by man's own work and volition. Now, as we will note in the following section, there is an element of truth in this picture insofar as the

18. Th. Waitz, *Ueber die Einheit des Menschengeschlechts und den Naturzustand des Menschen* (Leipzig: Fleischer, 1859), 334ff.; O. Peschel, *Abhandlungen zur Erd und Völkerkunde*, 5th ed. (Leipzig: Duncker & Humboldt, 1878), 135ff.; F. Ratzel, *Völkerkunde* (Leipzig: Bibliographisches Institut), I, 4ff.; Steinmetz, *De Studie der Völkenkunde* (1907); W. Schneider, *Die Naturvölker* (Paderborn: Schoningh, 1885); C. Gutberlet, *Der Mensch* (Paderborn: Schoningh, 1903), 475ff.; *Froberger, *Die Schöpfungsgeschichte der Menschheit in der "voraussetzungslosen" Völkerpsychologie* (1903); O. Zöckler, *Geschichte der Beziehungen zwischen Theologie und Naturwissenschaft* (Gütersloh: C. Bertelsman, 1877–99), II, 744ff.; F. G. Vigouroux, *Les Livres Saints*, 4 vols. (Paris: A. Roger & F. Chernoviz, 1886–90), IV, 171ff.; J. Guibert, *In the Beginning*, trans. by G. S. Whitmarsh (London: Kegan Paul, Trench, Trubner, 1900), 366–79.
19. S. Hoekstra, *Wijsgerige Godsdienstwetenschap*, I, 1ff., 213ff.

first humans had not yet attained the highest good and hence still had to develop. But aside from this point, and for many reasons, this view is totally unacceptable.

In the first place, Scripture clearly teaches that humans were, both physically and psychically, created as adults at "an age of vigor."[20] The Genesis account of the first humans is very simple but their state was that of full-grown, aware, freely acting agents. Creation in the image of God (Gen. 1:27; Eccl. 7:29; Eph. 4:24; Col. 3:10), the blessing of procreation and multiplication (Gen. 1:28), divine approval (Gen. 1:31), the probationary command (Gen. 2:17), the naming of the animals (Gen. 2:19), the pronouncement about Eve (Gen. 2:23, 24), the manner of the temptation (Gen. 3:1ff.), and the attitude of Adam and Eve after the fall (Gen. 3:7ff.) all attest to the truth that the first humans were created positively good, not morally indifferent. The only counterargument could perhaps be based on the fact that the first humans knew no shame. This, accordingly, has always been brought up by the opposition as a very strong argument.[21] It does not hold water, however, because before the fall the sex life was very well known to the first humans (Gen. 1:27, 28; 2:23, 24), and because shame is derived specifically from the fall and not from the awakening of sexuality.

Second, this view suffers from irresolution and makes the problem before us even more complicated. It is irresolute insofar as, on the one hand, it favors evolution but, having arrived at a certain point, it again pays tribute to creation. It wants no part of a creation of the act but does assume a creation of potentiality. It speaks of an ability *(Fähigkeit)* without readiness *(Fertigkeit);* and considers the creation of a child, both in a physical and a psychic sense, simpler and more reasonable than that of an adult. This is as such inherently absurd, for one who believes in the creation rather than the evolution of potentiality can no longer in principle object to the doctrine of original justice and the state of integrity. But, on top of that, it makes the issue even harder to imagine. Potentiality does not automatically develop into actuality. Max Müller correctly stated: "If we would attempt to picture the first man created as a child and as gradually developing his physical and psychic powers, we cannot grasp how he managed even for a day without supernatural assistance."[22] Along the same lines is Schelling's comment: "I definitely consider the state of culture as being original for the

20. Augustine, *The Literal Meaning of Genesis,* VI, 13, 14; P. Lombard, *Sent.,* II, dist. 17.
21. H. Ellis, *Geschlechtstrieb und Schamgefühl* (Leipzig: Wigand, 1900); W. Francken, *Ethische Studiën* (Haarlem, 1903), 110–28.
22. M. Müller, *Vorlesungen über die Wissenschaft der Sprache,* 3rd ed. (Leipzig: Mayer, 1866), 410.

human race."[23] And also J. G. Fichte wrote: "One wonders—if indeed it
is necessary to assume an origin of the entire human race—who brought
up the first human couple? They had to be brought up—a human being
could not have educated them. Hence they had to be brought up by another rational being, one who was not a human. This naturally holds
true only up to the time when they could educate each other. A spirit
adopted them, quite in the manner pictured in a venerable ancient document, which, generally speaking, contains the profoundest and most
sublime wisdom and posits results to which in the end all philosophy has
to return."[24] To avoid one miracle, many miracles have to be assumed.

Third, underlying this view is the error that innate holiness cannot
possibly exist. Holiness, we are told, is always the product of struggle
and effort. If Adam had been created a positively holy being, he was
necessarily good and without freedom to be otherwise.[25] As a result,
these theologians have to dream up a state between good and evil, holiness and unholiness, an undifferentiated state which is anterior to the
moral dimension either in a good or a bad sense and from which humans then have to evolve by an act of free will in one direction or another. In that case man is robbed of all intellectual and ethical substance and the image of God is located in a purely naked, merely formal
personality.[26] Such a concept of personality, however, is a mere abstraction, to which nothing in reality corresponds. No human being can
be conceived without certain qualities of intellect and will. A completely undifferentiated state of the will, without any inclination in one
direction or another, is simply an impossibility. Just as in nature only a
good tree can produce good fruit, so also in ethical life a good nature
precedes good works. To act one must first *be (Operari sequitur esse)*.
Scripture, accordingly, teaches that both in creation and re-creation
holiness is a gift from God. One who has this gift can further develop it
in word and deed; but one who lacks it can never acquire it.

23. F. W. Schelling, *Ausgewählte Werke*, vol. 3 (Darmstadt: Wissenschafliche Buchgesellschaft, 1968), 520–29 ("Vorlesungen über die Methode des Akademischen Studi-
ums," [1803], *Werke* 1/5, 286–95); idem, vol. 3, 643–45 ("Philosophie und Religion,"
[1804], *Werke* 1/6, 57–59).

24. J. G. Fichte, *Grundlage des Naturrechts nach Principien der Wissenschaftslehre* (Jena: Gabler, 1796). English trans. by A. E. Kroeger, *The Science of Rights* (New York: Harper & Row, 1970 [1889]).

25. R. Rothe, *Theologische Ethik*, 5 vols., 2nd rev. ed. (Wittenberg: Zimmerman,
1867–71), §480ff.

26. C. E. Nitzsch, *System der Christlichen Lehre*, 5th ed. (Bonn: Adolph Marcus, 1844)
211; J. Müller, *Die Christliche Lehre von der Sünde*, I, 154ff., 493ff. [*The Christian Doctrine
of Sin*]; F. A. Kahnis, *Die Luthersche Dogm.*, I, 432; G. Thomasius, *Die Christliche Dog-
mensgeschichte als Entwicklung-geschichte des Kirchlichen Rehrbegriffs*, 2 vols. (Erlangen:
A. Deichert, 1886–89), I, 110ff.; G. Beck, *Christliche Glaube*, II, 333; J. I. Doedes, *De Leer
der Zaligheid*, 55ff.

Finally, this view does less than justice to the justice of God, who has then allowed his creature to be tempted beyond his power to resist. It also fails to do justice to the seriousness of the temptation, which then becomes a crafty piece of trickery, and to the character of the fall, which ceases to be an appalling sin and changes into a nonculpable misfortune, an almost unavoidable lot. It erases the boundaries that exist between the state of integrity and the state of corruption, and allows man to keep intact the image of God, which exists in something purely formal, even after the fall. It conceives the relation between the formal (personality, free will) and the material (the religious and ethical life) to be as loose and dualistic as Rome pictures it between purely natural things and the superadded gift, with the sole difference that in the case of Rome holiness is the fruit of grace and in the case of Pelagius and his followers it is a product of caprice.

Roman Catholic Supernaturalism

Alongside and over against this naturalistic view of the image of God there arose another view which we may call supernaturalistic. It did not arise from the distinction between "image" and "likeness," although it was later associated with this distinction as well. Nor is it based on the interpretation of Genesis 1 and 2, inasmuch as many theologians acknowledge that it does not occur there, at least not literally. It was derived from the idea—one that gradually came up in the Christian church—of the state of glory *(status gloriae)* to which believers are elevated by Christ and his Spirit (John 1:12; Rom. 8:14–17; 1 Cor. 2:7f.; Eph. 1:15ff.; 2 Pet. 1:2ff.; 1 John 3:1, 2, etc.).[27] Gradually, under Neo-Platonic influence, this state of glory was viewed as a condition that far transcended the state of nature, not only in an ethical but also in a corporeal sense. In christological disputes after the fourth century this idea became so prominent that the deity of Christ and of the Spirit was affirmed particularly with the argument that for humans they were the authors of their deification. The essence of the state of glory increasingly came to be the vision of God according to his essence *(per essentiam)*, deiformity or deification, a participation in the divine nature that was not only moral but corporeal, a "melting union" with God.[28] Added to this doctrine of "the state of glory" was that of the meritorious nature of good works. Infused grace, which was granted in baptism, was definitely necessary, but also enabled a person to do such good works as could *ex condigno* (by a full merit)[29] earn eternal blessedness, the vision of God *per essentiam.*

---

27. M. J. Scheeben, *Handbuch der Katholischen Dogmatik,* 4 vols. (Freiburg i.B.: Herder, 1933), II, 272–81.

28. See H. Bavinck, *Gereformeerde Dogmatiek,* II, 154–58.

29. *Ed. note:* Cf. Richard A. Muller, *Dictionary of Latin and Greek Theological Terms* (Grand Rapids: Baker, 1985), s.v. *meritum,* 190–92.

From these two ideas, the mystical view of man's final destiny and the meritoriousness of good works, was born the Catholic doctrine of the "superadded gift" *(donum superadditum)*. The first to formulate it was Alexander Hales. The heavenly blessedness and the vision of God, which is man's final destiny—and was so for Adam—can be merited *ex condigno* only by such good works as are in accord with that final destiny. In other words, like that destiny, they have a supernatural character and hence proceed from a supernatural principle: infused grace. The righteousness that Adam possessed as a human, earthly being by virtue of creation was not, of course, sufficient to that end. So for Adam to reach his final destiny he too needed to be given a supernatural grace, that is, the *gratia gratum faciens* ("the grace that renders one engraced or pleasing to God"), the image of God. "But this elevation of the rational creature is a supernatural complement; and therefore neither consecration nor adoption nor any elevation *(assumptio)* of this kind happens through any property of nature but only through a gift superadded to nature. This consecrates nature, so that it may be a temple, assimilating it to God, so that it may be a son or a daughter, allying it to God or making it one with God through a conformity to the will that it may be a bride. This, however, comes about by God's mediation as grace renders it pleasing to him."[30]

This doctrine found general acceptance among the Scholastics,[31] was incorporated in the Roman Catechism,[32] was later defended and maintained against the Reformers, Baius, Jansen, and Quesnel,[33] and constitutes one of the most important and characteristic *loci* in Roman Catholic theology.[34] But although in substance there was consensus, at

30. Alexander of Hales, *Summa Theol.*, II, qu. 91, membr. 1, art. 3.
31. T. Aquinas, *Summa Theol.*, I, qu. 95; Bonaventure, *The Breviloquium*, II, c. 11, 12, V, c. 1; Commentaries of T. Aquinas, Bonaventure, Duns Scotus, e.a., on *Sentences*, II, dist. 29.
32. *Roman Catechism*, I, 2, qu. 18, 3.
33. R. Bellarmine, *De Gratia Primi Hominis* (Heidelberg: Rosa, 1612); H. Denzinger, *The Sources of Catholic Dogma (Enchiridion Symbolorum)*, trans. by Roy J. Deferrari, 30th ed. (London and St. Louis: Herder, 1955), n. 881ff.
34. Cf. in addition to the above-mentioned works, M. Becanus, *Summa Theologiae Scholasticae* (Rothmagi: I. Behovrt, 1651), I, tract. 5; A. Casini, *Controv. de statu purae naturae*, printed as an appendix to librum II; Petavius, *Opera Omnia*, "de opif. sex dierum" (*Theol. dogm. ed.* [1868], IV, 587–653); *Theologia Wirceburgensi (Theologia Dogmatica: Polemica, Scholastica et Moralis)*, VII, 145ff.; G. Perrone, *Praelectiones Theologicae*, 9 vols. (Louvain: Vanlinthout & Vandezande, 1838–43), III, 166–82; M. J. Scheeben, *Handbuch der Katholischer Dogmatik*, II, 239–514; M. J. Scheeben, *Nature and Grace*, trans. by Cyril Vollert (St. Louis: B. Herder, 1954; C. Schäzler, *Natur und Uebernatur* (Mainz: Kirchheim, 1865) [*ed. note:* Bavinck's citation reads simply *Natur u. Gnade.*]; H. Th. Simar, *Lehrbuch der Dogmatik*, 2 vols., 3rd ed. (Freiburg i.B.: Herder, 1879–80), 326ff.; C. Pesch, *Praelectiones Dogmaticae*, III: De Deo creante et elevante (Freiburg i.B.: Herder, 1916–25), 76–111 enz.

subordinate points there was a variety of differences. Some, such as Hales, Bonaventure, Albert the Great, Duns Scotus, Biel, and others, asserted that the supernatural gift of *gratia gratum faciens* was distinct from the original righteousness that man immediately possessed by nature at the moment of his creation, and was bestowed later in time than this original righteousness.[35] According to them, man was first created with "original righteousness" *(iustitia originalis)*, which enabled him to earn the grace which makes acceptable by a merit of congruity *(gratia gratum faciens ex congruo);* and having received the latter, he could by it gain heavenly blessedness *ex condigno,* a condigned or full merit. But Thomas objected to this idea, because in that case the *gratia gratum faciens* was also grounded on merits if a personal gift to Adam could not have been lost or acquired for all his descendants and could not then be bestowed without merit on small children in baptism. Thomas, therefore, taught that at the moment of his creation Adam had received the *gratia gratum faciens* along with original righteousness.[36] The Council of Trent avoided taking sides in this dispute between Franciscans and Dominicans and only declared (Session V, 1) that Adam had "lost the holiness and justice in which he had been constituted." Although later theologians usually followed Thomas and let original justice coincide *in fact and in time* with the *gratia gratum faciens,* ideally and logically the position remained the same.

Roman Catholic theology has a dual conception of humanity: man in the purely natural sense, without supernatural grace, is indeed sinless but only possesses natural religion and virtue and has his destiny on earth; man endowed with the superadded gift of the image of God has a supernatural religion and virtue and a destiny in heaven. But with this dual notion of man the search was not over. As soon as one attempted to imagine what belonged to the former idea of man and what belonged to the latter, one got in trouble with the various gifts granted to the first human being. Immortality and impassibility could not strictly be called natural, for they are not qualities belonging to Adam's earthly body as such and could be lost. On the other hand, they could not be the consequence of the *gratia gratum faciens* either, for then man in his purely natural state without the superadded gift would have been susceptible to death and suffering, and in that case death would not be the penalty for sin. The same is true for inordinate lust (concupiscence). According to Rome, the conflict between flesh and spirit is natural. The subjection

35. Alexander of Hales, *Summa Theol.,* II, qu. 96 m. 1.; Bonaventure, *Sent.* II, dist. 29, art. 2, qu. 2 enz.

36. T. Aquinas, *Summa Theol.,* I, qu. 100, art. 1; *Sent.,* II, dist. 20, qu. 2, art. 3, dist. 29, qu. 1, art. 1.

of the flesh to the spirit, therefore, is something supernatural, not something given with creation as such. At the same time, it can also not be attributed only to the *gratia gratum faciens*, for in that case a sinless human being without the superadded gift would not be possible. Consequently, between the two ideas described above Rome had to insert a third notion—preternatural.

Human beings are, therefore, conceived as endowed with natural, preternatural, and supernatural gifts. There are three kinds of justice, a natural, a preternatural, and a supernatural kind. It is not surprising that some theologians, such as Berti, Norisius, and others, could not imagine a human being endowed only with natural and preternatural gifts. In terms of God's absolute power *(potentia absoluta)* such a human was indeed possible but not in terms of his ordained power *(potentia ordinata)* (i.e., power exerted in and through the natural order). The beatific vision actually properly belongs to man by nature "at least as far as inclination and appetite are concerned" *(saltem quoad inclinationem et appetitum).*[37] But even if the conceivability and possibility of a human being in his or her purely natural state is upheld, all sorts of differences in the doctrine of the image of God remain. Some theologies make a distinction between the "image" and the "likeness" such that the former embraces the natural gifts and the latter the supernatural. Others, like the Roman Catechism, apply both concepts to the supernatural gifts. Hales, Bonaventure, Thomas, and others, in considering original justice, thought of natural righteousness, but the Roman Catechism and most later theologians refer especially to the superadded gifts as original justice. Immortality, impassibility, free will, and the restraint of concupiscence were sometimes derived from a divine gift and at other times from the "image" or the "likeness," and also at times attributed to original righteousness.[38] The Roman Catechism simply lists all these things and does not achieve a consistent view of the whole: thanks to a divine gift, Adam was not susceptible to death and suffering; his soul was created in God's image and likeness; furthermore, his concupiscence was restrained and made subject to reason; then to all this God added original righteousness and dominion.[39] On top of all this, then,

---

37. G. Perrone, *Prael. Theol.*, III, 167; J. H. Oswald, *Religiöse Urgeschichte der Menschheit* (Paderborn: Ferdinand Schöningh, 1885), 52ff. (*ed. note:* cf. J. H. Oswald, *Die Schöpfungslehre im allgemeinen und in besonderer Beziehung auf den Menschen* [Paderborn: F. Schöningh, 1885]; C. Pesch, *Prael. Dogm.*, III, 109).

38. T. Aquinas, *Summa Theol.*, I, qu. 95, art. 1; *Sent*, II, dist. 19, qu. 1, art. 4; C. Pesch, *Prael. Dogm.*, III, 89ff.

39. Roman Catechism, I, 2, qu. 18, 3. For the doctrine of the Greek Orthodox Church, cf. Georgius B. Matulewicz, *Doctrina Russorum de Statu Justitiae Originalis* (Freiburg i.B.: Herder, 1904).

comes the disagreement over the nature of the *gratia gratum faciens*, its relation to the Spirit of God, to the soul and its faculties, to the theological virtues, to good works, and so forth. All this is enough to show that the Roman Catholic doctrine of the image of God is inherently incomplete and in part for that reason fails to satisfy the theological mind.

Critique of Supernaturalism

This doctrine is inadequate, in the first place, because it is based on a mistaken view of man's final destiny. The state of grace and of glory, in which the church of Christ is a participant both here and in the hereafter, is most splendidly described in Holy Scripture as the state of the children of God, as participation in the divine nature, as the vision of God, as eternal life, as heavenly bliss, and so forth. On this issue there is no disagreement between Rome and us: What no eye has seen, nor ear heard, nor the heart of man conceived, that is what God, in the New Testament dispensation of the covenant of grace, has prepared for those who love him (1 Cor. 2:9). But Rome views this final human destiny, which has been realized by Christ, as a Neo-Platonic vision of God and a mystical fusion of the soul with God.[40] And that is not what Scripture teaches. All those benefits which Christ has acquired for his own are not just bestowed in the state of glory but are in principle already granted here on earth (1 Cor. 2:9) and do not, even according to Rome, include the vision of God *per essentiam*. Becoming a child of God is the fruit of faith (John 1:12; Rom. 8:14f.; Gal. 4:6; 1 John 3:1, 2). Eternal life is our portion here already and consists in knowing God in the face of Christ (John 3:16, 36; 17:3). Christ is and remains the way to the Father, to the knowledge and vision of God (Matt. 11:27; John 1:18; 14:6; 1 John 3:2b). The vision of God can only be achieved in the way of ethical Christian living (Matt. 5:8; 1 John 3:6). Even participation in the divine nature is not something for the future alone but a goal envisaged already by the granting of God's promises here on earth (2 Pet. 1:4) and again ethically mediated (Heb. 12:10).

Second, Scripture nowhere teaches that this state of glory, which is already initiated in the state of grace on earth, is "supernatural" and "superadded" in the Roman Catholic sense. Certainly this state of grace and glory far surpasses the reach of human thought and imagination (1 Cor. 2:9; 13:12; 1 John 3:2). It must be remembered, however, that according to 1 Corinthians 2 it is the wisdom of this age and the spirit of this world and the unspiritual person (vv. 6, 8, 12, 14) from whom these divine benefits remain hidden; and this "unspiritual" person is the one who is

---

40. Cf. H. Bavinck, *Gereformeerde Dogmatiek*, II, 154.

guided only by animal instinct, devoid of the spirit of God, and hence darkened in mind. Add to this that what God bestows and will bestow on believers will also remain to them an unmerited gift of grace, a gift that will always and ever arouse them to amazement and worship. Remember further that Christ not only acquired what Adam lost but also what Adam, in the way of obedience, would have gained. The salvific benefits of the covenant of grace, therefore, far surpass the reach of all our thoughts; but nothing in Scripture even hints at the notion that it is all a "superadditive" which originally did not belong to our human nature.

Third, the conclusion drawn by Rome from these benefits of grace in Christ for Adam's state before the fall is incorrect. Rome reasons as follows: If the state of glory for restored human beings consists in conformity to God, it must have consisted in that state also in the case of the first human. And if that state of glory is now attained by believers only by way of the state of grace, the same must be true of Adam before the fall. The connection between the state of grace and that of glory, according to Rome, consists in the fact that in justification man receives infused grace and in virtue of this grace performs good works which *ex condigno* merit eternal life. This entire scheme is then transferred to the first human. His final destiny, too, was the state of glory, a state he could only attain by way of the state of grace by which he could *ex condigno* merit eternal life. Like the state of glory, so also the grace in question is by its very nature supernatural, on a level above the natural man, and therefore a superadded gift. This reasoning on the part of Rome is correct insofar as from the image of God in the case of the restored human it infers that of the first human. There is, in fact, only one image of God. It is also correct insofar as it assumes that Adam's final destiny was no other than that which the believer now receives through Christ: eternal life. There is, in fact, but one ideal for man. But this reasoning is also incorrect.

It is incorrect because between "grace" and "glory" it constructs a bridge of meritoriousness and proceeds by applying it also to Adam. The meritorious value of good works can only be treated later. At this point, however, it must be pointed out that, even if the Roman Catholic view of man's final destiny were correct, Rome still has no right to conceive of grace in an "adequated" supernatural sense. It is also possible, after all, to posit a connection forged by God between certain promises of reward and certain works such that the rewards are not in a strict sense merited *ex condigno* by those works. The promise of eternal life made to Adam in case of obedience, was of such a nature as Reformed theologians taught in their doctrine of the covenant of works.[41] There was a merit *ex pacto* (arising from a covenant), not *ex condigno*. The

41. Cf. the next chapter.

good works of man never merit the glory of heaven; they are never of the same weight and worth *(condignity)*. Rome, however, by introducing the idea of the meritoriousness of good works both in the case of the believer and that of Adam, fails to do full justice to grace. Grace, in Roman Catholic thought, entirely changes its character. It stands in physical, not in ethical, contrast to nature. It does not presuppose sin and guilt, only a lower nature. On the one hand, it transforms everything into grace and so ensures that there is no longer any grace at all. Grace in the case of Adam and the believer, though it is indeed grace, is grace only in the sense in which also life, intellect, wisdom, power, and so forth, are grace. There is here no reason to call only the superadded gift by the name "grace." The fact that Adam was created and received an intellect and will was also and equally grace, even though there are quantitative differences among the various gifts of grace. In that way, really everything that God initially grants to man in creation or in re-creation becomes grace. But that is true only in that initial moment. For the moment man has received those initial gifts, says Rome, he himself is moved by that grace to go to work, and everything he receives from here on he receives as a reward for his merits. Even eternal life is no longer a truly gracious gift of God but a fitting, worthy, proportionate reward for work done. It could still be called a gift of grace only because the power which enabled humans to perform meritorious works was a gift of grace. It is just as the Pelagians put it in ancient times: the enablement *(posse)* is from God, the will *(velle)* from man.[42]

Fourth, we have indicated above that the Roman Catholic doctrine of the superadded gift has led, and had to lead, to a threefold understanding of human nature. To Rome there is not just one idea and one moral law and one destiny for humanity. Just as in other creaturely realms, so in the human world, hierarchy and rankings persist as well. In the abstract conceivably there is one human with natural justice, another with preternatural justice, and a third with supernatural justice. The first of these three humans is only slightly above an animal, subject to inordinate lust, to the natural contrast between flesh and spirit, as well as to physical suffering and temporal death. But in his will there still remains the power to do good, not to let inordinate lust issue into sinful deeds, and thus indeed to live a natural but still sinless life. The human being after the fall virtually still corresponds to that image. Although original sin is still frequently construed not only in a negative but also in a positive sense, it is nevertheless consistently conceived as

42. The value of Bensdorp's statement needs to be judged in this light: "Catholic doctrine splendidly maintains the absolute gratuity of grace. It is not only *factually* but by its very nature entirely gratuitous." *De Katholiek* 115 (1898): 81.

weakened to the degree that the physical contrast between nature and grace replaces the ethical antithesis between sin and grace. According to many Catholic thinkers, it consists only negatively in a loss of the superadded gift that God in his good pleasure bestowed on the first human.[43] The human being lacking that gift therefore remains a complete and perfect human person in his kind—and however hard it might be for him, especially over time, to remain so, nevertheless, if he so desires, he can remain a sinless one. This explains Rome's mellow judgment concerning unbaptized dying children and the pagans who have made good use of the light and powers of nature. They have no guilt and will therefore not be punished; they receive a penalty of loss *(poena damni)*, not of the senses *(poena sensus)*.

God, however, did not create the first human as such a natural man. He immediately gave him a preternatural righteousness as well. Hence Adam was not subject to inordinate lust, suffering, and death, even physical death, apart from the actual superadded gift (i.e., *gratia gratum faciens*). This is a second idea of man that is conceivable and possible. Such a person could have kept God's commandments without resistance from the flesh (the gift of integrity) but his righteousness would nevertheless have remained natural and not have merited the vision of God *per essentiam*. This second conception of man is then once more taken a step further by the addition of the superadded gift which results in a human being complete with supernatural righteousness. As is the case throughout the Roman Catholic system, so also here in the doctrine of the image of God we encounter the contrast between the natural and the supernatural, between the human and the divine, between the terrestrial and the celestial, and within each of these categories a host of gradations. In the ethical and religious life there is a wide range of ranks and classes and standings. Not all people are on—or aspire to— the same level. If God is at the center, his creatures gather round him in ever widening circles. Most distant from him is the natural man; then comes the preternatural man; finally the supernatural man. And in the last class there again are all kinds of distinctions and degrees. There are clergy and laypersons, monks and ordinary people, precepts and counsels, a lower and a higher morality. On the highest level stands the mystic who by meditation, ascesis, and prayer already here on earth achieves contemplation. And above the humans stand the angels, in turn organized in all sorts of rankings. Everything tends to rise upward toward God in ever increasing proximity to him. The soul's fusion with God is the highest bliss. So, in Catholicism, there is a place for everyone. It takes account of each person's capacity and fitness. It has varying ide-

43. Cf., e.g., J. H. Oswald, *Religiöse Urgeschichte*, 59, 137ff.

als for different people. It does not make the same moral and religious demands on everybody. Pierson correctly highlighted this fact; only he regarded as the principle and essence what is no more than a consequence and appearance.[44] It was against this Neo-Platonic Areopagite philosophy that the Reformation, taking its stand in Scripture, took action. Scripture knows of no such contrast between the natural and the supernatural. It knows only one idea of humanness, one moral law, one final destiny, one priesthood which is the portion of all believers.

Fifth, it is clear from this that the reason why Rome teaches a preternatural and supernatural justice is not that otherwise the amissibility of original justice cannot be explained. It is true that Roman Catholic theologians keep advancing this objection against the teaching of the Reformation: original righteousness belongs to man's essence or it does not; if the former is true, it is amissible, or, if it is nevertheless lost, then man by that token loses a part of his essence and ceases to be a complete human being. But, however often this objection is repeated, it is not to escape this objection that Rome came to the doctrine of the superadded gift. The very same difficulty still adheres to the Roman Catholic view since Adam also had natural, original righteousness. This natural righteousness, though it is natural and flows from the basic principles and powers of the natural man without supernatural assistance (albeit not without the universal help of divine preservation), can nevertheless still be lost and is in fact lost by many persons. Still, even the most degenerate sinner, one devoid of all natural justice, is still a human being. The possibility of losing and the actual loss of original righteousness, therefore, can absolutely not serve as an argument against its natural character. If that were the case, also the natural justice that Rome teaches would have to be called supernatural. The question between Rome and us is a very different one.

Original righteousness can be lost because it is an incidental property (accident) of human nature, no part of its substance. But among the "accidents" which as such can be lost Rome again makes a distinction between that which is naturally an "accident" and that which is supernaturally an "accident."[45] In our view, however, all natural righteousness is a natural "accident"; according to Rome, the *gratia gratum faciens* is a supernatural "accident." Why is that? Not to make possible or clear the possibility of its being lost, but because without it man would be a defective creature. Rome expressly teaches that, given the fact that God wanted to make a being consisting of soul and body, spirit

---

44. A. Pierson, *Geschiedenis van het Roomsch-katholicisme tot op het Concilie van Trente*, 4 vols. (Haarlem: A. C. Kruseman, 1868–72), I, 24ff.

45. Bensdorp, *De Katholiek*, CX, 56.

and matter, he could no more fashion these two, soul and body, in complete harmony than he could make a square circle. Flesh and spirit by their very nature fight each other, and without supernatural grace God cannot prevent conflict between these two elements. Bellarmine clearly states that man is composed of flesh and spirit and therefore in part tends to a corporal good and in part to a spiritual good; and that "from these diverse or contrary propensities there exists a certain conflict in one and the same human being." He further taught that "from the beginning of creation divine providence, in order to apply a remedy *to this sickness or weakness of human nature that arises from its material condition*, added to man a certain noteworthy gift, namely, original righteousness, so as to hold, as though by a kind of golden bridle, the inferior part to the superior and the superior part, which is easily subjected, to God."[46] Here it is clearly stated that the flesh by its very nature is opposed to the spirit. Matter is a power that stands over against God, one that is not per se sinful as in Manicheism, but nevertheless of a very low order, moves totally in a direction of its own, and automatically tempts man to engage in struggle and sin. That power is even of such a magnitude that reason alone cannot, at least not without great difficulty, control the motion of the soul. Needed to that end is a special supernatural grace. As in the philosophy of Plotinus, matter here is a creation that is very far removed from God, by nature hostile to all that is spiritual, and therefore has to be forcibly restrained.

Finally, in the sixth place, Rome's doctrine of the superadded gift implies a peculiar view of Christianity. In Rome's view, the Christian religion indeed also serves to save [us] from sin; but primarily and most importantly its purpose is to restore to man the grace which had been granted to Adam as a superadded gift but was lost to him. This grace was as necessary to man before the fall as it is necessary to us now and was as supernatural then as it is now after the fall. Hence, according to Rome, grace is a supernatural gift as such and not incidentally *(per accidens)*, not only because of sin.[47] Sin has not in any way changed the nature of grace. Perhaps grace has been increased by sin; but both before and after the fall it was identically the same, namely, an *elevation* [of man] *above nature*. That is its character and essence. Christianity, accordingly, may also still be a religion of redemption; but preeminently it is not a *reparation* but an *elevation* of nature; it serves to elevate nature above itself, that is, to divinize humanity. In the case of Adam the *gratia gratum faciens* served that goal; now Christianity serves that

46. R. Bellarmine, *De Gratia Primi Hominis*, 5, cf. 7; Bensdorp, *De Katholiek* 115 (1898): 256.
47. R. Bellarmine, *De Gratia Primi Hominis*, 5.

goal. Hence then and now his grace is the same; that is, the essential element in Christianity was not necessitated by the fall; it was already necessary before the fall. As the elevation of nature, Christianity was already present to Adam prior to the fall. The reception of infused grace is now bound—aside from the preparations—specifically to belief in two dogmas: the Trinity and the incarnation.[48] Now then: the same was true in the case of Adam. Even before the fall he was familiar with both.[49] The incarnation, by this logic, was therefore necessary before the fall and apart from sin. In other words, in order that man might become like God, God had to become man. This law was in effect both before and after the fall. Now, solely as a subordinate component, the incarnation brings atonement with it. But for Rome the point of gravity does not lie in satisfaction for and the forgiveness of sin but in the humanization of God and the divinization of man.[50]

The Reformation View of the Image

The Reformers unanimously rejected this teaching, especially because it led to a weakening of [the doctrine of] original sin. Their opposition was primarily directed against the Scholastic thesis: "While the supernatural qualities are lost, the natural ones still remain whole." And from there they reasoned back to the image of God. If by sin, by the loss of the image of God, man had become totally corrupt, it must also have belonged to his nature. Thus Luther maintained "that righteousness was not a gift which came from without, separate from man's nature, but . . . was truly part of his nature, so that it was Adam's nature to love God, to believe God, to know God, etc."[51] But even the Reformers had to maintain a distinction between what was left and what was lost of the image of God. To that end they used the words "substance," "essence," "attributes," "gifts," even "supernatural gifts." The Apology of the Augsburg Confession calls the knowledge and fear of God in Adam "gifts" and the Formula of Concord speaks of the "properties concreated in the paradise of nature."[52] The Lutheran dogmaticians indeed called the image of God natural insofar as human nature could not be pure without that image and was immediately concreated with that image. But they de-

48. Cf. H. Bavinck, *Gereformeerde Dogmatiek,* I, 579.
49. Becanus, *Theol. schol.,* I, tr. 5, c. 2; H. Th. Simar, *Lehrbuch der Dogmatik,* 3rd ed., 332; C. Pesch, *Prael. Dogm.,* II, 89 enz.; T. Aquinas, *Summa Theol.,* II, 2, qu. 2, art. 7, qu. 5, art. 1.
50. Cf. H. Bavinck, *Gereformeerde Dogmatiek,* I, 324ff.
51. M. Luther, *Luther's Works,* vol. 1, *Lectures on Genesis 1–3,* 165.
52. J. T. Müller, *Die Symbolischen Bücher der Evangelische-Lutherischen Kirche,* 5th ed. (Gütersloh: Bertelsmann, 1898), 80, 81, 580.

nied that the image of God was natural in the sense that it automatically flowed from human nature as such and was therefore an inamissible and essential component of it. Some, such as Gerhard, Quenstedt, and others, also specifically called the supernatural favor of God, the gracious inhabitation of the holy Trinity and the resulting pleasure and enjoyment, supernatural gifts.[53] So also Calvin makes a distinction between the substance of the soul and its attributes, and, with Augustine, says: "the natural attributes were corrupted in man by sin, but the supernatural ones were removed"; he even calls the latter "extraneous, not an intrinsic part of nature."[54] And many Reformed theologians similarly drew a distinction between natural qualities and supernatural gifts.[55] Many of them derived immortality from the grace of God, not from Adam's nature.[56] Even the ancient distinction between "image" and "likeness" was taken over by many and also applied in that sense.[57] It soon became clear, however, that even where Protestants retained the expression "supernatural gifts," they meant something else by it. The idea among Roman Catholics is that one can very well conceive a human being without these supernatural gifts. Indeed, as a rational and moral being, man would also have some knowledge of God, the moral law, and righteousness. But [according to Rome] there is an essential difference among knowledge, love, and righteousness in a natural sense and these qualities in a supernatural sense, between the natural and the supernatural man, between a human being and a Christian, between the world and the church, between nature and grace. Grace is not merely restorative, but an elevation and completion of nature. It was this position which the Reformation opposed as a matter of fundamental principle. And so it had to come around, and in fact did come around, to the doctrine that the image of God essentially belonged to man by nature, and that without it man could only exist in an "impure nature," as a sinner.

But the scholars of the Reformation, too, held differing views of the image of God. In the early period some Lutherans still equated the image of God with the essence of man and the substance of the soul,[58]

53. J. Gerhard, *Loci Theol.*, VIII, c. 1–3; J. Quenstedt, *Theologia*, II, 1–48; D. Hollaz, *Examen Theol.*, 461–88.

54. J. Calvin, *Institutes of the Christian Religion*, I, 15, 2; II, 2, 12.

55. J. Maccovius, *Loci Comm.*, 105ff.

56. J. Zanchi, *Op. Theol.*, III, 497; A. Polanus, *Syn. Theol.*, V, 29; F. Junius, *Op. Theol. Select.*, I, 211; Bucanus, *Theol.*, XI, 12; Maccovius, *Loci*, 409.

57. J. Zanchi, *Op. Theol.*, III, 486; Justin Martyr on Genesis 1:26; J. Alsted, *Theol.*, 281.

58. M. Luther in J. Köstlin, *The Theology of Luther in Its Historical Development and Inner Harmony*, trans. by Charles E. Hay, 2 vols. (Philadelphia: Lutheran Publication Society, 1897), I, 144–55; Melancthon, Hemming, Selnecker in H. Heppe, *Dogmatik des deutschen Protestantismus im sechzehnten Jahrhundert*, 3 vols. (Gotha: F. A. Perthes, 1857), I, 338ff.

but Lutheran theology as such was grounded in another idea. Its subjective soteriological character necessarily led to an exclusive identification of the image of God with the moral qualities which the first man received and whose loss made man, religiously and ethically, a "block of wood." Luther already frequently put all the emphasis on the gifts, and completely equated the image of God with them.[59] The confessional writings followed the same lines,[60] and so did the theologians Heerbrand, Hunnius, Gerhard, Quenstedt, Hollaz, and others.[61] The Lutherans did not indeed deny that the essence of man also expresses something divine, but the actual image of God consists only in "original righteousness" with the associated qualities of "immortality, impassibility, dominion," and a "most blissful condition." Only the Son, after all, is essentially and substantially the image of God (Heb. 1:3); in man the image is an "accidental perfection," capable of being lost and in fact lost (Rom. 3:23) and only renewed and restored in the believer (Rom. 8:29; 2 Cor. 3:18; 5:17; Eph. 4:24; Col. 3:10).

Reformed theologians, however, from the beginning incorporated also the essence of man in the image of God. Heppe is wrong when he asserts that Calvin and Zanchius did not teach this.[62] While Calvin does make a distinction between the soul's substance and its gifts, he expressly states that the image of God consisted in "those marks of excellence with which God had distinguished Adam over all other living creatures" and that consequently it also consists in integrity.[63] All the Reformed theologians agreed with this;[64] only Cocceius,[65] presenting an alternative view, taught that while the soul and its properties were presupposed by the image of God, they were not its content but only the canvas, so to speak, on which God painted his image. The image itself, according to Cocceius, consisted only in the gifts, as taught by 2 Corinthians 3:18, Ephesians 4:24, and Colossians 3:10. Others put it this way: the image of God consists antecedently in man's spiritual nature, for-

59. M. Luther in J. Köstlin, *The Theology of Luther*, II, 339–61; Heppe, *Dogmatik des Deutschen Protestantismus*, I, 345.

60. J. T. Müller, *Die Symbolischen Bücher der Evangelische-Lutherischen Kirche*, 80, 576.

61. E.g., J. Gerhard, *Loci Theol.*, VIII, c. 1; J. Quenstedt, *Theologia*, II, 3–10, 17–23; D. Hollaz, *Examen Theol.*, 464ff.

62. H. Heppe, *Reformed Dogmatics*, rev. and ed. by E. Bizer, trans. by G. T. Thomson (Grand Rapids: Baker, 1978 [1950]), 232, 233.

63. J. Calvin, *Institutes of the Christian Religion*, I, 15, 2; II, 12, 6; *Commentary on Genesis* 1:26, 9:6; *Commentary on James* 3:9.

64. J. Zanchi, *Op. Theol.*, III, 486, 477ff.; Z. Ursinus, *Heidelberg Catechism*, qu. 7; Justin Martyr, *Loci*, c. 46ff.; A. Polanus, *Syn. Theol.*, V, 34; *Synopsis Purioris Theologiae*, XIII, 36; M. Leydekker, *Fax Veritatis*, 395 enz.

65. J. Cocceius, *Summa Theologiae ex Scripturis Repetita*, XVII, §§12–24; cf. also J. H. Heidegger, *Corpus Theologiae*, VI, 119; J. Braun, *Doctrina Foederum*, I, 2, 15, 5ff.

mally in sanctity, and consequently in dominion.[66] As a rule, however, Reformed theologians continued to speak of the image of God in a broader and a narrower sense. In Holy Scripture, they read that man, on the one hand, is still called the image of God after the fall and should be respected as such (Gen. 5:1; 9:6; Acts 17:28; 1 Cor. 11:7; James 3:9); and that, on the other hand, he had nevertheless lost the primary content of the image of God (i.e., knowledge, righteousness, and holiness) and only regains these qualities in Christ (Eph. 4:24; Col. 3:10). By observing this distinction in Scripture and incorporating it in their theology, Reformed theologians have maintained the bond between the physical and the ethical nature of man and thereby also at this point (the relation between nature and grace) kept themselves from falling into various errors. Soon an additional distinction arose which was especially worked out in the doctrine of the covenant of works. This distinction answered the question what Adam had to become, not what Adam was. It is only in these three areas—the image of God in the broad sense, the image of God in the narrow sense, and the development or destination of the image of God—that is, in the doctrine of the covenant of works—can the locus of the image of God be treated to the full extent.

Rome and the Reformation

Between the Roman Catholic doctrine of the image of God and that of the Reformation there is a profound difference which makes itself felt over the whole field of theology. This difference is not located in the expression "original justice or righteousness." For, though Roman Catholic theologians use this term in a variety of senses, later ones sometimes also describe the supernatural righteousness by means of it. The righteousness of the first human being can be called "original" since from his origin he was characterized by his positive correspondence to the law of God and since original righteousness can be distinguished as such from habitual or actual righteousness. Also, in the case of Adam, the original righteousness was the beginning and root of his actual righteousness. After Thomas there was not even disagreement over the question whether this original righteousness would, for all humanity, have been the source of its actual righteousness if Adam had remained standing, since Adam received it not as a private but as a public person. The dispute concerned the question whether that

66. F. Turretin, *Institutes* of *Elenctic Theology*, V, qu. 10, §§6; L. Ryssen, *Summa Theol.*, 178; H. Witsius, *The Oeconomy of the Covenants*, 1. 2, 11; W. Brakel, *The Christian's Reasonable Service*, trans. by Bartel Elshout, 4 vols. (Ligonier, Pa.: Soli Deo Gloria, 1992), I, 323–26.

original righteousness was *natural* or, at least in part, *supernatural.* Reformed theologians asserted the former. By that they did not mean to say that this original righteousness arose automatically from human nature understood in the sense of a union of spirit and matter, nor that it could not be called a gift—even of God's grace in a broad sense. Rather they used this term to maintain the conviction that the image of God, that is, original righteousness, was inseparable from the idea of man as such and that it referred to the normal state, the harmony, the health of a human being; that without it a human cannot be true, complete, or normal. When man loses that image of God, he does not lose a substance and does indeed remain human, but becomes an abnormal, a sick, a spiritually dead human being, a sinner. He then lacks something that belonged to his nature, just as a blind man loses his sight, a deaf man his hearing, and a sick man his health. In Rome's view a human being can lose the "supernatural righteousness" and still be a good, true, complete, sinless human, with a natural justice which, in its kind, is without any defect. But, according to Protestant theologians, a human being cannot. There is no intermediate state between man as image of God and man as sinner. He is either a son of God, his offspring, his image, or he is a child of wrath, dead in sins and trespasses. When that human being again by faith receives that perfect righteousness in Christ, that benefit is indeed a supernatural gift but it is supernatural "as an accident," "incidentally"; he regains that which belongs to his being, like the blind man who again receives his sight.

Now this doctrine is grounded in Holy Scripture, which nowhere speaks of "supernatural gifts" in connection with the creation of man. Rome, accordingly, does not appeal to Genesis 1:26–31, Ecclesiastes 7:29, and so forth, but to the New Testament representation of the state of grace and the state of glory, an appeal which can in no way serve as proof. Scripture everywhere proceeds from the assumption that humanity is akin to God and his offspring. The service of God, the love for God, fellowship with God is not a superadded gift but originally and integrally human. God claims all of man—mind, heart, soul, body, and all his or her energies—for his service and his love. The moral law is one for all humans in all times, and the moral ideal is the same for all people. There is no "lower" or "higher" righteousness, no double morality, no twofold set of duties. Original righteousness is so natural that, even according to most Catholic theologians, it would have been inherited by Adam's descendants in the event of his obedience, and that even now the pagans still do what the law requires (Rom. 2:15). Accordingly, the objection that the Reformed position is caught in an antinomy since, on the one hand, it calls original righteousness "natural" and, on the other, "amissible" and "accidental,"[67] is based solely on misunderstanding.[68] Original righteousness is called natural, not because it consists in a certain substance or essence, but because it is a natural attribute or quality. Just as good health belongs to the nature of man, but is still "amissible," that is, can still be lost, so it is with the image of God. Rome and the Reformation both agree that original righteousness is neither a material nor a spiritual substance, as the Manicheans taught, but an "accident," a quality. And the sole difference concerns the question whether it is naturally "accidental" or, at least in part, supernaturally "accidental."[69] Rome only says of natural justice that it is naturally accidental while the Reformation makes this claim for the whole of original righteousness.

67. Bensdorp in *De Katholiek*, CX, 43; cf. also D. F. Strauss, *Der Alte und der Neue Glaube* (Leipzig: Hirzel, 1872), I, 708; Lipsius, *Dogm.*, §434.
68. Cf. F. A. Philippi, *Kirchliche Glaubenslehre* (Gütersloh: Bertelsmann, 1902), III, 408.
69. Bensdorp, *De Katholiek*, CX, 56–60; Bensdorp later provides yet a more elaborate defense of the Roman Catholic teaching concerning original righteousness in *De Katholiek* CXII (September 1896), CXIV (July/August and October/November 1898), CXV (1899): 23–46, CXVI (1900): 22–42. However, Bensdorp cannot escape the objections brought against this view except by making all sorts of distinctions that serve no other purpose than to rescue the notion out of the difficulty. He not only distinguishes substance and essence on the one hand from attributes *(accidens)* and qualities *(qualitas)* on the other, but when it is pointed out to him that attributes *(accidentia)* that are *essential* to human nature such as health, unity of body and soul, mind, original righteousness *(justitia originalis)* are still amissable, he makes further distinctions between essential qualities *(qualitates essentialis)* that are *in* the essence *(essentia)* (such as rationality) and essential attributes *(accidentia essentialia)* that are outside the essence *(essentia)* but still necessarily flow forth from them. He also distinguishes qualities *(accidens)* over against essence *(substantia)* from qualities *(accidens)* over against properties *(proprium)*; between attributes of kind *(accidens speciei)* and individual attributes *(accidens individui)*; between natural righteousness *(justitia naturalis)* as *potentia*, that as an attribute of kind *(accidens speciei)* is not amissable and a natural righteousness *(justitia naturalis)* as act *(actus)* that as an individual attribute *(accidens individui)* flows forth from a contingent free will and is therefore amissable. He thus comes to the conclusion finally that the original supernatural righteousness *(justitia supernaturalis* [*originalis*]*)* was indeed an attribute of kind *(accidens speciei)* but "not a natural attribute of kind *(accidens speciei naturale)* (in other words, not an essential attribute [*accidens essentiale*], not an attribute of kind [*accidens speciei*], therefore, in a strict sense" (*De Katholiek* 115 [October/November 1898]: 251, cf. 261, note). He then proceeds to argue that the original righteousness *(justitia originalis)* was an attribute of kind *(accidens speciei)* and that the human nature notwithstanding the fact that it was lost remains undamaged. This demonstrates thus "that the original righteousness *(justitia originalis)* was not an attribute of kind *(accidens speciei)* in the ordinary sense of the term." In other words, at the end of all this argumentation, the thesis from which Bensdorp proceeded was simply reiterated and the one and only proof given was borrowed from Rome's teaching concerning the *donum superadditum.* It is this which is apriori infallible and the reason why the distinction *must* be made. The objections brought against it therefore remain as strong as before: Just as health, unity of body and soul, reason, natural righteousness (not substantial being in manichaean sense, but still) belong to the essence of humanity and are nonetheless still losable, so too the original righteousness is naturally and essentially proper to humans. When this is lost, one does not cease to be human but becomes an abnormal, fallen person.

But for that reason, as stated above, Rome's entire case against the teaching that the image of God is natural collapses, for Rome itself acknowledges that natural justice is natural and still amissible, and is therefore no longer in a position to lodge this objection against the teaching of the Protestants. Its doctrine, accordingly, did not arise from the objection that the naturalness of original righteousness cannot be squared with its amissibility, but it owes its origin to an entirely different rationale, namely, the Neo-Platonic view of the ideal for the Christian life. It is *that* Neo-Platonism which the Reformation, basing itself on Scripture, rejected. In that connection it took care not to fall into the trap of any form of Manicheism. Man lost none of his substance as a result of sin. In that sense humans are fully human even after the fall. But when man lost his original righteousness he lost the harmony and health of his nature, and became a sinner through and through. His nature in the sense of substance or essence remained, but the moral qualities naturally belonging to his nature were lost.[70]

Lutheran or Reformed

Now this splendid view of the image of God and of original righteousness has come more clearly into its own in the Reformed church and Reformed theology than in the Lutheran. In Lutheran theology the image of God is restricted to original righteousness and was therefore totally lost when the latter was lost. In this theology the lines of demarcation between the spiritual and the worldly, between the heavenly and the earthly, are so sharply drawn that the result is two hemispheres and the connection between nature and grace, between creation and re-creation is totally denied.[71] The supernaturalist view is still at work here;

---

70. Cf. J. H. Scholten, *De Leer der Hervormde Kerk*, I, 304–26; Cannegieter, "De Godsdienst in den Mensch en de Mensch in den Godsdienst," *Teylers Theologische Tijdschrift* (1904): 178–211, esp. 199f.; A. Bruining, "De Roomsche Leer van het donum superadditum," *Teylers Theologische Tijdschrift* (1907): 564–97. The last-mentioned correctly contends that the natural man *(homo naturalis)* as understood by Rome is indeed a religious being and that, therefore, religion (as natural religion) is not extrinsic to human nature or added to it as a *donum superadditum*. But he weakens the significance of the distinction that Rome makes between natural religion *(religio naturalis)* and supernatural religion *(religio supernaturalis)* when he says that the image of a rein "is merely an image and nothing more," that the *donum superadditum* in the Roman Catholic view in fact merges with the pure nature *(natura pura)*. From this Bruining also comes to the notion that the Roman Catholic viewpoint is more reasonable than the Old Protestant view and that the Roman Catholic Church has advantage of strength over her opposition. One could only come to this conclusion if one substantially misunderstood Roman teaching concerning the image of God in man and its significance for the Roman system and sees nothing in it but a peculiar, supernaturalistic form of the religious notion that it is not *my* work but a work of *God* in me that brings me to my highest goal. The Roman Catholic teaching was far better portrayed by De Bussy, "Katholicisme en Protestantisme," *Theol. Tijdschrift* (1888): 253–313.
71. Cf. H. Bavinck, *Gereformeerde Dogmatiek*, I, 276.

the image of God stands alongside of nature, is detached from it, and is above it. The loss of the image, which renders man totally deaf and blind in spiritual matters, still enables him in earthly matters to do much good and in a sense renders him independent from the grace of God in Christ. Reformed theology, on the other hand, by its distinction between the image of God in a broader and a narrower sense, has most soundly maintained the connection between substance and quality, nature and grace, creation and re-creation. It must be granted that this distinction has often been conceived too mechanically and needs to be further developed organically. Nevertheless, Reformed theology has most vividly brought out the fact that the image of God in the narrower sense is most intimately bound up with that in the broader sense, and that the two components together make up the full image of God. The whole being, therefore, and not *something in man* but *man himself*, is the image of God. Further, sin, which precipitated the loss of the image of God in the narrower sense and spoiled and ruined the image of God in the broader sense, has profoundly affected the whole person, so that, consequently, also the grace of God in Christ restores the whole person, and is of the greatest significance for his or her whole life and labor, also in the family, society, the state, art, science, and so forth.

The Whole Person as the Image of God

In our treatment of the doctrine of the image of God, then, we must highlight, in accordance with Scripture and the Reformed confession, the idea that a human being does not *bear* or *have* the image of God but that he or she *is* the image of God. As a human being a man is the son, the likeness, or offspring of God (Gen. 1:26; 9:6; Luke 3:38; Acts 17:28; 1 Cor. 11:7; James 3:9).

Two things are implied in this doctrine. The first is that not something in God—one virtue or perfection or another to the exclusion of still others, nor one Person—say, the Son to the exclusion of the Father and the Spirit—but that God himself, the entire Deity, is the archetype of man. Granted, it has frequently been taught that man has specifically been made in the image of the Son or of the incarnate Christ,[72]

72. Clement of Alexandria, *Stromateis*, V, 14; Tertullian, *On the Resurrection of the Flesh*, c. 6; Osiander, according to J. Calvin, *Institutes of the Christian Religion*, I, 15, 2; II, 12, 6; J. C. C. Hofmann, *Der Schriftbeweis*, 3 vols. (Nördlingen: Beck, 1857–60), I, 290; G. Thomasius, *Christi Person und Werk*, 3rd ed. (Erlangen: Theodor Bläsing, 1853–61), I, 126; *Beck, *Glaubenslehre*, II, 329; L. F. Schoeberlein in *Herzog*, 2nd ed., 4, 7; H. Martensen, *Christian Dogmatics*, trans. by William Urwick (Edinburgh: T. & T. Clark, 1871), §72, 136–37; F. Delitzsch, *A System of Biblical Psychology*, trans. by Robert E. Wallis, 2nd ed. (Edinburgh: T. & T. Clark, 1875), 86–87, etc.

but there is nothing in Scripture that supports this notion. Scripture repeatedly tells us that man was made in the image of God, not that we have been modeled on Christ, but that he was made in our likeness (Rom. 8:3; Phil. 2:7, 8; Heb. 2:14) and that we, having been conformed to the image of Christ, are now again becoming like God (Rom. 8:29; 1 Cor. 15:49; 2 Cor. 3:18; Phil. 3:21; Eph. 4:24; Col. 3:10; 1 John 3:2). It is therefore much better for us to say that the Triune Being, God, is the archetype of man,[73] while at the same time exercising the greatest caution in the psychological exploration of the trinitarian components of man's being.[74]

On the other hand, it follows from the doctrine of human creation in the image of God that this image extends to the whole person. Nothing in a human being is excluded from the image of God. While all creatures display *vestiges* of God, only a human being is the *image* of God. And he is such totally, in soul and body, in all his faculties and powers, in all conditions and relations. Man is the image of God because and insofar as he is truly human, and he is truly and essentially human, because, and to the extent, he is the image of God. Naturally, just as the cosmos is an organism and reveals God's attributes more clearly in some than in other creatures, so also in man as an organism the image of God comes out more clearly in one part than another, more in the soul than in the body, more in the ethical virtues than in the physical powers. None of this, however, detracts in the least from the truth that the whole person is the image of God. Scripture could not and should not speak of God in a human manner and transfer all human attributes to God if God had not first made man totally in his image. And it is the task of Christian theology to point out this image of God in man's being in its entirety.

God is, first of all, demonstrable in the human soul. According to Genesis 2:7, man was formed from the dust of the earth by having the breath of life *(nišmat hayîm)* breathed into his nostrils and so becoming a living soul *(nepeš hayām, psychē zōsa)*. The breath of life is the principle of life; the living soul is the essence of man. By means of this combination Scripture accords to man a unique and independent place of his own and avoids both pantheism and materialism. The names *rûaḥ* and *nepeš (pneuma* and *psychē)*, which in Scripture denote the invisible component of man, make this very clear. Trichotomism, which is fun-

---

73. Augustine, *The Trinity*, XII, 6; P. Lombard, *Sent.*, II, dist. 16; T. Aquinas, *Summa Theol.*, I, qu. 13, art. 5.

74. J. Calvin, *Institutes of the Christian Religion*, I, 15, 4; idem, *Comm. on Genesis* 1:26; J. Polyander, *Synopsis Purioris Theologiae*, XIII, 7; J. Quenstedt, *Theologia*, II, 4; D. Hollaz, *Examen Theol.*, 466.

damentally rooted in Plato's dualism, and repeatedly found acceptance in gnostic and theosophical schools of thought, sees here two distinct substances.[75] But this is wrong. Hebrews 4:12 and 1 Thessalonians 5:23 no more contain a list of all the essential constituents of man than, say, Luke 10:27, and therefore do not prove anything. Soul and spirit in Scripture repeatedly occur in parallelism and interchangeably. One moment "body and soul" constitute the nature of man, the next it is "body and spirit" (Matt. 10:28; 1 Cor. 7:34; James 2:26). Psychic activities are in turn attributed to the spirit and to the soul (Ps. 139:14; Prov. 19:2 and 17:27; Ps. 77:7; 1 Cor. 2:11; Num. 21:4; and Job 21:4; 1 Sam. 1:10 and Isa. 54:6; Luke 1:46 and 47, etc.). Dying is called both the surrender of the soul (Gen. 35:18; 1 Kings 17:21; Matt. 20:28; Acts 15:26; 20:10) and the surrender of the spirit (Ps. 31:6; Matt. 27:50; Luke 8:55; 23:46; Acts 7:59). Sometimes the spirit and sometimes the soul is called immortal (Eccl. 12:7; Matt. 10:28); the dead are called "souls" (Rev. 6:9; 20:4) as well as "spirits" (Heb. 12:23; 1 Pet. 3:19). Still, though not essentially different, they are by no means identical. Man is "spirit," because he did not, like the animals, come forth from the earth, but had the breath of life breathed into him by God (Gen. 2:7); because he received his life-principle from God (Eccl. 12:7); because he has a spirit of his own, distinct from the Spirit of God (Gen. 41:8; 45:27; Exod. 35:21; Deut. 2:30; Judg. 15:19; Ezek. 3:14; Zech. 12:1; Matt. 26:41; Mark 2:8; Luke 1:47; 23:46; John 11:33; Acts 7:59; 17:16; Rom. 8:16; 1 Cor. 2:11, 5:3–5; 1 Thess. 5:23; Heb. 4:12; 12:23 etc.); because as such he is akin to the angels, can also think spiritual or heavenly things, and if necessary exist also without a body. But man is "soul," because from the very beginning the spiritual component in him (unlike that of the angels) is adapted to and organized for a body and is bound, also for his intellectual and spiritual life, to the sensual and external faculties; because he can rise to the higher faculties only from a substratum of the lower ones; hence because he is a sensual and material being and as such related to the animals. Man is a rational animal, a thinking reed,

75. Trichotomism, in its first phase, passed from Platonic philosophy to certain Christian authors, but later, especially because of Appollinaris, fell into disrepute. Not until modern times did it again find acceptance in the work of Olshausen, Beck, Delitzsch, Auberlen, and others. In England it was particularly defended—in connection with conditional immortality—by J. B. Heard, *The Tripartite Nature of Man*, 2nd ed. (Edinburgh: T. & T. Clark, 1866), but refuted inter alia by J. Laidlaw, *The Bible Doctrine of Man* (Edinburgh: T. & T. Clark, 1895), 66ff. and in the art. "Psychology" in J. Hastings, *Dictionary of the Bible*, IV, 166 [ed. by J. Hastings, rev. ed. by Frederick C. Grant and H. H. Rowley (New York: Charles Scribner's Sons, 1963)]; cf. also H. Bavinck, *Beginselen der Psychologie* (Kampen: Kok, 1923), §3; W. Geesink, *Van 's Heeren Ordinantiën*, 3 vols. (Amsterdam: W. Kirchener, 1907–8), 310ff.; J. Köberle, *Natur und Geist nach der Auffassung des Alten Testaments* (Munich: Beck, 1900).

a being existing between angels and animals, related to but distinct from both. He unites and reconciles within himself both heaven and earth, things both invisible and visible. And precisely as such he is the image and likeness of God. God is most certainly "spirit," and in this respect also the angels are related to him. But sometimes there is reference also to his soul, and throughout Scripture all the peculiar psychic feelings and activities that are essentially human are also attributed to God. In Christ, God assumed the nature of humanity, not that of angels. And precisely on that account man, rather than the angels, is the image, son, and offspring of God. The spirituality, invisibility, unity, simplicity, and immortality of the human soul are all features of the image of God. This image itself emerges in the fact that he has a spirit *(pneuma)* which was from the beginning organized into a soul *(psychē)*.

Belonging to the image of God, in the second place, are the human faculties. While the spirit is the principle and the soul the subject of life in man, the heart, according to Scripture, is the *organ* of man's life. It is, first, the center of physical life but then also, in a metaphorical sense, the seat and fountain of man's entire psychic life, of emotions and passions, of desire and will, even of thinking and knowing. From the heart flow "the springs of life" (Prov. 4:23). This life, which originates in the heart, then splits into two streams. On the one hand, we must distinguish the life which embraces all impressions, awarenesses, perceptions, observations, thoughts, knowledge, and wisdom. Especially in its higher forms, the central organ of this life is the *mind (vous)*. This life further embodies itself in words and language. On the other hand, the heart is the seat of all the emotions, passions, urges, inclinations, attachments, desires, and decisions of the will which have to be led by the mind *(vous)* and express themselves in action.

In all these psychic capacities and activities of human beings we can see features of the image of God as well. The very diversity and abundance of these forces reflect God. To the degree that a given creature is on a lower level, it is also less intricately organized and hence less related to and less susceptible of the highest good, which is God. In this regard even angels are of a lower rank than humans. Precisely because man is so wonderfully and richly endowed and organized, he can be conformed to and enjoy God in the fullest manner—from all sides, as it were, in all God's virtues and perfections. In the heart, mind, and will *(memoria, intellectus, voluntas)* Augustine even saw an analogy of the Triune Being of God. Just as the Father gives life to the Son and the Spirit, and the Spirit proceeds from the Father through the Son, so in human beings it is the heart *(memoria)*, the deep, hidden life of the psyche, which gives birth and being to the intellect and the will, and specifically places the will second in order to the intellect. Rationalism and

Pelagianism detach the intellect and the will from the heart and equate with these two the total being of man. Mysticism, despising the conscious, active life of the will, retreats into the depths of the mind. The Greek Orthodox Church and Greek Orthodox theology place head and heart immediately side by side. But, thanks to the leadership of Augustine, Western theology has avoided all these errors. It discovered that the doctrine of God and the doctrine of man are most intimately related. In the doctrine of the Trinity, therefore, it held onto the unity of the being, the distinctiveness of the three Persons, and the *filioque,* and in psychology, accordingly, it taught that the deep, hidden life of the soul comes to expression through the cognitive and the conative capacities and that between these two the latter was led and guided by the former.[76]

In the third place, the image of God manifests itself in the virtues of knowledge, righteousness, and holiness with which humanity was created from the start. For a well-ordered arrangement we had to deal first with the nature and faculties of the soul, but this analysis was only meant to furnish certain logical distinctions. Man was not created as a neutral being with morally indifferent powers and potentialities, but immediately made physically and ethically mature, with knowledge in the mind, righteousness in the will, holiness in the heart. Goodness, for a human being, consists in moral perfection, in complete harmony with the law of God, in holy and perfect being, like God himself (Lev. 19:2; Deut. 6:5; Matt. 5:48; 22:37; Eph. 5:1; 1 Pet. 1:15, 16). That law is one and the same rule for all persons. Scripture knows of no two sorts of human beings, no double moral law, no two kinds of moral perfection and destiny. If man was created good, he must have been created with original justice. On the one hand, this is not to be conceived as childlike innocence, but it must not be exaggerated either, as though the original state of integrity *(status integratis)* were already equal to the state of glory *(status gloriae).* Adam's knowledge, though pure, was limited and capable of growth; he walked by faith, not by sight; he not only possessed intuitive knowledge but also discursive knowledge; he knew the future only by special revelation.[77] The same was true of his righteousness and holiness; they were his from the beginning, for otherwise he could have never done any good work. Good fruits presuppose a good tree; one must first *be* before he can *do (operari sequitur esse).* But that increased righteousness and holiness must nevertheless still be kept, developed, and converted into action.

---

76. In the interest of space, for further discussion on human psychology the reader is referred to H. Bavinck, *Beginselen der Psychologie,* 2nd ed. (Kampen: Kok, 1923) and the literature cited there. Also see W. Geesink, *Van 's Heeren Ordinantiën,* I, 310ff.

77. T. Aquinas, *Summa Theol.,* I, qu. 94, art. 1–3.

This does not mean that Adam, equipped as he was with the necessary gifts, now had to go to work apart from God. Original righteousness *(justitia originalis)* was a free gift of God and it was also from moment to moment maintained in man by the providence of God. It is not for a second conceivable without communion with God. Just as the Son was already the mediator of union before the fall, so also the Holy Spirit was even then already the craftsman of all knowledge, righteousness, and holiness in humanity. Some church fathers argued this point with the aid of Genesis 2:7, saying that man was first formed by the Logos and that after that he had the breath of life, that is, the Holy Spirit, breathed into him.[78] While this exegesis was incorrect, it is perfectly true that man in the state of integrity only possessed the virtues of knowledge and righteousness by and in the Holy Spirit. Granted, between the indwelling of the Holy Spirit in man before sin and in the state of sin there is a big difference. Now that indwelling, after all, is "above nature" *(supra naturam)* because the Holy Spirit has to come to humans as it were from without and is diametrically opposed to sinful nature. In the case of Adam that entire contrast did not exist; his nature was holy and did not, as in the case of believers, have to be made holy; it was from the very beginning fit for the indwelling of the Holy Spirit. In the case of Adam, therefore, this indwelling was entirely natural. No truly good and perfect human being is even conceivable apart from the fellowship of the Holy Spirit. There is no such entity as the natural man, in the Roman Catholic sense, between the sinful man after the fall and the perfect human being created after God's image. A human being, that is, a human being in a full and true sense, is and must be an image of God, a child of God, God's own offspring, living in communion with him by the Holy Spirit. Thus, also before the fall, a human being was the dwellingplace of the entire holy Trinity, a most splendid temple of the Holy Spirit.

In the fourth place, also the human body belongs integrally to the image of God. A philosophy which either does not know or rejects divine revelation always lapses into empiricism or rationalism, materialism or spiritualism. But Scripture reconciles the two. Man has a "spirit" *(pneuma)* but that "spirit" is psychically organized, and must, by virtue of its nature, inhabit a body. It is of the essence of humanity to be corporeal and sensual. Hence man's body is first (if not temporally, then logically) formed from the dust of the earth and then the breath of life is breathed into him. He is called "Adam" after the ground from which he was formed. He is dust and is called dust (Gen. 2:7; Ps.

---

78. Cf. J. Kleutgen, *Die Theologie und Philosophie der Vorzeit*, 2 vols. (Münster: Theissing, 1868), II, 541ff.; G. Thomasius, *Christi Person und Werk*, I³, 155.

103:14; Job 10:9; 33:6; Isa. 2:22, 29:16, 45:9; 64:8, "from the earth, a man of dust," 1 Cor. 15:47). The body is not a prison, but a marvelous piece of art from the hand of God Almighty, and just as constitutive for the essence of humanity as the soul (Job 10:8–12; Ps. 8:139:13–17; Eccl. 12:2–7; Isa. 64:8). It is our earthly dwelling (2 Cor. 5:1), our organ or instrument of service, our apparatus (1 Cor. 12:18–26; 2 Cor. 4:7; 1 Thess. 4:4), and the "members" of the body are the weapons with which we fight in the cause of righteousness or unrighteousness (Rom. 6:13). It is so integrally and essentially a part of our humanity that, though violently torn from the soul by sin, it will be reunited with it in the resurrection of the dead. The nature of the union of the soul with the body, though incomprehensible, is much closer than the theories of "occasionalism" or "preestablished harmony" *(harmonia praestabilitia)* or "a system of influence" *(systema influxus)* imagine. It is not ethical but physical. It is so intimate that one nature, one person, one self is the subject of both and of all their activities. It is always the same soul that peers through the eyes, thinks through the brain, grasps with the hands, and walks with the feet. Although not always present in every part of the body in its full strength *(secundum totalitem virtutis)*, it is nevertheless present in all parts in its whole essence *(secundum totalitatem essentiae)*. It is one and the same life that flows throughout the body but operates and manifests itself in every organ in a manner peculiar to that organ. Now this body, which is so intimately bound up with the soul, also belongs to the image of God. Granted, this fact must not be construed to mean that God himself also has a material body, as the Audians thought; nor that God, in creating man also assumed a body, as Eugubinus taught; nor that God created man in the image of the still-to-be incarnated Christ, as Osiander believed. God, after all, is "spirit" *(pneuma,* John 4:24) and has no body. The human body is a part of the image of God in its organization as instrument of the soul, in its formal perfection, not in its material substance as flesh *(sarx)*.[79]

Just as God, though he is spirit *(pneuma),* is nevertheless the Creator of a material world which may be termed his revelation and manifestation, with this revelation coming to its climax in the incarnation, so also the spirit of man is designed for the body as its manifestation. The incarnation of God is proof that human beings and not angels are created in the image of God and that the human body is an essential component

---

79. Augustine, *The Literal Meaning of Genesis,* VI, 12; Gregory of Nyssa, *On the Making of Man,* c. 8; T. Aquinas, *Summa Theo.,* I, qu. 93, art. 6, *Summa Contra Gentiles,* IV, 26; Petavius, *Opera Omnia,* "de sex dier. opif.," II, 4, 7ff.; J. Gerhard, *Loci Theol.,* VIII, 3; J. Calvin, *Inst.,* I, 15, 3; A. Polanus, *Syn. Theol.,* 328; J. Zanchi, *Op. Theol.,* III, 677ff.; M. Becanus, *Inst. theol.,* VIII, 13; *Synopsis Purioris Theologiae,* XIII, 13; P. Mastricht, *Theologia,* III, 9, 30.

of that image. From the beginning creation was so arranged and human nature was immediately so created that it was amenable to and fit for the highest degree of conformity to God and for the most intimate indwelling of God. God could not have been able to become man if he had not first made man in his own image. And precisely because the body, being the organ of the soul, belongs to the essence of man and to the image of God, it originally also participated in immortality. God is not a God of the dead, but of the living (Matt. 22:32). Death is a consequence of sin (Gen. 2:7; 3:19; Rom. 5:12; 6:23; 1 Cor. 15:21, 56). In the case of Adam, however, this immortality did not consist in a state of not being able to die *(non posse mori)*, in eternal, imperishable life, but only in the condition of being able not to die *(posse non mori)*, in a not going to die in case of obedience. This state was not absolute but conditional; it depended on an ethical precondition. It is not correct, therefore, to say with Pelagians, Socinians, Remonstrants (etc.) that man was created mortal and that death is a given with the material organism, and therefore the normal and natural state of man. On the other hand, there is nevertheless an essential difference between Adam's not-going-to-die as long as he remained obedient, and the not-being-able-to-die which he was to receive as the reward for his obedience. Just as in Adam's case knowledge, righteousness, and holiness are still devoid of the gift of perseverance *(donum perseverantiae)*, so immortality was not yet totally integrated into inamissible eternal life. Adam's human nature was created so that, in case of his violation of God's commandment, it could and had to die. Adam was still a man of dust from the earth; only Christ is the Lord from heaven; the natural is first, then the spiritual (1 Cor. 15:45f.). Now through his body man was bound to earth but could also exercise dominion over the earth. Dominion over the earth, like immortality, is a part of the image of God. True, the Socinians went much too far when they located the entire being of man and the entire content of the image of God in dominion. Nonetheless, Genesis 1:26, 28; 2:19, 20; 9:2, 3 and Psalm 8:7–9 clearly teach that this dominion is most closely tied in with the creation in God's image and given with it. It is not an external appendix to the image; it is not based on a supplementary special dispensation; but, being the image of God, man is thereby at the same time elevated above all other creatures and appointed lord and king over them all.

Finally also belonging to this image is man's habitation in paradise (Gen. 2:8–15). Holiness and blessedness belong together; every human conscience witnesses to the fact that there is a connection between virtue and happiness; the ethical dimension and the physical dimension, the moral and the natural order in the world, being and appearance, spirit and matter may not be opposites. Congruent with a fallen humanity, therefore, is an earth which lies under a curse; a place of darkness therefore awaits the wicked in the hereafter; the righteous will one day walk in the light of God's countenance; the not-yet-fallen but still earthy man makes his home in a paradise.

So the whole human being is image and likeness of God, in soul and body, in all human faculties, powers, and gifts. Nothing in humanity is excluded from God's image; it stretches as far as our humanity does and constitutes our humanness. The human is not the divine self but is nevertheless a finite creaturely impression of the divine. All that is in God—his spiritual essence, his virtues and perfections, his immanent self-distinctions, his self-communication and self-revelation in creation—finds its admittedly finite and limited analogy and likeness in humanity. There is a profound truth in the Kabbalah's idea that God, who is the Infinite in himself, manifests himself in the ten sefiroth or attributes and that these together make up the Adam Cadmon.[80] Among creatures human nature is the supreme and most perfect revelation of God. And it is that not just in terms of its pneumatic side but equally in terms of its somatic side; it is that precisely as human, that is, as psychic, nature. In the teaching of Scripture God and the world, spirit and matter, are not opposites. There is nothing despicable or sinful in matter. The visible world is as much a beautiful and lush revelation of God as the spiritual. He displays his virtues as much in the former as in the latter. All creatures are embodiments of divine thoughts and all of them display the footsteps or vestiges of God. But all these vestiges, distributed side by side in the spiritual as well as the material world, are recapitulated in man and so organically connected and highly enhanced that they clearly constitute the image and likeness of God. The whole world raises itself upward, culminates and completes itself, and achieves its unity, its goal, and its crown in humanity. In order to be the image of God, therefore, man had to be a recapitulation of the whole of nature. The Jews used to say that God had collected the dust for the human body from all the lands of the earth.[81] Though the image is strange, a true and beautiful thought is expressed in it. As spirit, man is akin to the angels and soars to the invisible world; but he is at the same time a citizen of the visible world and connected with all physical creatures. There is not a single element in the human body that does not also occur in nature around him. Thus man forms a unity

80. A. Franck, *The Kabbalah* (New York: Arno, 1973), 148.

81. F. W. Weber, *System der altsynagogalen palastinischen Theologie* (Leipzig: Dorffling & Franke, 1880), 202ff.; cf. J. te Winkel, "A Frisian Myth," in *Geschiedenis der Nederlandsche Letterkunde van Middeleeuwen en Rederijkerstijd* in *De Ontwikkelingsgang der Nederlandsche Letterkunde*, 7 vols., 2nd ed. (Haarlem: F. Bohn, 1922–27), I, 28.

of the material and spiritual world, a mirror of the universe, a connecting link, compendium, the epitome of all of nature, a microcosm, and precisely on that account also the image and likeness of God, his son and heir, a micro-divine-being *(mikrotheos)*. He is the prophet who explains God and proclaims his excellencies; he is the priest who consecrates himself with all that is created to God as a holy offering; he is the king who guides and governs all things in justice and rectitude. And in all this he points to One who in a still higher and richer sense is the revelation and image of God, to him who is the only begotten of the Father, and the firstborn of all creatures. Adam, the son of God, was a type of Christ.

Human Destiny

6

The ultimate destiny of humanity, individually as well as corporately, was Adam's goal and not yet a given of his creation. Christ, not Adam, is the first full, true, spiritual man. Even in the state of integrity, Adam was only the beginning; Christ is the "end" of humanity, the one who gives us the possibility of imperishable eternal life. The parallel between Christ and Adam prompted theologians to conceive the original state of integrity in terms of a covenant, a covenant of works. This doctrine is based on Scripture and is eminently valuable. Covenant is of the essence of true religion, making possible a relation between the Creator and the creature and underscoring the dependence of rational, moral human beings on God. The Roman Catholic doctrine of the donum superadditum, though it seeks to honor the conviction that eternal life is a gift of grace, in fact reintroduces meritorious good works. By contrast, Lutheran views exalt the original state of Adam as already a possession of highest possible blessing and thus tend to antinomianism—Adam was ex lex, outside the law. But, before the fall, our first parents did not yet enjoy the eternal heavenly Sabbath; the state of integrity was not yet the state of glory. Full and complete humanity is found in community; humanity as a whole is the image of God—-in creation and in redemption. This underscores the notion of federal headship: Adam's over creation, Christ's over redeemed humanity. This emphasis on the organic unity of the human race also sheds light on its origins and propagation. The theory of the preexistence of human souls is rooted in a pagan dualism between spirit and matter, destroys the unity of humanity, and erases the distinction between human beings and angels. The debate between creationism and traducianism is less fixed. Although both face insoluble difficulties, Reformed along with Orthodox and Roman Catholic theologians, almost unanimously embraced creationism while traducianism found acceptance mainly among Lutherans. Creationism alone sufficiently maintains the specific uniqueness of humanity since it fends off both pantheism and materialism and respects both the organic unity of the human race in its entirety and, at the same time, the independent value, worth, and mysterious individual personality of every single human being. The state of integrity is a preparation for eternal glory when God will be all in all.

Although Adam was created in God's image, he was not that image immediately in the full sense, nor was he that image by himself alone. The image of God will only present itself to us in all of its many-splendored richness when man's destiny, both for this life and the life to come, is included in it. In 1 Corinthians 15:45–49 Paul contrasts the two covenant heads, Adam and Christ, with each other and compares them, not so much (as in Rom. 5:21–22 and 1 Cor. 15:22) in terms of what they did as in terms of their nature and person. The comparison here reaches its greatest depth and penetrates to the root of the distinction between them. The whole Adam, both before and after the fall, is contrasted to the whole Christ, after as well as before the resurrection. In virtue of creation the first man became a "living being" *(psychē sōsa)*, "natural" *(psychikos)*, "of the dust of the earth" *(ek gēs choikos);* but by his resurrection the second man became a "life-giving spirit" *(pneuma zōopoioun)*, "spiritual" *(pneumatikos)*, "from heaven" *(ex ouganou)*.[1] Although Adam was created after God's image, since he was "from the earth, earthy," he was dependent on the earth. He, after all, needed food and drink, light and air, day and night, hence did not yet have a glorified spiritual body on a level transcending all those needs. His natural body had not yet fully become an instrument of the spirit. As such, Adam, by comparison to Christ, stood on a lower level. Adam was the first; Christ the second and the last. Christ presupposes Adam and succeeds him. Adam is the lesser and inferior entity; Christ the greater and higher being. Hence Adam pointed to Christ; already before the fall he was the type of Christ. In Adam's creation Christ was already in view. The whole creation, including the creation of man, was infralapsarian. The natural came first, the spiritual second.

What Paul is here setting forth in great depth and breadth is grounded in Genesis 1 and 2 itself. Man, though spirit *(pneuma)* and bearing a breath of life within him, became a living being (soul) like the animals. He was given the fruit of herbs and trees for food (Gen. 1:29), a paradise as his dwellingplace (Gen. 2:8f.), a woman as helper (Gen. 2:18f.), a command for guidance (Gen. 2:16, 17), a threat of punishment in case of transgression (Gen. 2:17). It is evident from this scenario that the first man, however highly placed, did not yet possess the highest humanity. There is a very great difference between the natural and the pneumatic, between the state of integrity and the state of glory. After the resurrection both the stomach and food will be done away (1 Cor. 6:13), but both were realities to Adam. In heaven God's children will no longer marry, but be like the angels (Matt. 22:30); Adam, however, needed the help of a wife.

1. Cf. W. Lütgert, "Der Mensch aus dem Himmel," in Samuel Oettl, ed., *Greifswalder Studien* (Gütersloh: C. Bertelsmann, 1895), 207–28.

Covenant with Adam: Only the Beginning

Adam, accordingly, stood at the beginning, not the end, of his "career." His condition was provisional and temporary and could not remain as it was. It either had to pass on to higher glory or to sin and death. The penalty for transgressing the command was death; the reward of keeping it, by contrast, was life: eternal life. Our common conscience already testifies that in keeping God's commands there is great reward and that the violation of these commands brings punishment, but Holy Scripture also expresses this truth over and over. It sums up all the blessedness associated with the doing of God's commandments in the word "life," eternal life. Both in the covenant of works and that of grace Scripture knows but one ideal for a human being, and that is eternal life (Lev. 18:5; Ezek. 20:11; Ps. 9:12; Matt. 19:17; Luke 10:28; Gal. 3:12). Hence Adam still stood at the beginning. As yet he did not have this reward of eternal life, but still had to acquire it; he could still err, sin, fall and die. His relation to God was such that he could gradually increase in fellowship with God but could also still fall from it. In Scripture this unique relation is perhaps compared to a covenant in *one* verse. In Hosea 6:7 the Lord says of Israel and Judah that, despite all the labor spent on them, they, like Adam, transgressed the covenant (*kᵓādām ʿābĕrû bĕrît*, LXX *ōs anthrōpos* Vulg., sicut Adam). The translation "like a man" is burdened by the objection that in that case it is said of people in general that they transgressed the covenant. Furthermore, the translation "like [the covenant of] a man" would in any case require that the word *kᵓādām* be placed after the word *bĕrît*, not after the subject *hēmâ*. So, unless the word is corrupt or refers to a place name ["at Adam"], there remains the translation "like Adam." Implied, then, is that the command given to Adam was at bottom a covenant because it was intended, like God's covenant with Israel, to convey eternal life to Adam in the way of [covenantal] obedience. This is further reinforced by the parallel that Paul draws in Romans 5:12–21 between Adam and Christ. As the obedience of one man, that is, Christ, and the grace granted to humanity in him, brought acquittal, righteousness, and life, so the one transgression and misdeed of the one man is the cause of condemnation, sin, and death for humanity as a whole. The relation between us and Adam is like that between us and Christ. We in fact stand to Adam in the same relation. He is a type of Christ, our head, from whom guilt and death accrue to us because of his transgression. He is the cause of the death of us all; we all die in Adam (1 Cor. 15:22). Here, too, Adam's relation to God is a covenant relation, described now not so much in the direction of God as in the direction of those who are included in that covenant under Adam as head.

This richly valuable idea of Scripture has not always come into its own in Christian theology. A naturalistic view located the image of God solely in aptitude, naked potential, the freedom of the will, formal personhood, and even considered death natural. The image or at least the likeness of God consisted much more in what human beings had to acquire by their own exertions than in what they were given immediately at the creation. The supranaturalistic view, by contrast, struck out toward another extreme, attributing a totally supernatural character to the state of integrity. Not only was original righteousness considered a supernatural gift; immortality was viewed as a special benefaction of the Creator, and all susceptibility to suffering and pain was denied to Adam.[2] Some, like Gregory of Nyssa, John of Damascus, Böhme, and others, however, judged that before the fall man had no need of food, seeing he was immortal.[3] In any case excretion would in any case have occurred without any taint of unseemliness.[4] According to most church fathers, Scholastics, Roman Catholic, Lutheran, Remonstrant and also certain Reformed theologians like Zwingli, Musculus, Martyr, Zanchius, Junius, Piscator, and so forth, human food consisted only in plants and not in meat. Procreation occurred without any sensual pleasure and children were not born unable to speak, and needy, but very swiftly grew up to adulthood.[5] Many, going even further, believed that procreation occurred entirely apart from coitus;[6] that humans were first created androgynous, that the creation of the woman was as such proof of the fall.[7] Hence women did not really participate in the divine image and in human nature.[8] Origen even derived corporeality and all inequality among men from a fall of preexistent souls; others attributed to

2. Augustine, *The City of God*, XIV, 26; T. Aquinas, *Summa Theol.*, I, qu. 97, art. 2.

3. Petavius, *Opera Omnia*, "de sex dier. opif.," 7.

4. T. Aquinas, *Summa Theol.*, I, qu. 97, art. 3.

5. Augustine, *On the Merits and Remission of Sins*, I, 37, 38; P. Lombard, *Sent.*, II, dist. 20; T. Aquinas, *Summa Theol.*, I, qu. 98, art. 1.

6. Augustine, *The Retractions*, I, 10; Gregory of Nyssa, *On the Making of Man*, 16, 17; John of Damascus, *Exposition of the Orthodox Faith*, II, 30.

7. So, already, the Jews thought; cf. F. W. Weber, *System der altsynagogalen palastinischen Theologie* (Leipzig: Dörffling & Franke, 1880), 202ff., and then also J. S. Erigena, *The Division of Nature*, II, 6, 10, 23, IV, 12, and many philosophers such as Böhme, Oetinger, Baader, Schelling, J. P. Lange, *Christliche Dogmatik*, 3 vols. (Heidelberg: K. Winter, 1852), II, 324ff.; F. Delitzsch, *A System of Biblical Psychology* (Edinburgh: T. & T. Clark, 1899), 102ff.; J. C. K. Hofmann, *Weissagung und Erfüllung im Alten und im Neuen Testamente*, 2 vols. (Nördlingen: C. H. Beck, 1841–44), I, 65ff.; idem, *Der Schriftbeweis*, 2nd ed., 3 vols. (Nördlingen: Beck, 1857–60), I, 403ff., enz.

8. Cf. Augustine, *The Trinity*, XII, 7; T. Aquinas, *Summa Theol.*, I, qu. 93, art. 4, qu. 99, art. 2; Bonaventure, *Sent.*, II, dist. 16, art. 2, qu. 2, dist. 20, art. 1, qu. 6; J. Gerhard, *Loci Theol.*, VIII, c. 6; J. Quenstedt, *Theologia*, II, 15; J. Janssen, *Geschichte des deutschen Volkes seit dem Ausgang des Mittelalters*, 8 vols. (Paris: Librairie Plon, 1887–1911), VI, S. 395–97.

man before the fall a body totally different from ours.[9] In connection with all this paradise was often construed in very idealistic terms and even interpreted allegorically: animals did not die there; no wild or unclean animals existed there; roses blossomed but had no thorns; the air was much cleaner, the water much softer, and the light much brighter.[10]

Still everyone acknowledges that Adam did not yet possess the highest humanity, a truth implicit in the probationary command, the freedom of choice, the possibility of sin and death. Especially Augustine made a clear distinction between the ability not to sin *(posse non peccare)* and not to die *(posse non mori)*, which Adam possessed, and the inability to sin *(non posse peccare)* and the inability to die *(non posse mori)*, gifts that were to be bestowed along with the glorification of the first man in case of obedience and now granted to the elect out of grace.[11] The relation in which Adam originally stood vis-à-vis God was even described by Augustine as a covenant, a testament, a pact;[12] and the translation of the words *kʾādām* by "like Adam" led many to a similar view.[13] Materially, therefore, the doctrine of what was later called "the covenant of works" also already occurs in the church fathers. Included in Adam's situation, as it was construed by the Scholastics, Roman Catholic and Lutheran theologians, lay all the elements that were later summed up especially by Reformed theologians in the doctrine of the covenant of works.[14] The relation in which believers have come to stand to God by Christ is repeatedly described in Scripture with the term "covenant." Zwingli and Bucer already seized upon these scriptural thoughts to defend the unity of the Old and New Testaments against the Anabaptists. Now when, following the example of Scripture, the Christian religion was portrayed as a covenant, Paul's parallel between Adam and Christ prompted theologians also to conceive the state of integrity as a covenant.

In distinction from the covenant of grace this was then called the covenant of nature or of works *(foedus naturae* or *operum)*. It was called "covenant of nature," not because it was deemed to flow automatically

9. Origen, *Against Celsus*, I, 32, 33; idem, *On First Principles*, II, 9; cf. K. Liechtenhau, "Ophiten," in *PRE*[3], XIV, 404–13 and also Böhme, Ant. Bourignon, Baader, et al.
10. Luther on Genesis 3; cf. D. F. Strauss, *Die Christliche Glaubenslehre in ihrer geschichtlichen Entwicklung und im Kampf mit der Moderne Wissenschaft*, 2 vols. (Tübingen: C. F. Osiander, 1840–41), I, 700ff.
11. Augustine, *The City of God*, XXII, 30; idem, *Admonition and Grace;* idem, *Enchiridion*, 104–7; idem, *The Literal Meaning of Genesis*, III, 2, VI, 25; idem, *Against Julian*, V, 58; VI, 5 enz.
12. Augustine, *The City of God*, XVI, 27.
13. J. Marck, *Historia Paradisi* (Amsterdam: Gerardus Borstius, 1705), II, 6, 7.
14. Cf. P. Lombard, *Sent.*, II, dist. 19, 20.

and naturally from the nature of God or the nature of man, but because the foundation on which the covenant rested, that is, the moral law was known to man by nature and because it was made with man in his original state and could be kept by man with the powers bestowed on him in the creation, without the assistance of supernatural grace. Later, when the term occasioned misunderstanding, it was preferentially replaced by that of "covenant of works"; and it bore this name inasmuch as in this covenant eternal life could only be obtained in the way of works, that is, in the way of keeping God's commandments. Now this covenant, as parallel to the covenant of grace, was taught and developed with special predilection by Reformed theologians.[15] The Reformed Confessions do not mention it in so many words. Materially, however, it is nevertheless embodied in articles 14 and 15 of the Belgic Confession, where we read that man's entire nature was corrupted by Adam's transgression of the command of life;[16] in Lord's Day 3 and 4 of the Heidelberg Catechism it is said that man was created in God's image, so that he might live with God in eternal happiness, but it is also described as totally corrupted by Adam's fall; and in chapter III/IV of the Canons of Dordt it is stated that Adam's corruption spread to all his descendants "by God's just judgment." Formally, the covenant of works is incorporated in the Irish Articles (1615), the Westminster Confession (1647), the Helvetic Consensus Formula (1675), and the Walcheren Articles (1693).[17] Although the doctrine of the covenant of works also found acceptance with some Roman Catholic[18] and Lutheran theologians,[19] it was vigorously op-

15. *Ed. note:* Bavinck here refers to the literature at the head of the chapter section in the Dutch edition. Check the following authors in the bibliography: Boston, Brahe, Cloppenburg, Coccejus, Comrie, De Moor, Gomarus, van den Honert, Junius, Marck, Mastricht, Olevianus, Polanus, Trelcatius, Trelcatius Jr., Ursinus, Vitringa, Walker, Wollebius.

16. In its original version art. 14 of the Belgic Confession read that God formed man "after his own image and likeness, good, righteous, and holy, *entirely perfect in all things (et tout parfait en toutes choses)."* Later these words were omitted and replaced by "capable in all things to will agreeably to the will of God."

17. *Ed. note:* For a description of the Helvetic Consensus Formula (1675), see P. Schaff, *The Creeds of Christendom,* 6th ed., 3 vols. (New York: Harper, 1919), I, 477–89. The five Walcheren Articles (1693) were adopted by the Dutch Reformed Classes of Walcheren against the liberal-rationalist views of Herman Alexander Roëll, Balthasar Bekker, and Johannes Vlak. Discussion of the articles and the views of the three rejected can be found in the respective essays of the *Christelijke Encyclopedie,* ed. by F. W. Grosheide and G. P. Van Itterzon (Kampen: Kok, 1961). The full text of the Walcheren Articles is found in *Documenta Reformatoria,* ed. by J. N. Bakhuizen van den Brink et al. (Kampen: Kok, 1960), I, 460–70.

18. M. J. Scheeben, *Handbuch der Katholischen Dogmatik,* 4 vols. (Freiburg i.B.: Herder, 1933), II, 500; C. Pesch, *Praelectiones Dogmaticae* (Freiburg i.B.: Herder, 1916–25), III, 136.

19. J. F. Buddeus, *Institutiones Theologiae Moralis* (Leipzig: T. Fritsch, 1715), 527 and others, cf. C. Vitringa, *Doctr. Christ.,* II, 242.

posed by Remonstrants and Rationalists.[20] Only in modern times was the doctrine of the covenant of works again understood and explained by a number of theologians in its true significance.[21]

One can certainly raise the objection against the doctrine of the covenant as it has been developed in Reformed theology that it was overly detailed and treated too scholastically. Although later theologians still defended the doctrine, they no longer felt its significance and its theological and religious importance. Since it had lost its vitality, it was easy to combat it. But the doctrine of the covenant of works is based on Scripture and is eminently valuable. Among rational and moral creatures all higher life takes the form of a covenant. Generally, a covenant is an agreement between persons who voluntarily obligate and bind themselves to each other for the purpose of fending off an evil or obtaining a good. Such an agreement, whether it is made tacitly or defined in explicit detail, is the usual form in terms of which humans live and work together. Love, friendship, marriage, as well as all social cooperation in business, industry, science, art, and so forth, is ultimately grounded in a covenant, that is, in reciprocal fidelity and an assortment of generally recognized moral obligations. It should not surprise us, therefore, that also the highest and most richly textured life of human beings, namely, religion, bears this character. In Scripture "covenant" is the fixed form in which the relation of God to his people is depicted and presented. And even where the word does not occur, we nevertheless always see the two parties as it were in dialogue with each other, dealing with each other, with God calling people to conversion, reminding them of their obligations, and obligating himself to provide all that is good. Later, when we discuss the covenant of grace, we will spotlight the biblical concept of *běrit*. Here we will confine ourselves to reminding the reader of the general idea of covenant. Even if the term "covenant" never occurred in Scripture for the religious relation between Adam and God, not even in Hosea 6:7, still the religious life of man before the fall bears the character of a covenant. Reformed scholars were

---

20. S. Episcopius, *Inst. Theol.,* II, c. 2; P. van Limborch, *Theol. Christ.,* III, c. 2; J. Alting, on Hebrews 8:6 and *Opera Omnia Theologica* (Amsterdam: Borst, n.d.), V, 392; Venema, *Korte Verdediging van zijn eere en leere* (Leeuwarden: van Desiel, 1735); N. Schiere, *Doctrina testamentorum et foederum divinorum omnium* (Leovardiaw: M. Ingema, 1718); J. Vlak, *Eeuwig Evangelie* (1684) [*ed. note:* title not given by Bavinck] who is disputed by H. Brink, *Toet-Steen der Waarheid en anderen* (Amsterdam, 1685); Even J. J. Van Oosterzee, *Christian Dogmatics,* trans. by J. Watson and M. Evans, 2 vols. (New York: Scribner, Armstrong, 1874), §75, saw it as a Jewish work of art.

21. A. Kuyper, *De Heraut,* 161ff.; Ch. Hodge, *Systematic Theology,* 3 vols. (New York: Charles Scribner's Sons, 1888), II, 117; G. Vos, "The Doctrine of the Covenant in Reformed Theology," in *Redemptive History and Biblical Interpretation,* ed. by Richard B. Gaffin Jr. (Phillipsburg: Presbyterian & Reformed, 1980), 234–70.

never so narrow as to insist on the word, if only the matter itself was certain: one may doubt the word, provided the matter is safe *(de vocabulo dubitetur, re salva)*. But hidden behind the opposition to the word was opposition to the matter itself. And this must never be surrendered inasmuch as covenant is the essence of true religion.

Why should this be? First of all, because God is the Creator, man a creature; and with that statement an infinite distance between the two is a given. No fellowship, no religion between the two seems possible; there is only difference, distance, endless distinctness. If God remains elevated above humanity in his sovereign exaltedness and majesty, then no religion is possible, at least no religion in the sense of fellowship. Then the relation between the two is exhaustively described in the terms "master" and "servant." Then the image of the potter and the clay is still much too weak to describe that relation because clay has existence—and hence rights—independently of and over against the potter, but human beings have nothing and are nothing apart from God. Accordingly, if there is truly to be religion, if there is to be fellowship between God and man, if the relation between the two is to be also (but not exclusively) that of a master to his servant, of a potter to clay, as well as that of a king to his people, of a father to his son, of a mother to her child, of an eagle to her young, of a hen to her chicks, and so forth; that is, if not just one relation but all relations and all sorts of relations of dependence, submission, obedience, friendship, love, and so forth, among humans find their model and achieve their fulfillment in religion, then religion must be the character of a covenant. For then God has to come down from his lofty position, condescend to his creature, impart, reveal, and give himself away to human beings; then he who inhabits eternity and dwells in a high and holy place must also dwell with those who are of a humble spirit (Isa. 57:15). But this set of conditions is nothing other than the description of a covenant. If religion is called a covenant, it is thereby described as the true and genuine religion. This is what no religion has ever understood; all peoples either pantheistically pull God down into that which is creaturely, or deistically elevate him endlessly above it. In neither case does one arrive at true fellowship, at covenant, at genuine religion. But Scripture insists on both: God is infinitely great and condescendingly good; he is Sovereign but also Father; he is Creator but also Prototype. In a word, he is the God of the covenant.

It is clear, in the second place, that a creature cannot bring along or possess any rights before God. That is implicitly—in the nature of the case—impossible. A creature as such owes its very existence, all that it is and has, to God; it cannot make any claims before God and it cannot boast of anything; it has no rights and can make no demands of any kind. There is no such thing as merit in the existence of a creature before God, nor can there be since the relation between the Creator and a creature radically and once-and-for-all eliminates any notion of merit. This is true after the fall but no less before the fall. Then too human beings were creatures: without entitlements, without rights, without merit. When we have done everything we have been instructed to do, we are still unworthy servants (*douloi achreioi*, Luke 17:10). Now, however, the religion of Holy Scripture is such that in it human beings can nevertheless, as it were, assert certain rights before God. For they have the freedom to come to him with prayer and thanksgiving, to address him as "Father," to take refuge in him in all circumstances of distress and death, to desire all good things from him, even to expect salvation and eternal life from him. All this is possible solely because God in his condescending goodness gives rights to his creature. Every creaturely right is a given benefit, a gift of grace, undeserved and nonobligatory. All reward from the side of God originates in grace; no merit, either of condignity or of congruity,[22] is possible. True religion, accordingly, cannot be anything other than a covenant: it has its origin in the condescending goodness and grace of God. It has that character before as well as after the fall. For religion, like the moral law and the destiny of man, is one. The covenant of works and the covenant of grace do not differ in their final goal but only in the way that leads to it. In both there is one mediator; then a mediator of union, now a mediator of reconciliation. In both there is one faith, then faith in God, now faith in God through Christ and in both there is one hope, one love, and so forth. Religion is always the same in essence; it differs only in form.

In the third place men and women are rational and moral beings. That is how God created them and that, therefore, is how he treats them. He maintains what he created. God, accordingly, does not coerce human beings, for coercion is inconsistent with the nature of rational creatures. He deals with them, not as irrational creatures, as plants or animals, as blocks of wood, but goes to work with them as rational, moral, self-determining beings. He wants human beings to be free and to serve him in love, freely and willingly (Ps. 100:3). Religion is freedom; it is love which does not permit itself to be coerced. For that reason it must by its very nature take the shape of a covenant in which God acts, not coercively, but with counsel, admonition, warning, invitation, petition, and in which humans serve God, not under duress or violence, but willingly, by their own free consent, moved by love to love in return. At bottom religion is a duty but also a privilege. It is not work by which we bring advantage to God, make a contribution to him, and have a

---

22. *Ed. note:* See note 29 in previous chapter.

right to reward. It is grace for us to be allowed to serve him. God is never indebted to us, but we are always indebted to him for the good works we do (*Belgic Confession*, Art. 24). On his part there is always the gift; on our part there is always and alone the gratitude. For that reason religion is conceivable only in the form of a covenant and comes to its full realization only in that form. God, accordingly, made such a covenant with the first human beings. We must completely set aside the fragmentary development of this doctrine. The matter itself is certain. After creating men and women after his own image, God showed them their destiny and the way in which alone they could reach it. Human beings could know the moral law without special revelation since it was written in their hearts. But the probationary command is positive; it is not a given of human nature as such but could only be made known to human beings if God communicated it to them. Nor was it self-evident that keeping that command would yield eternal life. In that sense the "covenant of works" is not a "covenant of nature." Initially the church did not yet clearly understand this[23] but gradually it became obvious— and was taught as such—that God was in no way obligated to grant heavenly blessedness and eternal life to those who kept his law and thereby did not do anything other than what they were obligated to do. There *is* no natural connection here between work and reward.[24]

Reformed and Other Views of Human Destiny

And *that* is the truth which inheres in Rome's doctrine of the added gift *(donum superadditum)*. Eternal life is and remains an unmerited gift of God's grace. But because Rome does not know the doctrine of the covenant of works, it infers from this gracious gift of eternal life that also the image of God in man has to be supernatural and, by virtue of the supernatural power granted with the image of God, has humans again meriting eternal life *ex condigno*. Under the guise of honoring grace, Rome, therefore, again introduces the meritoriousness of good works. But Reformed theologians maintained, on the one hand, that the image of God in man was natural and that man, who was this image of God,

23. F. Gomarus, *De Foedere.*
24. J. Coccejus, *Summa Doctrinae de Foedere et Testamento Dei* (Frankfurt: J. M. a Sande, 1704), II, 23ff.; F. Burmann, *Syn. Theol.*, II, 8, 2, 4; J. Marck, *Hist. Parad.*, 479; J. Cloppenburg, *Exerc. Theol.*, VI, disp. 5; idem, *De Foedere*, I, 8ff.; H. Witsius, *The Oeconomy of the Covenants between God and Man* (London, 1763), I, 4 §§10–23; M. Leydekker, *Fax Veritatis* (Lugdun Batavorum: Daniel Gaesbeeck & Felicem Lopez, 1677), 399ff.; A. Comrie and N. Holtius, *Examen van het Ontwerp van Tolerantie*, 10 vols. (Amsterdam: Nicolaas Byl, 1753), IX, 227ff.; X, 288ff., 318ff.; Brahe, *Aanm. over de vijf Walch. art.*, 125ff. 261ff.

could know as well as keep the moral law without supernatural power; and, on the other hand, they firmly asserted that a higher state of blessedness than that which prevailed in paradise on earth, could never, in the nature of the case, be merited, but only be granted by a free dispensation of God. And they combined these two ideas in their theory of the covenant of works. This covenant is rooted in a free, special, and gracious dispensation of God. It proceeds from him and he decrees all the parts of it: condition and fulfillment, compliance and reward, transgression and punishment. It is monopleuric (unilateral) in origin, and it is added to the creation in God's image. The first human beings, on their part, being created in God's image, rested in it and saw in this covenant a revelation of a way to a higher blessedness. The covenant of works, accordingly, does justice to both the sovereignty of God—which implies the dependency of creatures and the nonmeritoriousness of all their works—and to the grace and generosity of God which nevertheless wants to give the creature a higher-than-earthly blessedness. It maintains both the dependence as well as the freedom of mankind. It combines Schleiermacher [dependence] and Kant [freedom]. The probationary command relates to the moral law as the covenant of works relates to man's creation in God's image. The moral law stands or falls in its entirety with the probationary command, and the image of God in mankind in its entirety stands or falls with the covenant of works. The covenant of works is the road to heavenly blessedness for the human beings who were created in God's image and had not yet fallen.

The covenant of works, accordingly, includes still another beautiful thought. It not only realizes the true and full idea of religion; it also gives expression to the fact that humanity before the fall, though created in God's image, did not yet possess the highest possible blessing. On this point there is a primary difference with Lutheran theologians. In their view, creation in God's image was the realization of the highest idea of man. In Adam that ideal was fully attained and a higher state was not possible. Adam did not have to become anything; he only had to remain what he was, namely, a participant in the full gracious indwelling of the Holy Trinity. Accordingly, he was not subject to a law that commanded him to do anything positive. The law that applied to him had only a negative thrust, and not until sin appeared was he brought under the dominion of the law. That is the reason why in the works of Lutheran theologians, as in those of the church fathers, the original state of man was frequently pictured in a very exaggerated manner. It is also why the state to which believers in Christ are elevated is essentially equated with that of Adam before the fall. In reference to the believer, everything is focused for the Lutheran on justification. Once the believer is justified he or she has enough and is completely satisfied and blessed. Salvation completely coincides with forgiveness. No need is felt to connect it backward with eternal election and forward with the whole of the Christian life, good works, and eternal life. Neither predestination nor perseverance is needed here. The Lutheran believer enjoys the new life in the present and feels no need for more.[25] For the Reformed, who walked in the footsteps of Augustine, things were different. According to them, Adam did not possess the highest kind of life. The highest kind of life is the material freedom consisting of not being able to err, sin, or die. It consists in being elevated absolutely above all fear and dread, above all possibility of falling. This highest life is immediately bestowed by grace through Christ upon believers. They can no longer sin (1 John 3:9) and they can no longer die (John 3:16) since by faith they immediately receive eternal, inamissible life. Theirs is the perseverance of the saints; they can no longer be lost. Hence Christ does not [merely] restore his own to the state of Adam before the fall. He acquired and bestows much more, namely, that which Adam would have received had he not fallen. He positions us not at the beginning but at the end of the journey that Adam had to complete. He accomplished not only the passive but also the active obedience required; he not only delivers us from guilt and punishment, but out of grace immediately grants us the right to eternal life.

Adam, however, did not yet have this high state of blessedness; he did not yet have eternal life. He received the possibility to remain standing *(posse stare)* but not the will *(velle stare)*. He could have it if he willed it *(posse si vellet)* but did not have the will to want that which he was able to have *(velle, quod posset)*. He had the possibility of not erring, sinning, and dying *(posse non errare, peccare, mori)*, but not yet the impossibility of erring, sinning, and dying *(non posse errare, peccare mori)*. He still lived in the state of one who could sin and die, and was therefore still in some fear and dread. His was not yet the invariable perfect love which casts out all fear. Reformed theologians rightly pointed out, therefore, that this possibility, this being changeably good, this still being able to sin and die was no part or component of the image of God, but its boundary, its limitation, its circumference.[26] The image of God therefore had to be fully developed—thereby overcoming and nullifying this

25. Luther in J. Köstlin, *Theology of Luther in Its Historical Development and Inner Harmony*, trans. by Charles E. Hay (Philadelphia: Lutheran Publication Society, 1897), II, 361; M. Schneckenburger and E. Güder, *Vergleichende Darstellung des lutherischen und reformirten Lehrbegriffs*, 2 vols. (Stuttgart: J. B. Metzler, 1855), I, 90ff., 120ff.; II, 185ff.; A. F. C. Vilmar, *Handbuch der Evangelishen Dogmatik* (Gütersloh: Bertelsmann, 1895), I, 340; F. H. Frank, *System der christlichen Wahrheit* (Erlangen: A. Deichert, 1878–80), I, 375.

26. H. Heppe, *Reformed Dogmatics* (Grand Rapids: Baker, 1978 [1950]), 249–50; W. G. T. Shedd, *Dogmatic Theology* (New York: Charles Scribner's Sons, 1888–89), II, 104, 150.

possibility of sin and death—and glitter in imperishable glory. In virtue
of this view of the state of integrity Reformed theologians, in distinction
from others, were able to observe a commendable sobriety in their account of the paradisal state. Adam was not Christ. The natural was not
the spiritual. Paradise was not heaven. However careful we must be to
resist the naturalism that denies the power of sin and considers death
natural, no less to be avoided is the supranaturalism that defines the
image of God as a supernatural addition to nature. Sin, according to
Reformed theologians, spoiled and destroyed everything, but because it
is not a substance it could not alter the essence or substance of the creation. The human being as sinner is still a human being. Similarly all
other creations (earth, heaven, nature, plant, animal), despite the curse
of sin and the rule of corruption, essentially and substantially remained
the same. As we noted above in the case of religion, so it is also in the
case of all the other things: sin did not take away the substance of
things, and grace therefore does not restore that substance either. The
stuff *(materia)* of all things is and remains the same. However, the form
(forma), given in creation, was *de*formed by sin in order to be entirely
*re*formed again in the sphere of grace.[27]

This serious, yet most wholesome, view of the paradisal state held by
the Reformed comes to expression at countless points. Against the
Lutherans and Remonstrants they defended the thesis that, aside from
the probationary command, Adam was also thoroughly bound to the
moral law. He was not "law-less" (*exlex*, bound by no law), even though
he fulfilled it without any coercion, willingly and out of love. Adam
knew the moral law by nature. Hence it did not, like the probationary
command, have to be revealed to him in a special way. It is essentially
the same as the Ten Commandments but differed in form, for the law
given on Sinai presupposes a catalogue of sins and therefore almost always speaks in the negative ("Thou shalt not . . ."), and the moral law
before the fall was much more positive. But precisely because in the
pre-fall life of Adam the moral law was in the nature of the case entirely
positive, it did not make clear to Adam's mind the possibility of sin.
Hence in addition to the *pre*scriptions there had to come a *pro*scription
and in addition to the commandments a positive law. In addition to the
commandments whose naturalness and reasonableness were obvious
to Adam, this command was, in a sense, arbitrary and incidental. In the
probationary command the entire moral law came to Adam at a single
throw, confronting him with the dilemma: either God or man, God's authority or one's own insight, unconditional obedience or independent
research, faith or skepticism. It was an appalling test which opened the

27. G. Voetius, *Select. Disp.*, I, 776.

way either to eternal blessedness or eternal ruin. Against the Cocceians, Reformed theologians maintained that also the Sabbath command belonged to that moral law. Before the fall our first parents did not yet enjoy the eternal heavenly Sabbath. Just as they were subject to the alternation of day and night they were also bound to the rule of six days of labor and one of rest. A day of rest and days of labor were therefore also distinct before the fall. Then, too, the religious life required a form and service of its own alongside the life of culture. Reformed theologians, with increasing unanimity and decisiveness, rejected the magical, theosophic notion that the two trees in the garden of Eden possessed the power to kill or to make alive of themselves, either by nature (Thomas, Suarez, Pererius), or in a supernatural manner (Augustine Bonaventure), either upon one-time use[28] or upon repeated use.[29] A few, however, such as Pareus, Rivet, and Zanchius,[30] initially still assumed that the eating of the fruit had an effect on the physical life of man.[31] This view, though it is consistent with the Roman Catholic doctrine of the sacraments, is, in part for that reason, unacceptable to the Reformed tradition since it makes life and death independent of the ethical condition, that is, of the act of obeying or disobeying God's command. Rather it assumes that human beings would continue to live even after the fall if only they had *ex opere operato* eaten of the tree of life. It thus implies that eternal life could be effected in humanity either at one stroke or gradually by the eating of a physical fruit, and thus denies the distinction between the natural and the spiritual. Reformed theologians, accordingly, preferred to view the tree of life as sign and seal of the covenant of works which bestowed life in a sacramental manner.

Similarly, Reformed theologians unanimously rejected,[32] as contrary to Scripture, all theosophic speculations concerning an androgynous maiden, the absence of the sex drive, and magical generation. The creation of the woman does not presuppose a kind of fall in Adam's life, nor did any new species emerge in the plant or animal kingdom after the entry of sin. According to Voetius, wild animals and creeping things were already created on the sixth day and predate the fall.[33] And, finally,

28. R. Bellarmine, *De Gratia Primi Hominis* (Heidelberg: Rosa, 1612), c. 14.

29. T. Aquinas, *Summa Theol.*, I, qu. 97, art. 4; cf. also A. Kuyper, *De Heraut*, 941 (5 January 1896): 1.

30. J. Zanchi, *Op. Theol.*, III, 501.

31. J. Calvin, *Institutes*, IV, 14, 12, 18; idem, *Commentary on Genesis*, trans. by John King (Grand Rapids: Baker, 1979), 115–18, 182–84 on Gen. 2:9, 3:22; J. Marck, *Historia Paradisi*, I, c. 17; cf. further literature in C. Vitringa, *Doctr. Christ.*, II, 220ff.

32. J. Marck, *Historia Paradisi*, 279ff.

33. G. Voetius, *Select. Disp.*, V, 191.

Calvin and most Reformed theologians were of the opinion that eating meat was permitted to humans even before the flood and the fall.[34] The fact that Genesis 1:29 does not expressly mention it cannot, as an argument from silence, be of service here. In Genesis 1:30 only the plant world is divided between man and animal, nothing is said about man's dominion over and claims upon the animal world. The animal world had already been placed under human dominion in Genesis 1:28, an act which certainly includes, especially with respect to the fish of the sea, the right to kill and use animals. Immediately after the fall God himself made garments of animal skins (3:21) and Abel made a sacrifice that was surely followed by a sacrificial meal. The practice of eating meat, moreover, was certainly in use before the flood and, if God did not authorize it before Genesis 9:3, it would have been unlawful and sinful before that time. Genesis 9:1–5 does not present a new commandment, but renews the blessing of creation; a new feature is only the prohibition to eat meat with its life, that is, its blood. The ground for the injunction against killing human beings (Gen. 9:5–7) is not present in the case of animals, for they were not made in God's image. Incomprehensible, finally, is why of all times God should permit mankind to eat meat *after* the fall and *after* the flood; one would expect the contrary, namely, that the rights and rule of man would be restricted after the fall. One would expect that, to counter lawlessness and degradation, the use of meat would be abolished and that vegetarianism would be considered much more in accord with the post-fall and post-flood state of mankind than the practice of eating meat.[35]

In all these issues Reformed theology was able to make such sound judgments because it was deeply imbued with the idea that Adam did not yet enjoy the highest level of blessedness. Sin undoubtedly has cosmic significance. As is evident from the phenomenon of death, sin also impacts our physical existence and has brought the entire earth under the curse. Without sin the development of humanity and the history of the earth would have been very different—though still unimaginable. Still, on the other hand, the state of integrity cannot be equated with the state of glory. We may not draw conclusions from the former for the

34. J. Calvin, *Commentary on Genesis,* 98–100, 291–93, on Genesis 1:29, 9:3; Heidegger, *de libertate Christianorum a re cibaria* (1662); Voetius, *Disp.,* IV, 387; V, 194; Coccejus, *S. Theol.,* XX, 17; J. Marck, *Historia Paradisi,* 341; B. De Moor, *Comm. Theol.,* III, 35–38 enz.

35. O. Zöckler, *Die Lehre vom Urstand des Menschen* (Gütersloh: C. Bertelsmann, 1870), 273ff.; *Köhler, *Biblische Geschichte,* I, 33ff.; R. Kraetzschmar, *Die Bundesvorstellung im Alten Testament in ihrer geschichtlichen Entwickelung* (Marburg: N. G. Elwert, 1896), 193ff.; V. Zapletal, *Der Schöpfungsbericht der Genesis* (Regensburg: G. J. Manz, 1911), 65.

conditions of the latter. Isaiah 11:6 and 65:25 can no more be applied
to the state of human life before the fall than Mark 12:25; Luke 20:36;
1 Corinthians 6:13 (etc.). Though the form *(forma)* has changed, the
matter *(materia)* of humankind, plant, animal, nature, and earth is the
same before and after the fall. All the essential components existing
today were present also before the fall. The distinctions and dissimilar-
ities between men and women, parents and children, brothers and sis-
ters, relatives and friends; the numerous institutions and relations in
the life of society such as marriage, family, child rearing, and so forth;
the alternation of day and night, workdays and the day of rest, labor and
leisure, months and years; man's dominion over the earth through science and art, and so forth—while all of these things have undoubtedly
been modified by sin and changed in appearance, they nevertheless
have their active principle and foundation in creation, in the ordinances of God, not in sin. Socialism and communism, also the socialism and communism of many Christian sects, are right in combating
the appalling consequences of sin, especially also in the sphere of society. But these systems do not stop there; they also come into conflict
with the nature of things, the creation ordinances, and therefore consistently take on, not a reformational, but a revolutionary character.

Human Destiny in Community

The doctrine of the covenant of works, finally, contains a third idea, an
idea of the richest religious and ethical significance. Adam was not created *alone*. As a man and by himself he was incomplete. He lacked
something for which no lower creature could make up (Gen. 2:20). As
a man by himself, accordingly, neither was he yet the fully unfolded
image of God. The creation of mankind in God's image was only completed on the sixth day when God created both man and woman in
union with each other (cf. *ʾwtm*, Gen. 1:27), in his image. Still even this
creation in God's image of man and woman in conjunction is not the
end but the beginning of God's journey with mankind. It is not good
that the man should be alone (Gen. 2:18); nor is it good that the man
and woman should be alone. Upon the two of them God immediately
pronounced the blessing of multiplication (Gen. 1:28). Not the man
alone, nor the man and woman together, but only the whole of humanity is the fully developed image of God, his son, his offspring. The image
of God is much too rich for it to be fully realized in a single human being, however richly gifted that human being may be. It can only be
somewhat unfolded in its depth and riches in a humanity counting bil-
lions of members. Just as the traces of God *(vestigia dei)* are spread over
many, many works, in both space and time, so also the image of God

can only be displayed in all its dimensions and characteristic features in a humanity whose members exist both successively one after the other and contemporaneously side by side. But just as the cosmos is a unity and receives its head and master in man; and just as the traces of God *(vestigia dei)* scattered throughout the entire world are bundled and raised up into the image of God of humankind, so also that humanity in turn is to be conceived as an organism which, precisely as such, is finally the only fully developed image of God. Not as a heap of souls on a tract of land, not as a loose aggregate of individuals, but as having been created out of one blood, as one household and one family, humanity is the image and likeness of God. Belonging to that humanity is also its development, its history, its ever-expanding dominion over the earth, its progress in science and art, its subjugation of all creatures. All these things as well constitute the unfolding of the image and likeness of God in keeping with which man was created. Just as God did not reveal himself just once at the creation, but continues and expands that revelation from day to day and from age to age, so also the image of God is not a static entity but extends and unfolds itself in the forms of space and time. It is both a gift *(Gabe)* and a mandate *(Aufgabe)*. It is an undeserved gift of grace that was given the first human being immediately at the creation, but at the same time the grounding principle and germ of an altogether rich and glorious development. Only humanity in its entirety—as one complete organism, summed up under a single head, spread out over the whole earth, as prophet proclaiming the truth of God, as priest dedicating itself to God, as ruler controlling the earth and the whole of creation—only it is the fully finished image, the most telling and striking likeness of God.

Scripture clearly teaches all this when it says that the church is the bride of Christ, the temple of the Holy Spirit, the dwelling of God, the new Jerusalem to which all the glory of the nations will be brought. This is a picture, to be sure, of the state of glory which will now be attained through the thickets of sin; but religion, the moral law, and man's final destiny are essentially the same in both the covenant of works and the covenant of grace. In both the goal and end is a kingdom of God, a holy humanity, in which God is all in all.

Only one point in this presentation requires further discussion. Humanity cannot be conceived as a completed organism unless it is united and epitomized in one head. In the covenant of grace Christ has that position and he is the head of the church; in the covenant of works that position is occupied by Adam. Eve was created from Adam so that he could be the first principle of the whole race *(principium totius speciei)* and so that the unity of the human race would be rooted in the unity of its origin. The woman, accordingly, is very much a partaker of human nature and of the image of God, and she represents that nature and image in accordance with her own nature and in a manner uniquely her own; but she is a partaker of both human nature and the image, not over against, but alongside of others, and in solidarity with the man. She is "from man," "for the man," and "the glory of man," and not independent of man but also the man, though head of his wife and "the image and glory of God" because he, in the first place, is the bearer of dominion, is nevertheless incomplete without the woman, for she is the mother of all living (1 Cor. 11:7–12; Eph. 5:22ff.). Paul above all points out to us this unity of humanity when he opposes Adam to Christ (Rom. 5:12–21; 1 Cor. 15:22, 45–49). The human race is not only physically of one blood (Acts 17:26), for that would not be enough for humanity. The same thing is true, after all, of all the animal species created in the beginning. Furthermore, Christ, the antitype of Adam, is not our ancestor; we did not physically descend from him. He himself is a descendant of Adam according to the flesh. In this respect Adam and Christ are not alike. But the similarity consists in the fact that in a juridical and ethical sense humanity stands in the same relation to Adam as to Christ. Just as Christ is the cause of our righteousness and our life, so Adam is the cause of our sin and our death. God considers and judges the whole human race in one person.

Now Reformed theologians have expressed this idea in their doctrine of the covenant of works. Only in this covenant does the ethical—not the physical—unity of mankind come into its own. And this ethical unity is requisite for humanity as an organism. Generally speaking, the law of architectonics everywhere requires the monarchical system. A work of art must be controlled by a single thought; a sermon must have a single theme; a church comes to completeness in a steeple; the man is the head of the family; in a kingdom the king [or queen] is the bearer of authority; as an organic whole, an ethical community, the human race is not conceivable without a head. In the covenant of works Adam had that position. The probationary command is proof that he occupied an entirely exceptional post. He was not only the ancestor but also the head and representative of the entire human race and his conduct was decisive for all. Just as the fate of the whole body rests with the head, which thinks and judges and decides for all the organs; just as the well-being of a family depends on the husband and father; just as a sovereign ruler can be a blessing or a curse for thousands and millions of his subjects, so the fate of humanity was put in the hands of Adam. His transgression became the fall of all his descendants but his obedience would also have been the life of all his descendants, as Christ, his antitype, proves. If we could not be subjected to condemnation in Adam without our knowledge, neither could we have been ac-

cepted unto grace in Christ without our participation. The covenant of
works and the covenant of grace stand and fall together. The same law
applies to both. On the basis of a common physical descent an ethical
unity has been built that causes humanity—in keeping with its nature—to manifest itself as one organism and to unite its members in
the closest possible way, not only by ties of blood but also by common
participation in blessing and curse, sin and righteousness, death and
life.

From this vantage point fresh light falls on the question of the propagation of the human race. At all times opinions have been divided on
this issue. The preexistence theory of Pythagoras, Plato, Plotinus, Philo,
and the later Jews found little acceptance among Christians,[36] but was
revived in a more or less modified form in modern times,[37] and today,
under the influence of Buddhism and the doctrine of evolution, it even
has many strong advocates.[38] If there exists no personal God and no
Creator, if evolution can only develop what is, and cannot produce anything absolutely new, and if for some reason one nevertheless wants to
maintain the immortality of the soul, it is natural to think that the souls
which continue to exist forever in the future also existed eternally in the
past. Just as Haeckel, for want of an explanation via the theory of evolution, made matter and energy, movement and life, consciousness and
feeling eternal, so in the same way others draw the conclusion that the
souls of humans at no time originated but have always existed in the
cosmos. But since the Christian religion arises from very different premises and is based on the confession of God's personal existence and
creative activity, it has no room for this doctrine of the eternal preexistence of souls. Nor is our soul in any way conscious of such preexistence and, rather than viewing the body as a prison and place of pun-

---

36. Origen, *On First Principles*, I, 6, 2; 8, 3; II, 9, 2; idem, *Against Celsus*, I, 32, 33; H.
More, *Mysterium pietatis* (1660).
37. G. E. Lessing, *Erziehung des Menschengeschlechts und andere Schriften* (Stuttgart: Reclam, 1997), §§91–95; I. Kant, *Religion Within the Limits of Reason Alone*, trans.
by T. M. Greene & H. H. Hudson (New York: Harper and Brothers, 1934), 145–51 [*Ed.
note:* For a fuller bibliographic note on Kant's views of preexistence and immortality, see
R. Eisler, s.v. "Unsterblichkeit," *Kant-Lexikon* (Berlin: Mittler & Sohn, 1930), 555–57];
F. W. Schelling, *Ausgewählte Werke* (Darmstadt: Wissenschaftlichle Buchgesellschaft,
1968) IV, 329ff. (*Werke*, I/7, 385ff., "Philosophische Untersuchungen über das Wesen der
menschlichen Freiheit und die damit zusammenhängenden Gegenstände"); I. H. von
Fichte, *Anthropologie* (Leipzig: Brockhaus, 1860), 494; J. Müller, *The Christian Doctrine
of Sin*, 5th ed., 2 vols., trans. by Wm. Urwick (Edinburgh: T. & T. Clark, 1868), ch. 3, par.
3; C. Sécrétan, *La Philosophie de la Liberté*, 2 vols. (Paris: G. Balliere, 1849), II, 204; cf.
also F. E. Daubanton, *Het Voortbestaan van het Menschelijk Geslacht* (Utrecht: Kemink,
1902), 4–54.
38. Cf. esp. John McTaggart and Ellis McTaggart, *Some Dogmas of Religion* (London:
E. Arnold, 1906), 112ff.

ishment, shrinks from the event of death. The theory of the preexistence of the soul, moreover, is rooted in a pagan dualism between spirit and matter, destroys the unity of the human race, and erases the distinction between human beings and angels.[39]

Creation and Traducianism

By contrast, the argument between traducianism and creationism remained undecided in Christian theology. In the ancient period the former had many advocates, such as Tertullian, Rufinus, Makarios, Eunomius, Appolinaris, Gregory of Nyssa, and, according to a probably highly exaggerated statement by Jerome, even "by the majority of the Westerners." Later, however, with a few exceptions, it was only embraced by the Lutherans: by Luther himself (though he was initially a creationist[40]), then by Melanchthon, Gerhard. Quenstedt (etc.).[41] Creationism, which already occurs in Aristotle, in the Christian church received the early endorsement of Clement of Alexandria, Lactantius, Hilary, Pelagius, Cassian, Gennadius, Theodoret, Athanasius, Gregory of Nazianzu, Cyril, Alexandrinus, Ambrose, and others, so that Jerome could already speak of it as a church doctrine. Greek scholastic and Roman Catholic theologians, accordingly, have all adopted creationism,[42] and only a few, such as Klee, show some sympathy for traducianism.[43] Also the Reformed theologians, with few exceptions,[44] opted for creationism.[45] Some, such as especially Augustine and Gregory the

39. F. E. Daubanton, *Het Voortbestaan*, 55–78.

40. J. Köstlin, *Luther's Theology*, II, 348.

41. J. Gerhard, *Loci Theol.*, VIII, c. 8; J. Quenstedt, *Theologia*, I, 519; D. Hollaz, *Examen Theol.* 414; F. A. Philippi, *Kirchliche Glaubenslehre* (Gütersloh: Bertelsmann, 1902), III, 103; A. F. C. Vilmar, *Handbuch der Evangel. Dogm.* (Gütersloh: Bertelsmann, 1895), I, 348; Frank, *System der Christliche Wahrheit*, I, 400; F. Delitzsch, *A System of Biblical Psychology*, 106ff.; H. Cremer, "Seele," in *PRE*[2], XIV, 27; A. Von Oettingen, *Lutherische Dogmatik*, 2 vols. (München: C. H. Beck, 1897), II, 370, 390ff.; W. Schmidt, *Christliche Dogmatik*, 4 vols. (Bonn: E. Weber, 1895–98), II, 260.

42. P. Lombard, *Sent.*, II, 17, 18; T. Aquinas, *Summa Theol.*, qu. 90 and 118; idem, *Summa Contra Gentiles*, II, 86–89; R. Bellarmine, *De Amiss. gr. et Statu Pecc.*, IV, 2; M. J. Scheeben, *Dogmatik*, II, 172ff.; J. Kleutgen, *Philosophie der Vorzeit*, 2nd ed. (Munster: Theissing, 1860), II, 583ff.; J. B. Heinrich and C. Gutberlet, *Dogmatische Theologie*, 2nd ed. (Mainz: Kirchheim, 1881–1900), VI, 265–315.

43. H. Klee, *Katholische Dogmatik*, 2nd ed. (Mainz: Kirchheim, 1861), II, 313ff.

44. G. Sohn, *Opera Sacrae Theologiae* (Herborn: C. Corvin, 1593), II, 563; Justin Martyr, *Loci*, 81; W. G. T. Shedd, *Dogmatic Theology* (New York: Charles Scribner's Sons, 1888–89), II, 22, 75; III, 250.

45. J. Calvin, *Commentary on Hebrews*, trans. by John Owen (Grand Rapids: Baker, 1979), 163–65, on Hebrews 12:9; J. Zanchi, *Op. Theol.*, III, 609; A. Polanus, *Syn. Theol.*, V., 31; G. Voetius, *Select. Disp.*, I, 798; B. De Moor, *Comm. Theol.*, II, 1064, III, 289; J. Marck, *Historia Paradisi*, II, 4 §§7–9 enz.

Great, prefer to leave the question undecided,[46] and others look for a compromise.[47]

Indeed, in the strength of their arguments traducianism and creationism are almost equal. Traducianism appeals to the creation of Eve of whose soul there is no special mention and who is therefore called "from" or "out of man" (*ex andreos;* 1 Cor. 11:8; Gen. 2:23); to the language of Holy Scripture which says that descendants were included in and sprang from the loins of their fathers (Gen. 46:26; Heb. 7:9, 10); to the word *yd^c*, to know, which is said to include a spiritual act; to the completion of creation on the seventh day (Gen. 2:2); to the fact that also animals can reproduce their own kind (Gen. 1:28; 5:3; 9:4; John 3:6); and especially to the hereditary transmission of sin and all sorts of psychological attributes.[48] Creationism, on the other hand, derives its support from the creation of Adam's soul (Gen. 2:7); many texts such as Ecclesiastes 12:7, Zechariah 12:1, and especially Hebrews 12:9 (cf. Num. 16:22), of which even Franz Delitzsch says: "There can hardly be a more classical prooftext for creationism";[49] and above all from the simple, indivisible, immortal, spiritual nature of the soul.

And just as both traducianism and creationism advance weighty arguments for their respective positions, so both are incapable of solving the difficulties present in this area. Traducianism neither explains the origin of the soul nor the hereditary transmission of sin. As for the first difficulty, there are two possibilities: the first is to end with the theory that the soul of the child already existed in the parents and their ancestors—hence to a kind of belief in preexistence—or that the soul was potentially present in the seed of the man or the woman or in both (i.e., to come up with a materialist view). The second is that the parents themselves somehow produced it (i.e., to a creationist view) with the human

---

46. Augustine repeatedly revisited the issue of the origin of the soul (*The Literal Meaning of Genesis*, I, 10; *The Retractions*, II, 45) but always ended with the statement that he did not know. Also, Leo the Great, Isodore, Chemnitz, Buddeus, Musculus, Piscator, Maresius, Van Oosterzee, Böhl, et al., refrained from taking a position.

47. G. W. Leibniz and J. C. Gottsched, *Theodicee* (Leipzig: Foerster, 1744), I, 91; R. Rothe, *Theologische Ethik*, 5 vols., 2nd rev. ed. (Wittenberg: Zimmerman, 1867–71), §136; J. H. A. Ebrard, *Christliche Dogmatik*, 2 vols. 2nd ed. (Konigsberg: A. W. Unser, 1862–63), I, 327ff.; H. Martensen, *Christian Dogmatics*, trans. by William Urwick (Edinburgh: T. & T. Clark, 1871), 164–70; F. E. Daubanton, *Het Voortbestaan*, 195ff.

48. All these arguments are set forth at length by Daubanton, 125ff. His main objection to creationism is that it is bound up with the doctrine of the covenant of works, which to him is an ingenious juridical invention (132, 141). He all too easily dismisses creationism when he writes that "the theologian of our day who does not practice his discipline in isolation from its sister disciplines as though in a cloister . . . has finished with this theory. He bequeaths to it a place of honor in the archives of the history of dogma" (150). Cf. Bierens de Haan, *in loco,* 187.

49. F. Delitzsch, *A System of Biblical Psychology*, 137–38.

agent in the place of God. As for the second difficulty, traducianism cannot help resolve it because sin is not material, not a substance, but a moral quality, moral guilt and moral corruption.[50] To obviate these difficulties Daubanton pictures the new body originating as a result of material contact between the procreative products, and the new spiritual soul similarly originating as a result of spiritual (metaphysical) contact between the psychic potencies inherent in the procreative products. Both the ovum and the sperm are "ensouled" prior to this contact and both are bearers of psychic life. Now when the two touch and penetrate each other both physically and psychically (metaphysically) in the mother's body, they have the capacity not only to produce a material fetus but also to produce in that fetus a new and newly become pneumatic human soul.[51] This scenario is of course [partially] correct.

[It is true that] insofar as both the ovum and the sperm, for as long as they are part of the living body, are "animated" [*bezieled*, lit. "ensouled," ed.]. But the crucial question here is what the nature of that "animated" life is. One can hardly imagine that in each of the two components, the ovum and the sperm, there is a "spiritual immortal" soul, as Daubanton himself describes the essence of the soul, for then the souls would be preexistent, every human being would possess countless souls, and each time the sperm and ovum would decompose, a soul would be lost. Daubanton, accordingly, does not speak of souls but of psychic potencies inherent in the sperm and ovum. But it is hard to tell what this expression—"psychic potencies"—means; capacities and powers can be potential as long as they do not begin to act, but a psychic potency is an impossible notion. A soul, as Daubanton himself defines it, either exists or doesn't exist. Presumably the idea is that the sperm and the ovum, both of them alive and "animated," possess the capacity to produce a fetus which is itself alive and "animated." But then the same question recurs, namely, what is the nature of the life which the fetus possesses in its initial stages? If one answers that that life is already present thanks to the individual immortal spiritual soul that indwells the fetus, one faces the question of where such a soul came from. It was present neither in the sperm nor in the ovum, nor can the union of the two produce it. If one answers that God gave to the sperm and the ovum the *capacity*, on being united, to produce a soul that neither of them had prior to the union but is still spiritual and immortal, then we are actually dealing with another form of creationism. For then both sperm and ovum possess the actual *creative* power to impart existence

50. The objections to traducianism and the grounds for creationism are unfolded at length by A. G. Honig, *Creationisme of Traducianisme?* (Kampen: J. H. Bos, 1906).
51. F. E. Daubanton, *Het Voortbestaan*, 194, 205–7, 211, 240.

to an immortal spiritual soul from within a life that, though "animated," is devoid of such a soul. And if one's answer to the question posed above is that sperm and ovum possess the capacity, upon being united, to produce a fetus which, though animated and alive, doesn't yet possess an immortal spiritual soul but which is so organized that, after a period of development, it can attain the possession of an immortal spiritual soul, then one has only managed to shift the locus of the difficulty. For then one immediately faces the further questions of *when* and *how* the fetus becomes a human being, *when* and *how* psychic life becomes pneumatic life. And then one can only answer *either* in one of two ways. The first is that this occurs gradually in keeping with the laws of evolution. In that case, however, the *essential* difference between the psychic and the pneumatic life, between the vital soul and the immortal spiritual soul, between animal and man, vanishes. The alternative is that the fetus itself has the capacity at a given moment to raise the psychic life into a spiritual soul. What we have then is another form of creationism, with this modification that now it is not God but a human (or better still a fetus) who becomes the creator. When traducianism pursues its own logic, it either lapses into materialism or again smuggles creationism into its tent under another label.

Another objection must be added. The moment an immortal spiritual soul dwells in an organism, there exists a human being, an individual, a personality, be it only germinally. Now somebody will say that either the sperm as such, or the ovum as such, or the fetus which originated from the union of the two in the first days of its life, is a human being who has a self of his or her own and will always exist. So there has to be a moment in which the fetus becomes a human being who will have his or her own independent and continuing existence. *When* this happens or *how* this happens is a mystery. Science has no idea when or how this happens, and theology with its conjecture of the fortieth or sixtieth day is only guessing. Creationism can no more explain this mystery than traducianism. But it has the advantage over the latter theory in that it is prepared respectfully to leave this mystery alone and not to subject it to a spurious explanation. The latter is the danger to which traducianism exposes itself. For if—as was stated above—it does not again smuggle in creationism under another name, it may nevertheless equip the sperm and ovum jointly or the fetus alone with a creative power, and so lapse into an evolutionary theory which implies that animal life can gradually and of itself develop into human life. But evolutionary theory here, as in many other cases, is totally unable to explain the phenomena. This already applies in a chemical sense. A union of different atoms or substances exhibits properties that are very different from those which are unique to those of each of the components. For that reason—to cite an example—Sir Oliver Lodge states: "there is no necessary justification for assuming that a phenomenon exhibited by an aggregate of particles must be possessed by the ingredients of which it is composed; on the contrary, wholly new properties may make their appearance simply by aggregation."[52]

Even in inanimate creatures the process of combining, uniting, or mixing elements already produces something new and, as it were, raises creation to a higher level. That is even much more powerfully true in the case of animate and rational beings. No person and particularly no person like, say, Goethe can be explained purely by genetics from his parents or ancestors. "Neither the physical stature of Goethe's father, nor his mother's happy disposition, give us any indication for understanding how this extraordinary personality came about. And just as genius suddenly makes its appearance, so also its marks soon disappear."[53] Granted, for years now an intense study has been made of the laws of heredity, but until now the result only consists in the knowledge that heredity is a complex question. The theories and hypotheses that have been posited in recent years have shed little or no light on the extent and manner of hereditary transmission.[54] No one taking account of the uniqueness of the human soul and its frequently unique and outstanding gifts will therefore be able to avoid acknowledging—in addition to and in connection with the truth of traducianism—an important creationist component in the formation of the soul. This creative activity of God which, although we do not know it, undoubtedly makes its power felt in various other areas of nature and history as well, surely ties in as intimately as possible with what is given in the tradition: *by creating,* said Lombard already, God influenced them and by influencing creates them.[55] He does not first create a soul apart from the body in order then to introduce it into the body from without but—at the proper time[56] and in a manner incomprehensible to us[57]—he elevates the existing psychic life to the level of a higher human spiritual life.[58] In keeping with this, accordingly, the hereditary transmission of sin cannot be explained by

52. O. J. Lodge, *Life and Matter,* 4th ed. (London: Williams & Norgate, 1907), 49–50 and cf. further cap. 5 and 10.

53. *Lexis, "Das Wesen der Kultur," *Die Kultur der Gegenwart,* I/1, 16.

54. W. H. Nieuwhuis, *Twee Vragen des Tijds* (Kampen: Kok, 1907), 76ff.

55. P. Lombard, *Sent.,* II, dist. 17.

56. Cf. A. Polanus, *Syn. Theol.,* V, 31; Bucanus, *Inst. Theol.,* VIII, 26.

57. T. Aquinas, *Summa Theol.,* I, qu. 118, art. 2; idem, *Summa Contra Gentiles,* 59, 68.

58. Also Rabus writes that the "psychic life principle of the sensory organism—originally passed down by generation—" can only be raised to a higher and independent human life "by the assumption of a divine act of creation," in an article entitled: "Vom Wirken und Wohnen des göttlichen Geistes in der Menschenseele," *Neue Kirchliche Zeitschrift* (November 1904): 828.

saying that the soul, though first created pure by God, is polluted by the body,[59] for in that case sin would be materialized. It is rather to be understood by the idea that the soul, though called into being as a rational spiritual entity by a creative activity of God, was nevertheless preformed in the psychic life of the fetus, that is, in the life of parents and ancestors, and thus receives its being, not from above or outside but under the conditions of, and amidst, the sin-nexus that oppresses the human race.[60]

Although creationism and traducianism both face insoluble difficulties, it is remarkable nevertheless that Eastern Orthodox, Roman Catholic, and Reformed theologians almost unanimously embraced the former view, while the latter found acceptance only among the Lutherans. This cannot be an accident; there has to be a reason for it. That reason lies in a different view of the nature and destiny of man. For, in the first place, Lutheran theology locates the image of God solely in a number of moral qualities, in original righteousness. As always, so here as well it limits its focus to the ethical-religious life of humanity and feels no need to relate this life to the whole of cosmic existence and to view it as a link in the whole counsel of God. As a result, human nature comes into its own neither vis-à-vis the angels nor vis-à-vis the animals. For if human beings possess this image of God we are virtually equal to the angels. The difference between us and them, by comparison with what we have in common, is negligible. The angels also bear the image of God. And if humans lack this image, they fall to the level of the animals and become "blocks and stones."[61] That which still distinguishes us from animals has so little theological and religious value that it is almost negligible. The crucial distinction, after all, consisted in possessing the image of God, an image humanity totally lost. Hence the boundaries between human beings and angels and between human beings and animals are no longer sharply drawn here. Original righteousness is everything; all else in humanity is subordinate and virtually of no theological value. But for that reason it is also a matter of indifference to Lutheran theology *how* the human race originated. Rather, it is more correct to say that which human beings have in common with the angels, namely, the image of God, "original righteousness," can and must come into being only by an act of creation. *That,* in an absolute sense, is a gift. But everything else a human being possesses is passed down

59. P. Lombard, *Sent.,* II, dist. 31.

60. G. Voetius, *Select. Disp.,* I, 1097; F. Turretin, *Institutes of Elenctic Theology,* IX, 12; B. De Moor, *Comm. Theol.,* III, 289.

61. *Ed. note:* Bavinck's phrase here is taken from *Canons of Dordt,* III/IV, 16, which insists that "regeneration does not act in people as if they were blocks and stones; nor does it abolish the will and its properties or coerce a reluctant will by force, but spiritually revives, heals, reforms and—in a manner at once pleasing and powerful—bends it back."

from one generation to the next in the same way as in the animal world. But Roman Catholic and Reformed theologians, even if they sometimes still denominated the angels "image of God," from the beginning sought the image of God in the total and entirely unique nature of human beings. It certainly consisted in the virtues of knowledge, righteousness, and holiness but these qualities, even in human beings, nevertheless bore a different character from those in the angels, and it not only consisted in those virtues but extended to all of our humanness. Hence it also consisted in the fact that the human spirit *(pneuma)* was from the beginning adapted to union with a human body *(sōma)* and that the body *(sōma)* was from the beginning designed for the spirit *(pneuma)*. Before and after the fall, in the state of integrity and that of corruption, in the state of grace and that of glory—human beings always are and always remain essentially distinct from the angels and the animals.

If human beings have the image of God, they do not become angels and if they lose it, they do not become animals. Always and forever they remain human and to that extent are always and forever the image of God. This is the reality which is sufficiently preserved only in creationism. Because human beings *exist* as wholly unique beings, they also *originate* in an entirely special way. Though related to angels and animals, they are nevertheless essentially different from them. Differing from them in their nature, they consequently differ from them also in their origin. Adam's creation was different from that of the animals and also different from that of the angels. Creationism alone sufficiently maintains the specific uniqueness of humanity since it fends off both pantheism and materialism and respects the boundaries between humanity and animals.

In the second place, a consequence of the Lutheran view of the image of God is that the moral unity of the human race has to take a back seat to physical descent. As a result of the fall human beings lost all spiritual and moral unity when they lost the entire image of God. Natural religion and natural morality, and the like, is of almost no importance. Only physical descent holds them together and is at the same time the cause of their moral depravity. The sin, which has robbed humanity of all religion and morality and of the entire image of God, for that very reason cannot be passed on to all human beings by ethical means but only by physical descent. Granted, it is not a substance (though Luther and others, especially Flacius, used very strong language in this connection). It is still primarily a stain, a form of decay, which affects the whole of a human being and above all kills the religious and ethical human faculties. In response and by contrast, Roman Catholic and Reformed theology, each in its own way, posited that the unity of mankind was not only of a physical but also of an ethical nature. Physical descent, certainly, is not enough; if it were, also animal species would constitute a unity. Similarity in moral virtues by itself is also insufficient; if it were sufficient, the angels among themselves and angels collectively with humanity would also constitute a unity. Animal species, though they are physically of one blood, are not a moral body *(corpus morale);* and angels, though they form a unity, are not related by blood. Human uniqueness, therefore, requires that the unity of humankind be both physical and ethical. And because original sin is not physical in nature but only ethical, it can only be rooted in the ethical and federal unity of the human race. Physical descent is not sufficient to explain it and runs the danger of materializing it. The so-called realism, say of Shedd,[62] is inadequate both as an explanation of Adam's sin and as an explanation of righteousness by faith-in-Christ. Needed among human beings is another kind of unity, one that causes them to act unitedly as a moral body, organically connected as well as ethically united. And that is a federal unity. Now on the basis of a physical unity an ethical unity has to be constructed. Adam as our ancestor is not enough: he must also be the covenant head of the human race, just as Christ, though he is not our common ancestor in a physical sense, is still able, as covenant head, to bestow righteousness and blessedness upon his church. Now this moral unity of the human race can only be maintained on the basis of creationism, for it has a character of its own, is distinct from that of animals as well as that of the angels, and therefore also comes into being in its own way, both by physical descent and by a creative act of God, the two of them in conjunction with each other.

Finally, in the third place, in virtue of its view of the image of God Lutheran theology does not trouble itself much about human destiny. Adam had everything he needed; he only had to remain what he was. The distinction between the "able not to sin" *(posse non peccare)* and the "not able to sin" *(non posse peccare)* carries little weight. Perseverance is not a higher good granted in Christ to his own. Thus Adam did not have to gain anything higher for his descendants. For that purpose traducianism is sufficient; there is no room for a covenant of works or creationism.

Again, Roman Catholic and Reformed theology thought otherwise, arguing as they did from another perspective. The destiny of man consists in heavenly blessedness, eternal life, the contemplation of God. But he can only reach this destiny in the way of obedience. There is no proportion between this obedience and that prospect. How then can

---

62. *Ed. note:* See W. T. Shedd, *Dogmatic Theology,* 3 vols., 3rd ed. (New York: Scribner, 1891–94), II, ch. 1, "Anthropology."

that heavenly blessedness nevertheless be granted to a human being as a reward for his or her works? Rome says: because in the image of God he or she is supplied with a supernatural grace which enables him or her to merit eternal life *ex condigno*. The Reformed theologian says: because God has established a covenant with humanity and desires to give it eternal life, not in proportion to the value of works, but in accordance with his own gracious dispensation. Both parties, however, agree that the destiny of man lies in eternal blessedness and that this blessedness can only be reached in the way of moral obedience, and that on behalf of the whole human race God put the decision in this matter in the hands of Adam. And for that reason these two parties also arrived at creationism. Needed to this end was (1) that all human beings should be included under the covenant head Adam, and (2) that at the same time they themselves should remain persons, individuals, having their own independence and responsibility. Physical descent alone would have resulted in a situation where the sin we received from Adam would be a deterministic fate, a process of nature, a sickness which had nothing to do with our will and hence did not imply any guilt on our part. That is not what sin is. Nor is the righteousness which Christ as the last Adam confers on us of that nature. Both the *sin* and the *righteousness* presuppose a federal relation between humanity as a whole and its heads.

Thus creationism maintains that every human person is an organic member of humanity as a whole, and at the same time that, in that whole, he or she occupies an independent place of his or her own. It upholds the unity of the human race in its entirety and at the same time the independent significance of every individual. Human beings are not specimens, not numbers of a kind, nor are they detached individuals like the angels. They are both parts of a whole and individuals: *living stones* of the *temple* of God. Creationism preserves the organic—both physical and moral—unity of humanity and at the same time it respects the mystery of the individual personality. Every human being, while a member of the body of humanity as a whole, is at the same time a unique idea of God, with a significance and destiny that is eternal! Every human being is himself or herself an image of God, yet that image is only fully unfolded in humanity as a whole! Whereas in virtue of that unity humanity as a whole fell in Adam, its progenitor and its head, that fall is nevertheless not a fate, a natural process, but, on the contrary, based on a free and sovereign dispensation of God. And this dispensation, however free and sovereign, is nevertheless so far removed from being arbitrary that it rather presupposes the physical connectedness of humankind, brings about and maintains its ethical unity, and is able to reveal and manifest in all its splendor not only the severity of God but also the riches of his grace. For when Adam falls Christ stands ready to take his place. The covenant of grace can replace the covenant of works because both are based on the same ordinances. If we could not have been condemned in Adam, neither could we have been acquitted in Christ. Hence, however the first human being should choose, creation could not miss its destiny. In Genesis cosmogony immediately passes over into geogony and geogony into anthropogony. The world, the earth, humanity are one organic whole. They stand, they fall, they are raised up together. The traces of God *(vestigia Dei)* in creation and the image of God in humanity may be mangled and mutilated by the sin of the first Adam; but by the last Adam and his re-creating grace they are all the more resplendently restored to their destiny. The state of integrity—either through the fall or apart from the fall—is a preparation for the state of glory in which God will impart his glory to all his creatures and be "all in all."[63]

63. *Ed. note:* Reference to 1 Cor. 15:28 is not given by Bavinck.

III
God's Fatherly Care

Providence 7

God's work of preserving needs to be distinguished from that of creation, though they are inseparable. Preservation is a great and glorious divine work no less than creating new things out of nothing. Creation brings forth existence; preservation is persistence in existence. Providence in some form is known to all people, though not as the gracious care of a loving Heavenly Father. Providence is not merely foreknowledge but involves God's active will ruling all things and includes preservation, concurrence, and government. The notion of concurrence was developed to ward off pantheism on the one side and Deism on the other. In the former providence coincides with the course of nature as blind necessity; in the latter providence is replaced by pure chance and God is removed from the world. In this manner an attempt was made to exalt human autonomy; for humanity to have freedom God must be absent or powerless. God's sovereignty is viewed as a threat to humanity. Though the doctrine of God's providence logically covers the entire scope of all God's decrees, extending to all topics covered in dogmatics, it is preferable to restrict the discussion to God's relation to his creation and creatures. Providence includes God's care through the secondary causality of the created order of law as he maintains it. A miracle is thus not a violation of natural law since God is no less involved with maintaining the ordinary order of the natural created world. It is the high respect Christianity has for the natural order of creation that encouraged science and made it possible. The Christian posture toward creation's order is never fatalism; astrology is appalling superstition. The providence of God does not cancel out secondary causes or human responsibility. Governance points to the final goal of providence: the perfection of God's kingly rule. While it is correct on occasion to speak of divine "permission," this must not be construed in such a way as to deny God's active sovereignty over sin and judgment. While riddles remain for human understanding of providence, this doctrine affords the believer with consolation and hope. God is Almighty Father: able and desirous of turning everything to our good.

When on the seventh day God completed his work that he had done, he rested on the seventh day from all his work (Gen. 2:2; Exod. 20:11; 31:17). Thus Scripture describes the transition from the work of creation to that of preservation. As Scripture also makes very clear (Isa. 40:28), this resting was not occasioned by fatigue, nor did it consist in God standing idly by. Creating, for God, is not work, and preserving no rest. God's "resting" only indicates that he stopped producing new kinds of things (Eccl. 1:9, 10); that the work of creation, in the true and narrow sense as producing things out of nothing *(productio rerum ex nihilo)*, was over; and that he delighted in this completed work with divine pleasure (Gen. 1:31; Exod. 31:17; Ps. 104:31).[1] Creation now passes into preservation.

The two are so fundamentally distinct that they can be contrasted as labor and rest. At the same time they are so intimately related and bound up with each other that preservation itself can be called "creating" (Pss. 104:30; 148:5; Isa. 45:7; Amos 4:13). Preservation itself, after all, is also a divine work, no less great and glorious than creation. God is no indolent God *(deus otiosus)*. He works always (John 5:17) and the world has no existence in itself. From the moment it came into being it has existed only in and through and unto God (Neh. 9:6; Ps. 104:30; Acts 17:28; Rom. 11:36; Col. 1:15; Heb. 1:3; Rev. 4:11). Although distinct from his being, it has no independent existence; independence is tantamount to nonexistence. The whole world with everything that is and occurs in it is subject to divine government. Summer and winter, day and night, fruitful and unfruitful years, light and darkness—it is all his work and formed by him (Gen. 8:22; 9:14; Lev. 26:3f.; Deut. 11:12f.; Job 38; Pss. 8, 29, 65, 104, 107, 147; Jer. 3:3; 5:24; Matt. 5:45, etc.). Scripture knows no independent creatures; this would be an oxymoron. God cares for all his creatures: for animals (Gen. 1:30; 6:19; 7:2; 9:10; Job 38:41; Pss. 36:7; 104:27; 147:9; Joel 1:20; Matt. 6:26, etc.), and particularly for humans. He sees them all (Job 34:21; Ps. 33:13, 14; Prov. 15:3); fashions the hearts of them all and observes all their deeds (Ps. 33:15; Prov. 5:21); they are all the works of his hands (Job 34:19), the rich as well as the poor (Prov. 22:2). He determines the boundaries of their habitation (Deut. 32:8; Acts 17:26), inclines the hearts of all (Prov. 21:1), directs the steps of all (Prov. 5:21; 16:9; 19:21; Jer. 10:23, etc.), and deals according to his will with the host of heaven and the inhabitants of the earth (Dan. 4:35). They are in his hands as clay in the hands of a potter, and as a saw in the hand of one who pulls it (Isa. 29:16; 45:9; Jer. 18:5; Rom. 9:20, 21).

God's providential government extends very particularly to his people. The entire history of the patriarchs, of Israel, of the church, and of

---

1. Augustine, *The City of God*, XI, 8, XII, 17; idem, *The Literal Meaning of Genesis*, IV, 8ff.; P. Lombard, *Sent.*, II, dist. 15; T. Aquinas, *Summa Theol.*, I, qu. 73; J. Calvin, *Commentary on Genesis*, trans. by J. King (Grand Rapids: Baker, 1979), 103–5 (on Gen. 2:2); J. Zanchi, *Op. Theol.*, III, 537.

every believer, is proof of this. What other people meant for evil against them, God turned to their good (Gen. 50:20); no weapon fashioned against them will succeed (Isa. 54:17); even the hairs on their head are all numbered (Matt. 10:30); all things work together for their good (Rom. 8:28). Thus all created things exist in the power and under the government of God; neither chance nor fate is known to Scripture (Exod. 21:13; Prov. 16:33). It is God who works all things according to the counsel of his will (Eph. 1:11) and makes all things serviceable to the revelation of his attributes, to the honor of his name (Prov. 16:4; Rom. 11:36). Scripture beautifully sums up all this in repeatedly speaking of God as a king who governs all things (Pss. 10:16; 24:7, 8; 29:10; 44:5; 47:7; 74:12; 115:3; Isa. 33:22, etc.). God is King: the King of kings and the Lord of lords; a King who in Christ is a Father to his subjects and a Father who is at the same time a King over his children. Among creatures, in the world of animals, humans, and angels, all that is found in the way of care for, love toward, and protection of one by the other is a faint adumbration of God's providential order over all the works of his hands. His absolute power and perfect love, accordingly, are the true object of the faith in providence reflected in Holy Scripture.

Added to this witness of Scripture is the testimony of all peoples. The doctrine of divine providence is a "mixed article," known in part to all humans from God's revelation in nature. It is an article of faith in every—even in the most corrupt—religion. One who denies it undermines religion. Without it, there is no longer any room for prayer and sacrifice, faith and hope, trust and love. Why serve God, asks Cicero,[2] if he does not at all care about us? For that reason all religions agree with the statement of Sophocles:[3] "Still great above is Zeus who oversees all things in sovereign power." Philosophy, too, has frequently recognized and defended this providence of God.[4] Nevertheless the doctrine of providence as it comes to expression in pagan religion and philosophy was not identical with that doctrine in Christianity. Among pagans belief in providence was more theory than practice, more a matter of philosophical opinion than of religious dogma. It proved inadequate in time of distress and death and always swung back and forth between

2. M. T. Cicero, *On the Nature of the Gods,* I, 2.
3. Sophocles, *Electra,* 173 [trans. by D. Grene (Chicago: University of Chicago Press, 1957)].
4. E.g., Socrates in Xenophon, *Memorabilia and Oeconomicus,* I, 4; IV, 3; Plato, *Leg.,* X, 901; idem, *Rep.,* X, 613 A.; Aristotle, *Eth. Nic.,* X, 9; *De Stoa* in M. T. Cicero, *On the Nature of the Gods,* II; L. A. Seneca, *De Providentia;* idem, *De Beneficiis;* M. T. Cicero, *On the Nature of the Gods,* I, 2; III, 26; Plutarch, *De Fato.;* Plotinus, *peri eiwmaruenhs* (*Enneads,* III, 1), and *peri pronoias* (*Enneads,* III, 2, 3); Philo, *peri pronoias,* cf. E. Schürer, *The History of the Jewish People in the Age of Jesus Christ (175 B.C.–A.D. 135),* vol. 3., rev. and ed. by Geza Vermes, Fergus Miller, and Matthew Black (Edinburgh: T. & T. Clark, 1979 [1885]), 531ff.

chance and fate. Since in Plato, for example, God was not the creator but only the shaper of the world, his power found its limit in finite matter.[5] Although Aristotle repeatedly mentions his belief in divine providence, for him it nevertheless totally coincides with the working of natural causes; the deity as "thought thinking itself" *(noēsis noēseōs)* exists in solitary self-contemplation outside the world, devoid of both will and action; a creature must expect neither help nor love from it.[6] In the teaching of the Stoa *foreknowledge (pronoia)* was identical with *destiny (eimarmenem)* and *nature (physis)* and, according to Epicurus, providence was inconsistent with the blessedness of the gods.[7] While some, like Plutarch and Plotinus, did their best to escape both chance and fate, in actual fact fate always again took a position behind and above the deity, whereas chance crept into the lower creatures and minor events from below. "The big things the gods take care of; the little ones they ignore" *(magna Dii curant, parva negligunt).*[8]

Christian belief in God's providence, however, is not of that kind. On the contrary, it is a source of consolation and hope, of trust and courage, of humility and resignation (Pss. 23; 33:10ff.; 44:5ff.; 127:1, 2; 146:2ff. etc.). In Scripture belief in God's providence is absolutely not based solely on God's revelation in nature but much more on his covenant and promises. It rests not only on God's justice but above all on his compassion and grace and presupposes the knowledge of sin (much more profoundly than is the case in paganism) but also the experience of God's forgiving love. It is not a cosmological speculation but a glorious confession of faith. Ritschl, accordingly, was right in again closely linking faith in providence to faith in redemption. In the case of the Christian, belief in God's providence is not a tenet of natural theology to which saving faith is later mechanically added. Instead, it is saving faith which for the first time prompts us to believe wholeheartedly in God's providence in the world, to see its significance, and to experience its consoling power. Belief in God's providence, therefore, is an article of the *Christian* faith. For the "natural" human being, so many objections can be raised against God's cosmic government that he or she can only adhere to it with difficulty. But the Christian has witnessed God's

---

5. E. Zeller, *Outlines of the History of Greek Philosophy,* 13th ed., trans. by L. R. Palmer (New York: Humanities, 1969), 139, 147–48.

6. Ibid., 180, 198.

7. Ibid., 217, 237.

8. M. T. Cicero, *On the Nature of the Gods,* II, 167; cf. T. Pfanner, *Syst. Theol. Gentilis Purioris* (Basel: Joh. Hermann Widerhold, 1679), c. 8; F. Creutzer, *Philosophorum Veterum Loci de Providentia Divina ac de Fato* (Heidelberg, 1806); R. Schneider, *Christliche Klänge aus den Griechischen und Römischen Klassikern* (1865), 231ff. [Leipzig: Siegismund & Volkening, 1877].

special providence at work in the cross of Christ and experienced it in the forgiving and regenerating grace of God that has come to his or her own heart. And from the vantage point of this new and certain experience in one's own life, the Christian believer now surveys the whole of existence and the entire world and discovers in all things, not chance or fate, but the leading of God's fatherly hand. Still, though all this has been unfolded by Ritschl with complete accuracy, saving faith may not be equated with, or dissolved in, faith in providence. Special revelation is distinct from general revelation and a saving faith in the person of Christ is different from a general belief in God's government in the world. It is above all by faith in Christ that believers are enabled—in spite of all the riddles that perplex them—to cling to the conviction that the God who rules the world is the same loving and compassionate Father who in Christ forgave them all their sins, accepted them as his children, and will bequeath to them eternal blessedness. In that case faith in God's providence is no illusion, but secure and certain; it rests on the revelation of God in Christ and carries within it the conviction that nature is subordinate and serviceable to grace, and the world to the kingdom of God. Thus, through all its tears and suffering, it looks forward with joy to the future. Although the riddles are not resolved, faith in God's fatherly hand always again arises from the depths and even enables us to boast in afflictions.[9]

The Language of Providence

It is noteworthy in this connection that Scripture does not use the abstract word "providence." Attempts have indeed been made to give to this word a scriptural character by appealing to Genesis 22:8; 1 Samuel 16:1; Ezekiel 20:6; Hebrews 11:40. A few times the word also occurs with reference to human forethought (Rom. 12:17; 13:14; 1 Tim. 5:8). But all this does not alter the fact that Scripture, speaking of God's providence, uses very different words. It does not compress the activity of God expressed by this word into an abstract concept and does not discuss its theological implications. But it depicts the activity itself in a most splendid and vital way and exhibits it to us in history. Scripture in its totality is itself the book of God's providence. Thus depicting this providence, it refers to creating (Pss. 104:30; 148:5), making alive (Job 33:4; Neh. 9:6), renewing (Ps. 104:30), seeing, observing, letting (Job 28:24; Ps. 33:15); saving, protecting, preserving (Num. 6:24; Pss. 36:7; 121:7); leading, teaching, ruling (Pss. 25:5, 9; 9:31, etc.), working (John 5:17), upholding

9. Cf. *Ulrich, "Heilsglaube und Vorsehungsglauben," *Neue Kirchliche Zeitschrift* (1901): 478–93; *Winter, *Neue Kirchliche Zeitschrift* (1907): 609–31.

(Heb. 1:3), caring (1 Pet. 5:7). The word "providence" is derived from philosophy. According to Laertius, Plato was the first person to use the word *pronoia* in this sense.[10] The Apocrypha already use the word (Wisdom 14:3; 17:2; 3 Macc. 4:21; 5:30; 4 Macc. 9:24; 13:18; 17:22) alongside of *diatērein* (Wisdom 11:25), *diakubernan* (3 Macc. 6:2), *dioikein* (Wisdom 8:1, etc.). The church fathers took it over and gave it legitimacy in Christian theology.[11]

In the process, however, the word underwent a significant change in meaning. Originally "providence" meant the act of foreseeing *(providentia)* or foreknowing *(pronoia)* that which was to happen in the future. "Providence is that through which some future event is seen."[12] Thus conceived, the word was absolutely not fit to encompass everything the Christian faith confesses in the doctrine of God's providence. As advance knowledge of the future, the providence of God would of course solely belong under the heading of "the knowledge of God" and be fully treated in the locus on the attributes of God. But the Christian faith does not understand the providence of God to mean a mere foreknowledge *(nuda praescientia);* it confesses that all things are not only known by God in advance but also determined and ordained in advance. For that reason providence was not only at an early stage attributed to the intellect but also to the will of God and described by John of Damascus as "that will of God by which all existing things receive suitable guidance through to their end."[13] Understood in that sense, the providence of God would belong to the doctrine of the decrees of God and have to be treated there. But again the Christian faith confesses more than is indicated by the word in that sense. For the decrees of God are carried out and the creatures who thereby come into being do not for a moment exist on their own but are only sustained from moment to moment by God's almighty hand. The origination and existence of all creatures have their origin, not in foreknowledge, nor even in a decree, but specifically in an omnipotent act of God. Hence, according to Scripture and the church's confession, providence is that act of God by which from moment to moment he preserves and governs all things. It is not only "pre-vision" *(Fürsehung)* but also "pro-vidence" *(Vorsehung).*

These different meanings attributed to the word "providence," however, were the reason why the place and content of this doctrine kept shifting in Christian dogmatics and were subjected to all kinds of

10. E. Zeller, *Outlines of the History of Greek Philosophy,* 148.

11. J. C. Suicerus, s.v. pronoia in *Thesaurus Ecclesiasticus, e Patribus Graecis Ordine Alphabetico* (Amsterdam: J. H. Wetsten, 1682).

12. "Providentia est, per quam futurum aliquid videtur." M. T. Cicero, *De Inventione,* II, 53.

13. John of Damascus, *Exposition of the Orthodox Faith,* II, 29.

changes. Sometimes it was counted among the attributes, then again among the decrees *(opera Dei ad intra)*, then to the outgoing works of God *(opera ad extra)*.[14] John of Damascus defines it as "the solicitude which God has for existing things," and though he treats it after the doctrine of creation, he does so in close connection with "foreknowledge" and "predestination."[15] Lombard discusses it in the chapter on predestination but before creation.[16] Thomas offers a very clear exposition. First, he describes the doctrine in general as "the exemplar of the order of things foreordained towards an end" and considers it the primary part of prudence whose precise task it is to order other things to an end. He then further adds that "two things pertain to the work of providence, namely the *exemplar* of the order, which is called 'providence' and 'disposition' and the *execution* of the order which is called 'government.'"[17] In line with these and other examples the doctrine of providence was either treated in Roman Catholic theology along with predestination under the will of God,[18] or only as "preservation" *(conservatio)* or "government" *(gubernatio)*, each by itself, subsequent to the creation,[19] or in its entire scope and in its broadest sense after the locus of creation.[20]

Similarly, in the theology of the Reformation providence was sometimes viewed as a "counsel" *(consilium)* according to which God governs all things,[21] then again as an external work of God.[22] The differ-

---

14. Cf. H. Bavinck, *Gereformeerde Dogmatiek*, II, 336.

15. John of Damascus, *Exposition of the Orthodox Faith*, II, 29, 30.

16. P. Lombard, *Sent.*, I, dist. 35.

17. T. Aquinas, *Summa Theol.*, I, qu. 22, art. 1; cf. Bonaventure, *Sent.*, I, dist. 35 and Victor Hugo, *Sent.*, tr. 1, c. 12.

18. D. Petavius, *Opera Omnia*, "de deo," VIII, c. 1–5; M. Becanus, *Summa Theologiae Scholasticae* (Rothmagi: I. Behovrt, 1651), I, c. 13; *Theologia Wirceburgensi (Theologia Dogmatica: Polemica, Scholastica et Moralis)*, 5 vols. (Wirceburgensi: 1852–53), III, 175; G. Perrone, *Praelectiones Theologicae*, 9 vols. (Louvain: Vanlinthout & Vandezande, 1838–43), II, 233; C. Pesch, *Praelectiones Dogmaticae*, II, 158 [Freiburg i.B.: Herder, 1916–25)]; P. Mannens, *Theologiae Dogmaticae Institutiones* (Roermand: Romen), II, 105ff.

19. T. Aquinas, *Summa Theol.*, I, qu. 103–5; idem, *Summa Contra Gentiles*, III, 65; idem, *Commentatores op Sent.*, II, dist. 37; J. B. Heinrich and C. Gutberlet, *Dogmatische Theologie*, 10 vols., 2nd ed. (Mainz: Kirchheim, 1881–1900), V, 279.

20. J. Schwetz, *Theologia Dogmatic Catholica* (Vienna: Congregatio Mechitharistica, n.d.), I, 405; P. C. A. Jansen, *Prael. Theol.*, II, 329; H. Th. Simar, *Lehrbuch der Dogmatik*, 2 vols. (Freiburg i.B.: Herder, 1879–80), 252; M. J. Scheeben, *Handbuch der Katholischer Dogmatik*, 4 vols. (Freiburg i.B.: Herder, 1933), II, 12; F. Dieringer, *Lehrbuch der Katholischen Dogmatik*, 4th ed. (Mainz: Kirchheim, 1858), 266ff.

21. *Second Helvetic Confession*, art. 6; Z. Ursinus, *Commentary on the Heidelberg Catechism*, trans. by G. W. Willard (Grand Rapids: Eerdmans, 1954), qu. 27; J. Zanchi, *Op. Theol.*, II, 425; S. Maresius, *Syst. Theol.*, IV, §19; J. Alsted, *Theol.*, 174.

22. J. Calvin, *Institutes of the Christian Religion*, I, 16, 3, 4; A. Polanus, *Syn. Theol.*, VI, 1; F. Junius, *Theses Theologiae* in *Opscula Theol. Select.*, XVII, 1, 2; *Synopsis Purioris Theologiae*, XI, 3; J. H. Heidegger, *Corpus Theologiae*, VII, 3 enz.

ence, as Alsted and Baier correctly remarked,[23] pertained more to the term than to the matter itself. If God really maintains and governs the world, he must have foreknowledge of it *(providentia)*, will it, and be able to care for it *(prudentia)*, and also actually so preserve and govern it in time that the end he had in mind would be attained. Taken in this broad sense, providence embraces (1) an internal act *(actus internus)* which can further again be differentiated as "foreknowledge" *(prognōsis)*, a purpose or proposed end *(prothesis)*, and a plan *(dioikēsis)*;[24] and (2) an external act *(actus externus)* which, as the execution of the order *(executio ordinis)*, was described as preservation *(conservatio)*, concurrence *(concursus)*, and government *(gubernatio)*. However, the internal act of this providence has already been completely treated earlier in the doctrine of the attributes and decrees of God. Hence here—after the doctrine of creation—providence can only be discussed as an external act, an act of God *ad extra*. Although providence in this sense can never be conceived in isolation from the internal act (the foreknowledge, purpose and plan), it *is* distinct from it, just as the execution of a plan is distinct from that plan.

With that the word "providence" underwent a major modification. One may well ask therefore whether the word can still serve to describe the matter itself. In the past, when providence was still treated in the doctrine of the attributes or decrees of God, it retained its original meaning; but since it has increasingly been understood as preservation and government and was discussed subsequent to creation, that original meaning has almost been totally lost. Providence in this latter, narrow sense is no longer a true *providentia*, no "exemplar of the order of things foreordained toward an end," for this precedes it and is assumed by it. It is itself the execution of the order. This, accordingly, was further defined in dogmatics as preservation *(conservatio)* or as government *(gubernatio)* or as a combination of the two.[25]

Later, to ward off pantheism and deism, concurrence or cooperation was inserted between the two. Materially, this doctrine has always been treated as part of the doctrine of providence[26] but later also formally ac-

23. J. Alsted, *Theol.*, 175; J. W. Baier, *Comp. Theol.* (St. Louis, 1879), I, 5, 2.
24. J. Gerhard, *Loci. Theol.*, VI, c. 2.
25. L. C. Lactantius, *De Ira Dei* (1543) (Darmstadt: Gentner, 1957), ch. 10; T. Aquinas, *Summa Theol.*, I, qu. 103, 104; Bonaventure, *Breviloquium*, pt. II; *Belgic Confession*, art. 13; *Heidelberg Catechism*, Lord's Day 10; J. Zanchi, *Op. Theol.*, II, 425; *Synopsis Purioris Theologiae*, XI, 3.
26. Augustine, *The Trinity*, III, 4; idem, *The City of God*, V, 8–11; Theodoret, Bishop of Cyrrhus, *On Divine Providence*, X; Boethius, *The Consolation of Philosophy*, IV and V; John of Damascus, *Exposition of the Orthodox Faith*, II, 29; T. Aquinas, *Summa Theol.*, I, qu. 48, 49, 104, art. 2, qu. 105, art. 5, I, 2, qu. 19, art. 4; idem, *Roman Catechism*, I, c. 2, qu. 20; U. Zwingli, *On Providence and Other Essays*, trans. by S. M. Jackson, ed. by W. J.

quired a place of its own between preservation and government.[27] This shows that the word "providence" as a term for the execution of the order was not adequate and was further defined as "preservation" and "government." These terms are undoubtedly more precise, more graphic, and more in keeping with scriptural usage as well. Especially when the word "providence" is used abstractly and put in the place of God, as Plutarch already started doing,[28] with the rationalism of the eighteenth century following suit, it is open to objection. Still the word, which gained legitimacy in the language of theology and religion, may be kept, provided only that the matter described by it is understood in the scriptural sense.

Non-Christian Competitors

The Christian doctrine of providence as an omnipotent act of God by which he preserves and governs all things must be distinguished not only from pagan "fate" and "chance" but consequently also from the pantheism and Deism, which keep cropping up in revived form over the centuries of Christianity. After all, "there are but three alternatives for the sum of existence: chance, fate or Deity. With chance there would be variety without uniformity, with fate uniformity without variety, but variety in uniformity is the demonstration of primal design and the seal of the creative mind. In the world as it exists, there is infinite variety and amazing uniformity."[29]

The Problem of Pantheism

Pantheism knows of no distinction between the being of God and the being of the world and—idealistically—lets the world be swallowed up

---

Hinks (Durham, N.C.: Labyrinth, 1983), c. 3; *Op.*, IV, 86; J. Calvin, *Institutes of the Christian Religion*, I, 16, 2; idem, *Treatises against the Anabaptists and Libertines* (*C.R.* 186), trans. and ed. by B. W. Farley (Grand Rapids: Baker, 1982), 242–49; idem, "Providence," ch. 10 (*C.R.* 347–66), *Concerning the Eternal Predestination of God*, trans. by J. K S. Reid (London: James Clarke, 1961); J. Zanchi, *Op. Theol.*, II, 449; Justin Martyr, *Loci C.*, 56, 59; J. Wollebius, *Compendium Theologiae*, c. 30; *Synopsis Purioris Theologiae*, XI, 13; J. Gerhard, *Loci Theol.*, VI, c. 9 enz.

27. P. van Mastricht, *Theologia*, III, 10, 10.29; F. Turretin, *Institutes of Elenctic Theology*, VI, qu. 4; A. Comrie and N. Holthuis, *Examen van het Ontwerp van Tolerantie*, VI, 270; IX, 210. W. Brakel, *The Christian's Reasonable Service*, XI, 6, trans. by B. Elshout (Ligonier, Pa.: Soli Deo Gloria, 1992); J. Marck, *Godg.*, X, 9; J. Quenstedt, *Theologia*, I, 531; D. Hollaz, *Examen Theologicum Acroamaticum* (Rostock and Leipzig: Russworm, 1718), 421; J. F. Buddeus, *Institutiones Theologiae Moralis* (Leipzig: Lipsiae, 1715), 409.

28. Cf. H. Cremer, *Biblico-theological Lexicon of New Testament Greek*, trans. by D. W. Simon and William Urwick (Edinburgh: T. & T. Clark, 1872), s.v., *pronoia*.

29. James Douglas in H. B. Smith, *System of Christian Theology* (New York: Armstrong, 1890), 107.

in God or—materialistically—lets God be swallowed up in the world. On that position there is no room for the [act of] creation and therefore no room, in the real sense, for preservation and government. Providence then coincides with the course of nature. The laws of nature are identical with the decrees of God, and the rule of God is nothing other than "the fixed and immutable order of nature" or "the concatenation of natural things."[30] On that view there is no room for miracle, the self-activity of secondary causes, personality, freedom, prayer, sin, and religion as a whole. While pantheism may present itself in ever so beautiful and seductive a form, it actually takes its adherents back into the embrace of a pagan fate. On its premises there is no other existence than the existence of nature; no higher power than that which operates in the world in accordance with iron-clad law; no other and better life than that for which the materials are present in this visible creation. For a time people may flatter themselves with the idealistic hope that the world will perfect itself by an immanent series of developments, but soon this optimism turns into pessimism, this idealism into materialism.

Over against this pantheism it was the task of Christian theology to maintain the distinction between creation and preservation, the self-activity of secondary causes, the freedom of personality, the character of sin, the truth of religion. It did this by rejecting fate and by clearly elucidating the confession of God's providence in distinction from it. The distinguishing feature of the theory of fate is not that all that exists and occurs in time is grounded and determined in God's eternal counsel, but the idea that all existence and occurrence is determined by a power which coincides with the world and which, apart from any consciousness and will, determines all things through blind necessity. According to Cicero, the fate of the Stoa was "an order and series of causes with one cause producing another from within itself."[31] A further distinction made was that between a *mathematical* or *astral* fate when events on earth were thought to be determined by the stars and a *natural* fate when they were deemed to be determined by the nexus of nature. It is in this latter form that the theory of fate presently appears in pantheism and materialism. It is noteworthy, however, that in recent times also belief in astral fate has been reinvigorated and has its enthusiastic advocates.[32] Now Christian theology by no means op-

---

30. B. Spinoza, *Tractatus Theologico-Politicus*, trans. by S. Shirley (Leiden: Brill, 1991), c. 3; cf. D. F. Strauss, *Die christliche Glaubenslehre in ihrer geschichtlichen Entwicklung und im Kampfe mit der modernen Wissenschaft*, 2 vols. (Tübingen: Osiander, 1840–41), II, 384; F. Schleiermacher, *The Christian Faith*, ed. H. R. MacIntosh and J. S. Steward (Edinburgh: T. & T. Clark, 1928), §46; cf. ch. 1, above.
31. M. T. Cicero, *De Divinatione*, 1; cf. Seneca, *De Beneficiis*, IV, 7; idem, *Nat.*, II, qu. 36.
32. Cf. *Wetenschappelijke Bladen*, IV (1896): 453; *De Holl. Revue* (25 September 1905).

poses the idea that all things were known and determined by God from eternity. To that extent it even recognized a "fate" and some theologians believed they could also use the word in a good sense. If we remember, says Augustine, that *fatum* is a derivative of *fari* and then describe by means of it the eternal and unchanging word by which God sustains all things, the name can be justified.[33] Boethius referred to fate as "a disposition inherent in changeable things by which Providence connects all things in their due order."[34] And even Maresius believed he could make Christian sense of the word.[35] But as a rule people were more cautious. Belief in fate, after all, proceeded from the idea that all things happen as a result of an irresistible blind force having neither consciousness nor will and those events were called *fatalia* which happen apart from the will of God and men by the necessity of a certain order.[36] In this sense, "fate" was most firmly opposed by all Christian theologians, by Augustine and his followers no less than by those who championed free will. "So far from saying that everything happens by fate, we say that nothing happens by fate."[37] On the Christian position, the only "necessity of order" is the wise, omnipotent, loving will of God. This is not to deny, as will appear later, that in the world of creatures there is a nexus of causes and consequences and that there are firm ordinances. However, the natural order is not behind and above, nor outside of and opposed to, God's will, but grounded in the will of an omnipotent and loving God and Father, governed by that will and serviceable to that will. Nor does it stand, as a blind coercive power, outside of and in opposition to our will, for "the fact is that our choices fall within the order of the causes which is known for certain to God and is contained in his foreknowledge."[38]

The Problem of Deism

On the other side of this spectrum stands Deism, which separates God and the world. This position is one which, in total or in part, separates the creatures, once they have been created, from God and then,

---

33. Augustine, *The City of God*, V, 9.
34. Boethius, *The Consolation of Philosophy*, Bk. IV, 6.
35. S. Maresius, *Syst. Theol.*, 149.
36. Augustine, *The City of God*, V, 3.
37. Ibid.
38. Ibid. and following comment on *Sent.*, I, dist. 35; T. Aquinas, *Summa Theol.*, I. qu. 116; idem, *Summa Contra Gentiles*, III, 93; Petavius, *de Deo*, VIII, 4; J. Gerhard, *Loci Theol.*, VI, 13; J. Calvin, *Inst.*, I, 16, 8; T. Beza, *Volumen Tractationum Theologicarum* (Geneva, 1573–76), I, 313ff.; J. H. Alting, *Theologia Elenctica Nova* (Amsterdam, 1654), 290; J. H. Heidegger, *Corpus Theologiae*, VII, 2; Turretin, *Institues of Elenctic Theology*, VI, 2; C. Vitringa, *Doctr. Christ.*, II, 170, 177–81; K. G. Bretschneider, *Systematische Entwicklung aller in der Dogmatik* (Leipzig: J. A. Barth, 1841), 472.

again in larger or smaller part, it allows them to exist and function on their own power, a power received at the time of creation. Deism thus basically revives the pagan theory of chance. Jerome once stated—more or less echoing Aristotle, Epicurus, Cicero, the Sadducees,[39] and others whose slogan was that "the gods take care of the big things but ignore the small"—that God's providential care did not cover all small insects.[40] Pelagianism, like Cicero,[41] attributed virtue to people's own will and power, while Semi-Pelagianism divided the work, attributing some to both God and man. Later, when this system penetrated Catholic theology, no small dissension arose over God's cooperation in providence. The Thomists conceived it as a "natural predetermination," "an application of energy for the purpose of making it work."[42] The Molinists, on the other hand, understood by it a kind of "simultaneous concourse, a merely formal cooperation, by which God—with the concurrence of the other—exerted influence on the same act and effect."[43]

Socinianism so abstractly and dualistically opposed the infinite to the finite that God could not even create the world out of nothing but only from an eternally existing finite substance. In accordance with this view it also withdrew a large area of the world from God's providence, leaving it to the independent insight and judgment of mankind. By nature the human will is so free that God cannot even beforehand calculate what a person will do in a given case. Only when a decision has been made does God adapt his own action to it. Free causes, accordingly, function in complete independence alongside and outside of God. The relation between God and the world is like that between a mechanical engineer and a machine. After making it and starting it, he leaves it to its own devices and only intervenes if something has to be repaired.[44] The Remonstrants similarly judged that at the creation creatures were endowed with powers that enabled them to live independently. Preservation, therefore, was a negative act of God, implying that he did not wish to destroy the essences, powers, and faculties of created things but to leave them to their own vigor to the extent they were able to flourish and endure by the power with which they had been endowed by cre-

39. On the Sadducees, see E. Schürer, *The History of the Jewish People*, II, 392ff.

40. See H. Bavinck, *Gereformeerde Dogmatiek*, II, 163.

41. M. T. Cicero, *On the Nature of the Gods*, III, 36.

42. T. Aquinas, *Summa Theol.*, I, 2, qu. 9, art. 6 to 3, qu. 79, 109; idem, *Summa Contra Gentiles*, III, 67–70, 162.

43. Cf. Daalman, *Summa S. Thomae*, II, 286–314; *Theologia Wirceburgensi*, I, c. 2; P. Dens, *Theologia Moralis et Dogmatica*, 8 vols. (Dublin: Richard Coyne, 1832), I, 66ff.; M. Liberatore, *Institutiones Philosophicae* (Rome, 1861), III, c. 4a. 1, 2; M. J. Scheeben, *Handbuch der Katholischer Dogmatik*, II, 22ff.; P. C. A. Jansen, *Prael.*, II, 334.

44. J. Volkel, *De Vera Religione Libri Quinque* (Racoviae: 1630), II, c. 7; J. Crell, *De Deo et Ejus Attributis*, c. 2–6; O. Fock, *Der Socinianismus* (Kiel: C. Schröder, 1847), 496ff.

ation—at least this view was not judged incorrect. In this connection, concurrence, defined "as a certain natural influence in all things emanating from the perfection of the divine nature," was rejected. The idea of the predestination of the number of people, of marriages, of the end of life, of the elect and of the lost, was contested, free will defended, and all "efficacious providence with respect to sin" replaced by a negative "permission" or "nonobstruction."[45] Although Arminianism was condemned at Dordtrecht and expelled from the Reformed domain, as an intellectual trend it found acceptance everywhere and penetrated all Christian countries and churches.

The period beginning in the middle of the seventeenth century was marked by a powerful effort to emancipate nature, world, humanity, science, and so forth from God and to make them self-reliant in relation to him, to Christianity, church, and theology. In this respect latitudinarianism, Deism, rationalism, and the Enlightenment were all in agreement.[46] This is the best of all possible worlds; humanity endowed with intellect and will, is self-sufficient; natural law, the forces of nature, natural religion, and natural morality together comprise a reserve of energies with which God endowed the world at the creation and which are now entirely adequate for its existence and development. Revelation, prophecy, miracles, and grace are totally redundant. Deism did not deny the existence of God, nor creation or providence. On the contrary, it loved to refer to the "Supreme Being" and discoursed at length on providence. But there was no longer any vitality in this belief. Deism in principle denied that God worked in creation in any way other than in accordance with and through the laws and forces of nature. Thus it was, from the outset, antisupranaturalistic. Preservation was enough; a kind of cooperation or divine influx operative along with every act of a creature was unnecessary.[47]

In its eighteenth-century form, this deism indeed belongs to the past. But in substance in both theory and practice it still holds sway in wide circles. Since, especially in the present century [the nineteenth], our knowledge of nature has greatly expanded and the stability of its laws

45. S. Episcopius, *Inst. Theol.*, IV, sect. 4; idem, *Apol. Conf.; Conf. Remonstr.*, in S. Episcopius, *Op. Theol.*; P. van Limborch, *Theol. Christ.*, II, 25ff.

46. On deism, cf. G. V. Lechler, *Geschichte des Englischen Deismus* (Tübingen, 1814); idem, "Deismus," *PRE*[2]; E. Troeltsch, "Deismus," *PRE*[3], IV, 532–59; B. Pünjer, *Geschichte der christlichen Religionsphilosophie seit der Reformation* (Brussels: Impression Anastaltique Culture et Civilisation, 1880–83), I, 209ff.; J. W. Hanne, *Die Idee der Absoluten Personlichkeit*, 2nd ed. (Hannover: C. Rumpler, 1865), II, 76ff.; T. Pesch, *Die Grossen Welträthsel*, 2 vols., 2nd ed. (Freiburg i.B.: Herder, 1892), II, 534ff.; J. I. Doedes, *Inleiding tot de Leer van God* (Utrecht: Kemink, 1870), 80ff.

47. F. V. Reinhard, *Grundriss der Dogmatik* (Munich: Seidel, 1802), §61; J. A. L. Wegscheider, *Institutiones theologiae christianae dogmaticae* (Halle: Gebauer, 1819), §106.

has been recognized, many people are inclined to separate nature in its pitiless and unchanging character from God's government, to let it rest independently in itself, and to restrict the providence of God to the domain of religion and ethics. But here, of course, providence cannot be taken absolutely either and finds its limit in human freedom.[48] It is not surprising that with such a view the old doctrine of "concurrence" was no longer understood and set aside as superfluous or incorrect.[49]

On those premises it even follows naturally to do what the "ethical" modernists[50] have done in our country, namely, juxtapose and contrapose natural power and moral power as it were like two deities in the Manichean manner. This runs the risk that the domain of the latter, like that of the Native Americans, will increasingly shrink and finally be taken over completely by blind irrational forces.[51] This consequence is probably the most serious objection to deism. By separating God from the world, the infinite from the finite, and placing them dualistically side by side, it turns the two into competing powers that are continually at loggerheads as they vie for sovereignty. That which is ascribed to God is taken from the world. The more God's providence is expanded, the more the creature loses its independence and freedom and, conversely, the creature can only maintain its self-activity if it drives God back and deprives him of his sovereignty. Peace between the two is therefore possible only on condition of complete separation.

Deism is essentially irreligious. For the Deist the salvation of humanity consists not in communion with God but in separation from him. The Deist's mind is at ease only in detachment from God, that is, if he can be a practical atheist. And because he realizes he can never free himself from God, he is a fearful creature, always afraid that he will be deprived of a part of his domain. For that reason there are always gradations in Deism; the boundaries between God's activity and that of the

48. Cf. G. Kreibig, *Die Räthsel der göttlichen Vorsehung* (Berlin, 1886); W. Schmidt, *Die göttl. Vorsehung und das Selbstleben de Welt* (1887); W. Schmidt, *Christliche Dogmatik*, 4 vols. (Bonne: E. Weber, 1895–98), I, 216ff.; W. Beyschlag, *Zur Verständigung über den christlichen Vortsehungsglauben* (Halle: Eugen Strien, 1888).

49. R. Rothe, *Theologische Ethik*, 5 vols. 2nd rev. ed. (Wittenberg: Zimmerman, 1867–71), §54; J. Müller, *The Christian Doctrine of Sin*, I, 318 [trans. by W. Urwick, 5th ed. (Edinburgh: T. & T. Clark, 1868)]; A. F. C. Vilmar, *Handbuch der Evangelischen Dogmatik* (Gütersloh: Bertelsmann, 1895), I, 255; R. L. Lipsius, *Lehrbuch der evangelisch-protestantischen Dogmatik* (Braunschweig: C. A. Schwetschke, 1893), §397ff.; W. Schmidt, *Christliche Dogmatik*, II, 210ff.; J. J. van Oosterzee, *Christian Dogmatics*, trans. by J. Watson and M. Evans, 2 vols. (New York: Scribner, Armstrong, 1874), §59, 5, 7; cf. also F. Philipi, *Kirchliche Dogmatik*, 3rd ed., II, 266, and J. Köstlin, "Concursus," in *PRE*³, IV, 262–67.

50. *Ed. note:* Bavinck's reference here is to a mediating school of Dutch theology known as the *"Ethischen."* See H. Bavinck, *De Theologie van Daniel Chantepie de la Saussaye* (Leiden: D. Donner, 1884).

51. See H. Bavinck, *Gereformeerde Dogmatiek*, I, 510.

world are ever being drawn differently. There are entire, one-half, and three-quarters Pelagians, and so forth, depending on whether the world and humanity are completely or in greater or smaller part withdrawn from God's control. In principle, Deism is always the same: it deactivates God, but one Deist will walk that road further than another. A Deist is a person who in his short life has not found the time to become an atheist.[52] Now the area which Deism takes out from under God's rule then falls under the sway of another power, be it fate or chance. Also in this regard, Deism constantly gets into conflict with itself. Especially today, now that everyone is so deeply convinced of the stability of the natural order, there is no room in it for chance, and Deism again falls back into the embrace of ancient fate while chance is mainly reserved for the domain of religious and ethical concerns. But the doctrine of chance is no better than that of fate. "Fate" could, in a pinch, still have a good meaning in the Christian world-and-life view; but chance *(casus)* and fortune *(fortuna)* are un-Christian through and through. Something is "fortuitous" only in the eyes of people when at that moment they are ignorant of its cause. But nothing is or can be objectively "fortuitous." All things have a cause and that cause is ultimately a component in the almighty and all-wise will of God.[53]

An Attempt at Definition

The providence of God, thus distinguished from God's knowledge and decree and maintained against pantheism and deism, is—in the beautiful words of the Heidelberg Catechism—"the almighty and ever present power of God by which he upholds, as with his hand, heaven and earth and all creatures and so rules them that . . . all things, in fact, come to us, not by chance but from his fatherly hand" (Lord's Day 10, Q. 27). Even thus defined, the doctrine of providence has enormous scope. It actually encompasses the entire implementation of all the de-

---

52. *Quack, *Port Royal*, 180.
53. Cf. Augustine, qu. 83, qu. 24 (*ed. note:* This reference is cryptic; Bavinck may be referring to Augustine's *De diversis quaestionibus octoginta tribus liber*); idem, *Against the Academics*, I, 1; idem, *Divine Providence and the Problem of Evil*, I, 2; idem, *The City of God*, V, 3; T. Aquinas, *Summa Theol.*, I, qu. 22, art. 2, qu. 103, art. 5; *Summa Contra Gentiles*, III, 72; J. Gerhard, *Loci Theol.*, VI, 3; J. Calvin, *Inst.*, I, 16, 2, 9; D. Chamier, *Panstratiae Catholicae* (Geneva: Rouer, 1626), II, 2, 4ff.; F. Turretin, *Institutes of Elenctic Theology*, III, qu. 12; P. Mastricht, *Theologia*, III, 10, 30; J. Müller, *Sünde*, II, 34ff.; C. H. Weisse, *Philosophische Dogmatik oder Philosophie des Christentums*, 3 vols. (Leipzig: Hirzel, 1855–62), I, 518; Kirchner, *Ueber den Zufall* (Halle: Pfeffer, 1888); G. Rümelin, *Ueber den Zufall, Deutsche Rundschau* (März, 1890), 353–64; R. Eisler, "Zufall," in *Wörterbuch der Philosophischen Begriffe*, 3 vols. (Berlin: E. S. Mittler und Sohn, 1910); E. Dennert, *Natuurwet, Toeval, Voorzienigheid* (Baarn, 1906).

crees which have bearing on the world after it has been called into being by creation. If the act of creation is excepted from it, it is as full as the free knowledge of God *(scientia libera)*, the decrees of God, as everything that exists and occurs in time. It extends to everything that is treated in dogmatics after the doctrine of creation and includes both the works of nature and of grace. All the works of God *ad extra*, which are subsequent to creation, are works of his providence. Only, the locus of providence does not discuss these works themselves but describes in general the nature of the relation in which God stands to the created world and which is always the same, notwithstanding the many different works which he in his providence accomplishes in the world. For that reason it is also not desirable for us to bring up in this locus a vast array of topics such as miracles, prayer, the end of life, the freedom of the will, sin, theodicy and so forth, for in part these topics have already been treated earlier in the context of the doctrine of the attributes and decrees of God, and in part they will be fully treated in their own place. The task of theodicy is not confined to the locus of providence alone but rests on the whole field of dogmatics. Hence the doctrine of providence does not include the material to be considered in the following loci but limits itself to a description of the relation—one that remains the same in all the various works—in which God stands toward his creatures. That relation is expressed by the words "preservation," "concurrence," and "government," which over time were viewed as aspects of providence. Whatever God may do in nature and grace, it is always he who preserves all things, who empowers them by the influx of his energy, and who governs them by his wisdom and omnipotence. Preservation, concurrence, and government, accordingly, are not parts or segments in which the work of providence is divided and which, being materially and temporally separate, succeed one another. Nor do they differ from one another in the sense that preservation relates only to the existence of creatures, concurrence only to their activities, and government exclusively to guidance toward the final goal of these creatures. But they are always integrally connected; they intermesh at all times. From the very beginning preservation is also government, and government concurrence, and concurrence preservation. Preservation tells us that nothing exists, not only no substance, but also no power, no activity, no idea, unless it exists totally from, through, and to God. Concurrence makes known to us the same preservation as an activity such that, far from suspending the existence of creatures, it above all affirms and maintains it. And government describes the other two as guiding all things in such a way that the final goal determined by God will be reached. And always, from beginning to end, providence is one simple, almighty, and omnipresent power.

Conceived as such a power and act of God, providence is most inti-mately connected with, while nevertheless being essentially distinct from, the activity of God in creating the world. Pantheism and Deism, in addressing the problem which is present here, seek to solve it by de-nying either creation [pantheism] or providence [Deism]. But theism maintains both and attempts to elucidate for theoretical as well as prac-tical reasons both the unity and the distinction between the two. Always to be a theist in the full and true sense of the word, that is, to see God's counsel and hand and work in all things and simultaneously, indeed for that very reason, to develop all available energies and gifts to the high-est level of activity—*that* is the glory of the Christian faith and the secret of the Christian life.

Scripture itself leads the way in taking this approach. On the one hand, it describes the activity of providence as an activity of creation (Ps. 104:30), of making alive (Neh. 9:6), of speaking (Pss. 33:9; 105:31, 34; 107:25; Job 37:6), of sending out his Word and Spirit (Pss. 104:30; 107:26), of commanding (Ps. 147:15; Lam. 3:37), of working (John 5:17), of upholding (Heb. 1:3), of willing (Rev. 4:11), so that all things without exception exist from, through, and to God (Acts 17:28; Rom. 11:36; Col. 1:17). God is never idle. He never stands by passively looking on. With divine potency he is always active in both nature and grace. Providence, therefore, is a positive act, not a giving permission to exist but a causing to exist and working from moment to moment. If it con-sisted merely in a posture of nondestruction it would not be God who upheld things, but things would exist in and by themselves, be it with power granted at the creation. And this is an absurd notion. A creature is, by definition, of itself a completely dependent being: that which does not exist *of* itself cannot for a moment exist *by* itself either. If God does not do anything, then nothing exists and nothing happens. "For the power and might of the Creator, who rules and embraces all, makes every creature abide, and if this power ever ceased to govern creatures, their essences would pass away and all nature would perish."[54] And just as providence is a power and an act, so it is also an almighty and every-where present power. God is immanently present with his being in all creatures. His providence extends to all creatures; all things exist in him. Scripture posits with the utmost certainty that nothing, however insignificant, falls outside of God's providence. Not just all things in general (Eph. 1:11; Col. 1:17; Heb. 1:3), but even the hairs of one's head

54. Augustine, *The Literal Meaning of Genesis,* IV, 12; idem, *Confessions,* IV, 17; cf. T. Aquinas, *Summa Theol.,* I, qu. 104, art. 1–4; idem, *Summa Contra Gentiles,* III, 65ff.; J. Calvin, *Institutes of the Christian Religion,* I, 16, 4; M. Leydekker, *Fax Veritatis* (1677), VI-II, 2; J. Alsted, *Theol.,* 304.

(Matt. 10:30), sparrows (Matt. 10:29) the birds of the air (Matt. 6:36), the lilies of the field (Matt. 6:28), the young ravens (Ps. 147:9), are the objects of his care. In any case, what is small or large to him who is only great? In the context of the cosmos that which is small is as important in its setting as that which is large, as indispensable and as necessary, and often of even greater significance and of weightier consequence.[55] While providence may be differentiated as "general" (Pss. 104; 148:1–3), "special" (Ps. 139:15f.; Job 10:9–12; Matt. 12:12; Luke 12:7), and "most special" (1 Tim. 4:10), as a power of God it nevertheless encompasses every single creature. Though Habakkuk (1:14) complains that God by his chastisements makes people like the fish of the sea that are caught in a net and like crawling things that have no ruler (i.e., to protect them from their enemies), he is not thereby saying that God's providence does not extend to all his creatures. In defense of the limited scope of God's providence people appeal with greater semblance of veracity to 1 Corinthians 9:9 ("Is it for oxen that God is concerned?"). Still Paul, who everywhere else takes God's sovereignty to be absolute (Acts 17:28; Rom. 11:36; Col. 1:17), by no means denies here that God's concern also includes oxen, but only indicates that this saying is included in the law of God for humanity's sake, not for the sake of oxen. Also this saying concerning the oxen is there "for our sakes" (*di nuas;* vs. 10; cf. Rom. 4:23, 24; 15:4; 2 Tim. 3:16) so that we might learn from it that the gospel worker is worthy of his wages. So then providence as an activity of God is as great, all-powerful, and omnipresent as creation; it is a continuous or continued creation. The two are one single act and differ only in structure.[56]

When earlier theologians used this language, it was by no means their intention to erase the distinction which exists between creation and providence, as Hodge for one fears.[57] Scripture, on the other hand, represents providence as a resting from the work of creation (Gen. 2:2; Exod. 20:11; 31:17), and further as a seeing (Pss. 14:2; 33:13), and observing (Pss. 33:15; 103:3), all of which presuppose the existence, the self-activity, and the freedom of the creature. *These* scriptural givens may not be neglected either. Creation and providence are not identical.

---

55. Cf. Calvin cited by Paul Henry, *The Life and Times of John Calvin,* trans. by Henry Stebbing, 2 vols. (New York: Robert Carter & Brothers, 1853), I, 358.

56. Augustine, *The Literal Meaning of Genesis,* IV, 15; idem, *Confessions,* IV, 12; idem, *The City of God,* XII, 17; T. Aquinas, I, qu. 104, art. 2; J. Quenstedt, *Theologia,* I, 351; Z. Ursinus, *Commentary on the Heidelberg Catechism,* qu. 27; C. Vitringa, *Doctr. Christ.,* II, 183; H. Heppe, *Dogmatik des deutschen Protestantismus im sechzehnten Jahrhundert,* 3 vols. (Gotha: F. A Perthes, 1857), 190.

57. Charles Hodge, *Systematic Theology,* 3 vols. (New York: Charles Scribner's Sons, 1888), I, 577ff.

If providence meant a creating anew every moment, creatures would also have to be produced out of nothing every moment. In that case, the continuity, connectedness, and "order of causes" would be totally lost and there would be no development or history. All created beings would then exist in appearance only and be devoid of all independence, freedom, and responsibility. God himself would be the cause of sin. Although many theologians called providence a "continuous creation," they by no means meant to erase the difference between the two. They all regarded providence rather as simultaneously an act of causing creatures to persist in their existence, as a form of preservation that presupposes creation. Augustine, for example, writes that God rested on the seventh day and no longer created any new species, and continues by describing the work of providence in distinction from that of creation as follows: "God moves his entire creation by a hidden power. . . . It is thus that God unfolds the generations which He laid up in creation when first He founded it; and they would not be sent forth to run their course if He who made creatures ceased to exercise His provident rule over them."[58] Providence may sometimes be called a creation, therefore, but it is always distinguished from the first and actual creation by the fact that it is a "continuous creation."

So the two agree in that it is the same omnipotent and omnipresent power of God that is at work both in creation and in providence. The latter act is not inferior to the former since power, divine power, is required for both. Also, creation and providence are naturally not distinct in God himself either for in him, the Eternal One, there is no variation or shadow due to change. He did not pass from not-creating to creating, nor from creating to preserving. He is invariably the same.[59] Creation and preservation, accordingly, are not objectively and materially distinct as acts of God in God's being but only in reason. But that is not to say that the distinction is arbitrary and only exists in our mind. No: that distinction is most definitely grounded in God's revelation and derived from it by our thinking. There is a difference between creation and preservation, but that difference does not lie in God's being as such but in the relation which God assumes toward his creatures. What happens to things as a result of creation is one thing; what happens with them as a result of preservation is another. The relation in which God's creatures are placed vis-à-vis God by these two actions differs in each case. This difference cannot be indicated by saying that creation is "out of nothing" and preservation concerns that which exists. Rather creation calls into being the things that are not, things which have no other ex-

58. Augustine, *The Literal Meaning of Genesis*, V, 20.
59. Cf. above, p. 48.

istence than that of ideas and decrees in the being of God. By preservation, with the same power, God summons those things which have received an existence which is distinct from his being and are nevertheless solely and exclusively from, through, and to God. Creation yields existence while preservation is persistence in existence. The difficulty for the mind to maintain both creation and preservation always arises from the fact that by creation God's creatures have received their own unique existence which is distinct from God's being and that that existence may and can never even for a moment be viewed as an existence of and by itself, independent from God.

We are confronted here by a mystery that far surpasses our understanding, and we are always inclined to do less than justice to either one or the other. It is this inclination which underlies pantheism and Deism. Both of these trends proceed from the same error and oppose God and the world to each other as two competing entities. The former sacrifices the world to God, creation to providence, and believes that God's existence can only be a divinely infinite existence if it denies the existence of the world, dissolves it into mere appearance, and allows it to be swallowed up by divine existence. The latter sacrifices God to the world, providence to creation, and believes that creatures come into their own to the extent that they become less dependent on God and distance themselves from God. The Christian, however, confesses that the world and every creature in it have received their own existence, but increase in reality, freedom, and authenticity to the extent that they are more dependent on God and exist from moment to moment from, through, and to God. A creature is the more perfect to the degree that God indwells it more and permeates it with his being. In that respect preservation is even greater than creation, for the latter only initiated the beginning of existence but the former is the progressive and ever increasing self-communication of God to his creatures. Providence is "the progressive expression in the universe of his divine perfection, the progressive realization in it of the archetypal ideal of perfect wisdom and love."[60]

Concurrence: Secondary Causes

With that we have now indicated the manner in which God exercises his providential rule in the world and which in former times was expressed by the doctrine of concurrence. This is as richly diversified as the diversity with which God distinguished his creatures at the time of creation. The variety exhibited in God's manner of government is just as great as

60. S. Harris, *God the Creator and Lord of All* (Edinburgh: Clark, 1897), I, 532.

that exhibited in his creation.[61] By creation God called into being a world which simultaneously deserves to be called a "cosmos" *(kosmos)* and an "age" *(aiōn)* and which in both space and time is "a most brilliant mirror of the divine glory."[62] Now providence serves to take the world from its beginning and to lead it to its final goal; it goes into effect immediately after the creation and brings to development all that was given in that creation. Creation, conversely, was aimed at providence; creation conferred on creatures the kind of existence that can be brought to development in and by providence. For the world was not created in a state of pure potency, as chaos or a nebulous cloud, but as an ordered cosmos and human beings were placed in it not as helpless toddlers but as an adult man and an adult woman. Development could only proceed from such a ready-made world, and that is how creation presented it to providence. In addition, that world was a harmonious whole in which unity was coupled to the most marvelous diversity. Every creature received a nature of its own and with it an existence, a life and a law of its own. Just as the moral law was increated in the heart of Adam as the rule for his life, so all creatures carried in their own nature the principles and laws for their own development.

All things are created by the word. All things are based on thought. The whole creation is a system grounded in the ordinances of God (Gen. 1:26, 28; 8:22; Pss. 104:5, 9; 119:90; 91; Eccl. 1:10; Job 38:10f.; Jer. 5:24; 31:25f.; 33:20, 25). On all creatures God conferred an order, a law which they do not violate (Ps. 148:6).[63] In all of its parts it is rooted in the counsel of God, a design that emerges in things great and small. This all comes from the Lord of hosts; he is wonderful in counsel, and excellent in wisdom (Isa. 28:23, 29).

This is how Scripture teaches us to understand the world, and this is also how Christian theology has understood it. Augustine said that "hidden seeds" *(semina occulta)*, "original principles" *(originales regulae)*, "seminal reasons" *(seminariae rationes)* were implanted in creatures, which, being concealed in the secret womb of nature, are the principles of all development. "Whatever things, by being born, become visible to our eyes receive the principles of their development from hidden seeds, and take the increases in size appropriate to them, as well as the distinctiveness of their forms as though from these original causes."[64] The world, accordingly, is pregnant with the causes of beings. "For as mothers are pregnant with unborn offspring, so the world

---

61. J. Alsted, *Theol.*, 315 ("Sicut creationis magna est varietas, ita et gubernationis").
62. Cf. above, section 259 (*GD*, 399ff.).
63. Cf. H. Bavinck, *Gereformeerde Dogmatiek*, I, 307–8.
64. Augustine, *The Trinity*, III, 7; idem, *The Literal Meaning of Genesis*, IV, 33.

itself is pregnant with the causes of unborn beings, which are not created in it except from that highest essence, where nothing is either born or dies, begins to be or ceases to be."[65]

The world is a tree of things *(arbor rerum)*, bringing forth branch and blossom and fruit.[66] God so preserves things and so works in them that they themselves work along with him as secondary causes. This is not to say that we must stop there. On the contrary, we must always ascend to the cause of all being and movement, and that is the will of God alone. "The 'nature' of any particular created thing is precisely what the supreme Creator of the thing willed it to be."[67] To that extent providence is not only a positive but also an immediate act of God. His will, his power, his being is immediately present in every creature and every event. All things exist and live together in him (Acts 17:28; Col. 1:17; Heb. 1:3). Just as he created the world by himself, so he also preserves and governs it by himself. Although God works through secondary causes, this is not to be interpreted, in the manner of Deism, to mean that they come in between God and the effects with their consequences and separate these from him. "God's immediate provision over everything extends to the exemplar of the order."[68]

For that reason a miracle is not a violation of natural law and no intervention in the natural order. From God's side it is an act that does not more immediately and directly have God as its cause than any ordinary event, and in the counsel of God and the plan of the world it occupies as much an equally well-ordered and harmonious place as any natural phenomenon. In miracles God only puts into effect a special force which, like any other force, operates in accordance with its own nature and therefore also has an outcome of its own.[69]

But at the creation God built his laws into things, fashioning an order by which the things themselves are interconnected. God is not dependent on causes, but things do depend on one another. That interconnectedness is of many kinds. Although in general it can be called "causal," the word "causal" in this sense must by no means be equated with "mechanical," as materialism would have us do. A mechanical connection is only one mode in which a number of things in the world relate to each other. Just as creatures received a nature of their own in the creation and differ among themselves, so there is also difference in

65. Augustine, *The Trinity*, III, 9.
66. Augustine, *The Literal Meaning of Genesis*, VIII, 9.
67. Augustine, *The City of God*, XXI, 8; idem, *The Trinity*, III, 6–9.
68. T. Aquinas, *Summa Theol.*, I qu. 22, art. 3, qu. 103, art. 6, qu. 103, art. 2; *Summa Contra Gentiles*, III, 76ff.
69. Cf. H. Bavinck, *Gereformeerde Dogmatiek*, I, 163; P. Mezger, *Räthsel des christlichen Vorsehungsglaubens* (Basel: Helbing & Lichterbahn, 1904), 20ff.

the laws in conformity with which they function and in the relation in which they stand to each other.

These laws and relations differ in every sphere: the physical and the psychological, the intellectual and the ethical, the family and society, science and art, the kingdoms of earth and the kingdom of heaven. It is the providence of God which, interlocking with creation, maintains and brings to full development all these distinct natures, forces, and ordinances. In providence God respects and develops—and does not nullify—the things he called into being in creation. "It does not pertain to divine providence to corrupt the nature of things but to preserve it."[70] Thus, therefore, he preserves and governs all creatures according to their nature, the angels in one way, humans in another, and the latter again in a way which differs from animals and plants. But insofar as God in his providence maintains things in their mutual relatedness and makes creatures subserve each other's existence and life, that providence can be called mediate. "God immediately provides for all things as it pertains to the exemplar of the order but as it pertains to the execution of the order he, to be sure, provides through other means."[71] Thus he created all the angels simultaneously but lets humans spring from one blood; thus he preserves some creatures individually and others as species and families. In each case, then, he employs all sorts of creatures as means in his hand to fulfill his counsel and to reach his goal.

Christian theology did not deny these things. On the contrary, following the example of Scripture, it has always emphatically upheld the natural order and the causal nexus of the phenomena. It is not true that Christianity with its supernaturalism was hostile to the natural order and made science impossible, as Draper, for example, and others have sought to demonstrate with such relish.[72] Much more in line with the facts is the judgment of Du Bois Reymond when he wrote: "Modern natural science, however paradoxical this may sound, owes its origin to Christianity."[73] In any case, Christianity made science—specifically natural science—possible and prepared the ground for it. For the more the natural phenomena are deified—as in polytheism—and viewed as

70. T. Aquinas, *Summa Theol.*, II, 1, qu. 10, art. 4.

71. T. Aquinas, *Summa Theol.*, I, qu. 22, art. 3

72. J. W. Draper, *History of the Conflict between Religion and Science* (New York: D. Appleton, 1897).

73. E. H. Du Bois Reymond, *Culturgeschichte und Naturwissenschaft* (Leipzig: Veit, 1878), 28; cf. also F. A. Lange, *Geschichte des Materialismus und Kritik seiner Bedeutung in der Gegenwart* (1882), 129ff. [8th ed. Leipzig: Baedekker, 1908]; H. Martensen-Larsen, *Die Naturwissenschaft in inhrem Schuldverhältniss zum Christenthum* (Berlin, 1897); E. Dennert in W. H. Nieuwhuis, *Twee Vragen des Tijds* (Kampen: Kok, 1907), 9–52; idem, *De Verdiensten der Kath. Kerk ten opzichte der Natuurwet*, foreword, F. Hendrichs (Amsterdam, 1906).

the visible images and bearers of deity, the more scientific inquiry is
made impossible since it becomes automatically a form of desecration
which disturbs the mystery of Deity. But Christianity distinguished
God and the world and, by its confession of God as the Creator of all
things, separated God from the nexus of nature and lifted him far above
it. The study of nature, therefore, is no longer a violation of Deity. At
the same time and by this very fact it has made human beings free and
given them independent status vis-à-vis nature, as is clearly demonstrated by the splendid view of nature we find in the psalmists and
prophets, in Jesus and the apostles. For the believer nature is no longer
an object of worship and dread.[74] Whereas before God he bows down
in deep humility and is utterly dependent on him, in relation to the
earth he has the calling to exercise dominion over it and to subject all
things to himself (Gen. 1:26). Dependence on God is something very
different from living conformably to nature and adapting oneself to circumstances. Many writers argue either in such a way that they attribute all things and events to the will of God and consider resistance
impermissible, or they limit God's providence, and place many things
in the hands of humans.[75]

Scripture, however, warns us both against this antinomianism and
this Pelagianism and cuts off at the root all false fatalistic resignation
on the one hand and all presumptuous self-confidence on the other.
Bowing before the powers of nature is something very different from
childlike submission to God, and exercising dominion over the earth is
a matter of serving God. The sea captain who went to his cabin to pray
and read the Bible during a storm did submit to the power of the elements, but not to God.[76] There is much more real piety in Cromwell's
dictum: "Trust God and keep your powder dry." It is, moreover, the confession of God as the Creator of heaven and earth which immediately
brings with it the one absolute and never self-contradictory truth, the
harmony and beauty of the counsel of God, and hence the unity of the
cosmic plan and the order of all of nature. "If in a free and wonderful
way, on the basis of the full scope of nature, one attributes to the one
God also a unified manner of working, then the connectedness of things

74. "The Hebrews faced the world and nature with sovereign self-awareness—being
without fear of the world—but also with a sense of the utmost responsibility. As God's
representative, humanity exercises dominion over the world but only as such. Human beings may not follow their arbitrary impulses but only the revealed will of God. Paganism,
in contrast, alternates between presumptuous misuse of the world and childish dread before its powers." R. Smend, *Lehrbuch der alttestamentlichen Religionsgeschichte* (Freiburg
i.B.: J. C. B. Mohr, 1893), 453.

75. So, e.g., W. Beyschlag, *Vorstehungsglauben*, 24ff.

76. S. Harris, *God the Creator and Lord of All*, I, 545.

in terms of cause and effect not only becomes conceivable but even a necessary consequence of the assumption."[77] Scripture itself models to us this recognition of such a natural order, of a wide range of ordinances and laws for created things. And miracle is so far from making an inroad on that natural order that it rather presupposes and confirms it. At all times the Christian church and theology have generously acknowledged such an order of things. Augustine repeatedly appealed to the saying in Wisdom 11:20: "You have arranged all things by measure and number and weight." At least in the early period they energetically opposed the appalling superstition that crested in the third and fourth centuries, and especially fought against astrology.[78] The controversy which often erupted was not a conflict between Christianity and natural science; the alignments were very different; it was usually a struggle between an earlier and later worldview, with believing Christians on both sides.[79]

This fundamentally correct view of nature which Christian theology advocated is nowhere more clearly in evidence than in its doctrine of "concurrence" and "secondary causes." In neither pantheism nor Deism can this doctrine come into its own. In the former there are no longer any *causes* and in the latter any *secondary* causes. In pantheism the secondary causes, that is, the immediate causes of things within the circle of created things, are identified with the primary cause, which is God. Between the two there is no distinction of substance and effect. Both materially and formally God is the subject of all that happens, hence also of sin. At best the so-called secondary causes are opportunities and passive instruments for the workings of God. Whereas this theory only sporadically surfaced in earlier times, in the more modern philosophy of Descartes it came to dominance and so led to the idealism of Berkeley and Malebranche, and to the pantheism of Spinoza, Hegel, Schleiermacher, Strauss, and others. So Malebranche, for example, posits that "there is only one true cause because there is only one true God; that the nature or power of each thing is nothing but the will of God; that all natural causes are not *true* causes but only *occasional* causes." The true cause can only be God because he alone can create

77. F. A. Lange, *Geschichte des Materialismus*, 130.

78. Augustine, *The City of God*, V, 1–8; T. Aquinas, *Summa Contra Gentiles*, III, 84ff.; J. Calvin, "A Warning Against Judiciary Astrology and Other Prevalent Curiosities," trans. by Mary Potter, *Calvin Theological Journal* 18 (1983): 157–89 (*Corpus Ref.*, 35, 509–44); F. Turretin, *Institutes of Elenctic Theology*, VI, qu. 2; B. De Moor, *Comm. Theol.*, II, 435; C. Vitringa, *Doctr. Christ.*, II, 180 enz.; cf. also A. von Harnack, *The Expansion of Christianity in the First Three Centuries*, 2 vols., trans. by James Moffatt (New York: G. P. Putnam's Sons, 1904), I, 152–80.

79. Cf. above, pp. 106–7.

and he cannot communicate that power to a creature. If creatures could be the true cause of motions and phenomena, they themselves would be gods. But "all these insignificant pagan divinities and all these particular causes of the philosophers are merely chimeras that the wicked mind tries to establish to undermine worship of the true God."[80] Accordingly, there are only phenomena, representations, and the only reality, power, substance behind these phenomena is that of God himself.[81]

Conversely, in Deism the secondary causes are separated from the primary cause and made independent. The primary cause is totally restricted to the creation, the communication of the possibility *(posse)*, and totally excluded in the case of the "willing" *(velle)* and the doing *(facere)*, as in the original Pelagianism. Or the two causes are conceived as associated causes which work with and alongside of each other, like two draft horses pulling a wagon, even though the one is perhaps stronger than the other, as in Semi-Pelagianism and synergism. In this view the creature becomes the creator of his or her own deeds. Scripture, however, tells us both that God works all things so that the creature is only an instrument in his hand (Isa. 44:24; Pss. 29:3; 65:11; 147:16; Matt. 5:45; Acts 17:25, etc.) *and* that providence is distinct from creation and presupposes the existence and self-activity of creatures (Gen. 1:11, 20, 22, 24, 28, etc.). In keeping with this witness, Christian theology teaches that the secondary causes are strictly subordinated to God as the primary cause and in that subordination nevertheless remain true causes. The odd theologian, to be sure, diverged from this position, such as the nominalist Biel in the Middle Ages and Zwingli in the time of the Reformation, who believed that secondary causes were mistakenly so-called and preferred to call them instruments.[82]

The constant teaching of the Christian church, nevertheless, has been that the two causes, though they are totally dependent on the primary cause, are at the same time also true and essential causes. With his almighty power God makes possible every secondary cause and is present in it with his being at its beginning, progression, and end. It is he who posits it and makes it move into action *(praecursus)* and who further accompanies it in its working and leads it to its effect *(concursus)*. He is

80. N. Malebranche, *The Search after Truth. Elucidations of the Search after Truth* (Columbus: Ohio State University Press, 1980), 448, 451.

81. Cf. J. Kleutgen, *Philosophie der Vorzeit vertheidigt,* 2nd ed. (Munster: Theissing, n.d.), II, 336–47; Hodge, *Systematic Theology,* I, 592.

82. U. Zwingli, *On the Providence and Other Essays,* IV, 95ff.; cf. the American theologian Emmons in A. H. Strong, *Systematic Theology* (New York, 1890), 205 [Philadelphia: Griffith & Rowland, 1907–09]; Ch. Hodge, *Systematic Theology,* I, 594; H. B. Smith, *System of Christian Theology,* 103.

at work [in us] both to will and to do for his good pleasure (Phil. 2:13). But this energizing activity of the primary cause in the secondary causes is so divinely great that precisely by that activity he stirs those secondary causes into an activity of their own. "The providence of God does not cancel out but posits secondary causation."[83] Concurrence is precisely the reason for the self-activity of the secondary causes, and these causes, sustained from beginning to end by God's power, work with a strength that is appropriate and natural to them. So little does the activity of God nullify the activity of the creature that the latter is all the more vigorous to the degree that the former reveals itself the more richly and fully. Hence the primary cause and the secondary cause remain two distinct causes. The former does not destroy the latter but on the contrary confers reality on it, and the second exists solely as a result of the first. Neither are the secondary causes merely instruments, organs, inanimate automata, but genuine causes with a nature, vitality, spontaneity, manner of working, and law of their own. "Satan and evildoers are not so effectively the instruments of God that they do not also act in their own behalf. For we must not suppose that God works in an iniquitous man as if he were a stone or a piece of wood, but He uses him as a thinking creature, according to the quality of his nature which He has given him. Thus when we say that God works in evildoers, that does not prevent them from working also in their own behalf."[84]

In relation to God the secondary causes can be compared to instruments (Isa. 10:15; 13:5; Jer. 50:25; Acts 9:15; Rom. 9:20–23); in relation to their effects and products they are causes in the true sense. And precisely because the primary and the secondary cause do not stand and function dualistically on separate tracks but the primary works through the secondary, the effect that proceeds from the two is one and the product is one. There is no division of labor between God and his creature but the same effect is totally the effect of the primary cause as well as totally the effect of the proximate cause. The product is also in the same sense totally the product of the primary as well as totally the product of the secondary cause. But because the primary cause and the secondary cause are not identical and differ essentially, the effect and product are *in reality* totally the effect and product of the two causes, to be sure, but *formally* they are only the effect and product of the secondary cause. Wood burns and it is God alone who makes it burn, but formally the burning process may not be attributed to God but must be attributed to the wood as subject. Human persons speak, act, and believe,

---

83. J. Wollebius in H. Heppe, *Reformed Dogmatics,* 258.
84. J. Calvin, *Treatises against the Anabaptists and Libertines,* trans. by B. W. Farley (Grand Rapids: Baker, 1982), 245.

and it is God alone who supplies to a sinner all the vitality and strength he or she needs for the commission of a sin. Nevertheless the subject and author of the sin is not God but the human being. In this manner Scripture draws the lines within which the reconciliation of God's sovereignty and human freedom has to be sought.

Providence as Government

Implicitly included in providence conceived as preservation and concurrence is divine government. One who so preserves things that he not only, by his will and being, sustains existent beings but even their powers and effects is absolutely sovereign: a true king. Government, therefore, is not a new element added to preservation and concurrence. Rather, it is as such like each of these two, the whole of God's providence, only now considered from the perspective of the final goal toward which God by his providence is guiding the whole created world. It is a beautiful and evocative thought when Scripture over and over calls God "king" and describes his providence as a kind of government. There are many people in our time who reject every idea of sovereignty in the family, the state, and society and want nothing to do with anything other than democracy and anarchy. Under the influence of this view there are also those who in theology find the idea of God as king too reminiscent of the Old Testament and antiquated and who at most still want to speak of God as Father. But this judgment is shallow and untrue. In the first place, the name "Father" for God is not limited to the New Testament but is used also in the Old Testament and even among the Gentiles. The New Testament may have a deeper and richer understanding of it but it was not the first to accord this name to God.[85] Conversely, the name "king" is not only repeatedly used for the divine being in the Old but also in the New Testament (Matt. 6:10, 13, 33; 1 Tim. 1:17; 6:15; Rev. 19:6, etc.). And in the second place, the name "king" is no less fitting for God than the name Father. All *patria* (lit., "fatherhood") in heaven and on earth derives its name from him who is the Father of our Lord Jesus Christ (Eph. 3:15). All relations that exist among creatures between superiors and inferiors are analogies of that one original relation in which God stands to the works of his hands. What a father is for his family, what an educator is for the young, what a commander is for the army, what a king is for his people—all that and much more God is in a totally original way for his creatures. Not just one but all his attributes come to expression in the world and therefore need to be honored by us. Now "kingship" for one is a glorious divine institu-

85. Cf. H. Bavinck, *Gereformeerde Dogmatiek*, II, 118.

tion as well. It not only confers on a people a unity symbolized in a person but as a hereditary kingship it also assumes the character of originality, loftiness, independence, and constancy. In all this it is a beautiful—albeit a weak—image of the kingship of God.

All sovereignty on earth is derivative, temporary, and limited and, in the case of abuse, more a curse than a blessing. But God is king in the absolute and true sense. The government of the universe is not democratic, nor aristocratic, nor republican, nor constitutional, but monarchical. To God belongs the one undivided legislative, judicial, and executive power. His sovereignty is original, eternal, unlimited, abundant in blessing. He is the King of kings and the Lord of lords (1 Tim. 6:15; Rev. 19:6). His royal realm is the whole of the universe. His are the heavens and the earth (Exod. 19:5; Pss. 8:2; 103:19; 148:13). He possesses all the nations (Pss. 22:29; 47:9; 96:10; Jer. 10:7; Mal. 1:14) and is supreme in all the earth (Pss. 47:3, 8; 83:19; 97:9). He is king forever (Ps. 29:10; 1 Tim. 1:17); no opposition stands a chance against him (Ps. 93:3, 4). His kingdom will surely come (Matt. 6:10; 1 Cor. 15:24; Rev. 12:10); his glory will be revealed and his name feared from the rising of the sun to its going down (Isa. 40:5; 59:19); he will be king over the entire earth (Zech. 14:9). Also in this government God deals with each thing according to its kind. "God rules over all things conformably to their nature."[86] Consequently, that rule of God is variously represented in Scripture and described with various names. By his rule he upholds the world and establishes it so that it will not be moved (Ps. 93:1); he ordains the light and the darkness (Ps. 104:19, 20), commands the rain and withholds it (Gen. 7:4; 8:2; Job 26:8; 38:22f.), gives snow, hoarfrost, and ice (Ps. 147:16), rebukes and stills the sea (Nah. 1:4; Pss. 65:8; 107:29), sends curses and destruction (Deut. 28:15ff.). All things fulfill his command (Ps. 148:8). With equal sovereign power and majesty he rules in the world of rational creatures. He rules among the Gentiles and possesses all nations (Pss. 22:29; 82:8); he deems the nations as less than nothing and emptiness (Isa. 40:17), deals with the inhabitants of the earth according to his will (Dan. 4:35) and directs the hearts and thoughts of all (Prov. 21:1).

And this government of God over his rational creatures extends not only to the good things of which he is the Giver both in nature and in grace (James 1:17); nor only to the beneficiaries of his favor, whom he chooses, preserves, cares for, and leads to eternal salvation, but also to evil and to those who love evil and do it. Granted, God hates sin with his whole being, as all of Scripture testifies (Deut. 32:4; Ps. 5:5–7; Job 34:10; 1 John 5, etc.), and by the prohibition of sin in law and in the human conscience as well as and by its judgments, God's government, gives un-

---

86. J. Alsted, *Theol.*, 301.

deniable witness to this aversion. At the same time the whole of Scripture also teaches that sin, from beginning to end, is subject to God's rule.[87] At its inception God sometimes acts to stop it (Gen. 20:6; 31:7), destroys the counsel of the wicked (Ps. 33:10), gives strength to resist temptation (1 Cor. 10:13), and always thwarts sin in that he prohibits it and inhibits the sinner through fear and trembling in his conscience.

But this prevention *(impeditio)* is by far not the only form in which God governs sin. Many times he allows it to happen and does not stop it. He gave Israel up to their stubborn hearts to follow their own counsels (Ps. 81:12), allowed the nations to walk in their own ways (Acts 14:16; 17:30), gave people up to their own lusts (Rom. 1:24, 28). And it can similarly be said that God permitted the fall of Adam, the murder of Abel, the iniquity of the people before the flood (Gen. 6:3), the sale of Joseph (Gen. 37), the condemnation of Jesus, and so on. But this permission *(permissio)* is so little negative in nature that even from its earliest beginning sin is subject to God's governing power and sovereignty. He creates and arranges the opportunities and occasions for sinning to test humans, thereby either to strengthen and to confirm them or to punish and to harden them (Gen. 27; 2 Chron. 32:31; Job 1, Matt. 4:1; 6:13; 1 Cor. 10:13). Although at first a given sin seemed to be nothing but an arbitrary act of humans, it turns out later that God had his hand in it and that it happened according to his counsel (Gen. 45:8; 2 Chron. 11:4; Luke 24:26; Acts 2:23; 3:17; 18; 4:28). It is sometimes materially—though not formally and subjectively—even attributed to God in its inception. God is the potter and humans are the clay (Jer. 18:5; Lam. 3:38; Isa. 45:7, 9; 64:7; Amos 3:6). He hardened and blinded certain persons (Exod. 4:21; 7:3; 9:12; 10:20, 27; 11:10; 14:4; Deut. 2:30; Josh. 11:20; Isa. 6:10; 63:17; Matt. 13:13; Mark 4:12; Luke 8:10; John 12:40; Acts 28:26; Rom. 9:18; 11:8); he turned a man's heart so that it was hateful and disobedient (1 Sam. 2:25; 1 Kgs. 12:25; 2 Chron. 25:20; Ps. 105:24; Ezek. 14:9). He sent an evil spirit or a lying spirit (Judg. 9:23; 1 Sam. 16:14; 1 Kgs. 22:23; 2 Chron. 18:22). By Satan he incited David to number the people (2 Sam. 24:1; 1 Chr. 21:1), prompts Shimei to curse David (2 Sam. 16:10), gives people over to their sins, allows them to fill the full measure of their iniquity (Gen. 15:16; Rom. 1:24), sends a strong spirit of delusion (2 Thess. 2:11), set Christ for the fall and rising of many (Luke 2:34; John 3:19; 9:39; 2 Cor. 2:16; 1 Pet. 2:8, etc.).[88]

---

87. C. Clemen, *Die Christliche Lehre von der Sünde* (Göttingen: Vandenhoeck und Ruprecht, 1897), I, 123–51.

88. Cf. H. Bavinck, *Gereformeerde Dogmatiek*, II, 306ff., and additional literature about God's activity in relation to the sinful deeds of humans in C. Vitringa, *Doctr. Christ.*, II, 196ff., 206ff.

Not only at the outset but also upon its continuation God keeps sin under his omnipotent control. Repeatedly he restrains or restricts it, inhibits its momentum and puts a stop to it by his judgment (Gen. 7:11; Exod. 15; Matt. 24:22; 2 Pet. 2:9), but also in cases where he allows it to continue he directs it (Prov. 16:9; 21:1), and, whether forgiving or punishing it, he ultimately makes it subservient to the fulfillment of his counsel, the glorification of his name (Gen. 45:7, 8; 50:20; Ps. 51:6; Isa. 10:5–7; Job 1:20, 22; Prov. 16:4; Acts 3:13; Rom. 8:28; 11:36).

Like sin (a culpable evil), so also suffering (a punitive evil), is subject to the dominion of God. He is the creator of light and darkness, of good and evil (Amos 3:6; Isa. 45:7; Job 2:10). Death, which was God's punishment and came at his command (Gen. 2:17), and all disasters and adversities, all sorrow and suffering, all afflictions and judgments, are imposed on humanity by God's omnipotent hand (Gen. 3:14ff.; Deut. 28:15ff. etc.). Already in the days of Israel people observed the dissonance which exists in this life between sin and punishment, holiness and blessedness (Ps. 73; Job; Eccl.). Faith struggled with this appalling problem but also again raised its head in victory over it, not because it saw the solution to it, but because it continued to cling to the royal power and fatherly love of the Lord. The prosperity of the wicked is a mere illusion and in any case temporary, while the righteous, even in their deepest suffering, still enjoy the love and grace of God (Ps. 73; Job). The suffering of the faithful is frequently rooted not in their personal sin but in the sin of humankind, and has its goal in the salvation of humankind and the glory of God. Suffering serves not only as retribution (Rom. 1:18, 27; 2:5, 6; 2 Thess. 1:2) but also as testing and chastisement (Deut. 8:6; Job 1:12; Ps. 118:8; Prov. 3:12; Jer. 10:24; 30:11; Heb. 12:6ff.; Rev. 3:19); as reinforcement and confirmation (Ps. 119:67, 71; Rom. 5:3–5; Heb. 12:10; James 1:2–4); as witness to the truth (Ps. 14:23; Acts 5:41; Phil. 1:29; 2 Tim. 4:6); and to glorify God (John 9:2). In Christ justice and mercy embrace; suffering is the road to glory; the cross points to a crown, and the timber of the cross becomes the tree of life.[89] The end toward which all things are being led by the providence of God is the establishment of his kingdom, the revelation of his attributes, the glory of his name (Rom. 11:32–36; 1 Cor. 15:18; Rev. 11:15; 12:13, etc.).

In this consoling fashion Scripture deals with the providence of God. Plenty of riddles remain, both in the life of individuals and in the history of the world and humankind. From this point on systematic theology's sole concern is with the mysteries that the providence of God has

---

89. We later revisit the problem of suffering in the section on the punishment of sin, *Gereformeerde Dogmatiek*, III, 139–73.

put on our docket in sin, freedom, responsibility, punishment, suffering, death, grace, atonement, reconciliation, prayer, and so forth, and therefore does not have to discuss all these topics here.

But God lets the light of his Word shine over all these enigmas and mysteries, not to solve them, but that "by steadfastness and the encouragement of the Scriptures we might have hope" (Rom. 15:4). The doctrine of providence is not a philosophical system but a confession of faith, the confession that, appearances notwithstanding, neither Satan or a human being or any other creature, but God and he alone—by his almighty and everywhere present power—preserves and governs all things. Such a confession can save us both from a superficial optimism that denies the riddles of life, and from a presumptuous pessimism that despairs of this world and human destiny. For the providence of God encompasses all things, not only the good but also sin and suffering, sorrow and death. For if these realities were removed from God's guidance, then what in the world would there be left for him to rule? God's providence is manifest not only, nor primarily, in the extraordinary events of life and in miracles but equally as much in the stable order of nature and the ordinary occurrences of daily life. What an impoverished faith it would be if it saw God's hand and counsel from afar in a few momentous events but did not discern it in a person's own life and lot? It leads all these things toward their final goal, not against but agreeably to their nature, not apart from but through the regular means; for what power would there be in a faith that recommended stoical indifference or fatalistic acquiescence as true godliness? But so, as the almighty and everywhere present power of God, it makes us grateful when things go well and patient when things go against us, prompts us to rest with childlike submission in the guidance of the Lord and at the same time arouses us from our inertia to the highest levels of activity. In all circumstances of life it gives us good confidence in our faithful God and Father that he will provide whatever we need for body and soul, and that he will turn to our good whatever adversity he sends us in this sad world, since he is able to do this as almighty God and desires to do this as a faithful Father.[90]

---

90. *Ed note:* cf. Lord's Day, 9 and 10, *The Heidelberg Catechism.*

Appendix

Cross-Reference with *Gereformeerde Dogmatiek*

This appendix cross-references the paragraph and subparagraph sections in the fifth chapter of Bavinck's *Gereformeerde Dogmatiek* ("Over de Wereld in haar oorspronkelijken Staat" ["Concerning the World in Its Original State"]) with the pages of this separate volume on creation. Bavinck divided this material into seven major sections (paragraphs 33–39), which constitute the seven chapters of this volume, and subdivided those sections into fifty-seven additional sections (#s 250–306). This method of cross-referencing was chosen rather than using the pagination of any particular edition since it is consistent from the second, revised printing through the fifth edition though the pagination is not the same in all editions. In the list that follows the first number under *G.D.* (33–39) is the paragraph number and the second (250–306) is the subparagraph number.

	G.D.[a]	I.B.[b]		G.D.	I.B.		G.D.	I.B.
33	#250	p. 24		#261	p. 65		#272	p. 108
	#251	p.25		#262	p. 69		#273	p. 112
	#252	p. 30		#263	p. 73		#274	p. 114
	#253	p. 34		#264	p. 77		#275	p. 120
	#254	p. 36		#265	p. 80		#276	p. 122
	#255	p. 39		#266	p. 83		#277	p. 126
	#256	p. 42		#267	p. 88		#278	p. 131
	#257	p. 45	35	#268	p. 95	36	#279	p. 137
	#258	p. 50		#269	p. 100		#280	p. 140
	#259	p. 56		#270	p. 102		#281	p. 147
34	#260	p. 61		#271	p. 105		#282	p. 151

a. *Gereformeerde Dogmatiek* (Vol. 4)
b. *In the Beginning*

Bibliography[1]

This bibliography includes the items Bavinck listed at the head of sections 33–39 in the *Gereformeerde Dogmatiek* as well as any additional works cited in his footnotes. Particularly with respect to the footnote references, where Bavinck's own citations were quite incomplete by contemporary standards—with titles often significantly abbreviated—this bibliography provides fuller information. In some cases full bibliographic information was available only for an edition other than the one Bavinck cited. Where English translations of Dutch or German works are available, they have been cited rather than the original. In a few instances where Bavinck cited Dutch translations of English originals the original work is listed. In cases where multiple versions or editions are available in English (e.g., Calvin's *Institutes*) the most recent, most frequently cited, or most accessible edition was chosen. In spite of best efforts to track down each reference to confirm or complete bibliographic information, some of Bavinck's abbreviated and cryptic notations remain unconfirmed or incomplete. Where information is unconfirmed, incomplete, and/or titles have been reconstructed, the work is marked with an asterisk.

Abbreviations

ANF   *The Ante-Nicene Fathers. Ed. by Alexander Roberts and James Donaldson. 10 vols. New York: Christian Literature, 1885–96. Reprint ed., Grand Rapids: Eerdmans, 1950–51.*

NPNF (1)   *A Select Library of Nicene and Post-Nicene Fathers of the Christian Church. First Series. 14 vols. Ed. by Philip Schaff. New York:*

---

1. The improvement of this bibliography over Bavinck's original in the *Gereformeerde Dogmatiek* is largely thanks to a valuable tool he did not have available to him—the Internet—and its diligent perusal by Calvin Theological Seminary graduate students Raymond Blacketer and Claudette Grinnell (who worked on the eschatology section, previously published as *The Last Things* [Baker, 1996], and Calvin Seminary Students Colin Vander Ploeg, Steven Baarda, and Marcia De Haan-Van Drunen, who worked on this creation section. This section was also carefully checked and extensively revised by Dr. Roger Nicole, whose work greatly helped reduce the number of mistakes, not to mention the amount of asterisks that still appear. The assistance of all is gratefully acknowledged here.

Christian Literature, 1887–1900. Reprint ed., Grand Rapids: Eerdmans, 1956.

NPNF (2) *A Select Library of Nicene and Post-Nicene Fathers of the Christian Church. Second Series. 14 vols. Ed. by Philip Schaff and Henry Wace. New York: Christian Literature, 1890–1900. Reprint ed., Grand Rapids: Eerdmans, 1952.*

PG   Migne, J. P. *Patrologia Graeca.*

PL   Migne, J. P. *Patrologia Latina.*

PRE   *Realencyklopädie für protestantische Theologie und Kirche. 24 vols. Ed. by Albert Hauck. 3rd ed. Leipzig: J. C. Hinrichs, 1896–1913.*

Books

Abelard, Peter. *Introductio ad Theologiam,* in *PL* 178.

Agassiz, Louis. *Essay on Classification.* Ed. by Edward Lurie. Cambridge, Mass.: Belknap Press of Harvard University Press, 1962.

Alexander of Hales. *Summa Theologica.* 4 vols. Quarracchi: Collegium S. Bonaventurae, 1924–58.

Alsted, Johann Heinrich. *Praecognita theologiae,* I–II, in *Methodus,* as books I and II: *Methodus sacrosanctae theologiae octo libris tradita.* Hanover: C. Eifrid, 1619.

———. *Theologia scholastica didactica exhibens locos communes theologicos.* Hanover: C. Eifrid, 1618.

Alting, Heinrich. *Theologia Elenctica Nova.* Amsterdam: J. Jansson, 1654.

Alting, Jacob. *Opera Omnia Theologica.* 5 vols. Amsterdam: Borst, 1687.

Ambrose, Saint. *Hexameron, Paradise, and Cain and Abel.* Trans. by John J. Savage. New York: Fathers of the Church, 1961.

Andree, Richard. *Die Flutsagen, ethnographisch betrachtet.* Braunschweig: F. Vieweg, 1891.

Anselm. *Basic Writings.* LaSalle, Ill.: Open Court, 1962.

———. *Why God Became Man, and The Virgin Conception, and Original Sin.* Trans. by Joseph M. Colleran. Albany: Magi Books, 1969.

Aquinas, Thomas. *Summa Theologiae.* Trans. by Thomas Gilby et al. 61 vols. New York: McGraw-Hill, 1964–81.

———. *Summa Contra Gentiles.* Trans. by the English Dominican Fathers. London: Burns, Oates & Washbourne, 1924.

———. *Aquinas on Creation: Writings on the Sentences of Peter Lombard, Book II.* Trans. by Steven E. Baldner and William E. Carroll. Toronto: Pontifical Institute of Mediaeval Studies, 1997.

Aristotle. *Nicomachean Ethics.* Trans. by Terence Irwin. Indianapolis: Hackett, 1985.

Athanasius. *Against the Arians. NPNF* (2), IV, 303–447.

———. *Against the Heathens.* Ed. and trans. by Robert W. Thomson. Oxford: Clarendon, 1971.

———. *Letter to Serapion. NPNF* (2), IV, 564–66.

———. *On the Incarnation. NPNF* (2), IV, 31–67.

Athenagoras. *The Resurrection of the Dead. ANF,* II, 149–62.

Auberlen, Carl August. *The Divine Revelation: An Essay in Defence of the Faith.* Trans. by A. B. Paton. Edinburgh: T. & T. Clark, 1867.

Augustine, Aurelius. *Acts or Disputation Against Fortunatus the Manichaean.* *NPNF* (2), IV, 113–24.

———. *Admonition and Grace.* Trans. by J. C. Murray. Vol. 2. *The Fathers of the Church.* Washington, D.C.: Catholic University of America Press, 1968.

———. *Against the Academics.* Trans. by John J. O'Meara. Vol. 12, *Ancient Christian Writers.* Westminster: Newman, 1950.

———. *Against Julian.* Trans. by M. A. Schumacher. Vol. 16. *Writings of Saint Augustine.* Washington, D.C.: Catholic University of America Press, 1984.

———. *The City of God. NPNF* (1), II, 1–511.

———. *Confessions. NPNF* (1), I, 27–207.

———. *De Genesi contra Mainichaeos* I. II, PL 34, 173–220.

———. *Divine Providence and the Problem of Evil.* Trans. by Robert P. Russell. In *Fathers of the Church: Writings of Saint Augustine.* Vol. 1. New York: CIMA, 1948.

———. *Eighty-Three Different Questions.* Trans. by D. L. Mosher. Vol. 70, *The Fathers of the Church.* New York, 1982.

———. *Enchiridion. NPNF* (1), III, 229–76.

———. *The Literal Meaning of Genesis. Ancient Christian Writers.* Vol. 41. Trans. and ann. by John Hammond Taylor. New York: Newman, 1982.

———. *On the Grace of Christ and Original Sin.* Trans. by P. Holmes, ed. by Whitney Oates. Vol. 1. *Basic Writings of Saint Augustine.* New York: Random House, 1948.

———. *On the Merits and Remission of Sins. NPNF* (1), V, 12–79.

———. *The Retractions.* Trans. by Mary Inez Bogan. Vol. 60. *The Fathers of the Church.* Washington, D.C.: Catholic University of America Press, 1968.

———. *The Trinity.* Trans. by Stephen McKenna. Vol. 45, *The Fathers of the Church.* Washington, D.C.: Catholic University of America Press, 1963.

Baier, Johann Wilhelm. *Compendium Theologiae Positivae.* 3 vols. in 4. St. Louis: Concordia, 1879.

Basil of Caesarea. *On the Hexaëmeron. Exegetical Homilies.* Trans. by Agnes Clare Way. Washington, D.C.: Catholic University of America Press, 1963.

———. *On the Holy Spirit.* Trans. by David Anderson. Crestwood, N.Y.: St. Vladimir's Seminary Press, 1980.

Baumgartner, Alexander. *Geschichte der Weltliteratur.* Freiburg i.B.: Herder, 1897.

Baumstark, Chr. E. *Christliche Apologetik auf anthropologischen Grundlage.* Frankfurt a/m, 1872.

Bavinck, Herman. *Doctrine of God.* Trans. by William Hendriksen. Grand Rapids: Eerdmans, 1951.

———. *Beginselen der Psychologie.* 2nd ed. Kampen: Kok, 1923.

———. *Gereformeerde Dogmatiek,* 4 vols. 4th ed. Kampen: Kok, 1928.

———. *Schepping of Ontwikkeling.* Kampen: Kok, 1901.

———. Ed. *Synopsis Purioris Theologiae.* Leiden: D. Donner, 1881.

Becanus, Martin. *Summa Theologiae Scholasticae.* Rothmagi: I. Behovrt, 1651.

Beck, Gottlieb. *Der Urmensch.* Basel: A. Gaering, 1899.

Beck, J. T. *Einleitung in das System der christlichen Lehre.* 2nd ed. Stuttgart: J. F. Steinkopf, 1870.

Bekker, Balthasar. *De Betoverde Wereld, Zynde een Grondig Ondersoek van't Gemeen Geloeven Aangaande de Geesten, Deselver Aart en Vermogen, Bewind en Bedrijft: Als Ook't Gene de Menschen door Derselver Kraght en Emeenschap Doen.* 4 vols. Amsterdam: D. van den Dalen, 1691–93.

Bellarmine, Robert. *De Controversiis Chrisanae fidei adversus huius temporis haereticos.* Cologne: Gualtheri, 1617–20.

———. *De Gratia Primi Hominis.* Heidelberg: Rosa, 1612.

———. *Opera Omnia.* Ed. J. Fèvre. 12 vols. Paris: Vivès, 1870–74.

Bettex, Frederic. *Natuurstudie en Christendom.* 4th ed. Kampen: Kok, 1908.

———. *Das Lied der Schöpfung.* 5th ed. Stuttgart: J. F. Steinkopf, 1906.

Beyschlag, Willibald. *Zur Verständigung über den christlichen Vorsehungsglauben.* Halle: Eugen Strien, 1888.

Beza, Theodore. *Volumen I. Tractationum Theologicarum.* Geneva: Jean Crispin, 1570.

Biedermann, Alois Emanuel. *Christliche Dogmatik.* Zurich: Füssli, 1869.

Biegler, J. *Die Civitas Dei des heiligen Augustinus.* Paderborn: Junfermann, 1894.

Biesterveld, Petrus. *De Jongste Methode voor de Verklaring van het Nieuwe Testament.* Kampen: Bos, 1905.

Bilderdijk, Willem. *Opstellen van Godgeleerden en Zedekundigen Inhoud.* 2 vols. Amsterdam: Immerzeel, 1883.

Boethius. *The Consolation of Philosophy.* Trans. by Peter Glassgold. Los Angeles: Sun and Moon, 1994.

Böhl, Eduard. *Dogmatik.* Amsterdam: Scheffer, 1887.

Bonaventure. *The Breviloquium.* Vol. 2, *The Works of Bonaventure.* Trans. by Jose De Vinck. Paterson, N.J.: St. Anthony Guild, 1963.

Bosizio, Athanasius. *Das Hexaemeron und die Geologie.* Mainz: Franz Kircheim, 1865.

Bosse, A. *Untersuchungen zum chronologischen Schema des Alten Testament.* Cothen, 1906.

Boston, Thomas. *A View of the Covenant of Grace from the Sacred Records.* Edmonton, Alberta: Still Waters Revival Books, 1993 [1677].

Bovon, Jules. *Dogmatique chrétienne.* 2 vols. Lausanne: Georges Bridel, 1895–96.

*Brahe, J. J. *Aanmerkingen Over de Vijf Walchersche Artikelen.*

Brakel, Wilhelmus. *The Christian's Reasonable Service.* Trans. by Bartel Elshout. Ligonier, Pa.: Soli Deo Gloria, 1992.

Braun, Johannes. *Doctrina Foederum, Sive Systema Theologiae Didacticae et Elenchticae.* Amsterdam: A. Van Sommeren, 1668.

Bretschneider, Karl Gottlieb. *Handbuch der Dogmatik der Evangelischlutherischen Kirche, oder Versuch einer beurtheilenden Darstellung der Grundstze, welche diese Kirche in ihren symbolischen Schriften bei die Christliche Glaubenslehre ausgesprochen hat, mit vergleichung der Glaubenslehre in der Bekenntnisschriften der reformirten Kirche.* Leipzig: J. A. Barth, 1838.

————. *Systematische Entwicklung aller in der Dogmatik verkommenden Begriffe nach den symbolischen Schriften der evangelisch-lutherischen und reformirten Kirche und den wichtigsten dogmatischen Lehrbüchern ihrer Theologen.* Leipzig: J. A. Barth, 1841.

Brinck, Henricus. *Toet-Steen der Waarheid.* 2nd ed. Utrecht: W. Clerc, 1690.

Brunetière, Ferdinand. *La Science et la Religion, Réponse à Quelques Objections.* Paris: Firmin-Didot, 1895.

Bucanus, Guillaume. *Institutiones Theologicae, Seu Locorum Communium Christianae Religionis, ex Dei Verbo, et Praestantissimorum Theologorum Orthodoxo Consensu Expositorum.* Bernae Helvetiorum: Johannes & Isaias Le Preux, 1605.

Büchner, Ludwig. *Force and Matter; or Principles of the Natural Order of the Universe.* Trans. from 15th German ed., 4th ed. New York: P. Eckler, 1891.

Budde, Karl. *Die Biblische Urgeschichte.* Giessen: J. Ricker, 1883.

Buddeus, Johann Franz. *Institutiones Theologiae Moralis.* Leipzig: T. Fritsch, 1715.

Burmann, Frans. *Synopsis Theologiae & Speciatim Oeconomiae Foederum Dei: Ab Initio Saeculorum Usque ad Consummationem Eorum.* 2 vols. in 1. Amsterdam: Joannem Wolters, 1699.

Burmeister, Hermann. *Geschichte der Schöpfung: eine Darstellung des Entwickelungsganges der Erde und ihrer Bewöhner.* 7th ed. Leipzig: C. G. Giebel, 1872.

Busken Huet, Conrad. *Het Land van Rembrandt; studien over de Noordnederlandsche beschaving in de zeventiende eeuw.* 2 vols. Haarlem: H. D. Tjeenk Willink, 1886.

Calvin, John. *Commentary on Genesis.* Trans. by John King. Grand Rapids: Baker, 1979.

————. *Commentary on the Epistles of Paul the Apostle to the Galatians, Ephesians, Philippians and Colossians.* Trans. by T. H. L. Parker. Grand Rapids: Eerdmans, 1965.

————. *Commentary on Hebrews.* Trans. by John Owen. Grand Rapids: Baker, 1979.

————. *Institutes of the Christian Religion* (1559). Ed. by John T. McNeill, trans. by F. L. Battles. 2 vols. Philadelphia: Westminster, 1960.

————. *Treatises against the Anabaptists and Libertines.* Trans. and ed. by Benjamin W. Farley. Grand Rapids: Baker, 1982, 242–49.

Capito, Wolfgang. *Hexaemeron Dei Opus Explicatum.* Strasbourg: Vendelinus Richel, 1539.

Carneri, Bartholomew. *Sittlichkeit und Darwinismus. Drei Bücher Ethik.* Wien: W. Braumüller, 1903.

Casini, Antonio. *Controv. de statu purae naturae.* Appendix to librum II de opificio. sex dierum. In D. Petavius, *De Theologicus dogmatibus.* Paris: Vivès, 1866. IV, 512–96.

The Catechism of the Council of Trent. Trans. by J. Donovan. New York: Catholic Publ. Society, 1829.

Chamier, Daniel. *Panstratiae Catholicae, sive Controversiarum de Religione Adversus Pontificios Corpus.* 4 vols. Geneva: Rouer, 1626.

Chantepie de la Saussaye, Pierre Daniel. *Lehrbuch der Religionsgeschichte.* 2 vols. Tübingen: J. C. B. Mohr (Paul Siebeck), 1905.

Chemniz, M. *Loci Theologici.* 3 vols. Frankfurt and Wittenberg: T. Merius & E. Schumacher, 1653.

Cicero, Marcus Tullius. *De Divinatione.* Loeb Classical Library. Trans. by William A. Falconer. Cambridge, Mass.: Harvard University Press, 1923.

———. *De Inventione.* Loeb Classical Library. 4 vols. Trans. by H. M. Hubbell. Cambridge, Mass.: Harvard University Press, 1949.

———. *On the Nature of the Gods.* Loeb Classical Library. Trans. by H. Rackham. New York: G. P. Putnam's Sons, 1933.

Clemen, Carl. *Die Christliche Lehre von der Sünde.* Göttingen: Vandenhoeck und Ruprecht, 1897.

Clement of Alexandria. *Stromateis.* Trans. by John Ferguson. Vol. 85. *The Fathers of the Church.* Washington, D.C.: Catholic University of America Press, 1991.

Cloppenburg, Johannes. *Disputatio de Foedere Dei.* 1643.

———. *Exercitationes Super Locos Communes Theologicos.* Franeker: Black, 1653.

———. *Theologica Opera Omnia.* 2 vols. Amsterdam: Borstius, 1684.

Coccejus, Johannes. *Summa Doctrinae de Foedere et Testamento Dei.* 2nd ed. Leiden: Elsevier, 1654.

———. *Summa Theologiae ex Scripturis Repetita.* Amsterdam: J. Ravenstein, 1665.

*Coelestinus, Fr. *Het Aardsche Paradijs.* Tilburg.

Comrie, Alexander, and Nicolaus Holtius. *Examen van het Ontwerp van Tolerantie.* 10 vols. Amsterdam: Nicolaas Byl, 1753.

Crell, Johann. *Liber de deo euisque attributis.* In *Opera Omnia.* Vol. IV. Amsterdam: Irenicus Philalethes, 1656.

Cremer, Hermann. *Biblico-theological Lexicon of New Testament Greek.* s. v. pronoia. Trans. by D. W. Simon and William Urwick. Edinburgh: T. & T. Clark, 1872.

Creutzer, Friedrich. *Philosophorum Veterum Loci de Providentia Divina ac de Fato.* Heidelberg: 1806.

Darwin, Charles. *The Descent of Man.* New York: D. Appleton, 1871.

———. *The Expression of Emotions in Man and Animals.* London: John Murray, 1872.

———. *On the Origin of Species by Means of Natural Selection.* London: J. Murray, 1859.

———. *Het Voortbestaan van het Menschelijk Geslacht.* Utrecht: Kemink, 1902.

Davidson, Andrew Bruce. *The Theology of the Old Testament.* Edited from the author's manuscripts by S. D. F. Salmond. New York: Charles Scribner's, 1904.

Dawson, John William. *Nature and the Bible: A course of lectures delivered in New York on the Morse Foundation of the Union Theological Seminary.* New York: Wilbur B. Ketcham, 1875.

De Fremery, H. N. *Handleiding tot de Kennis van het Spiritisme.* Bussum, 1904.

———. *Het Spiritische Levensbeschouwing.* Bussum, 1904.

Delitzsch, Franz. *Biblical Commentary on the Psalms.* 3 vols. Trans. by Francis Bolton. Edinburgh: T. & T. Clark, 1871.

———. *A New Commentary on Genesis.* Trans. by Sophia Taylor. Edinburgh: T. & T. Clark, 1899.

———. *A System of Biblical Psychology.* Trans. by Robert E. Wallis. Edinburgh: T. & T. Clark, 1899.

Delitzsch, Friedrich. *Babel and Bible.* Trans. by W. H. Corruth. Chicago: Open Court, 1903.

———. *Mehr Licht.* Leipzig: J. C. Hinrichs, 1907.

Dennert, Eberhard. *At the Deathbed of Darwinism.* Trans. by E. V. O'Harra and John H. Peschges Burlington, Iowa: German Literary Board, 1904.

———. *Moses oder Darwin?* 2nd ed. Stuttgart: Kielmann, 1907.

———. *Natuurwetenschap, Toeval, Voorzienigheid.* Baarn: Hollandia, 1906.

———. *Die Religion der Naturforscher.* 4th ed. Berlin: Buchhandlung der Berliner Stadtmission, 1901.

———. *Die Weltanschauung des modernen Naturforschers.* Stuttgart: M. Rielmann, 1907.

Dens, Pierre. *Theologia Moralis et Dogmatica.* 8 vols. Dublin: Richard Coyne, 1832.

Denzinger, Heinrich. *The Sources of Catholic Dogma (Enchiridion Symbolorum).* Translated from the 30th ed. by Roy J. Deferrari. London and St. Louis: Herder, 1955.

de Vries, Hugo. *Species and Varieties; Their Origin by Mutation.* Ed. by Daniel Trembly MacDougal, 2nd ed., corrected and rev. Chicago: Open Court.

Dieringer, Franz. *Lehrbuch der Katholischen Dogmatik.* 4th ed. Mainz: Kirchheim, 1858.

Dillmann, August. *Genesis.* Edinburgh: T. & T. Clark, 1897.

Dilloo, F. W. J. *Das Wunder an den Stufen des Achas.* Amsterdam: Hoveker, 1885.

Dippe, Alfred. *Naturphilosophie.* München: C. H. Beck and O. Beck, 1907.

Documents of Vatican Council I, 1869–1870. Selected and translated by John F. Broderick. Collegeville, Minn.: Liturgical, 1971.

Doedes, Jacobus Izaak. *De Heidelbergsche Catechismus.* Utrecht: Kemink & Zoon, 1881.

———. *Inleiding tot de Leer van God.* Utrecht: Kemink, 1870.

———. *De Leer der Zaligheid Volgens het Evangelie in de Schriften des Nieuwen Verbonds Voorgesteld.* Utrecht: Kemink, 1876.

———. *De Nederlandsche Geloofsbelijdenis en de Heidelbergsche Catechismus.* Utrecht: Kemink & Zoon, 1880–81.

Dorner, Isaak August. *History of the Development of the Doctrine of the Person of Christ.* 3 vols. Trans. by Patrick Fairbairn. Edinburgh: T. & T. Clark, 1868.

———. *A System of Christian Doctrine.* Trans. by Alfred Cave and J. S. Banks, 4 vols. Rev. ed. Edinburgh: T. & T. Clark, 1888.

Draper, John William. *History of the Conflict between Religion and Science.* New York: D. Appleton, 1897.

Du Bois-Reymond, Emil Heinrich. *Kulturgeschichte und Naturwissenschaft.* Leipzig: Veit, 1878.

*Du Prel, C. *Die Planetenbewhohner.*

Ebrard, Johannes Heinrich August. *Apologetics: The Scientific Vindication of Christianity.* Trans. by William Stuart and John Macpherson. 3 vols. 2nd ed. Edinburgh: T. & T. Clark, 1886–87.

———. *Christliche Dogmatik.* 2 vols. 2nd ed. Königsberg: A. W. Unzer, 1862–63.

———. *Het geloof aan de Heilige Schrift en de uitkomsten van het onderzoek der natuur.* Trans. by A. v. d. Linde. Amsterdam, 1862.

Edwards, Jonathan. *Dissertation Concerning the End for Which God Created the World.* In *The Works of Jonathan Edwards,* vol. 8, *Ethical Writings.* Ed. by Paul Ramsey. New Haven, Conn.: Yale University Press, 1989.

Eisler, Rudolf. *Kant-Lexikon.* Berlin: Mittler & Sohn, 1930.

Ellis, Havelock. *Geschlechtstrieb und Schamgefühl.* Leipzig: Wigand, 1900.

Engelkemper, Wilhelm. *Die Paradiesesflüsse.* Münster, 1901.

Episcopius, Simon. *Apologia pro Confessione Sive Declaratione Sententiae Eorum, qui in Foederato Belgio Vocantur Remonstrantes, Super Praecipuis Articulis Religionis Christianae contra Censuram Quatuor Professorum Leidensium.* 1629. *Opera* II, 95–283.

———. *Institutiones theologicae,* in *Opera,* vol 1. Amsterdam: Johan Blaeu, 1650.

———. *Opera theologica.* 2 vols. Amsterdam: Johan Blaeu, 1650–65.

Erbkam, Heinrich Wilhelm. *Geschichte der Protestantischen Sekten im Zeitalter der Reformation.* Hamburg and Gotha: F. & A. Perthes, 1848.

Erigena, Johannes Scotus. *The Division of Nature* (1681). Trans. by Myra L. Uhlfelder. Indianapolis: Bobbs-Merrill, 1976.

Esser, T. *Die Lehre des heiligen Thomas von Aquino über die Möglichkeit einer anfanglosen Schöpfung.* Münster: Aschendorff, 1895.

Eusebius of Caesaria. *Praeparatio Evangelica.* PG, 21.

Fichte, Immanuel Hermann von. *Anthropologie.* Leipzig: Brockhaus, 1860.

Fichte, Johann Gottlieb. *Die Anweisung zum Seligen Leben.* Trans. by William Smith as "The Doctrine of Religion." In *Popular Works.* London: Trübner, 1873.

———. *The Science of Rights.* Trans. by A. E. Kroeger. New York: Harper & Row, 1970 [1889].

———. *The Vocation of Man.* Trans. by William Smith. 2nd ed. Chicago: Open Court, 1910.

Fischer, Engelbert Lorenz. *Heidenthum und Offenbarung.* Mainz: Kirchheim, 1878.

Flammarion, Camille. *La Pluralité des Mondes Habités.* Paris: Didier, 1862.

Fock, Otto. *Der Socinianismus nach seiner Stellung in der Gesammtentwicklung des christlichen Geistes, Nach Seinem Historischen Verlauf und Nach Seinem Lehrbegriff.* Kiel: C. Schröder, 1847.

Franck, Adolphe. *The Kabbalah.* New York: Arno, 1973.

Francken, Wijnaendts. *Ethische Studiën.* Haarlem, 1903.

Frank, Franz Hermann Reinhold. *System der christlichen Wahrheit.* 2 vols. Erlangen: A. Deichert, 1878–80.

Fraser, Alexander Campbell. *Philosophy of Theism.* New York: Scribner's, 1899.

Friderici, Johannes Gottlieb. *De Aurea Aetate Quam Poëtae Finxerunt.* Leipzig, 1736.

*Froberger. *Die Schöpfungsgeschichte der Menschheit in der "vorausset-zungslosen" Völkerpsychologie.* 1903.

Gander, Martin. *Naturwissenschaft und Glaube. Benzigers Naturwissenschaftliche Bibliothek.* New York: Benziger Bros., 1905.

———. *Die Sündflut in ihrer Bedeutung für die Erdgeschichte.* Münster: Aschendorff, 1896.

Geesink, Wilhelm. *Van 's Heeren Ordinantiën.* 3 vols. Amsterdam: W. Kirchener, 1907.

Geikie, Archibald S. *Geology.* New York: D. Appleton, 1880.

Gerhard, Johann. *Loci Theologici.* 9 vols. Ed. by E. Preuss. Berlin: G. Schlawitz, 1863–75.

Gierke, Otto. *Johannes Althusius.* Breslau: W. Koebner, 1880.

Girard, Raymond de. *Etudes de Géologie Biblique. Le Déluge Devant la Critique Historique.* 3 vols. Freiburg: Fragnière, 1893–95.

Gnandt, Albert. *Der mosaische Schöpfungsbericht in seinem Verhältnis zur modernen Wissenschaft.* Graz, 1906.

Godet, Frédéric. *Etudes Bibliques: Première Série: Ancien Testament.* 2nd ed. Paris: Sandoz & Fischbacher, 1873.

———. *Studies on the Old Testament.* 6th ed. Trans. by W. H. Lyttelton. London: Hodder & Stoughton, 1892.

Gomarus, Franciscus. "Oratio de Foedere Dei." In *Opera Theologica Omnia.* Amsterdam: J. Jansson, 1644.

Gordon, Alex. R. *The Early Traditions of Genesis.* Edinburgh: T. & T. Clark, 1907.

Grasset, Joseph. *Les limites de la biologie.* Paris: Alcan, 1902.

Gregory Nazianzus. *Apologia in Hexaëmeron. PL* 44, 61–124.

Gregory of Nyssa. *On the Making of Man, NPNF* (2), V, 387–427.

Gregory the Great. *Moralia in Iobum.* In *Corpus Christianorum,* Series Latina, # CXLIII A. Turnholti: Typographi Brepols Editores Pontifici, 1979.

Gretillat, Augustin. *Exposé de Théologie Systématique.* 4 vols. Paris: Fischbacher, 1885–92.

Guibert, Jean. *In the Beginning.* Trans. by G. S. Whitmarsh. London: Kegan Paul, Trench, Trubner, 1900.

Gumplovicz, Ludwig. *Grundriss der Sociologie.* 2nd ed. Wien: Manzsche Buchhandlung, 1905.

Gunkel, Hermann. *Die Genesis übersetzt und erklärt.* Göttingen: Vandenhoeck und Ruprecht, 1902. *Genesis.* English trans. by Mark E. Biddle. Macon, Ga.: Mercer University Press, 1997.

Gunkel, Hermann, and Zimmern, Heinrich. *Schöpfung und Chaos in Urzeit und Endzeit.* 2nd ed. Göttingen: Vandenhoeck und Ruprecht, 1921.

Gutberlet, Konstantin. *Der Mechanische Monismus.* Paderborn: F. Schöningh, 1893.

———. *Der Mensch.* Paderborn: Schöningh, 1903.

Güttler, C. *Natursforschung und Bibel in ihrer Stellung zur Schöpfung.* Freiburg i.B.: Herder, 1877.

Haeckel, Ernst. *The History of Creation, or, The Development of the Earth and its Inhabitants by the Action of Natural Causes* [*Natürliche Schöpfungsgeschichte*]. Translated from the German, revised by E. R. Lankester. 2 vols. New York: D. Appleton, 1883.

———. *Der Kampf um den Entwickelungs-Gedanken*. Berlin: G. Reimer, 1905.

———. *Der Monismus als Band zwischen Religion und Wissenschaft*. 6th ed. Leipzig: A. Kroner, 1908.

———. *The Riddle of the Universe at the Close of the Nineteenth Century*. Trans. by Joseph McCabe. New York: Harper & Brothers, 1900.

Hagenbach, Karl Rudolf. *Lehrbuch der Dogmengeschichte*. Leipzig: Hirzel, 1888.

Hahn, W. *Die Entstehung der Weltkörper*. Regensburg: Pustet, 1895.

Hanne, Johann Wilhelm. *Die Idee der Absoluten Persönlichkeit*. 2nd ed. Hannover: C. Rumpler, 1865.

Häring, Theodor. *The Christian Faith*. 2 vols. Trans. by John Dickie and George Ferries. London: Hodder & Stoughton, 1913.

Harnack, Adolf von. *History of Dogma*. 7 vols. Trans. by N. Buchanan, J. Millar, E. B. Speirs, W. McGilchrist, ed. by A. B. Bruce. London: Williams & Norgate, 1896–99.

———. *The Mission and Expansion of Christianity in the First Three Centuries*. New York: Harper, 1962.

Harris, Samuel. *God the Creator and Lord of All*. 2 vols. Edinburgh: Clark, 1897.

Hartmann, Eduard von. *Gesammelte Studien und Aufsätze*. Leipzig: Friedrich, 1891.

———. *Wahrheit und Irrthum im Darwinismus: Eine Kritische Darstellun der organischen Entwicklungstheorie*. Berlin: C. Duncker, 1875.

Heard, John Bickford. *The Tripartite Nature of Man: Spirit, Soul, and Body*. 2nd ed. Edinburgh: T. & T. Clark, 1868.

Hegel, Georg Wilhelm Friedrich. *The Encyclopaedia of Logic (with the Zusätze)*. Trans. by T. F. Geraets et al. Indianapolis/Cambridge: Hackett, 1991.

———. *Lectures on the Philosophy of Religion*. Trans. by E. B. Speirs and J. Burdon Sanderson. 3 vols. London: Kegan Paul, Trench, Trübner, 1895.

———. *Philosophy of Nature*. Trans. by M. J. Petry. London and New York: Allen Unwin, Humanities Press, 1970.

———. *Sämtliche Werke*. 26 vols. Stuttgart: F. Frommann, 1949–59.

Heidegger, Johann Heinrich. *Corpus Theologiae Christianae*. 2 vols. Zürich: J. H. Bodmer, 1700.

———. *De Libertate Christianorum a lege cibaria veteri*. 2nd ed. Zürich: Gessner, 1678.

Heinrich, Joann Baptist, and Constantin Gutberlet. *Dogmatische Theologie*. 10 vols. 2nd ed. Mainz: Kirchheim, 1881–1900.

Hengstenberg, Ernst Wilhelm. *Dissertations on the Genuineness of the Pentateuch*. 2 vols. Trans. by John D. Lowe. Edinburgh: Continental Translation Society, 1847.

Henry, Paul Emil. *Life and Times of John Calvin*. 2 vols. Trans. by Hans Stebbing. New York: Robert Carta & Brothers, 1853.

Heppe, Heinrich. *Dogmatik des deutschen Protestantismus im sechzehnten Jahrhundert*, 3 vols. Gotha: F. A. Perthes, 1857.

———. *Reformed Dogmatics: Set Out and Illustrated from the Sources.* Rev. and ed. by Ernst Bizer, trans. by G. T. Thomson. Grand Rapids: Baker, 1978 [1950].

Herder, Johann Gottfried. *Aelteste Urkunde des Menschengeschlechts.* Riga: Hartknoch, 1774–76.

Hertwig, Oskar. *Biological Problems of Today: Preformation or Epigenesis?* New York: Macmillan, 1900.

———. *Die Entwicklung der Biologie im neunzehnten Jahrhundert.* Jena: G. Fischer, 1908.

Hesiod. *Essential Hesiod (Works and Days).* Trans. by C. J. Rowe. Bristol, Eng.: Bristol Classical Press, 1978.

Hettinger, Franz. *Natural Religion.* Ed. by Henry Sebastian Bowden. London: Burns & Oats, 1892.

Hobbes, Thomas. *Leviathan.* London: J. M. Dent, 1924.

Hodge, Charles. *Systematic Theology.* 3 vols. New York: Charles Scribner's Sons, 1888.

Hoekstra, Sytse. *Bronnen en Grondslagen van het Godsdienstig Geloof.* Amsterdam: P. N. van Kampen, 1864.

———. *Grondslag, Wezen en Openbaring van het Godsdienstig Geloof.* Rotterdam: Altmann & Roosenburg, 1861.

———. *Wijsgerige Godsdienstleer.* Amsterdam: Van Kampen, 1894, 95.

Hofmann, Johann Christian Conrad von. *Der Schriftbeweis.* 3 vols. Nördlingen: Beck, 1857–60.

———. *Weissagung und Erfüllung im Alten und im Neuen Testamente.* 2 vols. Nördlingen: C. H. Beck, 1841–44.

Hofstede de Groot, Petrus. *De Groninger Godgeleerdheid in Hunne Eigenaardigheid.* Groningen: Scholtens, 1855.

Hollaz, David. *Examen Theologicum Acroamaticum.* Rostock and Leipzig: Russworm, 1718.

Holzhey, Carl. *Schöpfung, Bibel und Inspiration.* Mergentheim: Carl Ohlinger, 1902.

Hommel, Fritz. *Geschichte des alten Morgenlandes.* Leipzig: Göschen, 1895.

Honert, Johan van den. "Voorrede," for Zacharius Ursinus, *Schatboek der Verklaring over den Nederlandsche Catechismus.* Gorinchem: Nicholas Coetzee, 1736.

Honig, A. G. *Creationisme of Traducianisme?* Kampen: J. H. Bos, 1906.

Hoornbeeck, Johannes. *Summa controversiarum religionis, cum infidelibus, haeriticis et schismaticis.* Utrecht: J. à Waersberge, 1658.

Howard, Nikolas. *Neue Berechnungen über die Chronologie des Alten Testamets und ihrer Verhaltnis zu der Altertumskunde.* Bonn, 1904.

Howorth, (Sir Henry Hoyle). *The Glacial Nightmare and the Flood: A Second Appeal to Common Sense from the Extravagance of some Recent Geology.* London: S. Low, Marston, 1893.

———. *The Mammoth and the Flood.* London: S. Low, Marston, Searle, & Rivingon, 1887.

————. *Neue Berechnungen über die Chronologie des Alt. Test. und ihr Verhältnis zu der Altertumskunde.* Foreword by v. E. Rupprecht. Bonn, 1904.

Hugenholtz, P. H. *Ethisch Pantheisme.* Amsterdam: Van Holkema & Warendorff, 1903.

Hugh of St. Victor. *Summa sententiarum septem tractatibus distincta. PL* 176, cols. 41–174.

Hümmelauer, Franz. *Der biblische Schöpfungsbericht.* Freiburg i.B.: Herder, 1877.

————. *Nochmals der biblischen Schöpfungsbegriff.* Freiburg i.B.: Herder, 1898.

Irenaeus. *Against Heresies. ANF,* I, 309–567.

Jansen, G. M. *Theologia Dogmatica Specialis.* Utrecht, 1877–79.

————. *Praelectiones Theologiae Fundamentalis.* Utrecht, 1875–77.

Jansen, Johannes. *Geschichte des deutschen Volkes seit dem Ausgang des Mittelalters.* 8 vols. Paris: Librairie Plon, 1887–1911.

Jensen, Peter. *Das Gilgamesch-Epos in der Weltliteratur I. Die Ursprünge der alttestamentlichen Patriarchen-, Propheten-, und Befreien-Sage und der neutestamentlichen Jesus-Sage.* Strassburg: Trubner, 1906.

John of Damascus. *Exposition of the Orthodox Faith. NPNF.* (2), IX, 259–360. In *Writings, The Fathers of the Church.* Washington, D.C.: Catholic University of America Press, 1958.

Josephus, Flavius. *The Works of Josephus.* Trans. by William Whiston. New updated edition. Peabody, Mass.: Hendrickson, 1987.

Junius, Franciscus. *Opuscula Theologica Selecta.* Ed. by Abraham Kuyper. Amsterdam: F. Muller, 1882.

————. *Theses Theologicae* in *Opuscula,* vol. I.

Justin Martyr. *Loci Aliquot Selecti.* Zürich: Schulthess, 1824.

————. *Dialogue with Trypho. ANF,* I, 194–270.

————. *Discourse to the Greeks. ANF,* I, 271–73.

Kaftan, Julius. *Dogmatik.* Tübingen: Mohr, 1901.

Kähler, Martin. *Die Wissenschaft der Christlichen Lehre.* 3rd ed. Leipzig: A. Deichert, 1905.

Kahnis, Friedrich August. *Die Luthersche Dogmatik, historisch-genetisch dargestellt.* 3 vols. Leipzig: Dörffling & Francke, 1861–68.

Kalb, Ernst. *Kirchen und Sekten der Gegenwart, unter Mitarbeit verschiedener evangelischer Theologen.* 2nd ed. Stuttgart: Verlag für Buchhandlung der Evangelische Gesellschaft, 1907.

Kant, Immanuel. *Critique of Pure Reason.* Trans. by Norman Kemp Smith. New York: St. Martin's, 1965 [1929].

————. *Religion within the Limits of Reason Alone.* Trans. by Theodore M. Greene and Hoyt H. Hudson. New York: Harper & Brothers, 1934.

Kaulen, Franz Philipp. *Der biblische Schöpfungsbericht.* Freiburg i.B.: Herder, 1902.

————. *Die Sprachenverwirrung zu Babel.* Mainz: F. Kirchheim, 1861.

Keerl, P. F. *Der Gottmensch, das Ebenbild Gottes.* Vol. 2 in series *De Mensch, das Ebenbild Gottes.* Basel: Bahnmeier, 1866.

Keil, Carl Friedrich, and F. Delitzsch. *Bible Commentary on the Old Testament.* 24 vols. Edinburgh: T. & T. Clark, 1864–1901.

Kern, H. *Rassen, Volken, Staten.* Haarlem: Bohn, 1904.

Kirchner, J. *Ueber den Zufall.* Halle: Pfeffer, 1888.

*Kirn, O. *Vorsehungsglaube und Naturwissenschaft.* 1903.

Klee, Heinrich. *Katholische Dogmatik.* 2nd ed. Mainz: Kirchheim, 1861.

Kleutgen, Joseph. *Philosophie der Vorzeit vertheidigt.* 2 vols. Münster: Theissing, 1863.

———. *Die Theologie der Vorzeit vertheidigt.* 2nd ed. 5 vols. Münster: Theissing, 1867–74.

Köberle, Justus. *Natur und Geist nach der Auffassung des Alten Testaments.* Munich: Beck, 1900.

Köhler, Ludwig. *Old Testament Theology.* Trans. by A. S. Todd. Philadelphia: Westminster, 1957.

*Kohler, Ludwig. *Lehrbuchder Bibl. Geschichte des A. T.*

Köstlin, Julius. *Theology of Luther in Its Historical Development and Inner Harmony.* Trans. by Charles E. Hay. 2 vols. Philadelphia: Lutheran Publication Society, 1897.

Kraetzschmar, Richard. *Die Bundesvorstellung im Alten Testament in ihrer geschichtlichen Entwicklung.* Marburg: N. G. Elwert, 1896.

Kreibig, Gustav. *Die Räthsel der göttlichen Vorsehung.* Berlin, 1886.

Kuenen, Abraham. *De Voornaamste Godsdiensten: de Godsienst van Israel tot den Ondergang van den Joodschen Staat.* 2 vols. Haarlem: Kruseman, 1869–70.

———. *The Religion of Israel to the Fall of the Jewish State.* 3 vols. Trans. by Alfred Heath May. London: Williams & Norgate, 1882–83.

Kurtz, Johann Heinrich. *The Bible and Astronomy: An Exposition of the Biblical Cosmology, and Its Relations to Natural Science.* Trans. by T. D. Simonton. 3rd ed. Philadelphia: Lindsay & Blakiston, 1857.

Kuyper, Abraham. *De Engelen Gods.* Amsterdam: Höveker & Wormser, 1902.

———. *De Gemeene Gratie in Wetenschap en Kunst.* Amsterdam: Höveker & Wormser, 1905.

———. *De Vleeschwording des Woords.* Amsterdam: Wormser, 1887.

———. *The Work of the Holy Spirit.* Trans. by J. Hendrick De Vries. Grand Rapids: Eerdmans, 1941 [1900].

Kuyper, Herman Huber. *Evolutie of Revelatie.* Amsterdam: Höveker & Wormser, 1903

Lactantius, Lucius C. *The Divine Institutes.* Trans. by Mary Francis McDonald. Washington, D.C.: Catholic University of America Press, 1964.

———. *De Ira Dei.* Darmstadt: Gentner, 1957 [1543].

Laidlaw, John. *The Bible Doctrine of Man.* Edinburgh: T. & T. Clark, 1895.

Lang, Andrew. *Onderzoek naar de Ontwikkeling van Godsdienst, Kultus en Mythologie.* Trans. by L. Knappert. Haarlem: F. Bohn, 1893.

Lange, Friedrich Albert. *Geschichte des Materialismus und Kritik seiner Bedeutung in der Gegenwart.* 8th ed. Leipzig: Baedekker, 1908.

Lange, Johann Peter. *Christliche Dogmatik.* 3 vols. Heidelberg: K. Winter, 1852.

Lechler, Gotthard Victor. *Geschichte des Englischen Deismus.* Stuttgart: J. G. Cotta, 1841.

Leibniz, Gottfried Wilhelm, and Johann Christoph Gottsched. *Theodicee.* Leipzig: Foerster, 1744.

———. *A System of Theology.* Trans. by Charles William Russell. London: Burns & Lambert, 1850.

Lessing, Gotthold Ephraim. *Erziehung des Menschengeschlechts und andere Schriften.* Stuttgart: Reclam, 1997.

Lexis, Wilhelm. *Das Wesen der Kultur.* Vol. I. *Die Kultur der Gegenwart.* 2nd ed. Leipzig: B. G. Trübner, 1912.

Leydekker, Melchior. *Fax Veritatis, seu Exercitationes ad nonnullas Controversias quae Hodie in Belgio Potissium Moventur, Multa ex Parte Theologico-philosophicae.* Leiden: Daniel Gaesbeeck & Felicem Lopez, 1677.

Liberatore, Matteo. *Institutiones Philosophicae.* 8th ed. 3 vols. Rome, 1855.

Liebmann, Otto. *Zur Analysis der Wirklichkeit: Eine Erörterung der Grundprobleme der Philosophie.* 3rd ed. Strassburg: K. J. Trübner, 1900.

Limborch, Phillip van. *Theologia Christiana ad praxin pietatis ac promotionem pacis christianae unice directa.* Amsterdam: Wetstein, 1735.

Lipps, Theodor. *Naturwissenschaft und Weltanschauung.* Heidelberg: C. Winter, 1906.

Lipsius, Richard Adelbert. *Lehrbuch der evangelisch-protestantischen Dogmatik.* Braunschweig: C. A. Schwetschke, 1893.

Lodge, Oliver J. *Life and Matter.* 4th ed. London: Williams & Norgate, 1907.

Lombard, Peter. *Sententiae in IV Liberis Distinctae.* 2 vols. 3rd ed. Grottaferrata: Colleggi S. Bonaventurae et Claras Aquas, 1971–81.

Lotz, Wilhelm. *Die Biblische Urgeschichte.* Leipzig: A. Deichert, 1907.

Lotze, Hermann. *Mircrocosmus.* Trans. by Elizabeth Hamilton and E. E. Constance Jones. New York: Scribner & Welford, 1866.

Love, Christoph. *Theologia Practica.* 4th ed. Amsterdam: J. H. Boom, 1669.

Lucken, Wilhelm. *Michael, eine Darstellung und Vergleichling der jüdischen und der Morgenländisch-christlichen Tradition.* Göttingen, 1898.

Lüken, Heinrich. *Die Stiftungsurkunde des Menschengeschlechts.* Freiburg i.B.: Herder, 1876.

———. *Die Traditionen des Menschengeschlechts.* Munster: Aschendorff, 1869.

Luthardt, Christoph Ernst. *Apologetische Vorträge uber die Grundwahrheiten des Christenthums.* 8th ed. Leipzig: Dörffling & Franke, 1878.

Luther, Martin. *Luther's Works.* Vol. 1, *Lectures on Genesis 1–3.* St. Louis: Concordia, 1958.

McCosh, James. *The Method of Divine Government, Physical and Moral.* 4th ed. New York: Carter & Brothers, 1855.

Maccovius, Johannes. *Loci Communes Theologici.* Amsterdam, 1658.

*Mac Gillavry. *De Continuïteit van het Doode en het Levende in de Natuur.* Leiden, 1898.

McTaggart, John, and Ellis McTaggart. *Some Dogmas of Religion.* London: E. Arnold, 1906.

Maimonides, Moses. *More Nebochim.* Warsaw: Goldman, 1872.

Malebranche, Nicholas. *The Search after Truth. Elucidations of the Search after Truth.* Trans. by R. Sault. Columbus: Ohio State University Press, 1980.

Mannens, Paulus. *Theologiae Dogmaticae Institutiones.* 3 vols. Roermand: Romen, 1910–15.

Marckius, Johannes. *Compendium theologiae christianae didactico-elencticum.* Groningen: Fossema, 1686.

———. *Historia Paradisi.* Amsterdam: Gerardus Borstius, 1705.

Maresius, Samuel. *Collegium Theologicum sive Systema Breve Universae Theologiae Comprehensium Octodecim Disputationibus.* Groningen: Francisci Bronchorstii, 1659.

Martensen, Hans Lassen. *Christian Dogmatics: A Compendium of the Doctrines of Christianity.* Trans. by William Urwick. Edinburgh: T & T. Clark, 1871.

Martensen-Larsen, Hans. *Die Naturwissenschaft in ihrem Schuldverhältniss zum Christenthum.* Berlin, 1897.

Marti, Karl. *Geschichte der Israelitischen Religion.* Strassburg: F. Bull, 1903.

Mastricht, Peter van. *Theoretico-practica theologia.* Utrecht: Appels, 1714.

Matulewicz, Georgius B. *Doctrina Russorum de Statu Justitiae Originalis.* Freiburg i.B.: Herder, 1904.

Mayer, Emil Walter. *Das Christliche Gottvertauen und der Glaube an Christus.* Göttingen: Vandenhoeck und Ruprecht, 1899.

Mees, Rudof Pieter. *De Mechanische Verklaring der Levensverschijnselen.* 's Gravenhage, 1899.

Meyer, H. A. W. *Critical and Exegetical Handbook to the Epistle to the Galatians.* Trans. by G. H. Venables. Edinburgh: T. & T. Clark, 1884.

———. *Critical and Exegetical Handbook to the Epistles to the Phillipians and Colossians.* Trans. by John C. Moore, rev. and ed. by William P. Dickson. Edinburgh: T. & T. Clark, 1875.

Mezger, Paul. *Räthsel des christlichen Vorsehungsglaubens.* Basel: Helbing & Lichterbahn, 1904.

Michelis, Friedrich. *Entwicklung der beiden ersten Kapitel der Genesis.* Münster: Theissing, 1845.

Möhler, Johann Adam. *Symbolik: Oder Darstellung der Dogmatischen Gegensätze der Katholiken und Protestanten nach Ihren öffentlichen Bekenntnisschriften.* Mainz: F. Kupferberg, 1838.

Moor, Bernhard de. *Commentarius Perpetuus in Joh. Marckii Compendium Theologiae Christianae Didactico-elencticum.* 6 vols. Leiden: J. Hasebroek, 1761–71.

More, Henry. *Mysterium pietatis, An Explanation of the Grand Mystery.* 3 vols. London: J. Fletcher, 1660.

Müller, Joseph T. *Die Symbolischen Bücher der Evangelisch-Lutherischen Kirche.* 8th ed. Gütersloh: Bertelsmann, 1898.

Müller, Julius. *The Christian Doctrine of Sin.* Trans. by William Urwick. 5th ed. 2. vols. Edinburgh: T. & T. Clark, 1868.

Müller, Max. *Vorlesungen über die Wissenschaft der Sprache.* 3rd ed. Leipzig: Mayer, 1866.

Münscher, Wilhelm. *Lehrbuch des Christlichen Dogmengeschichte.* Ed. by Daniel von Coelln. 3rd ed. Cassel: J. C. Krieger, 1832–38.

Nägeli, Carl. *A Mechanico-physiological Theory of Organic Evolution.* Chicago: Open Court, 1898.

————. *Entstehung und Begriff der Naturhistorischen.* München: Köningliche Akademie, 1865.

*Nickel, J. *Die Lehre des Alten Testaments über die Cherubim und Seraphim.* Breslau, 1890.

Niemeyer, H. A. *Collectio confessionum in ecclesiis reformatis publicatarum.* 2 vols. Leipzig: Klinkhardt, 1840.

Nieuwhuis, W. H. *De Verdiensten der Katholieke kerk ten Opzichte der Natuurwet.* Translated from English with foreword by F. Hendrichs. Amsterdam, 1906.

————. *Twee Vragen des Tijds.* Kampen: Kok, 1907.

Nikel, Johannes Simon. *Genesis und Keilschriftforschung.* Freiburg i.B.: Herder, 1903.

Nitzsch, Carl Emmanuel. *System of Christian Doctrines.* Edinburgh: T. & T. Clark, 1849; *System der Christlichen Lehre.* 5th ed. Bonn: Adolph Marcus, 1844.

Nitzsch, Friedrich. *Lehrbuch der Evangelischen Dogmatik.* 3rd ed. Prepared by Horst Stephan. Tübingen: J. C. B. Mohr, 1902.

Oehler, Gustav Friedrich. *Die Engelwelt.* Stuttgart, 1890.

————. *Theology of the Old Testament.* Trans. by Ellen D. Smith and Sophia Taylor. Edinburgh: T. & T. Clark, 1892–93.

Oettingen, Alexander von. *Lutherische Dogmatik, I, Principienlehre, apologetische Grundlegung zur Dogmatik.* Munich: C. H. Beck, 1897.

Olevian, Caspar. *De Bediening van het Genade Verbond* [*De Substantia Foederis Gratiae* (1585)]. Rotterdam: Mazijk, 1939. Also in *Geschriften van Caspar Olevianus.* The Hague: Het Reformatorische Boekhandel, 1963.

Oorthuys, Gerardus. *De Anthropologie van Zwingli.* Leiden: E. J. Brill, 1905.

Oosterzee, J. J. van. *Christian Dogmatics.* Trans. by J. Watson and M. Evans. 2 vols. New York: Scribner, Armstrong, 1874.

Opzoomer, C. W. *Wet en Wijsbegeerte.* 1857.

Origen. *Against Celsus. ANF,* IV, 395–669.

————. *On First Principles. ANF,* IV, 239–384.

————. *Homilies on Genesis and Exodus.* Trans. by Ronald E. Heine. Washington, D.C.: Catholic University of America Press, 1982.

Orr, James. *God's Image in Man and Its Defacement in the Light of Modern Denials.* London: Hodder & Stoughton, 1906.

Oswald, Johan Heinrich. *Angelologie.* Paderborn: Schöningh, 1883.

————. *Eschatologie.* Paderborn: Schöningh, 1868.

————. *Moses oder Darwin?* Stuttgart, 1907.

————. *Religiöse Urgeschichte der Menschheit.* Paderborn: Schöningh, 1887.

————. *Die Schöpfungslehre.* Paderborn: Ferdinand Schöningh, 1885.

————. *Die Überwindung des Wissenschaftlichen Materialismus.* Paderborn: Schöningh, 1895.

Otto, Rudolf. *Naturalism and Religion.* Trans. by J. Arthur Thomson and Margaret R. Thomson, ed. by W. D. Morrison. London: Williams & Norgate, 1907.

————. *The Philosophy of Religion.* London: Williams & Norgate, 1931.

Ovid. *The Metamorphoses.* Trans. by Henry T. Riley. New York: G. Bell & Sons, 1889.

Pastor of Hermas. ANF, II, 1–58.

Perrone, Giovanni. *Praelectiones Theologicae.* 9 vols. Louvain: Vanlinthout & Vandezande, 1838–43.

Pesch, C. *Praelectiones Dogmaticae.* 9 vols. Freiburg i.B.: Herder, 1902–10.

Pesch, Tillman. *Die Grossen Welträthsel.* 2 vols. 2nd ed. Freiburg i.B.: Herder, 1892.

Peschel, Oscar. *Abhandlungen zur Erd und Völkerkunde.* 5th ed. Leipzig: Duncker & Humboldt, 1878.

Petavius, Dionysius. *De Theologicis Dogmatibus.* 8 vols. Paris: Vives, 1865–67.

Pfaff, Friedrich. *Schöpfungsgeschichte.* Frankfurt a.M.: Heyder & Zimmer, 1877.

Pfanner, Tobias. *Systema Theologiae Gentilis Purioris.* Basel: Joh. Hermann Widerhold, 1679.

Pfleiderer, O. *Grundriss der christlichen Glaubens und Sittenlehre.* Berlin: G. Reimer, 1888.

Philippi, Friedrich A. *Kirchliche Glaubenslehre.* 6 vols. Gütersloh: Bertelsmann, 1902.

Pierson, Allard. *Bespiegeling, Gezag, en Ervaring.* Utrecht: Kemink, 1885.

———. *Geschiedenis van het Roomsch-katholicisme tot op het Concilie van Trente.* 4 vols. Haarlem: A. C. Kruseman, 1868–72.

Plato. *The Laws.* Trans. by E. B. England. 2 vols. New York: Longmans, Green, 1921.

———. *The Republic.* Trans. by Benjamin Jowett. Oxford: Clarendon, 1888.

Platz, Bonifacius. *Der Mensch.* Würzburg and Leipzig: Woerls Rusenbucherverlag, 1898.

Plotinus. *Psychic and Physical Treatises; Comprising the Second and Third Enneads.* Trans. by Stephen MacKennna. London: Philip Lee Warner, 1921.

Plutarch. *On Fate.* In *Plutarch's Moralia,* vol. 15, pp. 303–60. Trans. by Phillip H. De Lacy and Benedict Einarson. Cambridge, Mass.: Harvard University Press, 1959.

Poertner, Balthasar. *Das biblische Paradies.* Mainz: Kirchheim, 1901.

Polanus, Amandus. *Syntagma Theologiae Christianae.* 5th ed. Hanover: Aubry, 1624.

Pressensé, Edomond de. *Les Origines: Le Problème de la Connaissance, le Problème Cosmologique, le Problème Anthropologique, l'Origine de la Morale et de la Religion.* 2nd ed. Paris: Libraire Fischbacher, 1883.

Pseudo-Dionysius the Areopagite. *Pseudo-Dionysius: The Complete Works.* Ed. by Paul Rorem, trans. by Colm Luibheid. New York: Paulist, 1987.

Pünjer, Bernhard. *Geschichte der christlichen Religionsphilosophie seit der Reformation.* Brussels: Impression Anastaltique Culture et Civilisation, 1880–83.

Quack, H. P. G. *Port Royal door Sainte-Beuve.* Amsterdam, 1872.

Quenstedt, Johann Andreas. *Theologia Didactico-polemica Sive Systema Theologicum.* 1685. English, Chapters 1–3, *The Nature and Character of Theology.*

Abridged, edited, and translated by Luther Poellot. St. Louis: Concordia, 1986.

Ranke, Johannes. *Der Mensch.* 2nd ed. Leipzig: Bibliographisches Institut, 1894.

Ratzel, Friedrich. *The History of Mankind.* 3 vols. Trans. by A. J. Butler. New York: Macmillan, 1896–98.

Rauch. *Die Einheit des Menschengeschlechts.* Augsburg, 1873.

Rauwenhoff, L. W. E. *Wijsbegeerte van den Godsdienst.* Leiden: Brill & van Doesburgh, 1887.

Reiche, Armin. *Die künsterlichen Elemente in der Welt- und Lebensanschauung des Gregor von Nyssa.* Jena: A. Kámpte, 1897.

Reinhard, Franz Volkmar. *Grundriss der Dogmatik.* Munich: Seidel, 1802.

Reinhardt, Ludwig. *Der Mensch zur Eiszeit in Europa und Seine kulturentwicklung bis zum Ende der Steinzeit.* München: Ernst Reinhardt, 1913.

Reinke, Johannes. *Die Entwicklung der Naturwissenschaften Insbesondere der Biologie im Neunzehnten Jahrhundert.* Kiel: Universitäts-Buchhandlung (p. Toeche), 1900.

———. *Die Natur und Wir.* Berlin: Gebruder Paetel, 1908.

———. *Die Welt als That: Umrisse Einer Weltansicht auf Naturwissenschaftlicher Grundlage.* 4 vols. 3rd ed. Berlin: Gebruder Paetel, 1905.

Renan, Ernest. *L'avenir de la science; Pensées de 1848.* Paris: Calmann-Levy, 1890.

Reusch, Franz Heinrich. *Nature and the Bible: Lectures on the Mosaic History of Creation in Its Relation to Natural Science.* Trans. by Kathleen Lyttelton from 4th ed. Edinburgh: T. & T. Clark, 1886.

Riedel, Wilhelm. *Alttestamentliche Untersuchungen.* Leipzig: A. Deichert (Georg Böhme), 1902.

Riehm, G. *Christentum und Naturwissenschaft.* 2nd ed. Leipzig: J. C. Hinrichs, 1896.

Riem, Johannes. *Die Sintflut in Sage und Wissenschaft mit 2 Zeichn. Und einer Weltkarte.* Hamburg: Rauhe Haus, 1925.

Ritschl, Albrecht. *Die Christliche Lehre von der Rechfertigung und Versöhnung.* 3 vols. 4th ed. Bonn: A. Marcus, 1895–1903.

Rivetus, Andreas. *Operum theologicorum.* 3 vols. Rotterdam: Leers, 1651–60.

Romanes, George John. *The Scientific Evidences of Organic Evolution.* London: Macmillan, 1882.

———. *Thoughts on Religion.* Ed. by Charles Gore. 6th ed. Chicago: Open Court, 1911.

Rothe, Richard. *Theologische Ethik.* 5 vols. 2nd rev. ed. Wittenberg: Zimmerman, 1867–71.

Rümelin, G. *Ueber den Zufall, Deutsche Rundschau.* März, 1890.

Ryssen, Leonardus. *Summa theologiae elencticae completa, et didacticae quantum sufficit.* Edinburgh: G. Mosman, 1692.

Schäfer, Bernhard. *Bibel und Wissenschaft.* Münster: Theissing, 1881.

Schaff, P. *The Creeds of Christendom.* 6th ed. 3 vols. New York: Harper, 1919.

Schanz, Paul. *Das Alter des Menschengeschlechts nach der Heiligen Schrift der Profangeschichte und der Vorgeschichte.* Freiburg i.B.: Herder, 1896.

————. *A Christian Apology.* Trans. by Michael F. Glancey and Victor J. Schobel. 4th rev. ed. Ratisbon: F. Pustet, 1891.

————. *Über neue Versuche der Apologetik gegenüber dem Naturalismus und Spiritualismus.* Regensburg: Nat. Verl-Anst., 1897.

Schäzler, Constantin von. *Natur und Uebernatur.* Mainz: Kirchheim, 1865.

Scheeben, Matthias Joseph. *A Manual of Catholic Theology: Based on Scheeben's "Dogmatik."* 4th ed. 2 vols. Joseph Willhelm and Thomas Bartholomew Scannell. London: Kegan Paul, Trench, Trubner/New York: Benziger Brothers, 1909.

————. *Handbuch der Katholischen Dogmatik.* 4 vols. Freiburg i.B.: Herder, 1933 (orig. pub. 1874–98).

————. *Natur und Gnade.* Mainz: Kirchheim, 1861.

Schell, Herman. *Der Gottesglaube und die Naturwissenschaftliche Welterkenntniss.* 2nd ed. Bamberg: Schmidt, 1904.

Schelling, F. W. J. *Ausgewählte Werke.* 4 vols. Darmstadt: Wissenschaftlichle Buchgesellschaft, 1968.

Schiaparelli, G. V. *Astronomy in the Old Testament.* Oxford: Clarendon, 1905.

Schiere, Nicolaus. *Doctrina testamentorum et foederum divinorum omnium.* Leovardiaw: M. Ingema, 1718.

Schleiermacher, Friedrich. *The Christian Faith.* Ed. by H. R. MacIntosh and J. S. Steward. Edinburgh: T. & T. Clark, 1928.

Schmid, Rudolf. *The Scientific Creed of a Theologian.* Trans. by J. W. Stoughton from the 2nd ed. New York: A. C. Armstrong, 1906.

Schmidt, Carl. *Das Naturereignis der Sintflut.* Basel: B. Schwabe, 1895.

*Schmidt, E. *Die aeltesten Spuren des Menschen in N. Amerika,* Nos. 38 and 39 van de *Deutsche Zeit- und Streitfragen, Wetenschappelijke Bladen.* 1895.

Schmidt, Wilhelm. *Christliche Dogmatik.* 4 vols. Bonn: E. Weber, 1895–98.

————. *Die Göttliche Vorsehung und das Selbstleben der Welt.* Berlin: Wiegandt & Grieben, 1887.

Schneckenburger, Matthew, and Eduard Gueeder. *Vergleichende Dartstellung des Lutherischen und Reformirten Lehrbegriffs.* 2 vols. Stuttgart: J. B. Metzler, 1855.

Schneider, R. *Christliche Klänge aus den Griechischen und Römischen Klassikern.* Leipzig: Siegismund & Volkening, 1877.

Schneider, Th. *Was ist's mit der Sintflut?* Wiesbaden, 1903.

Schneider, Wilhelm. *Die Naturvölker.* Paderborn: Schoningh, 1885.

Schöberlein, Ludwig. *Prinzip und System der Dogmatik.* Heidelberg: C. Winter, 1881.

Scholten, Johannes Henricus. *De Leer der Hervormde Kerk in Hare Grondbeginselen.* 2 vols. 2nd ed. Leyden: P. Engels, 1850–51.

Schultz, Herman. *Alttestamentliche Theologie.* 2 vols. Frankfurt a/M: von Heyder & Zimmer, 1869.

Schürer, Emil. *The History of the Jewish People in the Age of Jesus Christ (175 B.C.–A.D. 135).* Vol. 3. Rev. and ed. by Geza Vermes, Fergus Miller, and Matthew Black. Edinburgh: T. & T. Clark, 1979 [1885].

Schurtz, Heinrich. *Katechismus der Völkerkunde.* Leipzig: J. J. Weber, 1893.

Schwalbe, Gustav Albert. *Studien zur Vorgeschichte des Menschen.* Stuttgart: Schweizerbart, 1906.

Schwane, Joseph. *Dogmengeschichte.* 4 vols. Freiburg i.B.: Herder, 1882–95.

Schwarz, Franz v. *Sintfluth und Völkerwanderungen.* Stuttgart: Enke, 1894.

Schwetz, Johannes. *Theologia Dogmatic Catholica.* Vienna: Congregatio Mechitharistica, n.d.

Scipio, Conrad. *Des Aurelius Augustinus Metaphysik im Rahmen seiner Lehre von Gott.* Leipzig: Breitkopf & Hartel, 1886.

Sécrétan, Charles. *La Philosophie de la Liberté.* 3rd ed. Paris: G. Balliere, 1849.

Semisch, J. G. *Justin Martyr: His Life, Writings, and Opinions.* 2 vols. Edinburgh: T. & T. Clark, 1843.

Seneca, Lucius Annaeus. *De Beneficiis.* Loeb Classical Library. Trans. by John W. Basore. Cambridge, Mass.: Harvard University Press, 1928.

————. *Naturales Quaestiones.* Loeb Classical Library. 2 vols. Trans. by Thomas Corcoran. Cambridge, Mass.: Harvard University Press, 1971–72.

————. *De Providentia.* In *Moral Essays,* vol. 1, Loeb Classical Library. Trans. by John W. Basore. New York: G. P. Putnam's Sons, 1928.

Shedd, William Greenough Thayer. *Dogmatic Theology.* 3 vols. 3rd ed. New York: Scribner, 1891–94.

Simar, H. Th. *Lehrbuch der Dogmatik.* 2 vols. Freiburg i.B.: Herder, 1879–80.

Simons, Menno. *The Complete Works of Menno Simon.* Elkhart: John F. Funk & Brother, 1871.

Smend, Rudolph. *Lehrbuch der alttestamentlichen Religionsgeschichte.* Freiburg i.B.: J. C. B. Mohr, 1893.

Smith, George. *The Chaldean Account of Genesis.* New York: Scribner's 1880.

Smith, Henry Boynton. *System of Christian Theology.* Ed. by William S. Karr. 4th rev. ed. New York: A. C. Armstrong, 1892, © 1890.

Sohn, Georg. *Opera Sacrae Theologiae.* 2 vols. Herborn: C. Corvin, 1598.

Sophocles, *Electra.* Trans. by E. A. Heary, ed. and introduction by William-Alan Landes. Studio City, Calif.: Players Press, 1995.

Spanheim, Friedrich. *Opera.* 3 vols. Lugduni Batavorum: Apud Cornelium Boutestein [etc.] 1701–3.

Spinoza, Baruch. *Ethics.* Ed. and trans. by James Gutman. New York: Hafner, 1949.

————. *Tractatus Theologico-Politicus.* Trans. by Samuel Shirley. Leiden: Brill, 1991.

Splittgerber, Franz Joseph. *Tod, Fortleben und Auferstehung.* 3rd ed. Halle: Fricke, 1879.

Stave, Erik. *Über den Einfluss des Parismus auf das Judentum.* Haarlem: E. F. Bohn, 1898.

Steinmetz, S. R. *De Studie der Völkenkunde.* 1907.

Steude, E. Gustav. *Christentum und Naturwissenschaft.* Gütersloh: C. Bertelsmann, 1895.

————. *Der Beweis für die Wahrheit des Christentums.* Gütersloh: C. Bertelsmann, 1899.

Stöckl, Albert. *Philosophie des Mittelalters.* 3 vols. Mainz: Kirchheim, 1864–66.

———. *Die Speculative Lehre vom Menschen und Ihre Geschichte*. Würzburg: Stahel, 1858.

Strauss, David Friedrich. *Die Christliche Glaubenslehre in ihrer geschichtlichen Entwicklung und im Kampf mit der Moderne Wissenschaft*. 2 vols. Tübingen: C. F. Osiander, 1840–41.

———. *The Old Faith and the New*. Trans. by Mathilde Blind. New York: Holt, 1873.

Strodl. *Die Entstehung der Völker*. Schaffhausen, 1868.

Strong, Augustus Hopkins. *Systematic Theology*. 3 vols. Philadelphia: Griffith & Rowland, 1907–9.

Suess, Eduard. *Die Sintfluth*. Leipzig: G. Freitag, 1883.

Suicerus, J. C. *Thesaurus ecclesiasticus*. 2 vols. Amsterdam: J. H. Wetstein, 1682.

Swedenborg, Emanuel. *The True Christian Religion: Containing the Universal Theology of the New Church, Foretold by the Lord in Daniel VII.13,14 and in Revelation XXI.1,2*. New York: Swedenborg Foundation, 1952.

Talma, A. S. E. *De Anthropologie van Calvijn*. Utrecht, 1882.

Tertullian. *Against Hermogenes*. Westminster, Md.: Newman, 1956 in *Ancient Christian Writers*. Vol. 24.

———. *Against Marcion*. ANF, III, 269–475.

———. *Against Praxeas*. ANF, III, 597–632.

———. *The Apology*. ANF, III, 17–60.

———. *A Treatise on the Soul*. ANF, II, 181–235.

———. *On the Resurrection of the Flesh*. ANF, III, 545–95.

———. *The Prescription against Heretics*. ANF, III, 243–67.

Theodoret, Bishop of Cyrrhus. *On Divine Providence*. Trans. by Thomas Halton. New York: Newman, 1988.

Theologia Wirceburgensi (Theologia Dogmatica: Polemica, Scholastica et Moralis). 5 vols. Wirceburgensi, 1852–53.

Theophilus. *To Autolycus*. ANF, II, 85–121.

Thomasius, Gottfried. *Christi Person und Werk*. 3rd ed. Erlangen: Theodor Bläsing, 1853–61.

———. *Die Christliche Dogmengeschichte als Entwicklung-geschichte Kirchlichen Lehrbegriffs*. 2 vols. Erlangen: A. Deichert, 1886–89.

Tiele, Cornelis Petrus. *Inleiding tot de Godsdienstwetenschap*. Amsterdam: P. N. van Kampen, 1897–99.

*Totheringham. *The Chronology of the Old Testament*. Cambridge, 1906.

Trelcatius, Lucas, Jr. *Scholastica et methodica locorum communium institutio*. London, 1604.

Trissl, Alois. *Das Biblische Sechstagewerk vom Standpunkte der Katholischen Exegese und vom Standpunkte der Naturwissenschaften*. 2nd ed. Regensburg: G. J. Manz, 1894.

———. *Sündflut oder Gletscher?* Regensburg: G. J. Manz, 1894.

Turretin, Francis. *Institutes of Elenctic Theology*. 3 vols. Trans. by George Musgrove Giger, ed. by James T. Dennison. Phillipsburg, N.J.: Presbyterian & Reformed, 1992.

————. *"De necessaria Secissiones nostra ab Ecclesia Romana." Opera* IV, 1–203. New York: Carter, 1848.

Ulrici, Hermann. *Gott und die Natur.* Leipzig: T. O. Weigel, 1862.

————. *Gott und der Mensch.* Leipzig: T. O. Weigel, 1874.

Urquhart, John. *How Old Is Man? Some Misunderstood Chapters in Scripture Chronology.* London: Nisbet, 1904.

Ursinus, Zacharias. *Catechismus Major.* In *Opera Theologica.* Heidelberg: John Lancellot, 1612.

————. *The Commentary of Dr. Zacharius Ursinus on the Heidelberg Catechism.* Trans. by G. W. Willard. Grand Rapids: Eerdmans, 1954.

Usener, H. *Die Sintflutsagen,* Vol. 3 of *Religionsgeschichtliche Untersuchungen.* Bonn: Cohen, 1899.

Van Dijk, Isaac. *Aesthetische en Ethische Godsdienst.* 1895. In Vol. I of *Gesammelte Geschriften.*

van Eyck van Heslinga, H. *De Eenheid van het Scheppingsverhaal.* Leiden, 1896.

Van Leeuwen. *Bijbelsche Anthropologie.* Utrecht, 1906.

Venema, Herman. *Korte Verdediging van zijn eere en leere.* Leeuwarden: van Desiel, 1735.

Verworn, Max. *Naturwissenschaft und Weltanschauung.* 2nd ed. Leipzig: Barth, 1904.

Vigouroux, Fulcran Grégoire. *Les Livres Saints et La Critique Rationaliste, Histoire, et Réfutation Des Objections Des Incrédules Contre Les Saintes Ecritures.* 4 vols. Paris: A. Roger & F. Chernoviz, 1886–90.

Vilmar, August Friedrick Christian. *Dogmatik.* 2 vols. Gütersloh: C. Bertelsmann, 1874.

Vitringa, Campegius. *Doctrina Christianae Religionis.* 8 vols. Leiden: Joannis le Mair, 1761–86.

Vlak, J. *Eeuwig Evangelium.* Amsterdam: G. Borstius, 1684.

Voetius, Gisbert. *Selectae disputationes theologicae.* 5 vols. Utrecht, 1648–69.

Volkel, Johann. *De Vera Religione Libri Quinque.* Racoviae, 1630.

Von Oettingen, Alexander von. *Lutherische Dogmatik.* 2 vols. München: C. H. Beck, 1897.

Vos, Geerhardus. *Redemptive History and Biblical Interpretation.* Ed. by Richard B. Gaffin. Phillipsburg: Presbyterian & Reformed, 1980.

Voss, Gerhard Johannes. *De Origine et Progressu Idololatriae.* Amsterdam: Blaeu, 1641.

Waitz, Theodor. *Ueber die Einheit des Menschengeschlechts und den Naturzustand des Menschen.* Leipzig: Fleischer, 1859.

Walch, Johann George. *Bibliotheca Theologica selecta, litterariis adnotationibus instructa.* 4 vols. Jenae: vid. Croeckerianal, 1757–65.

Walker, James. *The Theology and Theologians of Scotland, 1560–1750.* Reprinted from the 1888 2nd ed. Edinburgh: Knox, 1982.

Wallace, Alfred Russel. *Man's Place in the Universe: A Study of the Results of Scientific Research in Relation to the Unity or Plurality of Worlds.* London: Chapman & Hall, 1903.

Wasmann, Erich. *Biology and the Theory of Evolution.* Trans. by A. M. Buchanan. 3rd ed. St. Louis: B. Herder, 1923.

———. *Instinkt und Intelligenz im Thierreich.* 8th ed. Freiburg i.B.: Herder, 1905.

Weber, Ferdinand Wilhelm. *System der altsynagogalen palastinischen Theologie: aus Targum, Midrasch und Talmud.* Leipzig: Dörffling & Franke, 1880.

Weber, Otto. *Theologie und Assyriologie. im Streite um Babel und Bible.* Leipzig: J. C. Hinrichs, 1904.

———. *Die Literatur der Babylonier und Assyrer.* Leipzig: J. C. Hinrichs, 1907.

Wegscheider, Julius August Ludwig. *Institutiones theologiae christianae dogmaticae.* Halle: Gebauer, 1819.

Weiss, Bernhard. *Theologie des Neuen Testaments.* 5th ed. Berlin: W. Hertz, 1888.

Weisse, Christian Herman. *Philosophische Dogmatik oder Philosophie des Christentums.* 3 vols. Leipzig: Hirzel, 1855–62.

Wellhausen, Julius. *Geschichte Israels.* 2 vols. Berlin: Reimer, 1878.

———. *Prolegomena to the History of Israel.* Trans. by J. Sutherland Black and Allan Menzies. Edinburgh: Adam & Charles Black, 1885.

Wellisch, Sigmund. *Das Alter der Welt und des Menschen.* Wien Hartleben, 1899.

Weygoldt, G. P. *Darwinismus, Religion, Sittlichkeit.* Leiden: E. J. Brill, 1878.

Wigand, Albert. *Der Darwinismus und die Naturforschung Newtons und Cuviers. Beiträge zur Methodik der Naturforschung und zur Speciesfrage.* 3 vols. Braunschweig: F. Vieweg & Sohn, 1874–77.

*Wigand, Paul. *Die Erde der Mittelpunkt der Welt,* Heft 144 of *Zeitfragen des Christlichen Volkslebens.*

Willmann, Otto. *Geschichte des Idealismus* (1894) [Braunschweig: F. Vieweg & Sohn, 1907].

Winckler, Hugo. *Keilinschriftliches Textbuch zum A. T.* 2nd ed. Leipzig: J. C. Hinrichs, 1903.

Winkel, J. te. "Eene Friesche mythe," *Geschiedenis der Nederlandsche Letterkunde.* 3 vols. Haarlem: F. Bohn, 1887– .

*Winkler. *Keilinschriftl. Textbuch zum Alte Testaments.* 2nd ed. 1903.

Winternitz, *Die Flutsagen des Altertums und der Naturvölker.* Wien, 1901.

Wisemann, Nicholas Patrick Stephen. *Zusammenhang zwischen Wissenschaft und Offenbarung.* Regensburg: Manz, 1866.

Witsius, Herman. *The Oeconomy of the Covenants between God and Man. Comprehending a Complete Body of Divinity.* 3 vols. New York: Lee & Stokes, 1798.

Wollebius, Johannes. *Reformed Dogmatics (1657).* Ed. and trans. by John W. Beardslee III. New York: Oxford University Press, 1965.

———. *Compendium theologiae christianae.* Basel, 1626; Oxford, 1657.

Wright, G. F. *Scientific Confirmations of Old Testament History.* Oberlin, Ohio: Bibliotheca Sacra, 1906.

Wundt, Wilhelm Max. *Vorlesungen über die Menschen- und Thierseele.* 2 vols. Leipzig: L. Voss, 1863.

Xenophon. *Memorabilia and Oeconomicus. Loeb Classical Library.* 7 vols. Trans. by E. C. Marchant. New York: G. P. Putnam's Sons, 1918–68.

Zanchi, Jerome. *Operum Theologicorum.* 8 vols. [Geneva] Sumptibus Samuelis Crispini, 1617.

Zapletal, Vincenz. *Der Schöpfungsbericht der Genesis.* Regensburg: G. J. Manz, 1911.

Zeller, Eduard. *Outlines of the History of Greek Philosophy.* 13th ed. Trans. by L. R. Palmer. New York: Humanities, 1969.

Zimmern, Heinrich. *Biblische und Babylonische Urgeschichte.* 2 vols. Leipzig: J. C. Hinrichs, 1901.

Zittel, Karl Alfred von. *Aus der Urzeit: Bilder aus der Schöpfungsgeschichte.* 2nd ed. Munchen: R. Oldenbourg, 1875.

Zöckler, Otto. *Biblische und Kirchenhistorische. Studien.* München: C. H. Beck, 1893.

———. *Geschichte der Beziehungen zwischen Theologie und Naturwissenschaft.* 2 vols. Gütersloh: C. Bertelsman, 1877–99.

———. *Die Lehre vom Urstand des Menschen.* Gütersloh: C. Bertelsmann, 1879.

Zollmann, Theodor. *Bibel und Natur in der Harmonie ihrer Offenbarungen.* Hamburg, 1869.

Zwingli, Ulrich. *On Providence and Other Essays.* Trans. by Samuel Macauley Jackson, ed. by William John Hinks. Durham, N.C.: Labyrinth, 1983.

Articles

Bachmann. "Der Schöpfungsbericht und die Inspiration." *Neue Kirchliche Zeitschrift* (May 1906): 383–405; (October 1907): 743–62.

Bavinck, H. "Evolutie." In *Pro en Contra.* Baarn: Hollandia, 1907. Republished in *Verzamelde Opstellen.* Kampen: Kok, 1921, 105–20.

Bensdorp. Articles on grace and justification. *De Katholiek* 110, 56; 114 (1898): 81.

*Brandt. *Der Beweis des Glaubens.* 1876.

Braun, Johannes. "Die Kant-Laplace'sche Weltbildungstheorie," *Neue Kirchliche Zeitschrift* 3 (September 1903).

Bruining, A. "Pantheisme of Theisme." *Teylers Theologische Tijdschrift* 5 (1907): 433–57.

———. "De Roomsche leer van het donum superadditum." *Teylers Theologische Tijdschrift* (1907): 564–97.

*Bumuller. *Beweis des Glaubens* 36 (1900): 80.

Calvin, John. "A Warning against Judiciary Astrology and Other Customs." Trans. by Mary Potter. *Calvin Theological Journal* 18 (1983): 157–89 ("Contre l'astrologie," in *Corpus Reformatorum* 35 [7]: 513–42).

———. "Providence." *Concerning the Eternal Predestination of God.* Trans. by J. K. S. Reid. London: James Clarke, 1961.

Cannegieter. "De Godsdients in den Mensch and de Mensch in den Godsdients." *Teylers Theologische Tijdschrift* (1904): 178–211.

Comrie, Alexander. "Verhandeling van het Verbond der Werken." In Thomas Boston, *Een Beschouwing van het Verbond der Genade.* Amsterdam: N. Bijl, 1741.

Cremer, Hermann. "Ebenbild Gottes." *PRE*[3], V, 113–18.

———. "Engel." *PRE*[3], V, 364–72.

———. "Geist." *PRE*[3], VI, 444–50.

———. "Gerechtigkeit." *PRE*³, VI, 546–53.

———. "Herz." *PRE*³, VII, 773–76.

———. "Himmel." *PRE*³, VIII, 80–84.

———. "Pronoia." In *Biblical-theological Lexicon of New Testament Greek*. Trans. by D. W. Simon and William Urwick. Edinburgh: T. & T. Clark, 1872.

———. "Seele." *PRE*³, XVIII, 128–32; *PRE*², XIV, 25–30.

Darwin, G. H. "Kosmische Evolutie." *Wetenschappelijke Bladen* 14 (June 1906): 406–34.

———. "Report on a Discourse in South Africa." *Glauben und Wissen* 4 (March 1906): 104–5.

*Daubanton, F. E. Article in *Theologische Studien* (1887): 429–44.

De Bussy, I. J. "Katholicisme en Protestantisme." *Theologische Tijdschrift* 36 (1888): 253–313.

*De Graf. Article in *Teylers Theologische Tijdschrift* 3 (1905): 165–210.

De Hollandische Revue. (25 September 1905).

*Dennert, Eberhard. Article in *Glauben und Wissen* 4 (September 1906): 304.

———. "Verhandlungen des letzten Anthropologen-Kongress in Lindau (3–7 September 1899). *Der Beweis des Glaubens* 36 (1900): 80.

*Diestel, "Die Sintflut," *Deutsche Zeit und Streitvragen*. No. 137.

Doedes, Jacobus Izaak. "Nieuwe Merkwaardigheden uit den Oude-boeken-schat." In W. Moll and J. G. De Hoop Scheffer, eds., *Studien en Bijdragen*. Amsterdam: G. L. Funke, 1880, IV, 238–42.

Du Bois-Reymond, Emil Heinrich. "Rede." *Sitzungsberichte der Berliner Akademie* (1894).

Eisler, Rudolf. "Zufall." *Wörterbuch der Philosophischen Begriffe*. 3 vols. Berlin: E. S. Mittler, 1910.

Gebhardt. "Der Himmel im Neuen Testaments." *Zeitschrift für Kirchliche Wissenschaft un Kirchliches Leben* 7 (1886).

Geesink, W. "De Bijbel en het Avesta." *De Heraut* 830 (November 1893).

Gunkel, H. "Die Judische und die Babylonische Schopfungeschichte." *Deutsche Rundschau* (May 1903): 267–86.

Handelsblad, November 17, 1905.

Hartmann, Eduard von. "Mechanismus und Vitalismus in der mod. Biologie." *Archiv für systematische Philosophie* (1903): 139–78, 331–77.

Haupt, Erich. "Der Christliche Vorsehungsglaube." *Der Beweis des Glaubens* 24 (1888): 201–28.

Heinze, M. "Evolutionismus." *PRE*³, V, 672–81.

Hengstenberg, Ernst Wilhelm. "Die Wohlvereinbarkeit der biblischen Kosmologie mit den feststehenden Resultaten der kosmologenischen Wissenschaft. *Der Beweis des Glaubens* 3 (1867): 400–418.

*Herrmann, W. "Die Lehre von den Göttlichen Vorsehung und Weltregierung." *Christliche Welt* (1887).

Hertwig, Oskar. "Das biogenetische Grundgesetz nach dem heutigen Stande de Biologie." *Internationale Wochenschrift* 1 (1907).

Herzog, J. J. "Paradies." *PRE*¹.

Himpel, F. Von. "Biblishe Chronologie. A–F." *Herders Kirchenlexikon*. Freiburg im Bresgau: Herder, 1884. III, col. 311–15.

Hodge, A. "The Relation of God to the World," *Presbyterian and Reformed Review* (1887).

Honert, Johan van den. "Voorrede." in Z. Ursinus. *Schatboek der Vaerlkaringen over den Nederlandschen Catechismus.* Gorinchem: Nic. Goetze, 1736.

Hoppe. "Geist oder Instinkt." *Neue Kirchliche Zeitschrift* 9 (1907).

Hubrecht. Article in *Gids voor den Onderwijzer* 17 (June 1896).

Jürgens. "War die Sintflut eine Erdbebenwelle?" *Stimmen aus Maria-Laach* (1884), Nos. 85, 86.

Keerl, K. "Die Fixsterne und die Engel; die Fixsterne unde die Spektralanalyse," *Der Beweis des Glaubens* 32 (June 1896): 230–47.

Kellog, Alfred H. "The Incarnation and Other Worlds" *Princeton Theological Review* 3/2 (April 1905): 177–79.

Kern, H. "Oud en Nieuw over de menschenrassen." *Wetenschappelijke Bladen* (June 1904): 337–57.

Kessler, K. "Mani, Manichaer." *PRE*[3], 193–267.

Kosters. "De Bijbelsche Zondvloedverhalen met de Babylonischen vergeleken." *Theologisch Tijdschrift* 11 (1885).

Köstlin, Julius. "Concursus Divinus." *PRE*[3], IV, 262–67.

Kuyper, Abraham. Articles in *De Heraut* (13 October 1895); (20 October 1895); (5 January 1896); (31 May 1896).

———. "Evolution." Trans. by C. Menninga. *Calvin Theological Journal* 31 (1996): 11–50.

———. "Pantheism's Destruction of Boundaries." *Methodist Review* 52 (1893): 520–35; 762–78; revised translation in James D. Bratt, ed., *Abraham Kuyper: A Centennial Reader* (Grand Rapids: Eerdmans, 1998), 363–402.

Kuyper, Herman Huber. "Egypte vóór den tijd der Piramiden," *Wetenschappelijke Bladen* (August 1907): 274–93; (September 1907): 436–53.

———. "'S Menschen Plaats in het Heelal." *Wetenschappelijke Bladen* (April 1905): 67–78.

Laidlaw, John. "Psychology." In *Dictionary of the Bible.* Vol. IV. Edited by James Hastings. Revised edition by Frederick C. Grant and H. H. Rowley. New York: Charles Scribner's Sons, 1963.

Lechler, G. B. "Deismus." *PRE*[3], III, 529–35.

Liechtenhau, R. "Ophiten." *PRE*[3], XIV, 404–13.

Linder. "Parismus." *PRE*[3], 699–703.

Lütgert, W. "Der Mensch aus dem Himmel." In *Greifswalder Studien.* Edited by Samuel Oettli et al. Gütersloh: C. Bertelsmann, 1895, 207–28.

*Nägeli, Carl. *Entstehung und Begriff der naturhist.* Art.[2], 1865.

Otto, R. "Die mechanistische Lebenstheorie und die Theologie." *Zeitschrift für Theologie und Kirche* (1903): 179–213.

Pfaff, F. "Das Alter der Erde." *Zeitschrift für des Christliche Volksleben* 7 (1882).

Pressel, Wilhelm. "Paradies." *PRE*[3], 20, 332–97.

Rabus. "Vom Wirken und Wohnen des göttlichen Geistes in der Menschenseele." *Neue Kirchliche Zeitschrift* (November 1904): 828.

*Riem. Article in *Glauben und Wissen,* 1905.

*Rolfes. Article in *Philosophisches Jahrbuch* 10 (1897), heft 1.

Rumelin, G. "Über den Zufall." *Deutsch Rundschau* 17 (March 1890).

Schmidt, H. "Das Gilgamesepoc und die Bible." *Theologische Rundschau* 10 (1907): 189–208.

Schöberlein, Ludwig. "Ebenbild Gottes." *PRE*[2], IV, 4–8.

Snijders, C. "Het ontstaan en de verbreiding der menschenrassen." *Tijdspiegel* (April 1897).

———. [Article on inhabitants of planets.] *Tijdspiegel* (February 1898): 182–204.

Steinmetz, S. R. "De rassenkwestie." *Gids* (January 1907).

Stölzle, R. "Newtons Kosmogonie." *Philosophisches Jahrbuch* 20 (1907): 54–62.

Suicerus, Johann Casper. "eikwn." In *Thesaurus Ecclesiasticus, e Patribus Graecis Ordine Alphabetico.* Amsterdam: J. H. Wetsten, 1682.

Tiele, C. P. *Verslag en Mededeelen van de Koninglijke Akademie van Wetenschappelijke Letterkunde.* 1895.

Troeltsch. E. "Deismus." *PRE*[3], IV, 532–59.

Turner, H. H. "Man's Place in the Universe: A Further Note on the Views of Dr. A. R. Wallace" *Fortnightly Review* (April 1907): 600–610.

Ulrich. "Heilsglaube und Vorsehungsglauben." *Neue Kirchliche Zeitschrift* 1 (1901): 478–93.

Ulrici, H. "Pantheismus." *PRE*[3], XI, 183–93.

Upham. "Die Zeitdauer der geologischen Epochen." *Gaea* 30 (1894).

*Urdritz. Article in *Neue Kirchliche Zeitschrift* 10 (October 1899): 837–52.

van der Waals, J. D. "Het Zeeman-verschijnsel." *De Gids* 67 (March 1903): 493–512.

Volck. "Eden." *PRE*[3], V, 158–62.

Vuilleumier. "La première page de la Bible." *Revue de théologie et de philosophie* (1896): 364–418.

Wetzel, G. "Die Zeit der Weltschöpfung." *Jahrbuch für die Theologie* 1 (1875).

Whitley, D. Gath. "What Was the Primitive Condition of Man." *Princeton Theological Review* 4 (October 1906): 513–14.

Winter, "Wesen und Charakter des Christliche Vorsehungsglaubens." *Neue kirchliche Zeitschrift* 7 (1907): 609–31.

Zeehandelaar. "Het spiritistisch Gevaar." *Gids* (August 1907): 306–37.

Zöckler, Otto. [Comments on E. Dubois-Reymond's address, The Berliner Akademie (1894)] *Beweis des Glaubens* 31 (1895): 77–80.

———. "Darwinismus und Materialismus beim Begin des 20e Jahrhunderts." *Beweis des Glaubens* 36 (1900): 161–75.

———. "Die einheitliche Abstammung des Menschengeschlechts." *Jahrbuch für die Theologie* (1863): 51–90.

———. "In eigener Sache." *Beweis des Glaubens* 36 (1900): 32–39.

———. "Mensch," *PRE*[3], XII, 624.

———. "Schöpfung." *PRE*[2], XIII, 647.

———. "Schöpfung und Erhaltung der Welt," *PRE*[3], XVII, 701ff.

———. "Spiritismus." *PRE*[3], XVIII, 654–66.

Select Scripture Index

Old Testament

Genesis
1:1–3 35
1:2 35, 99, 100–102, 110–11, 121–22, 124
6:2 75–76

Deuteronomy
32:8 85, 87

Joshua
10:12, 13 107, 123

2 Kings
20:9 107

Job
33:23 88

Daniel
10:13 85, 87

Hosea
6:7 199, 203

New Testament

Matthew
18:10 87

Romans
5:12–21 199

1 Corinthians
9:9 246
15:45–49 198

Ephesians
4:24 160–61, 181, 182

Colossians
3:10 160–61, 181, 182

Revelation
8:3 88

Note: This index only includes Scripture references discussed by Bavinck in some significant detail; it corresponds to the index in the original four-volume *Gereformeerde Dogmatiek* (ed.).

Herman Bavinck (1854–1921) taught theology at the Theological School in Kampen, The Netherlands, and at the Free University of Amsterdam for almost forty years. At the Free University he succeeded the famous theologian and politician Abraham Kuyper. Among Bavinck's most influential publications were *Reformed Dogmatics* and *Our Reasonable Faith.*

John Bolt is professor of theology at Calvin Theological Seminary (Grand Rapids, Michigan), an editor of *Calvin Theological Journal,* and executive editor of the Dutch Reformed Translation Society.

John Vriend has been a full-time translator since 1982. Among the authors he has translated are G. C. Berkouwer and Hendrikus Berkhof. Vriend was born in the Netherlands, moved to North America at the age of fourteen, then spent four years in Amsterdam studying at the Free University.